IDEAS
AND IMAGES IN
WORLD ART

Dialogue with the Visible

IDEAS
AND IMAGES IN
WORLD ART

Dialogue with the Visible

RENÉ HUYGHE

Professor, Collège de France · Honorary curator-in-chief, The Louvre, Paris

HARRY N. ABRAMS, INC., *Publishers*

NEW YORK

Library of Congress Catalog Card Number: 59-8097

Milton S. Fox, Editor

Translated from the French by Norbert Guterman

Published in the United States of America, 1959

Illustrations printed in France
Book printed and bound in The Netherlands

TABLE OF CONTENTS

AUTHOR'S ACKNOWLEDGMENT

In this book I wanted a very close and integral relationship between pictures and text. This was a difficult thing to accomplish and required unremitting efforts. I am deeply grateful to Mlle. Gisèle Polaillon-Kerven for her care and devotion in solving the often intricate problems involved.

I also owe thanks to the private collectors and museum curators who were kind enough to assist in the preparation of this work. Special acknowledgments go to Mme. Hours, head of the laboratory services of The Louvre, and to her assistant Mme. Faillant; to Mlle. Fabre and Mlle. Jacquiot, of the Cabinet des Médailles; to Mlle. Hauchecorne, of the Musée Guimet; to the archaeologists M. Hamelin and M. Salin; in Holland, to Dr. Röell, director of the Rijksmuseum in Amsterdam, and to Dr. De Vries, director of the Mauritshuis in The Hague; and in Switzerland, to Professor Pijoan and to Mr. Herzer who went to a great deal of trouble to supply me with rare or unpublished documents.

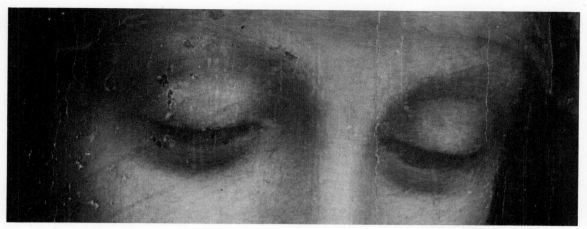

1. - *LEONARDO DA VINCI.* VIRGIN AND CHILD WITH ST. ANNE (detail). The Louvre, Paris

INTRODUCTION

The more exact our knowledge,
the greater our love.
Leonardo da Vinci

WHY write *more* about art? Why write about art at all? Have there not been too many comments already, too many explanations for objects that should simply be looked at, having been created to be looked at? We have no need of words, after all, in order to use our eyes; and paintings should have no need of theories of art.

True enough—if we really looked, if we were able to see with our own eyes, rather than with old habits, preconceived ideas, and beliefs. But too often we see only what we are accustomed to seeing, just as when we listen we hear only the echoes of our customary thoughts. For us all things are a mirror in which we search not for our real features (do we know what we really look like?) but for the visage we think we have or wish we had.

This is particularly true of civilized, overintellectual persons today. For generations we have been trained to perceive everything through the medium of ideas. We are fed to the teeth with dogmas about art, with definitions which have become convictions, and which we have so completely assimilated that we mistake them for instincts —whereas, though they have the same force, they are actually a screen between us and our instincts, keeping the latter well hidden. Without our being aware of it, the husks of this insubstantial nourishment have piled up around us, until they form a wall which shuts us in—and which in time we mistake for the horizon.

5

Yet what can we use, save ideas, to blast our way through the sedimentary deposits of ideas, to let in some fresh air and open up new vistas? With what can we kill the false authority of the word, if not with words? Inevitably we have to fall back on reflection to find, somewhere beyond the barriers of habit, the path to lucidity. Only thus can we discover what is still true—though deformed by systematization—in our theories and shibboleths; only thus reject all willful blindness, and so restore our sensations and emotions to freedom, by raising them to consciousness.

Such a task requires scrupulous intellectual honesty, in an age which scarcely encourages it. Our era has its own intellectual aberrations, not the least of which is the belief that an idea is justified solely by the ingeniousness of its formulation, and that it can do without a center of gravity. The contemporary intelligence resembles the miner who tunnels in any direction, only concerned that he bring something to the surface. No maps or blueprints are drawn, any longer; intellectual activities are beginning to seem a game, the responsibilities of the intellect forgotten. Words, whose function it once was to signify ideas, are giving in to their own vertigo. Ideas themselves, whose admirable function it is to shed light upon the obscurity that is present within us, are now merely deduced from their dialectical possibilities.

Now, a thought is not justified by the mere fact that someone has been able to think it: the brain does not secrete thoughts which attack reality for the mere purpose of producing iridescent bubbles, products of disintegration much like the bubbles that acid produces when poured on chalk. Thought does not exist merely as evidence of the agility of the mental mechanism: its purpose is to exert control over its own sources and to progress by keeping to what is verifiable.

Art, which has become a focal point of interest in our age, has suffered most from the jungle growth of "interpretation," which twists its branches about the arts and chokes off their life. Under these circumstances the need arises—yes, once again—to apply thought to art, but now in order to find our way out of this verbiage, to re-establish contact with the truths vouchsafed by facts. The only facts that count in such an enterprise are the works of art themselves. The aim of this book is not to create something that will take the place of these works, nor to use them tendentiously as a means of confirming some preconceived doctrine. Its humble goal is carefully to chart the boundaries of artistic reality, to clarify what has been attempted and achieved within these boundaries, and to grasp the human origin and import of art.

Such a task means keeping within a well-defined field. The field of painting, in which the visual image displays its multiple resources, both in what was created yesterday and in what is being created today, may prove most fertile for such an inquiry into the nature of the work of art, its purpose, and its potentialities.

As he scrutinizes the world and its appearances the painter asks questions of it; his manner of representing the world is an interpretation of the answers he has received—sometimes it is himself who gives the answers. Through painting, man carries on a dialogue with the visible world. Some artists confine themselves to listening to this world and to recording what it tells them: they are called Realists. Others raise their own voices, some to a thunderous pitch, to drown out the voice of the world: this is the special temptation of our contemporaries. The dialogue with visible reality has been going on for centuries, for millennia. The perpetually fresh exchanges, in a language all their own, echo both our dialogue with the universe and our dialogue with ourselves.

Only from an investigation that takes this dialogue into account can the outlines of a philosophy of art emerge. And only by carrying out a methodical examination of each segment of the field in its order, and by taking into account the many—sometimes contradictory—aspects of painting, shall we, in the last analysis, be able to arrive at some conception of the whole.

We shall not begin, then, with a particular formula invented for the occasion; we shall let our formula emerge, itself, out of the sum total of all such formulas. This book is itself a synthesis, the summing-up of lengthy studies undertaken piecemeal, over twenty-five years of lecturing and teaching. I have thought it desirable not to omit certain reflections, no longer so novel as they may once have been, which have occasionally been advanced elsewhere. It matters little whether an idea appears as a truism or a paradox, provided it helps us to understand art and its immense variety.

The mystery of art lies somewhere between the painter's hand and eye.
2. - *REMBRANDT*. SUPPER AT EMMAUS (detail). The Louvre, Paris

Photo Laboratory of The Louvre, Paris

To understand is not simply to acquire a few handy items of knowledge: it is to absorb these ideas, to penetrate them. Some essential problems will have to be returned to again and again, in the light of experience gained in subsequent chapters; even the windings of a path which seems to turn back on itself may in the end give us a clearer view of what at first glance was too sweeping a vista, and help us to situate this vista in the whole landscape, of which it is only one part.

We shall regard art as inseparable from the human species: it has existed since the birth of mankind. Perhaps it has never been greater than in those times when man was not aware of it, did not wonder about it as such, did not even suspect its existence.

By contrast, it has never seemed so important, to the point of becoming an obsession, as in our own day. Never before has it been so widely accessible, so greatly appreciated. Never before has it been so intensively analyzed and explained. In this it benefits (particularly as regards painting) from the major role visual images have come to play in our civilization. This fact, together with its causes and consequences, counts for far more than the theories of art which abound in our age in making possible the exploration of the mysterious power of images. Art merely puts this power to work. Thus our period provides us with the first of the experiments we have wished to make the basis for our investigation, and suggests the preamble which will open it.

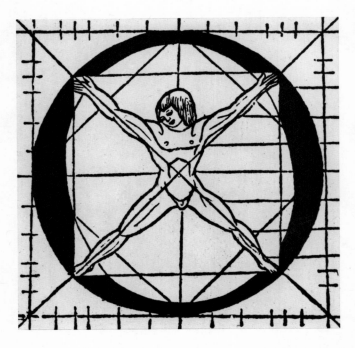

3. - *GEOFFROY TORY.* LETTER DESIGNED ACCORDING TO THE PROPORTIONS OF THE HUMAN BODY

Two rhythms: yesterday's reverie and today's frenzy.
4. - *TURNER.* RAIN, STEAM, AND SPEED (detail). National Gallery, London

PREAMBLE
ON THE POWER OF THE IMAGE [1]

More than ever people need visual images.
...Contemplation yields to quick visual impression.
A. de Monzie (1939)

1. THE SIGNS OF THE TIMES

THAT art, in the twentieth century, has come to occupy a greater place in our concerns than ever before, that it increasingly attracts the interest of the cultured, may be seen as part of a far larger development. The modern world is importuned, and obsessed, by the visual.

---

[1] In this Preamble I include certain views on the advent of a new civilization, "the civilization of the image," which I have advanced in many lectures and published papers since 1947 ("L'Art et la Civilisation moderne," *Bulletin de l'Institut National Genevois,* LII, etc.). I hope I may be forgiven for repeating these views here, in order to emphasize, at the outset, the crucial importance of art and of a lucid understanding of art for the present day.

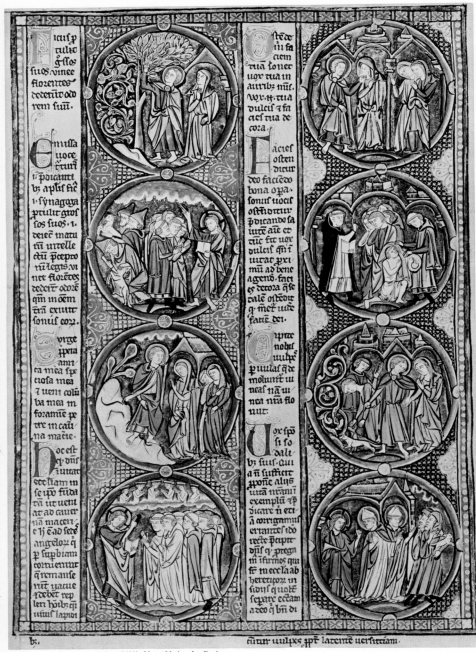

The evolution of the book illustrates the varying relationship between text and illustration over the centuries. In medieval manuscripts, miniatures and text are intimately related.

5. - BIBLE MORALISÉE (Moralized Bible). Thirteenth century. Commentary on the SONG OF SOLOMON. Bibliothèque Nationale, Paris

THE PRIMACY OF THE VISUAL.   Around 1900, books in the display windows of bookshops were disposed in a checkerboard arrangement, one next to the other, the subdued yellow and red covers contributing a bit of color: the display was primarily meant to be "read." Today's bookshop windows resemble exhibitions of pictures. Art books, with their illustrated dust jackets, have invaded the show cases, and other types of books have patterned their jackets on those of art books. A masterpiece of painting appears, for example, on the cover of each volume of a popular series of famous novels published in Italy. Window displays have become spectacles, with plaster casts, arrangements of objects, and décors worthy of the theater, all designed to catch the eye. There may even be a mechanical ballet, the pages of the latest best-seller turning as the volume revolves against a vivid backdrop of frosted glass illuminated from behind.

It is as though the written word were no longer expected to speak for itself, without

The earliest printed books look like medieval manuscripts.

6. - *At left:* FRENCH MASTER. Illumination for St. Augustine's CITY OF GOD: results of man's first disobedience. c. 1475. Bibliothèque Nationale, Paris

7. - *Below:* VERDUN MISSAL. Paris, 1481. Bibliothèque Nationale, Paris

421

LES VIES DE HANNIBAL, ET SCIPION
l'Africain, traduites par Charles Del'Eclvse.

Hannibal.

The classical book expresses itself through type and setting, and these give it its attractiveness.

8. - French translation of Plutarch's
LIVES. Lyons, 1572

the aid of some special visual appeal. Indeed, it occasionally no longer even tries to speak: there are one-time bookshops that now sell nothing but reproductions of masterpieces, as any pedestrian will have noticed.

But the shift of public attention from literature to the visual arts is also apparent in other, less obvious ways. To be sure, literature still holds the important place that rightly belongs to it, but it must often move over a little to make room for pictures. Quite a few weeklies now devote space to both. The names of great painters compete with and sometimes overshadow those of writers. Fifty years ago, Maurice Barrès and Anatole France were famous indeed, but they never enjoyed the celebrity of a Picasso, whom the proverbial man in the street looks up to, today, as to a figure of myth.

In the past, many a painter—Fromentin is one instance —dreamed of attaining public laurels as a novelist. Today, in France at least, there are few novelists who have not been tempted at one time or another to write art criticism. There are many art books in which the masters of the brush, the demigods, are commented on by the most prominent writers. Louis Aragon is the author of a book on Courbet; Paul Eluard has written numerous poems on contemporary painters, collected under the significant title *Voir* (To See). Jean Cocteau is nearly as well known for his drawings as for his writing.

A number of famous writers have followed the advice of Baudelaire, that great herald of the modern era: "Glorify the image (my great, single, primitive passion)."[1] Paul Claudel has shown us what "the eye can hear," and André Malraux makes us hear "the voices of silence."

Can these men be called "deserters"? Rather, I should call them "converts." The realm of the visual began to attract Malraux a long time ago. In 1936, when shooting his film *Man's Hope*, he discovered photographic expression; since then he has seen the history of civilization in terms of an "imaginary museum"—i.e., a museum which exists in the imagination, and is composed of images. It is to these images that he devotes the bulk of the space in the many art books which have been published under his editorship. More recently, the novelist André Chamson, who incidentally is the curator of a real museum, has joined the ranks of those who stress the increasing importance of visual expression. He has given many lectures on this subject and even taken to calling our era the "civilization of the image."

[1] That is what he says in *Mon cœur mis à nu* (Edition Crépet, *Oeuvres posthumes*, II, p. 114). According to an announcement in the *Magasin des familles* in 1851, he planned an essay on "The Power of Pictures Over the Mind." His own passion for them was so intense that he "could never be sated" ("Salon of 1859"), and in his "Autobiographical Notes" (*ibid.*, p. 136) he declares that he had, "from childhood on, an inveterate taste for all plastic representations." Silvestre reports that, stricken with aphasia shortly before his death, Baudelaire continued to gaze greedily at an engraving on the wall. Scarcely any other poet comes as close to the modern soul, to what Baudelaire himself called "modernity." This passion of his for visual art, which makes him a precursor of the present day, would provide a magnificent subject for a study.

Malraux has pointed out to what extent the widespread use of photography has affected our conceptions of art. One may ask whether it is not merely art, but our whole conception of life and the universe, that is changing. The invention of photography does not explain everything; it, too, has to be accounted for. For all great discoveries are made when the time is ripe for them; the climate has to be favorable and they will emerge. History shows that they appear in response to a need, that if they change the course of things, it is because the course of things urgently required that change. Photography was not invented until the nineteenth century; and while it is true that its discovery was made possible by scientific progress, the primary reason for that discovery was that the century required a mechanical method for the exact reproduction of objective reality. The triumph of naturalism, both in literature and in art, reflected the same trend; and just as science was ready with the new technique, so the century was ready to receive it.

In much the same way the fifteenth century gave rise to the discovery of printing.

TEXT GIVES WAY TO PICTURE. Photography—printing; the picture—the book. The trajectory of our culture is spanned in these two pairs of opposites. To fulfill its destiny, the West needed books; their multiplication and their dominance marked the intellectual stage of Western development. But in order to enter the visual stage, the West required photography.

The evolution of the book itself testifies to this shift. In medieval manuscripts, writing and illumination, reading matter and pictorial matter, were closely linked; after the advent of printing, typography ruled supreme. Since all things pass away gradually, the wood engravings in the early incunabula were survivals of illumination; but by the seventeenth century, the printed character by itself—italic or roman, set compactly or loosely—dominated the page with its black battalions. Borders and vignettes had a merely decorative function (figure 5, 6, 7, 8).

In the eighteenth century, however, the trend toward illustration, toward offering the reader food for his eyes as well as for his thoughts, reasserted itself. Moreau, Cochin, and others began to wield their burins. And in the nineteenth

Photo Flammarion

LA PEUR.   545

restait de sang-froid, je rebroussai doucement, et je me mis à siffler d'un

air dégagé. Quand un homme qui a peur en est à siffler, l'on peut compter qu'il est extraordinairement bas.

Je n'eus pas plutôt rebroussé, que le rapprochement se fit de la roue et du monstre aux vertèbres. Je l'entendis galoper, je sentis son haleine

The nineteenth-century pictures began to use images as well as words.
9. - *TOPFFER.* NOUVELLES GENEVOISES. Paris, 1845

Reproductions of paintings were done first in line—the most "intellectual" element; then light and shadow were supplied, today color is added.

10. - *At left:* TINTORETTO. SUSANNA AT THE BATH. From Landon, ANNALES DU MUSÉE, 1807

11. - *Below:* Reproduction from a photograph of the same painting in the Louvre

At right: Color reproduction of a portion of the painting

century, long before photography had found its way into books, lithographs and woodcuts were being used widely (figure 9).

It is significant that the early art books, even those dealing with paintings, made no attempt to show what they were commenting upon. Technical obstacles do not account for this. Nineteenth-century collections of prints, "books with figures" such as the *Temple des Muses* and the *Cabinet d'Or*, devoted to famous galleries, or the *Imagines ex antiquis marmoribus*, and *Tabellae selectae*, contain excellent reproductions. But they were the products of engravers; writers on art made do without them, and from Vasari to Bellori, historians of painting relied primarily on verbal description. Art was an object of thought; the visual appearance of the works was considered of secondary importance.

The nineteenth century began timidly enough. Illustrations of art books were line drawings that showed only the contours, reasonable approximations of the forms in paintings. It was only that the rendering of tones came to be expected, through engravings, and later, photographs. For a time black-and-white illustrations—halfway between intellectual convention and sensory reality—prevailed. Not until the twentieth century did color reproductions come to be taken for granted. It was not long ago that Salomon Reinach illustrated his *Répertoire*

des Peintures with old-fashioned line engravings. Scorning the new possibilities, he even chided those who demand color reproductions! There are still many amateurs today who turn up their noses at publishers' efforts to go beyond the rendering of values to achieve that of color, though without it the representation of a given painting is often inadequate or even misleading (figures 10 and 11, and plate 1).

It was only about a hundred years ago, in 1853, that Charles Blanc conceived the idea of issuing a volume on Rembrandt, in which the plates took precedence over the text. Six years later he ventured to found the first large magazine devoted to the visual arts, the still extant *Gazette des Beaux-Arts*, and to give some space in it—not very much, however—to illustrations. Periodicals had begun to use illustrations only shortly before that. In France, *Charivari* began to use them in 1830, and the *Magasin pittoresque* three years later; it was at this time that the *Penny Magazine* made its appearance in England. The movement developed slowly. In 1848 came *L'Illustration*, in 1857 *Le Monde Illustré*—these titles were to prove indicative of the contents. It was only natural that Constantin Guys, "the painter of modern life," should be one of the first artist-reporters. He contributed to the *Illustrated London News*—a title, again, that is significant (figure 12).

So far, only woodcuts had been used as illustrations. A little more than seventy years ago, photography made its appearance in newspapers, with snapshots coming ten years later. A great advance had been made when, early in the twentieth century, a French daily, *Excelsior*, reversed the usual ratio of text to pictures, and devoted

The newspapers of the nineteenth century, using illustrations, created the artist-reporter.

12. - *CONSTANTIN GUYS.* THE FUNERAL OF MARSHAL EXELMANS AT THE INVALIDES. Sketch for the *London Illustrated News.* Musée Carnavalet, Paris

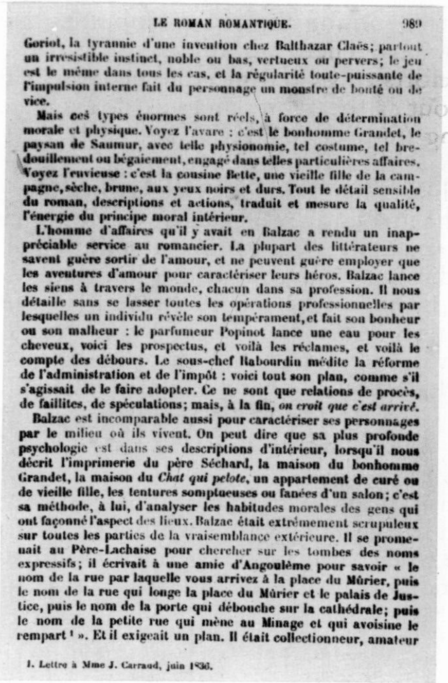

Goriot, la tyrannie d'une invention chez Balthazar Claës; partout un irrésistible instinct, noble ou bas, vertueux ou pervers; le jeu est le même dans tous les cas, et la régularité toute-puissante de l'impulsion interne fait du personnage un monstre de bonté ou de vice.

Mais ces types énormes sont réels, à force de détermination morale et physique. Voyez l'avare : c'est le bonhomme Grandet, le paysan de Saumur, avec telle physionomie, tel costume, tel déshabillé ou son bégaiement, engagé dans telles particulières affaires. Voyez l'envieuse : c'est la cousine Bette, une vieille fille de la campagne, sèche, brune, aux yeux noirs et durs. Tout le détail sensible du roman, descriptions et actions, traduit et mesure la qualité, l'énergie du principe moral intérieur.

L'homme d'affaires qu'il y avait en Balzac a rendu un inappréciable service au romancier. La plupart des littérateurs ne savent guère sortir de l'amour, et ne peuvent guère employer que les aventures d'amour pour caractériser leurs héros. Balzac lance les siens à travers le monde, chacun dans sa profession. Il nous détaille sans se lasser toutes les opérations professionnelles par lesquelles un individu révèle son tempérament, et fait son bonheur ou son malheur : le parfumeur Popinot lance une eau pour les cheveux, voici les prospectus, et voilà les réclames, et voilà le compte des débours. Le sous-chef Rabourdin médite la réforme de l'administration et de l'impôt : voici tout son plan, comme s'il s'agissait de le faire adopter. Ce ne sont que relations de procès, de faillites, de spéculations; mais, à la fin, on croit que c'est arrivé.

Balzac est incomparable aussi pour caractériser ses personnages par le milieu où ils vivent. On peut dire que sa plus profonde psychologie est dans ses descriptions d'intérieur, lorsqu'il nous décrit l'imprimerie du père Séchard, la maison du bonhomme Grandet, la maison du Chat qui pelote, un appartement de curé ou de vieille fille, les tentures somptueuses ou fanées d'un salon; c'est sa méthode, à lui, d'analyser les habitudes morales des gens qui ont façonné l'aspect des lieux. Balzac était extrêmement scrupuleux sur toutes les parties de la vraisemblance extérieure. Il se promenait au Père-Lachaise pour chercher sur les tombes des noms expressifs; il écrivait à une amie d'Angoulême pour savoir « le nom de la rue par laquelle vous arrivez à la place du Mûrier, puis le nom de la rue qui longe la place du Mûrier et le palais de Justice, puis le nom de la porte qui débouche sur la cathédrale; puis le nom de la petite rue qui mène au Minage et qui avoisine le rempart [1] ». Et il exigeait un plan. Il était collectionneur, amateur

[1]. Lettre à Mme J. Carraud, juin 1830.

Scènes de la vie de campagne : *Le Médecin de campagne* (1833), *Le Curé de village* (1839-1846), *Les Paysans* (1844).

Études philosophiques : *La Recherche de l'Absolu* (1834).

Théâtre : *Mercadet* (1838).

CARACTÈRE. — Pour se lancer dans une pareille entreprise, il fallait avoir la robuste organisation de Balzac.

1° *Le travailleur.* — Tous ces livres furent écrits dans une hâte fiévreuse. Très souvent, Balzac en avait touché le prix d'avance. Il s'enfermait chez lui, vêtu d'une robe de chambre, que le portrait et la caricature ont semblablement illustrée (FIG. 287, 288) et, à raison de quinze heures par jour, il achevait l'ouvrage, dans une sorte d'ivresse d'imagination que

FIG. 288. — Balzac en travailleur. (Caricature de 1838.) (Musée Balzac.)

le café entretenait. L'imprimeur venait chercher le manuscrit au fur et à mesure, et Balzac corrigeait sur les épreuves avec la même ardeur, jusqu'à désespérer les typographes (FIG. 293). Fier de cette puissance peu commune, il se considérait comme le « Napoléon des Lettres » (FIG. 291), et pouvait écrire :

Ce qui doit mériter la gloire dans l'art... c'est surtout le courage, un courage dont le vulgaire ne se doute pas. (*Cousine Bette*, éd. Calmann-Lévy, in-8°, t. X, p. 192.)

2° *L'imagination.* — Pendant ces sortes de retraites, il vivait réellement avec ses personnages. La façon dont il en parle dans ses lettres montre qu'ils existaient en effet pour lui, comme tout ce qui lui représentait son imagination. « Pour Balzac, le futur n'existait pas, tout était présent..., l'idée était si vive qu'elle devenait réelle en quelque sorte; parlait-il d'un dîner, il

FIG. 289. — Balzac en dandy. (Statuette de Dantan.) (Musée Carnavalet.) *Balzac y tient à la main un fameux canne, qui fut un des luxes dont il était le plus féru.*

Photos Flammarion

Today even books on literature are coming to rely more and more upon illustration.

13. - Lanson, HISTOIRE DE LA LITTÉRATURE FRANÇAISE. 1898 edition, with no illustrations

14. - Audic and Crouzet, HISTOIRE DE LA LITTÉRATURE FRANÇAISE. 1918 edition, illustrated by Abry

the bulk of its pages to photographs, citing the remark of Napoleon, that great initiator: "The sketchiest pen drawing tells me more than a long report!"[1] These words proclaimed the pre-eminence of the visual, and disclosed the main reason for it—the modern demand for speed.

VISUAL APPROACH. Bit by bit the printed word capitulated on every front. No books are as slow to change, as bound by tradition, as textbooks; and of all textbooks, those on the history of literature, the very purpose of which is to glorify the written word, might have been expected to remain the unconquerable bastion. But they, too, have surrendered. The old texts, with their compactly printed pages, filled with "the substantific marrow of the mind," had a grim aspect. In them, thought moved at a leisurely pace, the words creeping like centipedes along the

[1] The idea had been in the air ever since sensualist philosophy had begun its assault on intellectualism. As early as 1719 the Abbé Dubos, another precursor, observed in his *Réflexions critiques:* "A systematic discourse lasting an hour, no matter how attentively we listen to it, could not be more instructive than a single quick glance" (I, p. 379). The whole development had its beginnings in the eighteenth century.

In 1937 texts were almost entirely eliminated from an exhibition devoted to literature.
15. - PANEL FOR THE BALZAC EXHIBIT (Musée de la Littérature)

straight lines massed rigidly within the rectangular block of the page. This is how I remember the famous Lanson manual (figure 13). Yet, the same Lanson was to come out one day in a revised edition, which left room for pictures. And not only had the text been shortened: its whole aspect, its very nature, had been altered—it no longer simply "signified," it also "showed."

As early as 1912, the *Histoire illustrée de la Littérature Française*, by Abry, Audic, and Crouzet, took this new line. Students, the preface said, "encumber their memories with abstract formulas.... Therefore they must above all be given concrete realities." The text, too, yielded to the new force—visual appeal. A new type face, paragraphs of varying lengths, numbered headings in bold print supplemented the logic of the text with elements striking to the eye, and easily retained by the visual memory (figure 14).

At the 1937 Exposition, the *Musée de la Littérature* raised the white flag of surrender. The Musée had been conceived and was supervised by the Bibliothèque Nationale, with its chief librarian Julien Cain and his assistants—the elite guard of the printed word—in charge. In the displays at the exhibition, the word, defeated, was reduced to its simplest form of expression: a few selected phrases in large type caught the eye; photography and design did the rest. Thought was no longer conveyed by verbal constructions but by means of optical impressions (figure 15).

On posters, slogans yield to pictures.
16. - *DAUMIER*. L'ENTREPÔT D'IVRY. 1850. Bibliothèque Nationale, Paris

Photo Bibliothèque Nationale, Paris

Design in books, however, merely reflects what is happening around us, "under our very eyes." Open a newspaper—it, too, has evolved. It was the first to design a type page to attract the eye, by means of skillfully arranged headlines, and by exploiting the shock which results from the juxtaposition of photographs with type. The over-all aim is to make it unnecessary for the reader to read! We "glance through" the text, as the saying goes.

But the very streets we walk on have acquired visual appeal: store window displays, posters, and so on. These are directed at the pedestrian who does not stop, and therefore cannot read. They must get their message across in one sharp shock; and they, too, are in motion—witness the placards on buses.

And what effects such concentration achieves! The first notices posted in public, which appeared with the invention of printing, were successions of sentences decorated only with vignettes; and for a long time they remained so, down to the first half of the nineteenth century. Then more attractive ornamental designs began to make their appearance, followed by the use of color. The emergence of the true poster, which has become one of the visual arts, dates from the end of the last century, if we count Daumier, Gavarni, and Gustave Doré as mere forerunners (figure 16).

The new technique of psychic shock, which has taken the place of reflection, was well summed up by Maurice Denis in 1920: "The main thing," he said, "is to find an expressive outline, a symbol, which by the power of its forms and colors alone will forcibly catch the eye of the crowd, and tyrannize the passer-by. The poster is... a sign: *in hoc signo vinces!*" Denis wrote this before neon marked a further advance (figure 17 and the plate II).

Soon cities began to scintillate at night with electrically lighted advertisements, which were soon animated, made to revolve or flicker. The poster is in a hurry; it reproduces the rhythm of the passing minutes. Outside the cities, the billboards break up the serenity of the landscape, keeping the eye constantly on the alert. Advertisements attract the spectacle-greedy public as a flame attracts the moth. In the modern city everything is designed with this in mind. We are urged to live by the sensations that advertising evokes and, above all, by visual sensations (figure 18).

Such sensations no longer mean simply amusement, a passing impression, stimulation; by means of them contemporary man seeks to acquire knowledge that formerly was believed discoverable only in texts. What other explanation is there for the popularity of museums, for the pre-eminent place they hold in modern life—needless to say, above all in America? There we find educational services, some of them specially for children, which aim at nourishing the brain with information not only aesthetic, but also technical and historical, through visual contact with works of art, briefly commented upon. The public's avidity is such that the museums are obliged to enlarge the resources of their permanent collections by means of frequent temporary exhibitions. To see, to experience through sight, to obtain enjoyment through visual sensations—is there anything more urgently felt today?

In a few years advertising learned to condense images, aiming at visual shock.

17. - BONNARD. Poster for the *Revue Blanche*

A NEW CIVILIZATION AND NEW MEN.   Is it society that evolves? Or mankind? History teaches us that the world changes continually, but because of our intellectual laziness and pride we tend to view this change as taking place only in our

Modern man is hemmed in by city lights.
18. - STREET IN NEW ORLEANS. Photograph by Emil Schultess, with "fish-eye" lens

external circumstances; man, we imagine, is always true to himself, a universal norm. We regard the present stage, to which mankind progressed slowly, step by step, and which is our own, as the only truly normal, the more or less definitive one. Our ways of being, of thinking and feeling, and even our knowledge we look on as attainments that those who come after us will not be able to dispense with lightly.

And yet, both in his behavior and in his mental dispositions, man is constantly changing, and we in the present are but one wave in an endless series. A civilization is no more than the sum of the characteristics which the inhabitants of a given place exhibit at a given time, until their slow evolution enables them to take another step forward. Today even the quite recent past seems strange, barely conceivable to us. We must realize that to those who come after, we shall seem no less strange and inconceivable.

But how does what is so new today and will be so obsolete tomorrow differ from what has been? If the image is presently supplanting the text, it is because sensory life tends to occupy the place once held by intellectual life. In the past, the oral means of communication that had formerly prevailed gave way, similarly, to the printed word. From the Renaissance on new ideas were spread primarily by means of written sentences; in the nineteenth century the newspapers passed them on to the masses to whom public education had brought literacy. The millenary era of the oral transmission of knowledge, supplemented, in the field of religion, by the image of art, had come to an end. What we are experiencing today may be no more than an analogous mutation.

Whereas written texts obliged us to withdraw into ourselves in order to transform the words into thought, now sensations take us out of ourselves, irresistibly and continually. They demand compliance and an empty mind. Visual impressions are not subject to our will as the printed page was; we cannot accept or reject them as we please. They rush along at their own rapid pace, forcing us to keep up with them. On the movie or television screen, they are still more rapacious and tyrannical; because of the dark that surrounds them, they become, perforce, the focus of our attention, and we cannot tear our eyes away. Unlike the reader, the spectator is not free to absorb only what he chooses, assimilating his impressions later, in meditation or reverie; he becomes the prey of what he sees.

Everything today is absorbed through sense impressions; and, unlike thought, the senses do not enter into a dialogue with their object but, rather, identify themselves with it, record it, and submit to it. Not only the manner of acquiring knowledge but also the content of it is changing. The life of the mind as we have known it is threatened, at least in those incapable of defending themselves. The change has already become so pronounced, we have already become so "different," that we are conscious of it.

Some will find this hard to realize: they still look for the blank space at the bottom of the page, wait for the end of one chapter before turning to the next. But life has no such caesuras to serve as signposts. What has passed away remains a part of what is born, and quits it only reluctantly. More than that: what is entering into decline exhibits a deceptive hyperactivity that gives every evidence of life, so that this disorderly, cancerous proliferation, this morbid fecundity, is sometimes mistaken for vitality. The fact is that it is always difficult for us to tell what is dying away in us and what is emerging, as life carries us along.

Yet certain symptoms are clear enough. One of the most disquieting is the present uncontrolled eruption of words, swirling and eddying, recording every movement of thought, down to its feeblest stirrings. This phenomenon is particularly apparent in Europe, the fate of whose culture is intimately bound up with intellectualism. The nations that speak in the name of the future—a future which they are shaping in conformity with different standards—the Americans and the Russians, surrender much more willingly to the attraction of the sensory shock and to its violence: the former in their everyday life, the latter in their psychological theory, which assigns a central role to Pavlov's conditioned reflex.

The security which we, the children of an old civilization, find in purely intellectual activities is not evidence of the strength of the intellect, but rather of its exhaustion. Moreover, those who engage in such activities pay tribute to the very power which threatens them: never before have art and visual creations been so much talked about. The cloud of dust thrown up by these last-ditch efforts to verbalize envelops art, confusing it and sometimes even leading it astray. Such occurrences are characteristic of all mutations. The old skin is sloughed off, and since it is no longer attached to the reality it once clothed, it drifts hither and thither, forming complicated patterns that are actually meaningless. Meanwhile a new skin is forming, but the distracted eye has not yet perceived its delicate and fine texture.

This accounts for the present interest in ideas and words for their own sake, of the delight taken in their "gratuitous" (as we say in France) play; it also explains the giddiness in the form of expression, so scornful of all content as to degenerate into a cult of its own elements. "Words, words, words," says Hamlet; today we have a new literary movement, *"Lettrisme."* The letters rule the words that they were made to serve; the words, in turn, drag in their wake the ideas they were meant to obey. The primary function of language—that of expressing what is perceived and felt—has been forgotten; and it is this very function that the image now claims as *its* prerogative.

SPEED, INTENSITY.   The time has come to look deeper than at symptoms, to name the underlying reality to which they point. Behind the continual resorting to sense impressions, we have already discovered the demand for intensity. In this our age differs from past centuries which were interested above all in achieving the conditions under which mankind's most valuable qualities could attain harmony and perfection. In the past, moral thought sought to eliminate the imperfections that kept these qualities from reaching that ideal point at which they could at last be "realized," and at which mankind, having attained its longed-for consummation, could remain in repose.

Not so with us today. The seventeenth was perhaps the last century to cherish this dream of an ultimate state of fulfillment. Since then we have been in a continual rush, our only purpose being, it would seem, to achieve greater progress, to be ever more modern; far from aiming at a state of balance, we think only of avoiding any such possibility, which threatens us with immobility.

Life carries us along in a mounting rhythm, we drive ourselves from one position to the next, and the need for intensity that underlies all our desires, all our aspirations is reflected most clearly in our obsession with speed. F. T. Marinetti, self-styled

Some modern artists (Delaunay and the Italian Futurists) sought to render the rhythms and the intensity of our era.
19. - *DELAUNAY*. ELECTRIC MERRY-GO-ROUND

apostle of the quest for intensity, proclaimed in 1933: "There is no intensity without brevity; the strongest sensations are the briefest" (figure 19).[1]

From his beginnings down to the end of the eighteenth century, man measured speed by the rate of his own steps, or, at most, by the horse's gallop. But in less than two centuries—an insignificant space of time, set against all those millennia—he has passed from a maximum speed of about twenty miles per hour to the speed of sound; recently he has crossed the sonic barrier, approaching speeds of 800 miles per hour.

[1] *Futurist Manifesto*, 1933. *Synthetic aeronautics*, in collaboration with Aldo Giuntini.

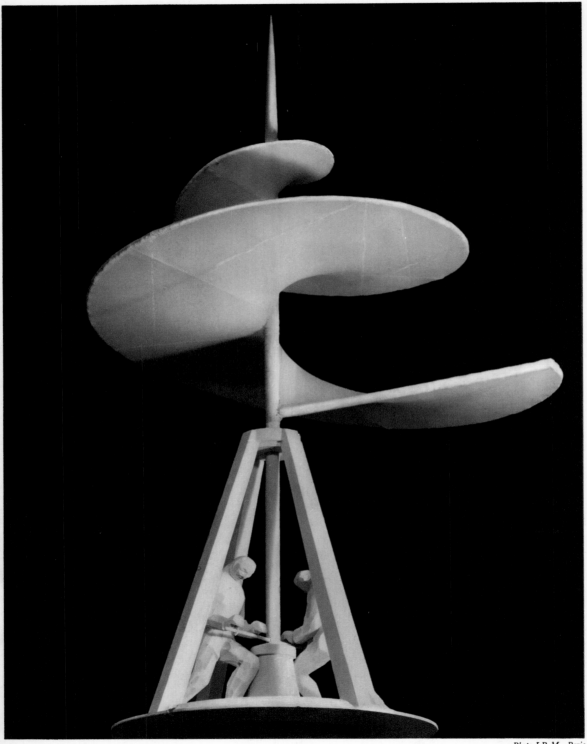

Such a development, which is frightening if you consider its implications, cannot have failed to affect our species profoundly. We have shaped a new world, and we are men of that new world, which in turn is shaping us.

Intensity and speed are the two faces of the new god we worship. Our life span having remained more or less unchanged, we have had to shorten the duration of our sections, to squeeze more and more of them into the same space of time. Man's avidity has always driven him in this direction: the tools he gradually evolved were aimed at giving his movements the maximum efficiency by eliminating error, and the maximum of promptness by multiplying their results. But his progress was slow, spread over thousands of years, until Western man, ruthless in his ambitions, succeeded in linking machines with sources of energy more powerful than his own muscles. From that day on he was able to transcend the natural limits of his organism.

Water, fire, and their result, steam, then electricity, and finally the fission of the atom have marked the stages of an amazing progress whose future is unforeseeable. Mechanics and energy have combined to launch the modern era on its constantly accelerating course.[1] They have merely carried to a height previously unknown man's natural aspiration to extend his power over the world and himself—an aspiration that runs through the entire course of our civilization.

2. THE CIVILIZATION OF THE BOOK

THE present stage of our civilization is the result of a long development. Man struggled for millennia to make an opening in the thick dam confronting him, in order to discover a new source of energy. For centuries upon centuries he kept on digging; and then suddenly one stroke of the pick, precisely aimed, caused a real break in the dam, releasing a force of hitherto unsuspected violence. And the spurting stream became a torrent, widening the narrow man-made breach, upsetting everything in its path, and thrusting aside the very men, now panic-stricken and helpless, who had for so long been struggling to find it and unleash it. Such is our history!

Although the brutality of the solutions we have found seems unprecedented, and

---

[1] How moving it is to see Leonardo da Vinci, on the threshold of the sixteenth century, groping for a way to bring the two forces together, and coming close to it. He had glimpsed into the mechanism of the automobile and of the airplane, but he lacked the sources of energy necessary to activate them; and yet he suspected the existence of that energy. When he conceived a cannon, the ball of which was to be propelled by steam obtained by pouring water into a chamber of copper heated very hot, he was close to the principle of the steam engine; but he did not conceive a machine capable of harnessing and using the energy thus released. Thus the two prime factors of the revolutions of the future were nearly brought together in Leonardo, but two more centuries were to go by before a new and more successful attempt to unite them projected us into the present age of machines (figure 20).

As early as the sixteenth century, with Leonardo, modern man embarked on the conquest of speed and of the world by means of the machine.

20. - *Opposite page:* PROJECT FOR HAND-DRIVEN FLYING MACHINE (HELICOPTER). From drawings by Leonardo da Vinci

may suggest the advent of an absolutely new era, we must realize that these developments were preceded by long and patient labor directed toward a single goal. Outwardly, man kept on inventing tools, to extend and multiply the activities of his hands; but at the same time, within himself, he kept trying to improve the organization of his mental capacities, to adjust them to the new conditions he aimed at achieving, and eventually also to the means he had discovered by which to attain this end. The relative slowness of thought when it was governed by the complicated rules of logic set modern man on a quest for some simpler, more direct mode of apprehension. He found it in sensation; yet abstract thought had itself been fashioned by the human species as a means of increasing its efficiency and speed of action.

THE PRE-LOGICAL AGE.   Early man found it natural to let himself be carried along by the stream of his sensory life. Sensations and emotions are the very substance of our inner life, a tide that bears us now lazily, now capriciously, with its current, seeming to demand of us no more than to be perceived. Our senses respond involuntarily to the external and internal stimuli that assail us. The child and the primitive do not go beyond such responses.

But the necessity to adjust, in order to survive, to the world around him soon compels the child, as it does the primitive, to form an idea of these stimuli that is enough to base an action on. From confused sensations and emotions he must derive concepts, if he is to find his way about in reality, and to make use of it. These concepts are at first mental images, memories of experiences whose significance lies in their emotional color—attraction, fear, repulsion. They point dimly toward practical application. Thus, neither the child nor the primitive sees reality as neutral, objective. Each impresses his affective tendencies on it, not distinguishing it from his dreams; each clothes it with the imaginary colors of his emotions. Where does the initial sense datum leave off and where does the concept, which lends the former a familiar aspect, denoting the attitude to be assumed toward it, begin?

In addition to what he perceives, the child feels, as does the primitive, the effects of invisible forces. Inevitably, he tends to endow each force with a material, recognizable appearance, usually that of the visible thing whose effects are most similar. By drawing an analogy with himself, early man conceived of every force as emanating from a conscious will, an organized being; and, again by analogy, he endowed such forces with material bodies, transforming them into gods or demons, human or animal figures (figure 21).

These invented images become as much a positive presence as the known forms whose aspects they assume. The child fashions for himself a thousand fantasies, the primitive a thousand superstitions and myths in which reality and his own responses to it are confused. Man attempts to fashion the endless, obscure actions of the powers that rule the world around him into an intelligible drama, to be played on his private stage. But he is necessarily confined to using décors and actors he has actually seen. This marvelous stage world, partly imaginary, that is interposed between himself and the real world helps him, despite its unreality, to form some idea—correct or incorrect—of what reality is, and to act upon it.

Early people represented invisible forces by embodying them in figures which spoke to the imagination.

21. - *Opposite page:* NAGA, GENIUS OF THE NETHER WORLD. Temple of Mukteshvara, Bhuvaneshvara, tenth century

Man's imaginary stage world is merely a projection of his natural inclinations. Every human group, like every individual, elaborates the fable that most suits its wishes; the subject common to all, reality, takes on a different appearance in each case. The interior image of nature is not distinguished from the exterior. But while the former can be and is infinitely variable, the latter is and must be identical for all, for otherwise irreparable confusion would follow. Purely mental images, fashioned according to dreams rather than ascertainable facts, are only for private use. They cannot easily be exchanged among different groups or different individuals.

The development of civilization could not for this reason be halted at the prelogical stage. If, after childhood, man continued to live only within his private fantasies, which reflect his own psyche more than they reflect "the other," the general, the universal, he would become increasingly bound by a convention suited only to himself and his most immediate surroundings; he would be alone in a stifling silence. In order to act upon things, to act with and on other living beings, he must acquire a means of communication, he must learn to understand others and make himself understood. He realizes, in time, that by remaining isolated and over-absorbed in his inner life, he runs the risk of being forever incapable of expressing himself, and thus inaccessible. The Romantics realized this: they constantly deplored the fact that one could not be completely oneself without experiencing the inability of communicating oneself to one's fellow man. "We shall all die unknown," Balzac observed.

In order to act, in order to enter into relations with other human beings, man must discover a mode of exchange whereby the signs he uses will be universally understood. This mode must be *neutral*, and therefore he cannot discover it in his emotions, for, however developed emotional expression may become, it remains forever an expression of his own intimate being, and hence obscure; the secret of man's inner life can be penetrated only by dint of long effort, which will never entirely dispel the uncertainty surrounding it.

THE LANGUAGE OF THE INTELLIGIBLE. Swift and efficient action requires an intelligible language. Such a language could develop only by establishing a kind of zone of neutrality in the sensory life, which had previously been too closely bound up with the particular, by digging beneath its changing surface to the bedrock. Details had to be eliminated, sacrificed, until, in response to the questioning blows of thought, there echoed the firm common ground of all knowledge, undisturbed by emotions and their interpretations. The goal was to uncover what might be called the common denominator of mental life.

This rigid skeletal framework, this bedrock of quasi-complete agreement about definitions, was the idea, and its covering was the word. The word and the idea represented a step toward the commonplace—the term is used here without its pejorative connotations—a step toward that which everybody could grasp in an identical way, without resorting to guesswork. The life of the senses, now under suspicion and repressed, was pushed into the background to make room for abstraction (*ab-trahere*, etymology says), for that which was literally extracted from the rich original confusion of subjective life. Every man could preserve his own sensory experiences within himself; social activity required abstraction.

The individual's inner possessions now became exchangeable, like goods. Society has long since given up the practice of barter; the farmer no longer takes his sacks of grain to the artisan to exchange them for, say, a piece of furniture. Instead, we have divested goods of their tangible worth, assessing their value in money, which is neutral and serves only as a means of exchange. Money became fictitious, then entirely abstract; it has assumed the form of the bank note whose value is conventional, determined by mutual agreement, but it is an ideal means of exchange. Similarly, ideas clothed in words make possible an exchange which would otherwise have remained impossible. But this result was achieved at a high cost—the real substance had to be sacrificed. The value of ideas is guaranteed by the reserve of sensory experiences (a value which is no longer verifiable, for the phenomena of inflation and compulsory rate of exchange exist in this realm too); ideas facilitate trade and, by tacit agreement, serve as substitutes for material and nontransferable values. They relieve us of the trouble of having to obtain direct, sensory knowledge of things.

By thus eliminating the personal factor from cognition, ideas marked an immense step forward on the way to speed and precision of action.

Civilized man has made increasing use of abstraction, which has many advantages to compensate for the loss of emotional content. Thanks to abstraction we can benefit from experiences that we have not undergone personally; it is enough to record the results of those that have been communicated to us by others. By substituting for the direct experience of a reality a designation, name, or even a sign, we keep our creative forces free for other tasks. Anything that has been ascertained once can be kept in reserve, filed in one's memory, and indicated by a brief label; the keenness of the searching mind is free to concentrate on the pertinent point. E. T. Bell has shown how mathematics, for example, progressed by becoming more abstract, more and more devoid of any positive concrete content.

The instrument that enabled civilization to gain this dominance was the book. When printing was invented, it became possible to multiply words and ideas, and to convey them to great numbers of people who had been living in the darkness of their sensory traditions. The "civilization of the book," as Lucien Febvre named it long ago, came into being. An ever-increasing number of people came to live on ideas, to change under their impact.

A new type of man developed, whose sensibility was inevitably atrophied, but whose intellectual powers were infinitely enriched; indeed, his mind was often jammed with notions that had made their way into language but were unintelligible to many who made use of them. The words, the outer shells of the ideas, were used identically by all, and at first look it was impossible to distinguish between persons who had grasped the inner substance and persons to whom words were empty shells, their use an *inanité sonore* (sonorous inanity), as Mallarmé might have said.

HAVENS FOR SENSIBILITY. Under such circumstances, what happened to sensibility? It found its voice only outside man's practical activities, in poetry and in art; and this voice is no longer rational, but suggestive. If each of us fails to communicate in direct proportion to his degree of emotional complexity, he can circumvent this difficulty by resorting to the ruse of evocation. There is nothing surprising about this. If we gave free rein to all those private resonances that make us individuals, communication would indeed be difficult, all things would be confusion.

Even assuming that we managed to obtain glimpses of one another's inner states, as we sometimes do through poetry and art, the task of communicating would involve a considerable strain on our intuitive faculties. It takes a great deal of time and effort to imagine what another person feels and to share feelings with him. Social life cannot adjust itself to this slowness, nor to the uncertainties and inevitable margin of error such a process entails.

That is why civilized societies, like the adult individual, have taken the emotional life out of circulation; it has been necessary to replace it with reason, to divest sensations of their personal overtones, and make them subject to the universal rules of logic. The West, following the model of Greece, developed this repressive social pattern with elegance and precision. It reached its apogee 2,500 years after the Greeks, in the scientific civilization, at once experimental and rational, of the nineteenth century.

Any man past childhood who perseveres in an existence dominated by his sensory reactions and fantasies is doomed to become maladjusted, isolated, to be by-passed and even crushed by modern society. That is the whole problem raised by recent psychology, with its distinction between the introvert and the extrovert. There is a way to escape from the dilemma, particularly for the man endowed with creative talents, and that is in art or poetry. The artist is admitted to and respected by society, for he fulfills the specialized task of feeling for others and of communicating to them the results of his adventures, saving them the trouble of living them themselves. The poet or the artist, to an ever-increasing extent, not only feels "more" than others, he also feels "for" others, who admire him but at the same time judge him to be a useless member of society, often secretly despising him. Society reveres in its artists a talent it no longer possesses itself, but at the same time it looks upon them as a symptom of its own weakness.

Not so among the primitives, in whose societies poetry and art are not reduced to a game, a luxury, an almost superfluous appendage, but reflect something divine. Carl Kiersmeier mentions a Negro kingdom in the Belgian Congo where, of the king's councilors, the most respected is the sculptor. How shocked we would be at the suggestion that we should grant a similarly high status to poets and artists in our governing bodies! On the contrary, it seems to us more proper to appoint to such bodies professional wielders of ideas and words, the professors and the lawyers.

Since the Renaissance, the civilization of the book has prevailed, as the high point of man's intellectual development. But the excesses of intellectualism have led us in the twentieth century to condemn this civilization as "bookish."

We must keep in mind that all this is true only of the West, although the East and other parts of the world are now trying forcibly to catch up with the West. But the West has made up its mind to be exclusively utilitarian: it is entirely oriented toward the mastery of the external world. It is obsessed by this: through science, through investigation of physical laws, it aims at acting upon the world, taming it, transforming it into the instrument of its desires. It aims at conquest of the universe and all its secrets, as well as of territories and nations![1]

In the West we value knowledge most when it is practical; its worth is determined by its positive consequences, by the hold it gives us over the forces surrounding us. As for interior knowledge, so highly prized by the Oriental, it has attracted us little,

[1] Claude Bernard, for instance, once said that the task of the human mind is "to conquer nature and wrest its secrets from it."

save as a means to mechanical efficiency, i.e., as rudimentary logic; aside from this, we are still novices in the field of inner development. To us progress is no more than the dream of an indefinitely expanding power over nature—a dream which in the nineteenth century became the true religion of European man.

The medieval era, still dominated by a Christianity conceived on the threshold of Asia, was less unlike the East. The rift has widened, most notably since the civilization of the book began to accelerate the speed of our progress, and it is a real gulf that the Eastern peoples, influenced by recent events, are now attempting to bridge.

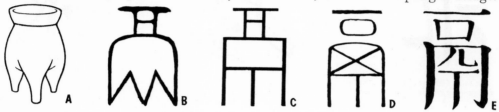

In China, as elsewhere, writing derives from the progressive schematization of figurative drawings.
22. - CALDRON. From A. Silcock, INTRODUCTION TO CHINESE ART

THE TESTIMONY OF WRITING.   This antithesis between East and West may be seen in the history of the written characters with which each culture records its thoughts. This analysis of the visual elements of writing leads into the revelations we hope to find in the works of art. In fact, it raises the essential problem of art.

It is, of course, possible to agree on a geometric form for each letter and to establish its so-called correct outline. The act of writing, however, involves a number of expressive movements governed by the nervous, muscular, and psychic systems. Written characters are a kind of seismographic chart, which only the expert graphologist can interpret; in writing, each of us makes his own the neutral and anonymous sign he intends only to reproduce. Thus each letter reveals not only its conventional meaning but also the nervousness, gentleness, or authoritativeness of the person who formed it. It comes closer either to abstraction or to the life of the senses, according to whether it follows the universal model exactly or interprets it by giving it an individual slant.

The prehistoric drawings of the Iberian Levant were degenerating into letterlike signs, resembling these inscribed pebbles from Mas d'Azil, as the Abbé Breuil and Obermaier have shown.
23. - *Left to right:* PREHISTORIC ROCK DRAWINGS AND A PEBBLE FROM MAS D'AZIL

The history of the alphabets reflects this evolution. In the beginning, the written character was a pictorial sign that developed out of the gradual schematization of drawings which were orginally intended as representations. Here, as elsewhere, the trend toward abstraction eliminates details, simplifies, tends toward the geometric, the diagram. Obermaier, the great student of prehistory, has patiently retraced the evolution of the spontaneous, almost Impressionistic Iberian rock drawings, dating from the late Paleolithic. The end result can be seen in the famous inscribed pebbles from Mas d'Azil. Significantly, Piette at first thought that the drawings on these

The same Chinese character varies in form according to circumstances. Here, the sign denoting eternity evokes the original image—the endless waves of the sea.

24. - VARIOUS STYLES OF CHINESE WRITING: "YUNG" (ETERNAL)

pebbles were alphabetical signs (figure 23). At all events, they cast light on the gradual formation of written characters.

In Egypt, as in China, the earliest letters represent recognizable objects; then, step by step, they are divested of their directly evocative power, and become mere conventional signs. Nevertheless, they often continue to carry a remote suggestion of the original pictures from which they derive (figures 22 and 24).

But of such survivals of the past, the last traces of sensory origins are in the end eliminated in the alphabets. Reason, by an inexorable process, detaches the sign from the word which it once represented, and reduces it to the mere designation of a sound, an element within the word; and eventually the sign comes to represent only an element detached from the sound—the letter. Then the alphabet is born, and

25. - *At left:* Another version of "YUNG"

In the West only artists are expected to produce beautiful lines and linear forms, but in the East—for instance, in China—the need for beauty has remained so universal that the same qualities are required in ordinary handwriting.

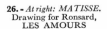

26. - *At right: MATISSE. Drawing for Ronsard,* LES AMOURS

finally typography, which reproduces letters mechanically, achieving the ultimate standardization of form, which cannot be achieved by handwriting. Under our very eyes, mankind has passed from the written character, which is a sensory, evocative image of the object, to a system of abstract signs that can be arranged at will to express the constructions of the intellect.

It is not surprising to note that the East has resisted this standardizing work of the intellect more stubbornly than the West. In Chinese calligraphy particularly, the suggestive elements rooted in the visual reality which the West has eliminated continue to make themselves felt. Until very recently the Chinese employed six styles of calligraphy; the abstract symbols varied according to circumstances: the traditional forms were used for official documents, and the modern forms for private correspondence.

Moreover, these signs explicitly preserve their connection with the representational images from which they derive. Referring to the character "yung" (eternal), on the basis of which the "Eight Laws of Writing" were formulated in the T'ang period, Hugh Gordon Porteus observes that it is a modification, in graphic style, of an ancient pictogram consisting of three waves and denoting "water."[1]

In the West, from the earliest medieval manuscripts to modern typography, the letters were progressively dehumanized and finally reduced to combinations of geometric elements.

27. - *Top to bottom:* CURSIVE WRITING, SIXTH CENTURY; MEROVINGIAN WRITING; CAROLINGIAN WRITING, NINTH CENTURY; GARAMOND TYPE FACE; DIDOT TYPE FACE; EUROPE TYPE FACE; BIFUR TYPE FACE

When we write the word "eternal," we trace a number of abstract conventional signs, whose meaning we must know in order to understand the word. But the Chinese written character "yung" graphically suggests the idea of eternity, since it consists of wavy lines, evocative of the ocean, which has no beginning or end. This idea is one of the themes of Chinese poetry, and like the magic of the verse, that of the brush, though silent, makes us experience directly the perpetual renewal of time (figure 24).

"Those marvelous ideograms," writes Grousset, "which seem to contain a mysterious charge of 'explosive' interpretations... are perhaps a more powerful

---

[1] *Background to Chinese Art*, p. 39. Faber and Faber, London, 1935.

stimulant to the mind than our barren alphabetic signs."[1] Western alphabets, stripped of such evocative power, were reduced to skeletons. In medieval books, the flexibility and communicative vibrancy of the hand lettering, the flourishes and *sigla*, all gave the copyist an opportunity to express his personality. During the Carolingian Renaissance this intrusion of the personal was checked, to some extent; the letters were standardized, geometrized, by being modeled on ancient inscriptions. In the fifteenth century, when the printed line made its appearance, abstraction continued its irresistible advance. Dürer and, shortly after him, Geoffroy Tory sought to discover "the proper and true proportion" of "good letters"; Tory taught that "among all the manual tools, the compass is the King and the ruler the Queen" (figure 3).

Nevertheless typography retained, through force of habit, some of the features of handwriting: for instance, forms corresponding to downstrokes and upstrokes. These were no more than a survival of the muscular motions necessary in handwriting, marking the points where the pen touched or was lifted from the page, suggesting a rhythm similar to that of breathing. Although the printed letter could have dispensed with such features, for some time no one thought of eliminating them.

In the nineteenth century, however, "Didot" type, austere and regular, almost wiped out the memory of a living hand; the trend toward mechanical neutrality which we call standardization is clearly manifested in it. That trend won the day in the twentieth century. The "Europe" type face is composed of simple straight lines and curves; however, the continuity of the letters is retained, reminding us of the original script. Nothing remains of it, however, in the more modern "Bifur" type, with its hachures and serifs which help to emphasize the more striking forms, playing down the others: the technique of the sensory shock makes it debut (figure 27).

This dehumanization of printed characters is so obvious that occasionally designers have attempted to react against it; the early Renaissance masters who gave the characters geometric forms tried at least to base their proportions on those of the human body. The investigations of Dürer, among others, bear witness to this. As late as the nineteenth century, letters were designed that suggested the silhouettes of people, animals, plants. These attempts are significant, psychologically, but they remained without influence and were not followed up.

More than this, handwriting itself began to succumb to the general trend. A new "script" is being taught, which imitates the inexpressive regularity of printed letters.

Certain teachers, particularly in Switzerland, have championed this type of handwriting, which induces the individual to imitate the effects of a machine, by outlawing slurs, variations of pressure, any kind of graphic interpretation. One of the advocates of this hand, M. Dottrens, condemns the traditional running hand, which reproduces the human gesture, in the following terms: "The hand reflects an obsolete artistic conception!" Thus, in the end, all survivals of personal expression are deliberately eliminated from handwriting (figure 29).[2]

[1] R. Grousset, *La Chine et son art*, p. vii.
[2] A lively debate on this subject took place between Pierre Foix and Delamain. Cf. *La Graphologie* Nos. 34 and 54, and *Figaro Littéraire* (August 15, 1953).

Typography has gradually freed itself from the domination of handwriting and its human characteristics; now handwriting has come to the point of negating itself and imitating typography and its mechanical aspects! It is as though we had reached an evolutionary stage in which only abstract elements, completely cut off from their sensory roots, would be tolerated. Thomas Reid, the eighteenth-century Scottish philosopher, in a text whose import has not been fully realized, foresaw this danger. According to him, artificial conventional signs *signify* but do not express; they speak to the understanding, as letters or algebraic figures, but they do not say anything to the heart, to the passions, to the affections, to the will. These signs have divested themselves and divested us of the language of nature that we bring with us into the world, but that we have forgotten because we did not use it. This language, Thomas Reid says, survives only in the arts.

Life and its necessities have taught us to eliminate the "useless," that is, the sensory element.

Photo Bibliothèque Nationale, Paris

In the sixteenth century, a page by Bourdichon combined the medieval miniature with the new conception of more regular and geometrical letters.

28. - *JEAN BOURDICHON*. ADORATION OF THE MAGI. Tours Missal. Fifteenth century. Bibliothèque Nationale, Paris

To restore it, we need the specialized efforts of poetry and art, which provide a compensation that society tolerates. Thomas Reid was less paradoxical than it may seem when he advised us to abolish the use of articulated sounds and writing for a century, for then every man would become a painter, actor, or orator.

THE ARTISTIC FACULTY. The momentary triumph of the intellect over the senses thus accounts for a surprising phenomenon, which has often been

Monsieur O. Lenoir
12 Avenue Foch
LAON (AISNE)

Recent attempts to eliminate all trace of the living hand from handwriting.

29. - SPECIMEN OF THE "SCRIPT" HAND

pointed out: in the oldest, most primitive societies, art was an essential element in everything, however humble, that was made. Why does it assume the status of a conscious quest, a luxury, as civilization develops? In every half-savage tribe in Africa or Polynesia, every archaic city brought back to life by excavations, even in every peasant community, however "backward," the most utilitarian objects —a crude vessel, ordinary cloth—are striking for their harmonious form, the sureness of their decorative taste. The beauty of these objects seems inseparable from their function, and the artisan who produces them does not distinguish between the two (figure 31).

Today, by contrast, it requires an effort to bring the two things together. The inexpensive article is merely efficient; the addition of beauty or what is claimed to be beauty increases the price, and transforms the article into a "de luxe" object: beauty is an optional superfluity. We are presently witnessing a reaction against this state of affairs, a reaction aroused by the too-provocative conspicuousness of a distinction that was formerly inconceivable. The curve of the lowliest ancient bowl was just as flawless as that of the vase made of the most precious metal (figures 30 and 32).

As soon as the machine made its appearance on the modern abstract scene, the object, fabricated according to an engineering blueprint, and produced by machine-made tools, ceased to be the product of sensibility, which animated the human hand. Any aesthetic qualities it possesses are now only a veneer, added deliberately. Under such circumstances art was inevitably reduced to passive imitation of accepted models or the application of formulas that have nothing in common with the irrepressible spontaneity of former days. Today we have only a "quest" for beauty; the term is revealing. And yet, as Picasso put it, beauty is not to be "sought"—it can only be "found."

The social consequences of this are tremendous: the traditional artisan, in whose work utilitarian fabrication was indistinguishable from aesthetic creation, is being gradually eliminated; he has become obsolete. His function is now divided between the worker, who cannot go beyond the limits of his machine—at best he is permitted to have some technical skills—and the artist, who, freed from specific duties, plunges ever more deeply into pure aesthetics, to the point of eventually losing contact with society.

Significantly, this division began to be felt during the Renaissance, when the "civilization of the book" was born. But for some time the artisan and the artist shared in each other's interests: the former continued to be concerned with art, the latter to feel obliged to satisfy the social demand. With the advent of the machine, however, the artisan's function was reduced to that of a living mechanism; he became a worker, a proletarian. As for the artist, he cut himself off from society in order to pursue, for himself and for a small elite, ever more specialized aesthetic explorations; he gradually lost interest in communicating with the public. This led to a dramatic cleavage, in which the worker's humanity became enslaved, while

31. - *Below:* SPOONS FROM BRITTANY. Nineteenth century. Musée des Arts et Traditions Populaires, Paris

Photos Flammarion

30. - SERVICE FOR TRAVELING

Before the reign of the machine, beauty and function were inseparable in objects of daily use. Today the object is exclusively utilitarian; what is called "beauty" is a "supplementary" luxury.

32. - SERVICE FOR FISH

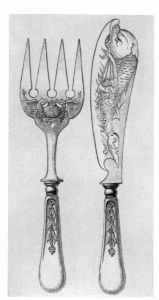

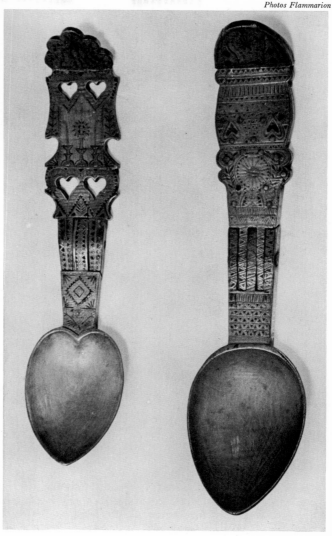

37

the artist preserved his own only by withdrawing into creative solitude. The proletarian unrest that has caused so many social convulsions in our era must perhaps be accounted for not merely by social causes, but also by a deep psychological cause—the fact that man has become unbalanced, thwarted in his normal development.

The effects of this cleavage on art were no less considerable: beauty thus separated, "extracted," from spontaneous creation, had to be defined more clearly. As a result, it lost its naturalness, and was exposed to all the risks of artificiality. It no longer emerged spontaneously out of an inner harmony, the fruit of talent developed by training; its sensory origin was forgotten, and it became the object of abstract formulas and definitions. Made the property of the lucid intelligence, it was too often cut off from its living sources.

Monstrously, art was reduced to theories of which the work itself became only an illustrative application; aesthetics, which the ancient world had only touched upon occasionally in its philosophical explorations, now became a full-fledged system, and even sought to rule the creative act. In the Middle Ages art was still *natural;* from the Renaissance on, it was thought necessary to *think* in order to create.

When the civilization of the book, which began in the Renaissance, reached its culmination in the nineteenth century, the shift had gone so far that art sought a reason for its existence outside its own nature; it was thought that art could be justified only if it were made to serve an ascertainable value. Middle-class society, brought to the fore by the French Revolution, imagined that the principle of art was richness: it found beauty, which it confused with luxury, in precious materials, lavish ornamentation, in ostentatious displays of learning—i.e., in conscious or unconscious imitations of recognized historical "styles" (figure 33).

Then, as the machine extended its rule, modern industrialized society, rejecting in the name of science everything that did not serve some positive purpose, reduced beauty to utility, and imagined that it could be found in perfect adjustment to practical functions, in so-called "functionalism." This was a praiseworthy reaction against the excesses of luxury. The perfectly efficient form was often harmonious in its bareness: beauty can indeed be discovered in the simplified lines that the mind imposes on the chance patterns of things. However, such instances of the beautiful do not obviate a basic confusion that is apparent in the very terminology of this aesthetics: the "useful" requires a complement. It is useful *to* something, it serves a purpose that is external to it. But the beautiful cannot have a purpose other than itself; it is not beautiful "for" something or "to" something, and this fundamental difference, which Socrates pointed out long ago, is enough to distinguish the two concepts, which can never coincide (figure 34).[1]

---

[1] Cf. Plato, *Hippias Major*, in which we also find the distinction between αὐτὸ τὸ καλόν, "the beautiful in itself," and καλὸν πρὸς τι, "the beautiful" (we should use the term "good") "for something." Aristotle retained this distinction (*Poetics*, VII, 13).

33. - THE FOYER OF THE OPÉRA, by *GARNIER*

Having lost the instinct for beauty, the modern era seeks beauty in secondary features: the nineteenth century in displays of wealth, the twentieth in functional bareness.

34. - THE FOYER OF THE THÉÂTRE NATIONAL DE CHAILLOT, by *CARLU*

Vlaminck's landscapes, pierced by high-speed roads, suggest the vision of the man at the wheel.
35. - *VLAMINCK.* LA NATIONALE

3. THE CIVILIZATION OF THE IMAGE

THE civilization of the book ends with the nineteenth century. The machine at first fostered its ascendancy; but soon, carried away by its own impetus, it forced this civilization to transcend itself. Man, obsessed with speed, had preferred thinking to experiencing; now thought in turn became too slow: swifter than sensibility, it still could not achieve instantaneousness. And this era of ours requires instantaneous apprehension! Thought is discursive; to express an idea in a sentence requires a subject and a predicate, at least, and often an object as well —the three elements must be juxtaposed to reveal the meaning. Thought is ana-

40

lytical: it breaks up a confused idea into its elements, which it puts together again in accordance with the laws of logic. We have to move faster!

What can we turn to? It acts as a sign which is spontaneously registered; and if the senses are trained to set off an instinctive response in the form of a reflex, considerable time is gained. The reflex saves the seconds that would have been wasted by the detour of the thought. A ringing bell acts more swiftly than an explication! The message of the senses elicits an immediate, a simultaneous perception.[1] All you have to do is open your eyes, and you perceive at a glance a complex whole, a totality. Contemporary man needs such total perceptions, which alone are compatible with the speed that governs his life.

THREATS TO INNER LIFE. The machine makes great demands upon us. Originally a means of action, a slave, it gradually left its imprint on its master. Man conceived and fashioned the machine in the likeness of his desires; but he invented it to make up for his own deficiencies; hence, it could not resemble him. Yet in order to control his machines man had to become adjusted to them. This was a dangerous temptation. Through successive surrenders, man has been led to nullify himself so as to comply with the laws of this creation of his, which was meant to act as his deputy, and on which he has come to depend. To meditate, to confront one's actions with the state of one's feelings involves hesitation, and this is a factor that has no place in the machine. Man's inwardness is incompatible with infallibility of action; that can be achieved only by uniformity, from which the unforeseen is excluded. And inwardness hinders the speed of action, since it requires a pause.

The horseman of the past was a living being manipulating another living being; although his horse was his inferior, it too had feelings and capacities. It was necessary for him to anticipate the horse's natural reactions, adjust his demands to them. This often required a great deal of psychology and intuition. These would merely be a hindrance to the motorist, who has no use for such subjective considerations. The faultless performance of his function—that of attaining speed—rests primarily on sure reflexes. In other words, under identical circumstances, he must perform identical motions, in order to achieve known results; he must repress his inner freedom along with his desire to take chances, and improve his automatic reflexes, protect them against the delays caused by reflection. Do you doubt this? Then read the following item, printed in the newspapers in 1949:

"The most dangerous drivers are the intelligent people, and more particularly the intellectuals. A New York Negro, medically classified as a moron, had just obtained his driver's license, and been hired by a bus line. The decision was taken on the strength of a report by Professor James Kaker, of the University of Chicago. According to him, the ideal driver is the 'high-grade moron.'" Disregarding the paradox and the ironical connotations of this item, we may say that it strikingly characterizes our present stage of development, in which reflective thought has been supplanted, for the sake of speed, by the organized reflex.

[1] Delacroix had observed this, comparing the poet with the painter: "The poet solves his problem by a succession of images; the painter, by a simultaneity of images" (*Journal*, Supplement, III, p. 417, December 16, 1843).

The identity of the machines results in the identity of their masters. Different conceptions, distinctive modes of feeling are but a handicap in the face of uniform instruments, and imply the risk of mishandling, of delay. Modern man accepts the laws of his tool; he calls it standardization. Man himself, as a component part of the social motor, tends to become interchangeable, predictable in his behavior, and usable without time-consuming psychological training.

This trend is universal; nations that we regard today as irreconcilable adversaries will be described by the future historian as competitors bent on achieving the same goal. We may venture to say that Nazism, Fascism, Marxist Russia, and capitalist America will some day appear to have been rivals seeking the same prize by varying methods. Behind their disparate ideologies, there is the same hidden motive—that of creating a homogeneous, neutralized individual, suited to play the part of a cog in powerful collective mechanisms. All of them strive, by means of external pressure and legislation, to cast the mold which will serve to produce the ideal citizen, whose reflexes can be predicted and controlled. Whether the objective is industrial efficiency or military power, to form this man is the major preoccupation of all "modern" societies. There are a thousand indications of this everywhere, but we have grown to accept them without realizing their significance.

THE SIGN REPLACES THE WORD.   Yesterday, the individual had explained to him the meaning of the motions required of him; notices or labels intelligibly stated it, and he performed the given motions after understanding their meaning. Today he is trained to respond rapidly and automatically to specific stimuli.

Not so long ago, on entering a village, the motorist was told by virtue of what municipal regulation he was forbidden to exceed a certain—incidentally, very moderate—speed. Elsewhere he was asked not to blow his horn, and the reason for the request—proximity to a hospital, for instance—was given. Today the traffic regulations are conveyed exclusively by lines or diagrams: an S rearing like a snake means a sharp turn; two stylized children holding hands, a school.

The sign catches the eye effectively. The smashed and charred body of a car that is occasionally placed on a concrete pedestal at the side of an American highway as a warning to drivers is more certain to make them take their feet off the accelerator than a long speech, more so even than a billboard with a skull and bones, which is used elsewhere. In this example, the sign still preserves an intelligible relation to what it stands for.

Our life centers around elementary sensations—bells ringing, red and green lights, a bar on a colored disk, etc.—to which we are trained to respond by appropriate actions. It might be objected that such responses are confined to the street, the area of collective life. But let us look into the domain of private life—even into the privacy of the bathroom. Not so long ago, the Victorian idea of convenience decreed two faucets, on which we could read the words "hot" and "cold." Choosing one or the other required a minimal effort of thought—but still, it was thought. Man in his hurry wanted to spare himself this trouble, so the words became signs, the initials H and C being substituted. But apparently even this moderate appeal to our reasoning faculties seemed excessive, for recently the letters have been replaced by two spots, one red and one blue. To grasp their significance we no longer follow the path of understanding, but that of sensation: red, associated with fire, with molten metal, is a hot color; blue is a cold color, that of water or ice. These signs have nothing to do with thinking: a bold short-cut made it possible to dispense with thought, to establish a direct line between the perception and the subsequent action.

Words, the all-powerful words which once ruled the civilization of the book, are yielding to the general thirst for speed: they abdicate, they shrivel, they go over to the enemy. It is possible to trace through history this progressive contraction of thought. The seventeenth-century sentence is long and complex. This is the period of the fully developed idea, of the dissertation in which thought seeks continually to expand, to the point of occasional redundance of expression. The eighteenth century, by contrast, sets out to pare down and abridge the form, and produces the "Voltairean" sentence, which serves as the model for modern language and its conciseness. Actually, it was in the eighteenth century, chiefly under the influence of England, where the machine first came into prominence, that the primacy of sensation over thought began to assert itself. Then the abstract and rationalist philosophies yielded to the sensualist doctrines which derived the human mind from sensation. It is enough to mention Locke and Hume, and the tremendous popularity of their theories, which spread all over Europe, and to which the nineteenth century that saw the rise of the "psychology of sensation" owes a great deal.

In the twentieth century came the vogue for artificially compressed texts published in special magazines, called digests, where the originals are handed over to teams of reducers rather than to editors. Moreover, the newspapers popularized the use of pictures, which make it possible to replace the text with a few simple sentences, a practice which previously had been confined to children's literature.

Parallel with this contraction of thought goes an abandoning of discursive features in favor of sudden effects, similar to those of sensation; avoiding lengthy commentaries, communication now aims at concentration, in order to end up with the modern slogan, in which the idea is so compressed that its effect resembles that of the sensory shock with its resultant automatism. The sentence yields to the visual shock. Stereotyped, it no longer aims at being understood, but merely recognized.

The word, too, succumbs to the pressures of the age; it evolves into the sign which presents a conventional aspect of the thing denoted, instead of an abstract meaning. The word is replaced by the initial. The day before yesterday, one said "The Holy Alliance of the Nations"; yesterday, the League of Nations was called the L.N. Today, the initials that have supplanted the words are further concentrated into an auditory sensation, even more simplified. Now we do not even say the U.N.O.; this succession of separate letters is molded into a single articulation— UNO. Similarly, we say IBM (for International Business Machines), while twenty-five years ago we still said Y.M.C.A. (for Young Men's Christian Association). Everywhere the "intelligible" yields to the "perceived," particularly to the visual, by which we take in at a glance a multiplicity of elements presented simultaneously.

In America, where the intellectual tradition is less deep-rooted than in Europe, this use of the sign is widespread. A surprising and characteristic example of it is the postcard which saves the tourist the trouble of writing. Printed on it are a score of stock remarks, to which modern society tends to reduce epistolary ex-

BUSY PERSON'S CORRESPONDENCE CARD

HELLO		I SPEND MY TIME	
PAL	SUGAR	MOTORING	
FOLKS	HUBBY	HIKING	
CHUM	WIFEY	BOATING	
THIS PLACE IS		FISHING	
QUIET	NOISY	READING	
IDEAL	GRAND	LOAFING	
NOTHING EXTRA		SIGHTSEEING	
BEST ON THE MAP		BORROWING MONEY	
THE WEATHER IS		I NEED	
WARM	COOL	MONEY	YOU
WET	DRY	SLEEP	REST
PLEASANT		A GOOD JOB	
DREARY		$1,000,000	
THE FOLKS ARE		WILL SEE YOU	
NICE	SILLY	SOON	
QUIET	NOISY	LATER	
ENTERTAINING		NEXT WEEK	
FULL OF PEP		ON	
I'M FEELING		GIVE MY REGARDS TO	
FINE	WELL	MA AND DAD	
BUM	SICK	THE CHILDREN	
BLUE	HAPPY	MY CHUMS	
VERY LONESOME		EVERYBODY	

U S CAPITOL WASHINGTON D C

CHECK ITEMS DESIRED

America invented the postcard that need not be written.

36. - AMERICAN POSTCARD FOR USE BY THE "BUSY PERSON"

changes among people. The user need merely check the sentences he wishes to say and cross out the others. Thus personal expression is subjected, in normal times, to a constraint as brutal as that to which correspondence between Frenchmen living in the free and occupied zones was subject during the German Occupation (figure 36).

This is not an isolated, exceptional case but the expression of a system. Another variation of it is found in the coded messages that were made available to the American troops in Korea. This time, sentences were eliminated altogether, and replaced by numbers. According to the *Figaro Littéraire* of February 3, 1951, the code comprised 300 typical messages, covering all human activities—love, finances, health, the family. Needless to say, love could be expressed with great precision: No. 42 conveyed "kisses," while No. 43 meant "love and kisses." But the most frequently used was No. 44: "fondest love and kisses." No. 74 does not refer to love; it stands for "thanks for your kind financial help."

THE IMPACT OF THE IMAGE. If sensation and the basic images that evoke it were put only to utilitarian purposes, one might regard the dominance of the visual as merely one effect of mechanization rather than as the symptom of a deep trend of our era. But the visual extends its sway much further: it seeks to bring the human mind into subjection, and the mind seems strangely compliant. Advertising, that obsession of our time, is the best proof of this: it both exploits the power of the visual and contributes to its spread. Now, advertising provides us with a particularly accurate picture of the contemporary mind, for if it did not understand this mind, it would be doomed to failure. Unlike literature or philosophy, advertising cannot afford to make mistakes: a single misstep would be fatal. To survive, advertising must be effective, and hence it must gratify a need of the minds it influences.

At its beginnings, a little over a century ago, advertising was verbal and ideological; it exploited the authority of the word. Balzac, who in 1837 outlined its "physiology" in *César Birotteau*, composed a stupendous prospectus for a "double cream of the Sultanas and carminative water," which he refers to as "what the historians call a 'corroborative document.'" "The ridiculous *phraseology* was one of the elements of its success," Balzac points out, as well as "the magic exerted by these *words*," evocative of the Orient (my italics). This is not merely a thesis invented

44

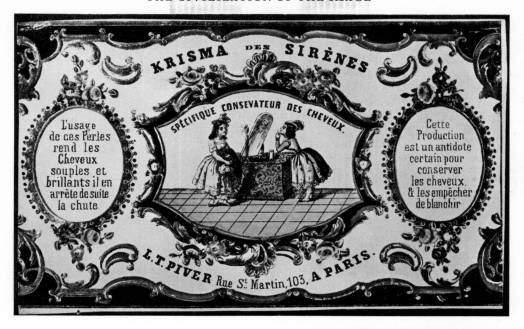

37. - ADVERTISEMENT FOR KRISMA DES SIRÈNES,
manufactured by *L. T. PIVER*

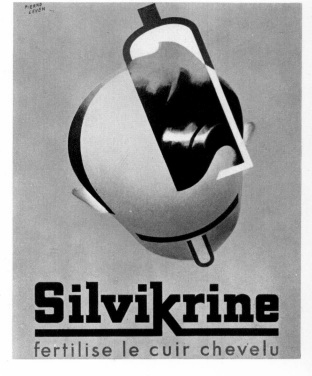

A century ago advertising appealed to the literary and artistic tastes of the public. Today, visual shock is used for quick effect.

38. - ADVERTISEMENT FOR SILVIKRINE (hair lotion)

45

By appealing to instinctual mental associations, advertising artificially creates a desire for given products.

39. - ADVERTISEMENT FOR THE SWISS SUN-TAN OIL HAMOL

by a novelist: it is easy to find contemporary documents not a bit less extravagant than the speeches of his great perfume-maker. There was, for instance, an advertisement for *Krisma des Sirènes*, which was couched in equally flowery language, exploiting not the romantic appeal of the East but the classical appeal of Greece. The advertising of the mid-nineteenth century was "literary." It praised the qualities of a product; eloquence and rhetoric, sometimes soaring to the heights of nonsense, were its most valuable instruments in its effort to reach the customer, for the aim was to persuade him. Pictures were used, but merely as an ornamental accompaniment (figure 37).

Today, the aim of advertising is different: it is necessary to shock the customer to implant in his visual memory, by the device of surprise or repetition, an image that will stay with him. The purpose is no longer to make him think or to obtain his conscious approval of a given product. The image forces a simple idea upon him by means of a visual attack; entering through the eye, it sneaks into his mind like a burglar, and establishes there a permanent connection between the product and the need it is alleged to gratify. Whether this association is justified or even rational is beside the point: to show is to prove.

Arguments pro and con are no longer weighed, nor can they be weighed: there are no arguments. The image creates an unbreakable link between a given remedy and the flourishing appearance of a healthy man; a bald pate is covered with thick hair when seen through a bottle of the advertised hair tonic, and so on. The visual impression assumes the character of a factual statement. It provides direct evidence, as no idea can, since ideas are subject to criticism (figure 38).

As I have said, the association of ideas thus implanted need not be rational. In the examples given above it still is. It is not logically impossible that chemical science should develop a substance that stimulates the growth of hair. The customer hopes for such a tonic, and that is sufficient to win his confidence. But actually the image can do more than this: it can create convictions that are completely unfounded. Since they are not subject to rational examination, they can be arbitrary and even absurd; the man who holds such convictions may be unaware of them, for his function has been merely to record them in his memory. Advertisers soon began to be aware of this irresistible power of images, and have not shrunk from exploiting it. For example, in the case of a sun-tan lotion, the older, still-rational method consisted in showing a section of magnificently golden skin seen through the miraculous

bottle. The new, improved method (figure 39) shows merely a young couple reclining together on a beach, their heads framed by a large red heart. The picture has no rational relation to the effectiveness of the lotion. But the advertiser, going deeper than the mere wish of the buyer to acquire a rich sun tan, attempts to arouse his obscure longings for romance, to get at his whole naïve fantasy life. In addition, he makes use of the magic appeal of the movies, which is surreptitiously suggested. (Similarly, the sirens in travel ads sing "Sunshine and romance.") This ad appeals to the prospective buyer's unconscious emotional urges that have nothing to do with the product in question.

THOUGHT AND REFLEX. Properly direct sensory stimuli by-pass the mind's rational areas, automatically releasing instinctual forces that are not consciously controlled. Writing in 1947, I suggested[1] that we have here an instance of Pavlov's conditioned reflex, the cornerstone of Russian psychology. Pavlov's experiment is well known; if for some days in succession a dog is given a piece of meat when a bell rings, this dog will salivate at the mere ringing of the bell, even when it is given no meat. A shift has taken place; the normal association has been replaced by an artificially induced one. In this experiment it is not the mind that is deceived but the biological reflex itself!

Once a man's intelligence has been lulled to sleep and the way opened to invading sensory stimuli, he docilely accepts the message they convey. André Malraux, in the Epilogue he added to his *Conquerors* in 1949, observes: "The aim is always to produce a conditioned reflex. A given set of terms is systematically connected with given names, and these names end up by evoking the emotions that the terms themselves habitually evoke."

It is hardly necessary to point out that such psychological technique can be used to mold people's minds, to set up in them a chain of unconscious associations, which will release the desired emotional responses. The individual exposed to this kind of collective hypnotism will acquire beliefs that are all the more impervious to rational criticism because they are unconscious, almost organic roots.

The effectiveness of the mechanism has often been demonstrated in the political sphere. In 1919, a poster showing a Bolshevik with a knife between his teeth, disheveled, his eyes staring ferociously, his hands dripping with blood, contributed more to the defeat of the French Communists than any rational argument. More recently, French Communist posters have linked the idea of Communism with pictures of young people enjoying the countryside, sunny weather, and flowering trees. Everybody knows that no political party can affect the weather or the rhythm of the seasons; but by means of the conditioned reflex, these posters implant such a belief in the viewer's unconscious mind. These instinctual forces can be mobilized with equal effectiveness in support of or against the same political group.

The continued use of such techniques undoubtedly reduces the power of the "self," whereas the civilization of the book had exalted the self to the point of egotism. And these techniques weaken the self for another reason: the self is the source of nuances, and individual variations, but the influence of sensory stimuli is

---

[1] *Bulletin de l'Institut National Genevois*, II, 1947.

based exclusively on the factor of intensity, which is a corollary of speed. To elicit the desired response, the stimulus must be strong, must produce a shock, must strike hard. It is not surprising that violent sensation has become a need of the modern era. The swifter the advance of civilization, the more such violence is valued, and America, which is not deterred by tradition, cultivates it more openly than Europe.

The history of the poster once again provides us with striking illustrations. In the nineteenth century, pictorial advertising, like the official art of the time, was based on the use of drawings, which applied the intellectual elements of form and outline. At the end of that century, color became the predominant factor in poster art, just as it had been victorious in painting from Delacroix to the Impressionists. Color triumphed

40. - *At left: FERDINAND HODLER.*
LE BÛCHERON. 1910

A comparison between the treatments of a given subject, Le Bûcheron ("Woodcutter"—name of a French furniture factory) by an early twentieth-century designer and by later specialists of the poster shows the gradual triumph of the schematic and the visual shock.

41. - *Above: CASSANDRE.*
POSTER FOR LE BÛCHERON. 1923

42. - *Center: CASSANDRE.*
POSTER FOR LE BÛCHERON. 1924

43. - *At right: LOUPOT.*
THE WOODEN MAN

49

For the last hundred years the evolution of art has revealed the same tendencies as the poster. Around 1850 Courbet sought primarily to produce an illusionistic rendering of what he actually saw.

Photo Flammarion

44. - *COURBET.* CLIFFS AT ÉTRETAT

not only over line but also over values, the subtle nuances of chiaroscuro. The earliest masterpieces of modern poster art, those of Lautrec and Bonnard, are based solely on the sensory appeal of the color spot and its contour: modeling and shading are eliminated and all that is left is a flatly painted area of color, surrounded by a thick black line, resembling the leaded outlines in a stained-glass window. This line ignores the traditional ideas of form—it is a continuous stroke developing into an arabesque, which impresses us by its originality and boldness (plate II).

In the twentieth century line and color have been further simplified and used more aggressively; today, their primary function is to give "punch," to compel the viewer's attention, to impress upon him, however much in a hurry he may be, the significance of the image he is confronted with. The drawing has been reduced to a mere diagram, a shorthand notation. Many familiar posters have evolved under our very eyes; in a few years they have passed from careful realism to near-abstraction. It would be instructive to observe the parallel evolution in modern art (figures 40 to 45).

In a chorus that grows ever louder, one must raise one's voice to make oneself heard. Thus it has come about that color has achieved unexpected intensity with the help of electric lights. Today color glows and flashes, it all but leaps off the surface, it assaults the eye. It has to catch the attention of the pedestrian hurrying past, and sometimes it is itself in motion, a placard borne by a bus and plunging with it through space.

SENSORY EXHAUSTION.   It is now necessary to take into account the sensory wear and tear on the overtaxed and blasé viewer. Habituation results in a thirst

A twentieth-century treatment of a motif similar to Courbet's shows the cliffs, the beach, and the boats disposed in successive planes. Here everything is subordinated to a concentrated synthesis of plastic effects.

45. - *BRAQUE.* CLIFFS

for greater violence, which becomes indispensable: a ceaseless drumming sound ends by dulling our ears.[1] We may ask whether the threshold of all our perceptions is not being raised. We observe that the color is rawer and, so to speak, more forced in American-produced motion pictures than it is in those originating in Europe, where the wearing-down process is less advanced, and American physiologists have indeed concluded that the level at which we register color has risen. Similarly it has been suggested that the modern ear has become incapable of hearing certain tones that were formerly audible to it. Nuances, now a thing of the past, are being eliminated in favor of intensity of expression.

There is evidence in support of this. When, after the collapse of Germany, the Agfa plant became the property of the victors, the formula for manufacturing the film was deliberately changed, in the United States, in order to obtain more glaring color, even though this meant less precise reproduction. This was done in answer to consumer demand. Even old Europe has now been affected by this trend: careful scrutiny shows that art-book publishers tend to exaggerate the colors in reproductions of paintings, aiming at more "flattering" effects.

The same trend accounts for the excesses indulged in (sometimes unwittingly) by some of the great Anglo-Saxon museums, where in restoring Old Masters, the paintings have been made to conform to current optical requirements by means of

[1] With his usual perspicacity Paul Valéry foresaw this. "Whether in politics, economy, social life, entertainment, motion, I notice that the pace of modernity is that of intoxication. We must increase the doses or shift to a new drug. Such is the law: ever more advanced, ever more intense, ever bigger, ever faster, and always newer. Such are the requirements, which are necessarily matched by a somewhat blunted sensibility" (*Degas, Danse, Dessin*, p. 136).

brutal scouring. And yet those responsible for such practices, as well as those who defend them, are acting in good faith; it is only that their eyes are not sensitive to the subtleties the painters once sought to express by infinitely light varnishes or even by seemingly murky patinas. Furthermore, the museum officials rely less on their own trained eyes than on the mechanical findings of their laboratories, which cannot record these fine nuances. Should not the laboratories be required, in the first place, to gauge the sensitivity of the restorers' and curators' eyes? That is the crux of the matter.

A servile faith in the physicist's instruments is a confession of sensory inadequacy, the mark of abdication; in fact, instruments, which measure quantity but not quality, cannot equal the human eye. No test-tube finding can even come close to the sensitivity of the professional taster when it comes to evaluating a wine. And yet our senses of smell and taste are less highly trained than our sense of sight. The blind recourse to measurements taken by instruments, a confession of human impotence, is a symptom of our era; it is also a confirmation of an irrevocable law.

Everywhere the typical, the average, replaces the refined variations of individual sensibilities. The eclipse of the nuance has as its consequence a lowering of taste, which is the faculty of perceiving and appreciating nuances. Its decline opens the way for an invasion of brilliant and often clashing colors into the realm of clothing, and in France neckties or sports shirts imported from America are worn which would formerly have been regarded as "loud." Men, whose perceptions are less keen, are the first to succumb to such things, while women still resist and continue to invoke the European tradition. "Beauty has died, so to speak," writes Paul Valéry. "Novelty, intensity, strangeness—in short, all the values of shock—have supplanted it."

The appetite for surprise and for crudeness manifests itself everywhere. Open your newspaper: from the headlines above the articles (and their spirit) to the last-page advertisements, the entire contents are aimed at "causing a sensation," as we unwittingly confess by the very use of this phrase. Go to a country fair: the attractions offer, physically, speed and shock—rapid, whirling, sudden, abrupt motions; psychologically, they arouse the most elementary emotions, those closest to the organic reflex—eroticism and fear. The horror story and sex have become the two mainsprings of public appeal, the two focal points.... One word, repeated over and over, dominates the billboards and the advertisements—Sensations! Sensational! —and is echoed by the Anglicism "Exciting!" That is what Valéry called "the rhetoric of shock."

· And visual device—the simplified image, flaunting, provocative, screaming with color and bold forms—becomes the instrument of a universal appeal, waited for by avid eyes and releasing in our nerve centers the reflexes of greed and appetite.

At the opposite extreme, the highest realms of thought show signs of a similar pressure; the present-day popularity of existentialism and phenomenology may be accounted for by the fact that these systems reject intellectual comprehension of the world in favor of direct intuitive apprehension. They aim at what might be called "the sensation of being," invoking a kind of metaphysical sensory shock.

If this is what we have come to, what consequences may be expected? We are heirs of the civilization of the book, and suffering from the diseases accompanying its decline; at the same time, we are the pioneers of the civilization of the image, and are carried along by its impetuous advance, which we do not yet understand well enough to control it. We are in the midst of an era of transition. Torn between our past and our future, discouraged by our contradictions and our excesses, we feel both too old and too young. The epoch is exhilarating for the observer, but crushing for those who must experience it and try to find their place in it.

DECLINE OF THE INDIVIDUAL. What is threatened, what shrinks each day—like the magic skin in Balzac's story *Peau de chagrin*— is the margin for individual existence that society grants to its members. One of the first effects of the systematic intellectualism that marked the civilization of the book was that authentic personal sensibility, nourished on actual experience, was submerged by a mass of ideas and words. Ideas and words enable us to think and to express not only what we ourselves experience but also that of which we have only an abstract, artificial, borrowed notion. The flood of prefabricated mental images silences the inner voice of the common man as well as that of the most refined intellectual. Hence, as a reaction against this, our interest in the poet and in the artist, the child and the madman, the heterogeneous, and sometimes outrageous, body of those who, actively or passively, still retain direct communication with their interior motivations, whose lives are not entirely swallowed up by collective rational activities.

The civilization of the image has gone one step further: by-passing reasoning and judgment, it has established a direct relationship between sensation and action. It has tremendous resources with which to shape human conduct, thanks to the system of co-ordinated sensory stimuli it employs. The difference between the free nations and those not free is actually no more than this—that in the former these resources of the visual are used by groups or parties in competition with one another, while in the latter they are controlled by the governments.

The civilization of the book, while systematizing the means of exchange among human beings, at least favored individualism. Reading is practiced in isolation; the book submits its intellectualized material to the judge who sits within each reader; safe in his private chamber, he can choose whatever he considers valuable enough to be stored in the memory.

But this civilization has been under attack for more than a century. As early as 1819, Lamennais, in his *Mélanges religieux et philosophiques*, sounded the alarm: "We have stopped reading, we have not the time. Our mind is solicited simultaneously from too many sides: it has to be spoken to quickly as it passes by. But there are things that cannot be said or understood in such haste, and these are the most important things for man. This accelerated movement, which makes coherent thought impossible, may alone be sufficient to weaken, and in the long run utterly destroy, human reason." 1819! This pronouncement was not heeded at the time. Today it stands illumined by a glaring light.

The civilization of the image invades and occupies the individual as it would conquer a territory. It leaves us no time for examining and assimilating things: it imposes on us its sudden and rapid intrusions and its authoritarian rhythm. The spectator (or the listener, as the case may be) is now only a cog in a machine. Aldous Huxley in *On the Margin* summed up the results of the development denounced by Lamennais. The book has been supplanted by the motion picture, by

46. - *DAVID.* THE RAPE OF THE SABINES. The Louvre, Paris

Art books direct the reader's attention by isolating details from their context.

47. - *Opposite page:* THE SHEAF OF WHEAT. Detail from the same painting

the radio, those providers of ready-made entertainment, which require on the part of the pleasure seekers no personal participation and no intellectual effort, however slight.

Long before Huxley, Kafka had analyzed the authoritarian tendency of the image with rare penetration: "I am a visual type. But the cinema disturbs vision. Because of the hurried rhythm of the motion and the rapid changing of the images, we inevitably fail to see what is projected. It is not the eye that takes hold of the images, it is the images that take hold of the eye. They envelop the mind. The cinema puts the eye, which up until now has been naked, into uniform." And, referring to the saying that the eye is the window of the soul, he concluded, "Motion pictures are the iron shutters on that window."[1]

Now, freedom is first of all the freedom to choose. What will be the fate of this freedom? Sensation as we know it today is not free but controlled, not only because it is imposed on us from all sides, but also because it tolerates no margin for judgment. Nothing is more revealing than its tendency to dictate even details. Formerly

[1] Interview reprinted in *Allemagne d'aujourd'hui,* July–August, 1951.

the viewer, confronted with a painting, was left to himself, and had an opportunity to form his own opinion. Today comments posted on the walls, or blared through the loud-speaker, which has made its way even into art galleries, direct the viewer's attention to particular aspects of what he sees.

The art book, by means of carefully chosen photographs, forces the eye to fix on one detail or another of the painting. As for the motion picture, it completely takes over the eye, dictates its rhythms and directions to it, tells it when to roam and when to pause, and sometimes even what path to follow. In Haesaerts' *Rubens*, this technique has been applied with great effectiveness. The eye, tamed, obeys; and thought, held on the leash, must follow. For alongside the fixed image of the illustration, the motion picture and television have placed the moving image, whose activity parallels that of the individual's inner life. The book does the same thing, but with it, we dictate the pace, and we can stop reading it at will, thus asserting our freedom (figures 46 to 48).

Now speed enters in, and we are no longer given a chance to rest between visual impressions. This is true not only of spectacles; it is also true of everyday life. The

Motion pictures lead the eye through a painting along an arbitrary path.

48. - *RUBENS.* KERMESSE. The Louvre, Paris. Diagram of the sequence of images in Paul Haesaerts' and Henri Storck's film on Rubens

landscapes speeding past the window of the train or the automobile only rarely give the overstrained eye an opportunity to relax—and to stop, never! Gradually we become insatiable for images; the eye, intoxicated with mobility, no longer knows the pause necessary for savoring a nuance of feeling or for meditation; it is bent only on hurriedly stilling its morbid hunger. Statistics show that Americans, who lead in this race for visual gratification, travel far more than Europeans. Modern man, this wandering Jew of sensations, can continually renew his sensory impressions but is unable to transform them into internal capital. Since he can no longer choose the objects of his attention, since he has renounced taste, which requires time to evaluate the object, he is at the mercy of psychic imperatives that make freedom an impossibility. Duhamel in his *Scènes de la vie future* warned us of this. It has become the great danger of our time.

4. TOWARD THE FUTURE

Is the civilization of the image, then, to be condemned? To do so would be to overlook the possibilities it affords for counteracting its dangers.

We shall not indulge in pessimistic oversimplifications aimed at disparaging our own era. In mankind's progress, losses are almost always compensated for by gains; every goal pursued requires sacrifices. The reduction of the intellectual operation to visual perception does not necessarily imply mental regression: while the average man becomes poorer in the process, thus paying the price for the greater intensity and speed he strives for, the superior individual achieves results that were formerly beyond his reach.

THE SIGN LIGHTENS THE WORK OF THE MIND. Just as the Arabic system of numbering, infinitely more convenient than the Roman, enabled mathematics to take a gigantic step forward, so the visual figuration of concepts, which formerly had to be developed by purely intellectual means, has tremendously lightened the work of the mind and released energies for use elsewhere.

At the forefront of our culture today are the scientists, directing the great enterprise of conquering the external world. By inventing analytical geometry, Descartes made algebra *visual*, illustrating its spatial concepts with what have since been called "graphs." Their advantage, as a mathematician once said strikingly, is that "they speak to our eyes." Descartes himself pointed out that with the help of these figures it would be possible "to construct all problems," i.e., to give them visual form, to translate them into images. He discovered that thanks to such images it was possible to perceive relations more rapidly, more completely, and more accurately than by means of concepts. Once functions are represented as curves, the knowledge they convey becomes visual, and since it is contained in the variations of a simple line, the mind can grasp a given phenomenon or even a given complex of ideas "at a glance," without having to follow the lengthy course of mental exposition.[1]

For instance, to express the variations in the responses of the human eye to different colors, all one has to do is mark on the abscissa the range of the spectrum, and on the ordinate the scale of the lumen units measuring optical sensibility, and then to make a graph indicating the modulations of this sensibility in relation to colors; in this way one can comprehend both the phenomenon as a whole and a complex mass of its details. To present even a part of such an explanation with equal clarity and precision in words would require an interminable speech.

By adding a third co-ordinate, registering another variable, to the figure, even richer results can be obtained. The phenomenon previously shown in one of its aspects will now be recorded with all the transformations brought about by the additional factor; and the mind's control over the object under investigation will be vastly extended.

On the other hand, certain dangers are apparent. Here is one: the graphs used by the press and propagandists to illustrate statistics tend to replace sound rational logic by a factitious "visual logic." Let us assume that the cultivation of a particular crop requires that the soil be given periodic rests; the graph recording the progress of this cultivation will naturally contain horizontal lines, so-called "plateaus." If this phenomenon is explained to the public, it will be understood at once. But if it is shown on a graph, with rising production indicated by a diagonal line into which the rest indispensable to keep up the fertility of the soil introduces the sudden horizontals, the eye will be disconcerted, for it expects the line to keep rising. The "plateaus" can be explained to the mind, but to the eye they look like an anomaly, a break, which, if stressed, might arouse anxiety or might even cause a panic, though there is no reason for it.

During election campaigns we often see such graphs used to show the relative strength of the contending parties. Attempts are made to deceive the eye by a tendentious arrangement of hatchings or grayed surfaces. In such cases an irrational visual logic supplants rational logic, preventing the latter from performing its proper function.

More generally, it may be asked whether the passive acceptance of ready-made ideas and the omission of the intermediate steps of conscious thought does not contribute to a progressive decline in the inner life. This question must certainly be answered in the affirmative, as regards the compliant masses; yet the technique of imparting such ideas, for those who know how to use it, makes new advances possible.

By gradually replacing particular sensory experiences with generalized abstractions, human intelligence developed, and transcended the animal stage. A further advance was achieved when concepts were expressed by signs and mathematical symbols: with the help of these signs, the human intelligence could range beyond its natural limits, entering areas that had previously seemed inaccessible because they were inconceivable. For instance, we cannot conceive of infinity except in the

---

[1] Paul Valéry, who has not overlooked anything, says: "The great invention of making the laws of nature perceivable by the eye and as though legible, has been incorporated into science, and in a way duplicates the world of experience by a visual world of curves, surfaces, and diagrams that translate properties into figures. The graph can achieve a consistency of which words are incapable, it is superior to them in clarity and precision" (Letter to Ferrero, in *Divers essais sur L. de Vinci*, 1931, p. 160).

artificial terms of a continually renewed addition. But once the concept is replaced by a conventional sign (∞), we are no longer dependent on a mental equivalent of infinity. Instead of trying to give substance to this ungraspable idea, we need only make use of it.

The sign, this embryo of the image, far from obstructing thought, may help us to transcend it. Thanks to the sign, the mind can progress beyond that which it is capable of imagining, and move at ease in a world in which it is blind. Without this artifice, it would certainly have hesitated before the mysteries of the universe which lie outside the human scale—the regions of the infinitely small and infinitely great. Our perceptions cannot reach these zones; our rational habits are useless there. But the scientist no longer has to form clear concepts of them (it is almost impossible to conceive of them in terms of images, much less ideas); instead, he attacks them with the help of mathematical symbols. The latter no longer speak to the senses, and do not correspond to mental concepts; completely impersonal, and more abstract than words—which, like plants torn from the ground with earth clinging to their roots, always retain traces of actual experience—the symbols enable us, as it were, to think the unthinkable. Being nothing more than the conventional names by which they are called, they are governed only by their own inner logic.

Thus, after transcending his own potentialities, after conquering those areas to which nature had seemed to deny him access, such as atomic energy, modern man soars above his own sphere—he penetrates into an alien world beyond the universe that is accessible to him, which is fashioned on his own scale and seems to conform to the laws of his mind. Equipped with signs, with manipulable mathematical symbols, science advances into ever new areas. Who can foretell to what new stage it will lead the future generations, what new mutations of our minds it will bring about?

The civilization of the book was incapable of such achievements. Descartes vowed never to judge anything that was not "so clearly and distinctly present in his mind that he could never doubt it"; he also said that "we must never let ourselves be convinced unless it is by the evidence of our reason." To admit only clear-cut and intelligible ideas, expressing primarily sensory experience and organizing it in accordance with a few principles of which the most intangible was that of contradiction—such was the program of those few centuries.

For the civilization of the image, the break with intellectual habits, if not with the essential laws of reason, is no longer impossible.[1] According to Le Roy, today we use concepts that were "shocking to the reason of the former era," and Louis de Broglie says: "The deeper we penetrate into the infinitesimal structure of matter, the more we realize that the concepts fashioned by our minds in the course of everyday experience, particularly the concepts of space and time, are inadequate to describe the new worlds we are exploring." But where logical thinking proves inadequate, we can resort to the fiction of the symbol.

By thus freeing us from the necessity to perceive or even directly to conceive of the realities under study, the civilization of the image, true enough, eliminates the

---

[1] The principle of contradiction itself is not immune. The contemporary philosopher Stefane Lupasco has founded a dynamic "logic of the contradictory": "Let us introduce," he writes, "contradiction into the the very workings of our explicit thought; more than that, let us erect a logical formalism, a deductive logic starting from the 'axiom of the fundamental contradiction,' and unexpected worlds will open before our minds...."

In the twentieth century, worship of the visual occasionally reduces the painting to a play of lines and colors, without reference to anything else.

49. - *MONDRIAN.* DIAGONAL. Museum of Modern Art, New York

individual's personal control and peculiarities but it also hurdles the barriers that would formerly have impeded our intelligence. Such is the situation confronting us, endangering the individual but at the same time opening new potentialities to him.

ART AS THE SAFEGUARD OF THE SOUL. Perhaps it lies only with us to see that the civilization of the image brings us back, in however roundabout a way, to that from which it seems to remove us. To be sure, man is not the master of his fate and is swept along by events. But he begins to control those events the moment he becomes conscious of them. Lucidity enables him to judge, and judgment to react. Fate accounts only for tendencies; it is up to man to recognize them, and then he will be able, if not to direct them, at least to direct himself amid them.

A passive acceptance of the shortcomings of one's era or even the attempt to go them one better implies a good deal of either frivolity or cowardice. To ignore them, to deny them systematically, implies stupidity. It is just as futile, when one is confronted with a runaway horse, to clutch at him and let him drag you along as to stand in his way and be trampled by him; a sensible man tries to catch up with the horse, to grasp the reins and at least attempt to guide him.

No one can compel time to reverse its course. The characteristics of our era, which are more evident each day, will continue to assert themselves, perforce. All we can do is to assess the consequences of change according to eternal human standards. Each generation, entirely absorbed by its own destiny, lightly tosses overboard the acquisitions of its predecessors: eager to get hold of the riches of the future, it does not hesitate to squander the resources slowly accumulated in the past—resources sometimes more valuable than the new acquisitions.

The task of those whose historical awareness enables them to rise above current involvements is to avoid the squandering of authentic values, without obstructing the new values in process of development.

Nothing will keep modern civilization from complying with the ever-growing demands of speed and the machine; nothing will stop the rule of sensation, which is better adapted to present conditions, from succeeding that of the idea, which itself succeeded that of sensory forces. Therefore we must put the tremendous powers of the visual to work in order to preserve the balance of man's inner life.

The public's growing curiosity about painting, ancient and modern, its interest in museums, in illustrated books on great artists, the glamour of some artists whose illustrious names compete in popularity with the most famous movie stars (don't you agree, Picasso?)—all this shows that culture still possesses powerful weapons, provided it does not withdraw into spiteful pride.

Art, which responds to the sensory avidity of our era, can make use of the opening wedge provided by modern psychology. Starting with the sensory appeal, which is familiar to everyone today, it can develop the emotional and spiritual values that the exclusive rule of that same sensory appeal seems to be threatening.

The function of an elite is not to indulge in solitary and disdainful dreams. Making use of the means that are momentarily favored, it should preserve, beyond the fashions, the awareness of a life in which the heart and the mind can achieve a constant flowering and balance expressed in the most various forms. This is the path of true and eternal humanism.

At present, art is the most suitable instrument for humanism. Owing to propitious circumstances, it happens to be equipped with a new weapon—with the very power of the image. The nineteenth century could hardly conceive that the image could be anything but a visual statement, a faithful reproduction of reality. At the most, that century occasionally sought to give support to the image through an idea and its figurative representation.

Only a few great minds went further, perhaps even further than our own era. Goethe was the profoundest of them, and he preceded Delacroix. In Goethe the old civilization, that of the book, found one of its major embodiments, and yet he anticipated everything that could be expected of the civilization that was to succeed his own. This lofty intellectual was, at that early date, a champion of the visual. "I prize Seeing a great deal," he declared. "In the visual image we possess life."

He elaborated this idea in prophetic words, which so struck Delacroix that he copied them: "We speak too much, we should speak less and draw more. As for myself," this master of the word

Contemporary art, however, also realizes that lines and colors possess an evocative force capable of appealing once more to the spirit.

50. - ROUAULT. *HEAD OF A CLOWN*

confessed, "I should like to renounce the word, and speak only in images, as does plastic nature. This fig tree, this snake, this cocoon, exposed to the sun in front of this window, all these things are secret signs; and those who could decipher their true meaning, could do without any spoken or written language in the future. There is in the word something so futile, so pointless, I am almost tempted to say, so ridiculous...."

Goethe teaches us that the sensations of the eye are not merely fleeting signs. It is up to us to transform them into a meaningful construction of the world and of ourselves: both the world and man are illumined in our images of them, in the images we make of them. They acquire meanings in these images, they disclose their meanings. This may be the task of art which our epoch has instinctively placed at the forefront of its preoccupations.

WHAT PAINTING CAN AND SHOULD DO.   The twentieth century has restored autonomy to the image. It knows that the image possesses powers that are its own and that need not be justified by the imitation of an object or the exposition of a subject. Intoxicated by this discovery, the century has applied itself to the study of the elements of the visual image, to line and color and to designs based on these elements. From Cubism to the abstract school, we have witnessed an irresistible tide of "plastic" explorations (figure 49).

At the same time, the twentieth century is beginning to realize the psychological power of the image. Fauvism, and to an even greater extent Expressionism, discovered that sensation, provided it achieves the maximum of intensity through concentration, releases a nervous shock that projects it into emotion (figure 50).

Surrealism, for its part, had a glimpse of a less known power: the image signifies not only thought, as the preceding centuries, in their intransigent intellectualism, imagined; the image can be, and almost always is, an emanation from areas over which thought does not extend its rule. It is set off by what is most resistant to thought, namely, the unconscious.

But we are scarcely beginning to take possession of all these resources. Their use remains fragmentary, often confused and torn by conflicts between schools. Those who discover the plastic potentialities of the image refuse to learn anything else; those who sense that it is capable of conveying deep psychic realities confine themselves exclusively to this function. Each, dazzled by his discovery, makes a cult of it, a superstition in which he bogs down.

What is needed is to achieve a total and balanced assessment of the powers of the image. All its elements have been recognized separately or anticipated, during the last hundred years; it would be enough if they were arranged in an order in which they would complement each other rather than cancel each other out; it would be enough if each one were made to contribute to the fullness of the whole. This book proposes to outline such a synthesis.

Art can make use of the means that the era extolls; by using them it can bring man back to the inner life that is increasingly threatened by their abuse. Thus art provides the easiest path toward the restoration of our shaken balance.

Modern art, in its Expressionist phase, makes use of the emotional reverberations of sensation.
51. - *Opposite page: ROUAULT.* CHRIST OF THE FACTORIES

The power of the image, recovered through art, should make that image master of its own fate. It should not be distorted by the exacerbated intellectualism which, in our day, harasses it with a string of theories; but this is not to say that we cannot or should not reflect on it and expect some help from our clear realization of it. The work of art, through the images it offers us, gives us a vision of the world; thought, through its lucid ideas, gives us conceptual knowledge. If the means used by each must not be confounded at any price, at least the results gained by one can support and strengthen the other, the ideal being that each should be the complement of the other.

We must guard against reducing art to ideas; but it is important to put ideas at the service of art in order to grasp its true nature and measure its potentialities as well as its limitations. Are we not justified in hoping that we shall thus be able to glimpse the task art is to be assigned in order to help us better to fulfill our lives?

Modern art, in its Surrealist phase, undertook the direct rendering of the unconscious.
52. - *MAX ERNST.* PETRIFIED FOREST

Photo Maurice Poplin

53. - *FRANCESCO DI GIORGIO MARTINI* (attrib.). THE IDEAL CITY. Ducal Palace, Urbino

CHAPTER ONE

REALITY, BEAUTY, AND POETRY

> *Painting isn't too difficult when one*
> *doesn't know ... but when one knows ...*
> *oh, then, it's something else again.*
>   *Degas*

MAN created works of art before he was able to discourse about art, and it was in an attempt to understand this essential activity, not comparable to any other despite the confusions to which it has only too often fallen prey, that he one day asked himself the question: What is art? Let us, therefore, go back to that beginning, to the initial fact: the work, and more particularly the painted work—the realm of images, where the intimate alliance of imitation and creation poses the problem fully and explicitly.

The question can now be restated in more specific terms: What is a painting? How, by what methods, has the painter contributed to the emergence of the idea of art? Reversing Socrates' objection to Hippias, we might say: "I am not asking you what Beauty is; I am asking what a beautiful thing is!" In what Malraux calls "the imaginary museum" we find displayed the works by which each civilization and generation has answered this question. It is up to us to decipher them; we must dismiss from our minds all preconceived ideas rising out of our own lives and temperaments, and try to understand the solutions the works themselves put forward, in their silent language.

65

THE RIDDLE OF PAINTING.   Confronted with a painting, a man of the West who is unaware of the questions raised by modern aesthetics will look for an image of reality, and will measure the painter's skill and the merit of the work by the degree of its conformity with its model. "What does it represent?" is the average man's first reaction. If his curiosity is aroused, he will wonder: "How was it done? By means of what techniques did the artist manage to create this illusion?" The general public, no matter what seeming concessions it makes to so-called advanced ideas whose implications it but dimly perceives, does not look deeper. How many visitors to museums and exhibitions, convinced that they enjoy art, make representation their sole criterion! They sense, to be sure, that the "connoisseur" of painting finds access to something that escapes them; they conclude that he knows the secrets of "technique." This term, "technique," is the magic formula of our era. As if the "how" could provide the answer to the "why"—as if a knowledge of the means of execution could replace insight into the deeper motives!

It is true that the Western artist has hardly ever sought to achieve his essential goal, beauty or poetry, outside the path of realism; the viewers of his work may be forgiven for not going deeper, for seeing only the path without suspecting whither it leads them. That is why, for a long time (and this is a view still held by many of our contemporaries), all art that deviated from realism was *ipso facto* suspected of being unable to achieve it, was regarded as clumsy, as "primitive." Highly advanced arts, such as those of Byzantium and China, are to this day secretly regarded as inferior, on the grounds that they neglect or despise natural appearance.

This conviction is stubborn, invincible, firmly rooted in the lower as well as in the middle classes, which reject all other interpretations of art as the fancies of literary men or the paradoxes of aestheticians. It is a view that is closely linked with Western man's innate disposition, with the fact that all his faculties and activities are aimed at mastering the outside world (figure 54). Man's striving for knowledge has come to be so completely identified with his efforts to explore the material universe, that he experiences, as Bergson pointed out, the greatest difficulty in coming to terms with the spiritual world, which is so different from the other.

Modern psychology has had to make a tremendous effort in order to free itself from this bondage to the material world and to fashion concepts valid for its domain. This effort is essentially parallel with that of contemporary art which has also sought to go beyond physical reality as it is perceived by our senses.

For centuries, almost every interpretation of art advanced in the West was based on the idea that art resembled nature. When ancient art strove, in effect, to go beyond reality and to transcend banal natural appearance by finding the source of ideal beauty in the mind rather than in things, the effort seemed to go unnoticed. The familiar anecdotes that have come down to us all have the same ring. The grapes that Zeuxis represented in the hands of a young boy were so much like nature that birds tried to pick them; the painter was congratulated for this, but he replied unhappily: "If the boy had been better painted, the birds would have been afraid of him!" Another story is that Alexander's horse neighed on seeing its own effigy. The aesthetic theories dating from that time are founded on the concept of imitation, mimesis: it is the basis of Aristotle's theory, and even for Plato imitation is the supreme law of art, although his philosophy holds that the essence of beauty lies elsewhere. After them, Xenocrates praised Lysippus for having rendered hair so exactly.

Two thousand years later, Leonardo da Vinci, the Renaissance artist who rendered a supernatural and poetic universe with the greatest lucidity, could still write: "There was once a painting representing the father of a family, which the grandsons learned to caress when they were still in swaddling clothes, and the cat and the dog of the house did the same thing; and this was marvelous to behold." He sums up the meaning of such anecdotes in this principle: "Painting represents to the senses, with truth and certainty, the works of nature. Is not this science, which represents the works of nature, more admirable than the science which gives us only the works of men, such as words, poetry, and its modes?"

Photo Braun

The realistic conception of art reached its culmination in the nineteenth century. Some paintings of that period vie with photography at its most banal.

54. - *GARNIER*. FLAGRANTE DELICTO

True, antiquity and the Renaissance evolved many notions of art besides the one of its achieving verisimilitude, but they never disavowed this one; it remained the foundation to which they always returned. Even those whose works demonstrate that art is situated in a realm that cannot be mistaken for reality, define art as the imitation of nature. We are confronted with a peculiar paradox. The successive preparatory sketches of painters whose finished works and theories seem to be governed by the aesthetics of realism prove clearly that they are pursuing other goals: stylized proportions and bold simplifications are evidence of this. It is only their thinking, cast in the Western mold, prisoner of habit, that does not dare to oppose the ruling dogma.

The works on painting that have reached us from China or India reveal quite different aims, pursued with full consciousness. Is it not admirable that Kuo Hsi, whose *Treatise on Landscape* dates from the eleventh century, could write: "The ancients said that a poem is a painting without forms, and that a painting is a poem with forms," a poem that causes us to "imagine the subtle feelings which it depicts.... It is not easy to discover its meaning." Among the Six Principles of Painting listed in the *Treatise on Painting* which Hsieh-Ho composed toward the end of the fifth century, "Rebirth of the spirit" comes first, while "Conformity with objects and likenesses" is given third place. According to the Six Canons of Hindu painting, which are also very ancient, the purpose of art is to reveal the spirit; and the *Alamkara Shastras* proclaimed that "the only excellent images are those which possess the Power of Suggestion." Thus the East fully understood the mission and the evocative powers of art a long time ago, while the West continued stubbornly to adhere to its obsession with realism.

It is true that today we have recognized this to be an error, but we tend now to go to the other extreme, and to think that the representation of reality is incompatible with art, that it can come only out of mediocrity or misunderstanding. Such sectarianism is also dangerous. We may smile at the ingenuousness with which recent converts to the new faith ascribe to old masters aesthetic intentions characteristic of our era, but which they certainly never had, even if the significance of their works transcends that of their ideas.

1. REALITY

FROM the thirteenth century to the twentieth, Western art consistently pursued the goal of realism, ever greater realism. This fact cannot possibly be contested; witness the attempts at illusionism which are a distinctive feature of Western art. From the insects that the primitives liked to paint on their panels to the *trompe-l'œil* curtains that the Dutchmen of the seventeenth century inserted in front of their paintings; from the beckoning figures that Veronese made to emerge from the wall at the Villa Maser to the deliberate confusion between painting and sculpture in which the Baroque decorators of Central Europe indulged, visual make-believe has been an innate temptation of Western schools of art. It would be rather presumptuous to decree that this superrealism has nothing to do with art (figure 55).

TROMPE-L'OEIL AND MIRROR.   In an article dealing with certain aspects of illusionism,[1] Robert Gavelle quotes the praise given by Lucas de Heere to the works of Van Eyck: "They are mirrors, yes, mirrors, not paintings." According to Emile Gavelle, father of Robert, the meaning of the famous inscription, *Johannes de Eyck fuit hic* on the rear wall of *Giovanni Arnolfini and His Bride*, is that the painter was identifying himself with the mirror above which these words are written, and should be translated as "Jan van Eyck was this mirror." This is perfectly plausible.[2]

In some Flemish cities, painters at the beginning of the fifteenth century belonged to the same guild as the mirror-makers. At Bruges, the St. John Guild included miniaturists and calligraphers and the St. Lucas Guild included both painters and glass- and mirror-makers. In the seventeenth century, Gerard Dou, so minutely exact, was the son of a glassmaker. In Italy, Leonardo explained "how the mirror

[1] "Aspects du trompe-l'œil" in *Amour de l'Art*, July, 1938, XIX, No. 6, pp. 231 ff.
[2] However, Salomon Reinach thinks that in correct Latin usage the word "*hic*" can only mean "here."

is the master of painters."[1]

Western painting was indeed fascinated by the sheet of glass which captures so totally and so exactly the appearance of the world. The artist prided himself on emulating its function, but he felt that he had an advantage over it, since he could record forever the objects that appear only ephemerally in the mirror. The competition, egged on by the mysterious properties of mirrors, came to an end only with the invention

[1] The passage in question is found in MS. 2038 at the Bibliothèque Nationale (fol. 24 v.); Leonardo advises the painter to place the object before a mirror, and then to compare its reflection with his painting. He insists on the fact that "mirrors have many points of resemblance to a picture; namely, that you see the picture made upon one plane showing things which appear in relief, and the mirror upon one plane does the same.... It is certain that if you but know how to compose your picture, it will also seem a natural thing seen in a great mirror" (*The Notebooks of Leonardo da Vinci.* New York, 1938, II, 254–255).

However, Leonardo knew that a painting is more than a mirror: "The painter who draws by practice and judgment of the eye without the use of reason, is like the mirror that reproduces within itself all the objects which are set opposite it without knowledge of the same" (*Op. cit.*, II, 275).

In the eighteenth century, artists sought to blur the distinction between reality and illusion, and between painting and sculpture.

55. - TROMPE-L'OEIL PAINTING.
Hôtel de Châteaurenard, Aix-en-Provence

56. - *JAN VAN EYCK.* GIOVANNI ARNOLFINI AND HIS WIFE (detail). National Gallery, London

57. - *QUENTIN MATSYS.* THE MONEYLENDER AND HIS WIFE (detail). The Louvre, Paris

In the early Renaissance, painting was haunted by the microcosm of the mirror....

59. - *SPANISH SCHOOL, SEVENTEENTH CENTURY.* OLD MAN LOOKING AT HIMSELF IN A MIRROR (detail)

of photography, with its mechanical and definitive recording of the image, for then painting was forced to share the superiority (i.e., its permanence) which formerly it alone had had over the elusive mirror reflections.

But before this happened, both northern painters (e.g., Van Eyck, Quentin Matsys with his *Moneylender*, Vermeer, Gerard Dou) and southern painters (Velázquez with his famous *Maids of Honor*, Titian with his *Allegory of Alfonso d'Avalos*, Tintoretto with his *Venus and Vulcan*, and many others) had not contented themselves with aping the mirror; they went further and reproduced not only the object before the mirror but also the image of the objects *in* the mirror! In a happy intoxication to which even later works, such as those of Ingres and the young Degas, bear witness, painters recorded reality as they saw it, and side by side with this, reality as reflected in a mirror, with its slightly different quality. The fact that artists of the caliber of these persistently indulged in such pursuits seems to indicate that the use of *trompe-l'œil* was hardly an aberration (figures 56 to 61).

BEYOND NATURAL APPEARANCE. Realism has its fascination and its justification: it would be presumptuous to exclude it from art. One must, however, be clear as to its rightful place. And it is precisely

58. - *GIOVANNI BELLINI.* ALLEGORY (detail). Accademia, Venice

... Later painters studied the subtle variations of reality as reflected in mirrors.

60. - *RUBENS.* TOILET OF VENUS (detail).
Gemäldegalerie, Vienna

61. - *DEGAS.* THE DANCING CLASS (detail). Collection
Harry Payne Bingham, New York

the mirror that raises this question: to look in a painting solely for the reproduction of the object it represents is like mistaking the ephemeral image in the mirror for the mirror itself. The mirror as such, with its substance and qualities, is not the deceptive image it reflects. It is not this face, these flowers whose forms strike its surface and rebound into our eye. The mirror exists behind this semblance, behind the phenomenon of reflection of which it is merely the vehicle.

The same is true of the painting, and this is what the deceived viewers fail to realize: if we wish to know the true nature of a painting, we must go beyond the world it reflects. The thin coating of reality, thanks to which we are able to perceive the painting, at the same time masks its true essence, the laws that actually govern its existence. We cannot claim that we know what a painting is unless we have penetrated as far as that essence. What does this mean? The painting is a flat surface covered with a certain substance, the pictorial medium, which forms lines and colors "assembled in a certain order," to quote Maurice Denis's famous formula. But it is much more than that. Unlike the mirror, it has, behind its visible surface, a psychological context—the life of the mind out of which the artist drew it, and of which these lines and colors are the visible sign. The background, the seeming depth in which the mirror-image is imbedded, is illusory, reflecting only the space in front of the mirror; in the painting the background leads into another "dimension," another world, to which the work invites us. A painting is in this sense the window of the artist's soul.

Whatever great artists, echoing the ideas current in their time, may have professed to believe, they have always more or less dimly perceived this truth; if they have not always expressed it, they have always behaved as though they knew it instinctively. The public too has always sensed it, whatever doctrines it may have professed. Otherwise how can we account for the fact that fame has not been bestowed on painters according to the degree to which they achieved that vaunted realism, but rather for something else that they offered and that aroused a sense of harmony or a pleasurable emotion in the viewer? Values became confused, temporarily, and certain facile painters, from Gerard Dou to Meissonier, owed their excessive and short-lived celebrity to such confusion; but in the last analysis, acclaim has always been given on the basis of less obvious qualities, of a revelation of something that the artists carried within themselves and that enabled them to be not "apes of nature," but poets, in the Greek sense of the word ποιεῖν, creators. The novelty of a painter's contribution, as well as the shock it produced, could cause hesitation at first, and yet the admiration of the centuries has in the end gone unquestionably to Rembrandt rather than to Gerard Dou, to Manet rather than to Meissonier. To be sure, the history of art has its great unrecognized figures, but how small their number is in comparison with that of the great artists who have been accorded renown!

We must learn, in our understanding of art, not to be beguiled by that coating of realism which makes the painting attractive to the viewer, but which distracts him from what lies beyond it.

What would we think of a man who, confronted with an admirable example of the jeweler's art, stupidly amused himself with observing the reflections sent back by the surface of the gem, not bothering to appreciate its substance, its design and form? Confronted with a painting, the ignorant layman behaves very similarly: he looks for everything except for painting.

2. BEAUTY

WHAT, then, is a painting "in itself," as the philosophers say? What is the living body beneath this covering that might just as well clothe a puppet? It is a being, a complex reality—like life, of which it is one of the highest and most concentrated expressions. This complexity is the source of many misunderstandings. People always have a tendency to simplify and to systematize; they cling exclusively, jealously, to the aspect of a thing that was the first to be revealed to them, and to which they are most attuned; therein is the source of all aesthetic quarrels!

How can we grasp the bewildering riches of art? "The eye listens," said Claudel, stressing the necessity to perceive what lies behind immediate appearance. What does the eye listen to? To the "voices of silence," is the answer given by Malraux, thus indicating the presence of a hidden meaning, one that is not where one expects to find it. Long ago, in the fourth century, Gregory of Nyssa said: "Silent painting speaks on the wall." Through the ages, the metaphor has not changed. It teaches us that we must go beyond the obvious.

PAINTING IS ALCHEMY. Every realistic painter, whatever the degree of his realism may be, has a "motif" for his picture. This word, even in his own mouth, suggests that nature provides him with no more than an occasion, a starting point; the proper meaning of "motif" is: that which sets something going, which moves and arouses emotion. He plans to create something that does not yet exist—a painting. For the time being, the work exists only potentially, in the flat regular surface that is before him—"an empty canvas protected by its whiteness" one might say, paraphrasing Mallarmé. In the painter's hand, the stick of charcoal or the

Torn between the demands of nature and those of painting, Corot chose the representation....
62. - *COROT*. THE COLOSSEUM IN ROME. The Louvre, Paris

brush prepares on its part the line of color—also potential—that will be born out of its encounter with the canvas.

Assuming that the artist confines himself to reproducing only what is before his eyes, his task is still not an easy one. On the one hand, he perceives a number of continually moving luminous spots, variously colored. These his eye has been habituated to distinguish and to recognize as forms, that is, objects, and to situate them in the space encompassed by his gaze. On the other hand, there is waiting before him that clear surface on which there is nothing as yet, which is merely a flatness ready to be used; the only thing he can put on it is a line drawn or painted by his hand or with a drawing or painting device responsive to his motions. He is suspended between these two extremes, and everything depends on him. He will have either to "cheat" or to compromise: cheat in order to give his canvas something of the appearance of nature; or compromise in order to adapt this appearance to the possibilities of the canvas.

This painter may be Corot. Imagine him standing before the Colosseum, which is bathed in light, with his hand raised and squinting his eye. For this Roman landscape from which the enormous mass rises is filled to its depths, to its farthest corner, with air, and the light is filtered through it. Mass, depth, light—none of these actually exist in the painting, which has only surface, height, and width, lines, and colors. Moreover, in the landscape everything is alive and changing; on the canvas everything will be fixed. It is up to the artist to find the point at which the two worlds meet. Thus each motion he makes will comprise a choice, a decision; he will have, at every step, to eliminate one of two alternatives. He may decide in favor of nature; then he must force his picture to violate its own natural conditions, to become artifice and illusion, a *trompe-l'œil* of the kind we have just discussed: flat, it will look

73

Unlike Corot, Gauguin forced the landscape to yield to the formal needs of his painting.

63. - *GAUGUIN.* TAHITIAN SHEPHERDESSES. 1892. Museum of Modern Art, Moscow

three-dimensional; substantial, opaque, rigid, it will seem ethereal, luminous, throbbing with life. That was what Corot set out to do, and he was successful (figure 62).

But the painter may be Gauguin. Then he will choose to follow the opposite course, to sacrifice the resemblance to nature, and even plausibility, for the sake of his canvas. He will compel the landscape transposed onto his canvas to surrender its depth, the mobility of its atmosphere, the vibrations of its lights and shadows; he will imprison it within heavy lines; with the help of his palette he will display it in sharply contrasting colors. Here nature, stunned, submits to laws that are not its own; it is digested, assimilated by the painting, of which it is merely the raw material, and modern art is born (figures 63 and 64).

For the first time, art consciously, deliberately formulates a task for itself, which it conceives of as that of organizing the elements that constitute its language. What is "thinkable" in terms of line and form (what we shall call the "plastic" elements) will contribute to the organization of the surface to be painted. What can be expressed in terms of light and pigment (what we shall call the "pictorial" elements) will determine its texture.

We have now reached the threshold of the domain of the plastic. This term, "plastic," unlike "pictorial," is not perfectly clear; far from it. It has had many meanings. We shall be using it constantly hereafter, and for this reason it is important that we define it accurately.[1]

[1] Originally, πλαστική (sc. τέχνη) meant the art of modeling or molding. In the first century A.D. Pliny the Elder introduced the term into Latin, translating it as *plastica*; it was used in this original sense by Vitruvius and others. As late as the seventeenth century, the *Encyclopédie* defines *la plastique* as the part of

74

Our contemporaries compel reality to capitulate completely to the demands of line and color.
64. - *MANESSIER*. WINTER. 1954

The sense in which we shall use this term is that which it has acquired in the twentieth century. We call "plastic explorations" the elaboration of the means sculpture concerned with modeling. This narrow technical sense has come to the fore today with the emergence of the so-called "plastics."

However, the same Vitruvius also used the term to denote sculpture as a whole—*plastica ratio* means the "principles of sculpture." At the same time the Greek verb *plasso* (πλάσσω) passed into Latin, where it was used in the sense of "to form, to shape." It was taken up by Tertullian, then by the Church Fathers, and medieval scholastics used the word "plastic" to denote "the power of giving form." This is the meaning that it has, essentially, in modern aesthetics.

In the meantime, classical French, in which the adjective appears toward the middle of the sixteenth century, i.e., during the Renaissance, adopted the term in the broader sense it had in Low Latin and in the Middle Ages; it uses *plastique* as a synonym for "that which is of the domain of form." But in line with the ideas on art current at the time, form was confined to its sculptural uses and, consequently, to the representation of the human body. This gave rise to a new meaning of the word; *une belle plastique* meant "an anatomy."

When the phrase "plastic arts" came into widespread use in the nineteenth century it denoted those arts which in contrast with music, for instance, aimed at imitating forms, primarily those of nature. Kant still applied the term only to the arts of form, properly used, i.e., as having volume—to architecture and sculpture. But Schopenhauer excluded the former, while he added painting; and the latter usage then became predominant. The doctrine of realism does not go further: at the most, writers spoke of, in addition to *plastique d'art*, a *plastique d'ornement*, in which form enjoyed to some extent the privilege of invention, while the other elements were exclusively figurative. Since color was officially regarded as a mere addition to form, it was casually included in this adjective, which strictly speaking it had nothing to do with. Thus the term "plastic" gradually came to be more or less synonymous with "visual." Baudelaire, in his *Peintre de la vie moderne*, refers to his pen as "accustomed to struggling against plastic representations."

Our own era, in its quest for a term adequate to express its new aesthetic concerns, has adopted the adjective "plastic," and even the noun "plasticity" (the latter having made its appearance at the end of the eighteenth century), to denote everything that falls within the province of form and color. But it no longer regards these as the means of reproducing natural appearance; they are a creation and, as such, the basis of art.

75

available to the painter when, no longer using such means solely to represent models he seeks to bring out the intrinsic beauty which they themselves contain. But while line and form formerly were accorded first place in such explorations, the emphasis has now been put upon color. The term "plastic," which originally applied only to sculpture, has thus come to denote, somewhat paradoxically, what the term "form" denoted earlier.

I shall follow this usage, unsatisfactory as it is, for the lack of a better word. However, I shall try whenever possible to distinguish that which is properly "plastic" (the domain of form) from that which is "pictorial" (the domain of effects exclusively derived from the various media). Color belongs in both realms: it performs a plastic function in so far as it serves to emphasize or qualify forms; its function is pictorial when it serves to enhance the texture.[1]

Photo Flammarion

At first sight, Van Eyck seems microscopically realistic— and yet his painting is constructed with geometric rigor. Here we see the structure of the painting.

65. - VAN EYCK. THE MADONNA OF CHANCELLOR ROLIN. The Louvre, Paris

With the advent of modern painting, the plastic and the pictorial elements boldly shake off the last restraints that seek to make them evoke what is outside themselves; they improvise freely with their own resources, opening the doors to abstract art. Between this free play of the elements and the other extreme, the art of illusionism, lies an immense range of possibilities, including all the historically developed varieties of art.

FROM REALISTIC TO PLASTIC ART. In actual fact, and despite everything that is said, the absolute extremes do not exist. There is no total realism; the painter has always had to make concessions to the means available to him. Nor is there such a thing as pure abstraction, for if the eye ceased to draw on its memories of visual reality, it would be left with a complete blank. In our day, Mondrian's inflexibility brought him almost to the point at which the absolute meets the absurd (figure 49).

On the other hand, every great artist practices, more or less openly, a kind of intellectual alchemy, enhancing his delight in visual reality by blending with it his joy in his own inventiveness. The layman is all too easily deceived by the painter's skill in concealing his personal contributions within plausibility, and from force of of habit asks of a pictorial work merely that it recall what he has seen or disclose to him what he may see.

[1] This accounts for the conflict between the Classical and the Romantic, between Ingres and Delacroix: the former regarded the function of color as exclusively "plastic," the latter as "pictorial."

66. - *VAN EYCK.* THE MADONNA OF CHANCELLOR ROLIN. Detail of the landscape background

77

Van Eyck is admired for his marvelous realism; and the viewer, his magnifying glass trembling with his emotion, explores the microcosm that is the Rolin Madonna, its every square inch filled with precise detail. But it is rarely noticed that in adapting his subject to the dimensions of his panel the artist has given his amazing evocation of space an exactly cubic form which, within the rectangular frame, greatly increases the illusion of depth. This illusionary space, once it is divested of its false appearance of reality, becomes the rigorous dream of a mathematician (figures 65 and 66).

Or take a look at Rogier van der Weyden's tumultuous *Entombment*, with its almost Gothic disorder. The spirit of the construction is different here: it is reminiscent of a rose window design; and it is just as apparent. The figures are placed within a pentagon formed by the lintel of the tomb, the lateral projections marked by the figures of the Virgin and St. John, and the two diagonals, meeting near the bottom, that of Mary Magdalene and the overturned stone. This pentagon is inscribed within a circle suggested by the curve of the tumulus, which is tangent to the three remaining sides of the frame; the center of the circle and of the pentagon coincide at the center of the body of Christ (figures 67 and 68).

Photo Giraudon

Van der Weyden is more Gothic than Van Eyck; he composes on a geometrical basis, too, but recalls the rose window of the cathedrals.

67. - *Opposite page: VAN DER WEYDEN.* ENTOMBMENT. Uffizi, Florence

68. - *Above:* Diagram of the composition

It might be objected that such regularities are purely accidental. Well, then, here is the case of a supposed realist who is, so to speak, caught red-handed in the act of betraying his faith. The nineteenth-century bourgeoisie had the greatest admiration for the meticulousness and lifelikeness of Ingres's representations. This was particularly true of his portraits. And yet it is Ingres who provides us with examples of the most deliberate violations of "reality." Who has not seen the additional vertebrae in the *Grande Odalisque* in the Louvre, or the neck swollen to the point of suggesting a goiter, in his *Jupiter and Thetis* at Aix? In both cases, the anatomical distortions were made for the sole purpose of enabling a line to display to the utmost its capacity for describing a harmonious arabesque. Like another Iphigenia, Thetis' body was sacrificed on the altar of merciless *plastique* (figure 69).

The sketches that show the successive stages of another work of Ingres, his *Raphael and La Fornarina*, are evidence of this intentional distortion. In this painting he started from nature. A first pencil sketch, unpublished if I am not mistaken, which is in the Museum of Bern, shows the painter submitting completely to visible reality, as though to inspire it with confidence so that he may ensnare it the more effectively. He tells his model to undress, he ties around her head the kerchief he plans for his figure, and now all he has to do is make an accurate sketch of her, without changing anything. True, her pelvis is heavy, her flesh, her belly, her breasts tend to sag—but can he do anything except record them as they are? Well, at least her face is beautiful. Ingres tries to make the best of it; he shifts the position of her hand —first it is on her shoulder, then on her chest, then finally below—and each time he passively records the result. There we have the perfect realist. Or have we? Suddenly his agile pencil alters the line of the breast, and sketches another breast that she *might have had*, whose form, less tired, is more in accord with his conception of the beautiful (figure 70).

One day he imagines the attitude that will embody the theme he intends to treat: a young woman inclining her face, with a caressing gesture, toward her lover's head.[1] There is nothing impossible in this, and the model assumes the prescribed pose, with a chair taking the place that will belong to Raphael in the painting. Unfortunately, in this position her body is slightly twisted, and Ingres must show the resulting folds and swellings in the drapery above her. But there is an unexpected compensation: her neck, now stretched, has lost the fatty corrugations that showed previously. It now has a delicate taut line, which forms an elegant and perfect curve (figure 71).

Ingres senses his opportunity: he sets to work, and soon produces the finished painting, in which everything is ordered around that concentrated, sharp curve, rising like the sound of a violin that soars above the din of the orchestra. The arabesque wins the day, and reality complies with its wishes. To focus the viewer's attention on it, to develop its harmony, Ingres eliminates everything that might detract from it; he renounces the modeling he had done, erasing the projecting edge of the shoulder on which he spent so much effort. He wants his design to be as smooth as possible, even if it has to be false, so that nothing may disturb the effect of this divine contour. At the same time, in order to set off the purity of this line, he gathers the material of the sleeve into folds, and at first even makes it look exaggeratedly heavy, to set off the fragile neck with its delicately undulating curve (figure 72).

The painting is finished: what was sacrificed was realism.

THE MATHEMATICS OF BEAUTY. Are such effects as the one described above deliberate? This is often doubted. But the fact is that artists do calculate them in advance. Proportions figured numerically, the obvious superposition of rigorous geometric forms on nature, preclude the supposition that we are being confronted by accidental effects. Dürer's *Adam and Eve* is a case in point. No one can deny the Nuremberg master's naturalism, which is occasionally even a bit ponderous: here, certainly, is an industrious, meticulous observer who would not need to fear a comparison with Lysippus on the grounds of his ability to render the thousand separate lines of a head of hair (figure 74)!

[1] Ingres produced several versions of this subject, revising it lovingly. In the painting at the Fogg Art Museum (Wildenstein Catalogue, No. 88) La Fornarina is still almost erect (1814); in the versions of 1840 and 1860 (Wild. Cat. 231 and 297), the spinal curve is as regular as if it had been drawn with a compass (figure 73).

Ingres often sacrificed truth to style.

69. - *INGRES.* JUPITER AND THETIS (detail). Museum, Aix

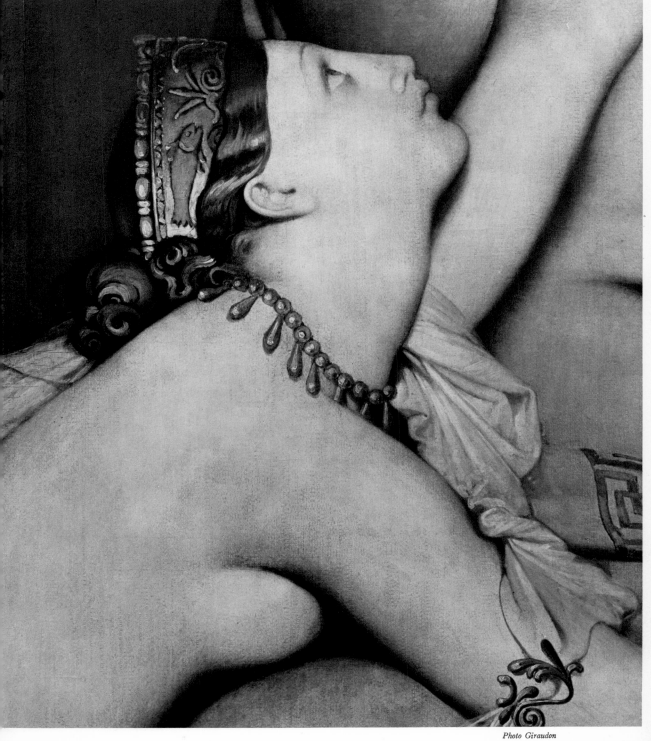

Ingres first scrupulously copied his model...

70. - *At left: INGRES.* Study for RAPHAEL AND LA FORNARINA. 1814. Museum, Bern

...an unexpected gesture or movement suggested a line...

71. - *Left below: INGRES.* RAPHAEL AND LA FOR-NARINA. Drawing. Museum, Lyons

...the whole painting was organized around the new, flowing curve...

72. - *Below:* RAPHAEL AND LA FORNARINA. Private collection

...in the last versions, the main concern is the arched line of the back.

73. - *Opposite page:* RAPHAEL AND LA FORNARINA. c. 1860. Private collection

Among the preliminary sketches Dürer made for his etching of *Adam and Eve* in 1504, there are two that will dispel all doubts as to the deliberateness of his intent to replace natural forms by forms originating in his mind, which avidly sought intricate proportions. The first sketch, now at Dresden, shows that Dürer, like Ingres later, did not content himself with imitating reality; he wanted to subject it to his own laws. Several times he shifts the position of his model's leg to make it conform to his idea of where it should be; more than that, he uses configurations of lines drawn with the help of a ruler and a compass and placed according to numerical computations, to arrive at structure and proportions that are purely abstract (figure 75).

Clearly we have here an application of the famous "golden section" theory which Fra Luca Pacioli, in his book *De divina proportione*, attributed to Plato. Leonardo da Vinci, who was interested in such problems, made illustrations for the treatise. Dürer was so engrossed in these matters that in 1506 (no doubt advised by Jacopo de' Barbari, who is regarded as the author of the admirable portrait of Fra Luca), he went on horseback from Venice, where the treatise on proportion was to be printed three years later, to Bologna, in order to meet its author, who was a Franciscan friar.

Dürer's engraving strikes the viewer by its minute realism...

74. - *ALBRECHT DÜRER*. ADAM AND EVE. Engraving

In drawing the figure of Adam, Dürer was obviously greatly inspired by these geometric theories. This figure seems to be built entirely of circles, squares, and triangles, intricately linked one with the other, which make it an entirely abstract construction (figure 76).

Thus the artist's will to achieve plastic effects is so strong that he goes beyond instinctively determined arrangements, submitting his forms to strict mathematical requirements. It would take us too far afield[1] to analyze in greater detail the use by artists, from antiquity on, of "ideal" proportions, such as the "golden section," the *sectio divina*, as Kepler called it (the division of a line segment in extreme and mean ratio), or the square root of two. These artists reproduced natural appearance in order to conceal the arid bareness of the work of art, and at the same time to make

[1] The various books Matila C. Ghyka devoted to this problem provide us with a complete general view, which is discussed below (cf. p. 174).

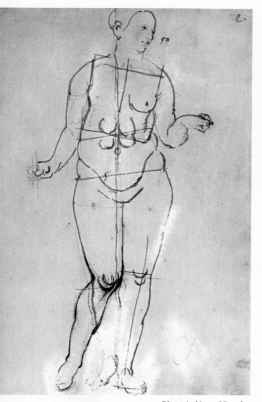

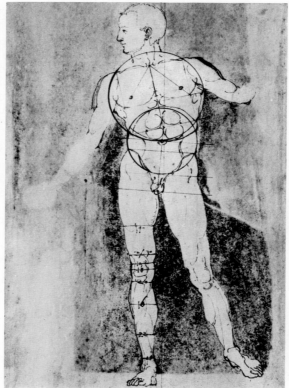

Photo Archives of Dresden   *Photo Albertina, Vienna*

...but the preliminary drawings disclose intricate calculations of proportion.

75. - *ALBRECHT DÜRER*. Drawing for EVE.   **76.** - *ALBRECHT DÜRER*. Study for ADAM. c. 1507. Albertina, Vienna
         Archives of Dresden

reality more desirable, as a body is when concealed under draperies. Paul Bourget, opposing the naturalist infatuation with truthfulness, demanded only plausibility in the novel. Many artists have been admired for their alleged realism who merely paid tribute to verisimilitude, using it as a pretext for constructing a system of lines and planes that met with their plastic requirements.

    Once the idea of beauty is introduced, that of reality must compromise with it. The artist cannot be expected to rely only on chance in order to obtain an effect which he has accurately conceived in advance; he must work it out deliberately. "Plastic" form provides the logical answer, as regards both means and end, to his need for beauty. Western tradition, however naturalistic, is not opposed to "plastic" form; as far back as the Greeks, this tradition had a concept of "idealized reality," a compromise between natural appearance and intellectual design. The two are not incompatible, for Western man turns his attention to the world with a view to conquering it, subjecting it to his order. It was inevitable that he should have attempted to imprint the seal of human reason even on natural appearance.

3. POETRY

CAN art then be summed up as a dialogue between reality, on the one hand, and plastic beauty on the other? No, for the two cannot be brought into agreement except through a third party, an interpreter capable of understanding them and mediating between them. An outside intelligence is required, not merely to conceive of the transition from natural appearance, the point of departure, to the painting, the point of arrival, but to bring this transition about.

ENTER THE ARTIST.   This outside intelligence, this mediator, is the artist. If nature is in a given landscape—for instance, a view of the Colosseum bathed in sunlight—it is because the artist (in this case Corot) stopped to look at it, because he chose to picture it. Why did he do so? In response to some inner inclination, to some summons from his thoughts or feelings.

Furthermore, if the scene he chose to portray suggested the possibility of a certain arrangement of lines and colors, it is because the desirability of that arrangement and the idea for it arose in him, because he

conceived it; he translated it into reality, imparting to it a given quality, his own—one among countless possible qualities; he executed the work in accordance with certain principles, unexpressed to be sure, but coherent, and reflecting his personal inclinations and predispositions. The memory of the Colosseum as it appeared at a certain moment and the organization of the canvas it inspired were unmistakably those of Camille Corot, a Parisian, aged thirty, who had been a resident of Rome for six months; but Corot in turn is defined by this memory and this organization.

Consciously or unconsciously—often both—the artist is the reason for the existence of the view he has chosen, of the image he has created; this, like any product of creation, obscurely and inevitably resembles its creator. Odilon Redon tells us: "I think I complied with the secret laws which led me to fashion—somehow or other, as best I could, and in accordance with my dream—*things* into which I put myself entirely!"[1] No, there are no true

[1] Odilon Redon, *A soi-même*, p. 11.

77. - *COURBET*. THE PAINTER'S STUDIO
(center section). The Louvre, Paris

86

realists; or, perhaps, the only person who could be one would be a man so devoid of character and personal reality as to be unable to manifest the fact of his own existence.

Courbet says: "I paint only what I see," but he does not give the reason for this, which is his delight in manipulating thick oily paint, in erecting with its help a monument to the voluptuous proteiform matter that gives rise to his moist foliage, his firm and rich flesh, his fawn-colored and dark furs, his fresh water. These things make us want to touch them with our fingers, to taste and smell them, and most of all to caress them lovingly with our eyes; they justify a new mode of perception—pictorial sensuality (figures 77 and 78).

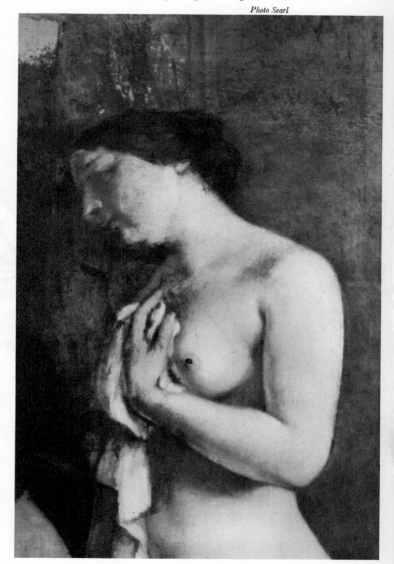

Photo Searl

Velázquez, even though more aristocratic than Courbet, and seemingly aloof from his object, was also one of the pioneers in this new mode of perception. Under the brush of such artists, who aim at "obscurity," a landscape or a face acquires an intensity previously known only in a few ancient still lifes and in some of the Venetian paintings. This intensity is the artist's own contribution; it is the energy he instills into the object through his translation of it into pictorial form.

Conversely, there is no exclusively "plastic" or, if you will, "abstract" art; the painter least open to any chance suggestions of nature will breathe life into his canvas through subtle combinations of lines and colors, in which he will be reflected. Matisse showed his awareness of this fact when he said in an interview: "Composition is the art of arranging decoratively the various elements available to the painter *for the purpose of expressing emotion.*" It has often been objected that the art of Braque and of Picasso sometimes moves so far away from nature that it becomes merely an

Closer examination shows that Courbet's seeming realism does not conceal his lyrical enjoyment of paint for its own sake.

78.- *COURBET*. Nude called "Reality." Detail from THE PAINTER'S STUDIO

amazing counterpoint of lines and colors, that these painters might just as well have produced Persian rugs. And yet the objector, provided he has an eye for such things and some slight training, can readily distinguish a Braque from a Picasso merely by its appearance. Asked how he can tell them apart, he will say it is easy, that Picasso has a violent and tragic quality, that he is more aggressive and even cruel, while Braque is calmer, more affectionate, that he loses himself in a kind of reverie of color. In other words, a human quality gives meaning to what might otherwise seem a chance arrangement of forms (figures 79 and 80).

The artist's presence, the expressive charge with which he loads everything fashioned by his hand, and which is like a weapon aimed at us, is conveyed *through* the plastic design of the work, as though it were breaking through the supposed

objective mirror of reality. Whether he skillfully copies what he sees or ingeniously combines elements that have nothing to do with natural appearance, every detail of his work, observed or imagined, represents a choice among an infinite number of possibilities. And this choice is determined by a secret and deep affinity between what he is and what attracts him.

Every image created by the human hand expresses a particular concept of beauty and a particular psychological presence; therefore it cannot be neutral— that is, it cannot be either purely plastic or purely realistic. Moreover, everything is so closely interrelated that the aesthetic concept expressed itself characterizes the epoch or the individual. The two possibilities we have just considered for art—the representation of what is, and a plastic construction (or, to use current terminology, the figurative and the abstract)—cannot be separated from each other, nor can they be opposed to each other, for they have a common feature: each of them always expresses the artist; he is, as it were, their common denominator.

The conflict between earlier and later styles is misleading, to the extent that it focuses our attention on this badly formulated problem. The nineteenth-century public gave to the imitation of reality an exclusive, disproportionate importance. Our century demands that reality be sacrificed altogether to abstract inventions. To do so is to forget that the problem of art is a human problem, that all of its elements relate to man, and that every element, realistic or plastic, that is introduced into art is inseparable from another factor, namely, *expression*.

Expression! This is the quality of art most difficult to isolate and to describe, the

The same subject treated by two modern masters shows that their individualities, far from being lost in decorative anonymity, strongly express themselves in that manner.

79. - *At left: PICASSO.* STILL LIFE WITH SKULL. 1945

80. - *At right: BRAQUE.* THE EASEL. 1938. Collection Paul Rosenberg, New York

least susceptible to dogmatic formulation or theoretical analysis. The natural and plastic elements are visible, hence verifiable: realism can always be tested by a comparison with the model; beauty often has a canon, can be formulated in terms of proportions or quantities, as has been done only too often in the course of history. But the element of expression conveys a human reality which is invisible. It is the imponderable presence, in the work, of the inner world of the artist, which cannot be measured by yardsticks or apprehended by the senses. With it we leave the domain of space to which realistic art and plastic art have confined us. What we are dealing with now is another faculty, the imagination, in the sense in which it was defined by Joubert: "I call imagination the faculty of making perceptible that which is intellectual, of embodying that which is spirit; in brief, of bringing to light, without distorting it, that which is in itself invisible."

Some aesthetic theories, for instance Plato's, define plastic beauty as a reflection of immaterial, divine realities. Through the medium of art, the soul, which by its very nature cannot occupy space, will nevertheless concretely manifest itself in space. How? By the traces it leaves on the visible world.

We are familiar with natural forces which, when spent, exhausted, leave their mark in the

A photograph of a landscape treated by Van Gogh shows how very ordinary it is...

81. - FARMYARD OF THE ASYLUM OF SAINT-RÉMY. Photograph

upheaval their passage has caused. The winter torrent leaves its traces in its bed of uprooted stones and hollowed-out earth, and the ocean wind in pine trees that are permanently bent as a result of its breath. But the soul, whose reality we experience within ourselves, and which cannot occupy space—where shall we look for its traces when it is the soul of another being? The answer is: in the mark left by its desires and passions, the imprint of its inner organization which shapes external reality in accordance with its own laws, in the countless allusions and references that point, in the work, to this phantom protagonist who has been its inspiration, its spiritual cause.

To be convinced of this it is enough to compare the neutral image of a landscape produced by a photographic lens and the vision (for this is the correct term) of it the painter gives us. This vision, which is also an interpretation, asserts itself when the artist, having mastered his subject, begins to fashion it, as the sculptor fashions a piece of clay, transforming it into an embodiment of his idea. Like the food which the organism attacks with its fluids in order to assimilate it, the initial theme taken from nature is subjected to the acids of sensibility, which strives to make it its own.

THE WORLD OF VAN GOGH. Let us open the windows of the little room Van Gogh used as his studio at the Saint-Rémy asylum: it gives on an ordinary garden in which barley is grown.[1] Nature is here in all its robust objectivity. It suggests a large suburban vegetable garden; a low wall separates it from pine and cypress groves, beyond which the plain extends to the soft hills on the horizon (figure 81).

Now let us watch Van Gogh as he faces this garden: like a wrestler he grips it, crushes it against his chest; he makes it resound with the pulsations of his furiously pounding heart; he dislocates nature, which under his hands becomes like a panting animal caught by its pursuer, ready to submit to his will.

[1] Not wheat, as we often read in descriptions of his paintings.

A force hitherto unseen, of which the photograph shows no trace, now rises like a wind, like a storm, overthrowing, carrying everything before it; the entire landscape, regardless of the solidity of its earth, stones, and trees, becomes a ragged, twisted flag, flapping in the mighty breath that torments it.

An irresistible surge breaks up the surface of the ground, makes it heave; as the lines of perspective no longer merely measure distance, they rush into the distance and disappear, are engulfed by the vanishing point as though swallowed up by a swirling tide; the dark foliage too is agitated, it undulates and twists like a dancing flame, and the far-off hills become animated, begin to stir under the tremendous impact. The sun, surrounded by luminous waves, turns the sky into a maelstrom. Yet so far we have described only Van Gogh's sketch, the preliminary bout between the two realities pitted against each other, the external one that submits passively and the inner one that is breaking out (figure 82).

In the painting, or rather the paintings, that Van Gogh did of this landscape, the brush describes the swirling motions of wind-lashed rain, indicating the frantic dance of the elements; the empty sky becomes the scene of a mad gyration, a cosmic

...his drawing transforms the landscape in passionate surge...

82. - *VAN GOGH.* FARMYARD, SEEN FROM THE ASYLUM OF SAINT-RÉMY. Black pencil. 1889. Neue Staatsgalerie, Munich

...the painting is a vision which is expressive of the artist's inward feeling.

83. - *VAN GOGH.* FIELD OF BARLEY. Saint-Rémy. June, 1889 Kröller-Müller Museum, Otterlo

eruption touched off by the sun, which sets the air on fire. And the color adds its brasses to this symphony of violence. "Instead of trying to reproduce exactly what is before my eyes, I use color arbitrarily *in order to express myself more strongly!*" (figure 83).

Van Gogh, aroused, torn by the forces that have been set in motion within him, has sensed, beneath the impassive crust of things, the same principle of life that is active in him. Is he looking beyond the surface of reality? Or is he reproducing the turmoil that fills his own breast and that he cannot make us see by any other means? "My great desire is to learn to make such inexactitudes, anomalies, revisions, changes, give birth to lies, yes, call them lies if you will, but lies that are truer than the literal truth" (To Théo, letter 418).

Every artist similarly treats the world as his own possession; he borrows its inflexible mask and, animating it by his own warmth, gestures, cries, he returns it to us more or less intact in appearance, but actually emptied of its substance, which he has replaced with his own. Re-enacting the story of Dr. Jekyll and Mr. Hyde, a new soul is born within nature's body; a stranger

Photo Vizzavona

Sometimes Mont Sainte-Victoire has for Cézanne the serenity of ancient architecture...

84. - *CÉZANNE.* **MONT SAINTE-VICTOIRE. Collection Lecomte**

Photo Vizzavona

...at other times it echoes the rhythms of the curving branches...

85. - *CÉZANNE.* **MONT SAINTE-VICTOIRE WITH THE GREAT PINE TREE. National Gallery, London**

sneaks in and remolds it from within, giving it a countenance on which we read expressions of a mind that it did not have before. What is the mysterious alchemy that causes this mutation, this transfiguration to take place before our eyes, that gives reality a new and unpredictable face?

THE WORLD OF CÉZANNE.   The face is different each time: if the viewer is shown Cézanne's version of reality instead of Van Gogh's, he finds himself in a different "ambiance," to use a term that has become fashionable. Both artists are painting Provence, but Cézanne sees the landscape not as a furiously blazing mass but as crystallized architecture; the forces he senses in it are not those of disorder but of order. In his *Estaque*, the water is implacably flat, horizontal, under the dazzling sun. Nothing stirs any longer; the profile of the distant hills, belying Van Gogh's undulating curves, is jagged, the better to suggest its stoniness.

Between the lines of the text of nature that was deciphered by Van Gogh, Cézanne reads the firmness of the underlying structure, product of subterranean forces at work. "To paint a landscape adequately, I must first discover its geological foundations." He often took long Sunday walks with his childhood friend Marion,

Photo Vizzavona

...or again it surges up as in an enormous cataclysm.

86. - *CÉZANNE.* MONT SAINTE-VICTOIRE. Museum of Modern Art, Moscow

93

professor of geology. But in questioning him, Cézanne was seeking to gain a better understanding of his own reality. He "recognized" the ordering spirit which he liked to divine in the formation of strata and rocks—it was his own. He echoed, in an entirely different tone, Van Gogh's statement, when he said, more coldly: "The landscape becomes human, is reflected, thinks itself in me."

Before our eyes, a rigorous law becomes perceivable by the senses, as masses of matter are refined and transformed into shapes which the mind caresses, delighting in the discovery that they resemble the forms conceived by geometry. Where others see in nature a chaos of vehement sensations, Cézanne finds stability, structure, regularity, and certainty, thus making the universe appear as the orderly conception of a higher intelligence.

However, a man is not all of a piece, even though some of his traits are constant; he is not identical at every moment with the simplified picture we have of him. He has his variations, his facets. Art, which records the differences between one individual's vision and another's, also discloses the minor divergencies that account for the complexity of a given artist's work (figures 84 to 86).

One of Cézanne's favorite subjects is Mont Sainte-Victoire. He sees it as a reflection of himself—but also of all his potential selves. As we look through the various versions, we see in them the divergent aspects of a single personality. In the one in the Lecomte Collection, the imperious order has a quality of harmony: nowhere else is Cézanne, the Latin, so close to the Greek soul; the mountain rises like an Acropolis, combining the severity of Rome with the refinement of Athens; the surrounding landscape rises with it toward its own apotheosis.

The painting of it at the National Gallery in London is no less austere, but it is slightly less rigid. The hard line of the contours against the sky is no longer tense; it relaxes into a rhythmic movement, accompanied in the foreground by the curve of a branch bending like a palm tree.

> *L'or léger qu'elle murmure*
> *Sonne au simple doigt de l'air*
> *Et d'une soyeuse armure*
> *Charge l'âme du désert.*

The light gold it whispers / Resounds at the slightest finger of air / And with a silken armor / Clothes the soul of the desert.

Valéry, like Cézanne, creates a crystalline structure, dazzling with light, and vibrant with melody.

Now look at the version of Mont Sainte-Victoire in Moscow: here Cézanne comes closer to Van Gogh because, at the source of this geology whose order he enjoyed, he divined the gigantic eruption, the upheaval of incandescent matter, whose cooling off was to result in order, in balance. Life explodes with virgin ardor in its beginnings, before arriving at the conclusion which will satisfy the mind.

Do we not see in this a parallel with Cézanne's career, which began with the torments of the Baroque and ended in an insatiable classicism? His final severity is that of lava grown cold. The Mont Sainte-Victoire of his last years shows us Cézanne in his entirety. Intensity and fixity are combined in this iridescent cliff, with the profile of a ship's prow, a sharp edge broken, like the plain above which it towers, into a thousand gemlike facets glowing with the infinite modulations of color.

Thus, as with the spokes of a wheel, every line that leads outward to a different

point on the periphery seems to contradict the directions of all the other lines; and yet all of them converge in a single center, from which each springs and which all together define.

This is a little like the analysis of painting we are attempting in this book: we shall outline different orientations, one after another; yet in the end all of them will meet to constitute a final unity.

4. TOWARD A SYNTHESIS

So far we have distinguished three principal "voices" taking part in the dialogue from which the work of art will issue. There is nature, the point of departure, the basic material. There is the painting, the terminal point, the plastic construction. Between them, lifting the first to the level of the second, borrowing from the one and giving to the other only in order to assert himself and define himself more clearly, is the painter, who runs the show.

This combination of three elements was concisely described by Rouault, who defined the three principal participants in the creative act: "The eye captures the fleeting vision. The mind orders, and the heart cherishes," he wrote in *Verve*, in 1938. According to the ideals of a given historical period, a given group, or a given individual, one of the three participants is brought forward, and another pushed into the background, but none of the three can ever be absent without destroying the natural harmony of the whole.

Imitation, Construction, Expression: those are the three orientations available to the painter. Reality, Beauty, Poetry, are the three goddesses, a trinity rather than a triad, whom he worships. According to his purposes at a given moment, as well as his own inclination, the great master may invoke one of the goddesses rather than another; but he is rarely without all three of them, and that, primarily, is what makes for his greatness.

DELACROIX'S MANY SIDES. Take Delacroix, for example. Reality, Beauty, Poetry—all are equally familiar to him. An analysis of one of his themes—one that appealed to him most, i.e., the female body—will show this clearly.

One day, when his model, Mlle Rose, began to show signs of weariness, and to slump, he was seized with the desire to test himself by putting on paper everything he saw. Nothing would escape, he decided, through the fine-meshed net of his vision—no slightest curve of the figure, no tonality of the flesh. He would be a realist. On February 20, 1824, he wrote that he wanted "to produce a painting of an entirely new kind, which will, so to speak, consist in a precise copy of nature,"[1] as a reaction against the prevailing conventions (figure 87).

And yet Delacroix is the author of the famous apostrophe: "Ah, you accursed realist, are you trying by chance to produce an illusion such that I will imagine I have actually witnessed the spectacle you pretend you are offering me? It is the cruel reality of things that I flee from, when I take refuge in the sphere of art's creations."[2]

[1] *Journal*, ed. Joubin, 1, p. 52.
[2] *Oeuvres littéraires*, 1, 59.

Delacroix knew how to be severely realistic when making his studies.

87. - *DELACROIX.* SEATED NUDE (MADEMOISELLE ROSE). The Louvre, Paris

96

Let us watch him closely then, on this occasion, when he draws on the paper a reclining nude, and his hand succumbs to the temptation of the harmonious line. He thinks of the subtle and firm development for which the rhythm of this supine body, the wavy contour of its form, could provide the incentive. "In portraits of women, above all," he wrote, "it is necessary to begin with the gracefulness of the whole." The lines must be, so to speak, "memorized," then "it will be possible in some way to reproduce them geometrically in the picture."[1] Here he actually makes his vision comply with the flowing line, which he emphasizes to the point of achieving a result similar to that of his old adversary, Ingres the draftsman.[2] At this moment he is a "plastic" artist (figures 88 and 89).

However, the effort he makes to develop this line born of his thought as well as his hand draws him away from his habitual range of emotions. He fears that he may become its prisoner, be restricted, paralyzed, for he also said: "Woe to the painting which shows nothing beyond the finite....What gives a painting its value is indefinable—it is precisely that which eludes precise definition." What is it then? "That which the soul has added to the colors and lines in order to make them reveal the soul," for (did he not copy this from Goethe?) "the soul, in drawing, delineates a part of its essential being";[3] it is the soul that the work must render. This had been his opinion in his youth: "The subject is oneself, one's impressions, one's emotions in the face of nature. It is within oneself that one must look, not around one."[4]

That is why, now, he closes his eyes; the heady fumes he has absorbed are allowed to suffuse and intoxicate his mind. His imagination takes hold of this body before him, this nude, and makes it the slave of his dream. He shows it, supple and full, bright in the intimacy of the shadow-filled room; he unfolds its forms to the rhythm of his desire; he scatters its hair, lets it fall in waves....

> *O Toison moutonnant jusque sur l'encolure!*
> *O boucles! O parfum chargé de nonchaloir!*
> *Extase! Pour peupler ce soir l'alcôve obscure*
> *Des souvenirs dormant dans cette chevelure*
> *Je la veux agiter dans l'air comme un mouchoir!*

Baudelaire, whose affinity to Delacroix is great, lends him his voice: lust and voluptuousness become a single image, reflected in a mirror; it conjures up the fragrance of flowers, revives in the mind the echoes of familiar sentiments. On one side of the mirror, we see the female body in its complacency, its vanity, its desires; on the other, we see the shadowy, sardonic figure of the devil, familiar to us from Delacroix's pencil sketch in which he is shown whispering to Gretchen. Life, the meaning of life, its joys and sorrows, seems here to emerge like some monstrous genie materializing out of the wisps of smoke that arise from a blazing fire (figure 90).

THE TOTAL PAINTING.   There is no great artist who, at one time or another, depending on the aim of a given work—illustration, exploration, or creation—does

---

[1] *Oeuvres littéraires*, p. 70.

[2] We reproduce (figures 88 and 89) an example previously published in *Formes* (vi, June, 1930), which Jacques Mathey has used again in an article in the *Gazette des Beaux-Arts* (January, 1953).

[3] Supplement to the *Journal* (ed. Joubin), iii, p. 402, 405.

[4] *Oeuvres littéraires*, i, 76.

88. - *DELACROIX*. RECLINING NUDE. Drawing. The Louvre, Paris

*The elegant curves of a female body could inspire Delacroix to produce plastic
harmonies rivaling those of Ingres.*

89. - *INGRES*. NUDE. Drawing. The Louvre, Paris

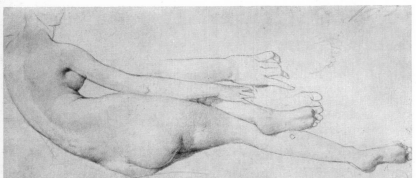

not take advantage of the three possibilities of art. There is practically no masterpiece, we might add, that does not contain an element of all three; and though exceptional success with one of them is sometimes sufficient to justify a work's being called a masterpiece, as a rule the finest works are those in which a balance between nature, painting, and the artist is achieved—sometimes by reducing the importance of one of them, sometimes by dint of exalting all three.

Almost all of Titian's paintings display a marvelous talent for making all three elements contribute to the final success of the work. His paintings provide the best illustration of Valéry's statement: "What I call 'great art' is merely an art that requires the use of *all of a man's faculties*, and that appeals to all the faculties of other men.... I believe that ... a work of art should be the act of the whole man."[1]

Which is more distinctly perceivable in Titian's *Entombment* (plate III)—the voice of nature, that of beauty, or that of the soul? It is difficult to separate them: the sumptuousness of the fabrics, the way in which they are draped in order to enhance their textures, produce a striking illusionistic effect; but their richness, their folds serve to emphasize the implacable whiteness of the shroud underneath the body of the Christ, and bring out the sharp lines of its creases. The curve formed by the winding sheet balances the curve formed by the heads and shoulders of the three bearers. The compositon is built around the powerful arch these figures make, the curve of which, if prolonged, would come to rest on the bottom edge of the picture. The slightly bent silhouette of the Virgin strongly expresses her grief and provides a parallel curve, reinforcing the arch formed by the central group. The head of St. John at the top indicates the axis of the canvas, but it also contributes to the expression of grief.

[1] Paul Valéry, *Degas, Danse, Dessin*, p. 137.

The composition may be seen as a rhythmic configuration of lines and colors, in which the warm red of Nicodemus' robe offsets the cold blue of the Virgin's, as the ruddy autumn foliage offsets the pale blue of the evening sky. But the painting also expresses, above all, the crushing weight of the divine body irrevocably abandoned by its soul; it sags heavily, and it is the weight of this body that compels the three men to hold themselves firmly and to form a supporting arch. The canvas also emphasizes the hard nakedness of the corpse and the linen that partly drapes it, for everything around it is painted in contrasting deep tones and shadows.

Finally, the striking presence of the sky, the woods, and the rich fabrics, the magnificent symphony of colors, the strong lines of the composition, the intense feeling of tragedy all combine to produce that mixture of sensuality and profundity, of enjoyment and melancholy, of force and feeling, which is Titian. Who would venture to isolate one of these elements and to say that it alone is valuable? Titian's art is a great symphony in which each of the elements is indispensable and inseparable from the impressive whole.

IS ART A LANGUAGE? Indeed, it may be asked whether this complex entity—which combines references to a reality familiar to all, with a beauty derived from a select vocabulary of images, and from associations between images, and finally from the uses to which they are put by the artist in order to express his ideas and feelings—whether this does not constitute a distinct language. The comparison is fruitful, provided it is not pushed too far.

Photo Hachette

The female body was at times no more than a stimulus to Delacroix the poet.

90. - *DELACROIX.* MORNING TOILETTE.
Collection David-Weill, Paris

Although the vocabulary of art consists of images rather than words, it is based on the store of common experiences that make human communication possible. Just as every word in use in a language corresponds to an idea that can be defined in a dictionary, every identifiable image evokes the memory of a familiar sensation. Speaking of Delacroix and quoting him in his *Salon of 1846*, Baudelaire says: "Nature is a vast dictionary of which he turns the pages and which he consults with a sure and profound eye." This implies a condemnation of exclusive, out-and-out realism. A painter concerned only with reproducing the images provided by reality would be no more interesting than a parrot which repeats human words. A handful of terms taken from a dictionary is not a text; nor can one properly call an assortment of borrowings from nature a work of art.

Language would be pointless if it did not *signify*. The same is true of art. Maurice Barrès, in the notes appended to his *Voyage de Sparte*, recalls the "important lesson Goethe gave us through the mediation of Eckermann, one night of April, 1827," when in discussing Rubens he defined the use the artist makes of nature. "He is in a dual relationship with nature: he is simultaneously its master and slave. He is the slave of nature in the sense that he must operate with terrestrial means in order to be understood; he is its master in the sense that he subjects these means to his lofty purposes. The artist wants to speak to the world through a combination of elements, but this combination he does not find in nature; it is the fruit of his own mind." And Rimbaud says: "Your memory and your senses shall be only the nourishment for your creative impulse."

However, it is important to define this concept further, and to dispel a widespread misunderstanding: what the artist expresses in his language of images does not fall within the same province as what is signified by verbal language. Nineteenth-century society tried stubbornly to reduce art to something which it is not, to curtail its powers: "If art cannot duplicate nature," the century said, in effect, "let it at least duplicate spoken language, make visible to the eye what can be described, narrated, or explained in sentences. Art must be either naturalistic or literary."

To be sure, when man could not read, society required of art that it show what should have been read; the Church wanted to make it "the Bible of the Poor." But such attempts were only makeshifts, dictated by specific historical circumstances. In the fourth century, St. Basil said: "What the word offers to the ear, painting shows through imitation." His brother, St. Gregory of Nyssa, referred to painting as "a speaking book." These men were not concerned with the interests and the truth of art, but with those of the Church. Moreover the artists instinctively went beyond the task that was assigned to them.

Beginning with the Renaissance, the civilization of the book contributed to the same misunderstanding: invoking sensory experience on the one hand and logical thinking on the other, this civilization was inevitably tempted to reduce art to realism and "literature." And the fact is that during that time art often was descriptive, narrative, or allegorical.

The twentieth century has reacted to this unhealthy tendency and rediscovered the path leading toward true artistic values, but it overshot the mark by sacrificing altogether the prevailing ideas of the past, by banning and suppressing elements in art that needed merely to be relegated to their proper place. Our century has brutally condemned both reality (as though reality existed only as an object for literal reproduction!) and the subject (as though all subjects must be inspired by literature!). Such oversimplifications, which have often been carried to the point of puerility, will no doubt be judged severely one day, and modern art held answerable for them by subsequent generations.

Our period, however, has one immense fact to its credit: it has liberated the image from misleading entanglements, rediscovered its true purpose—that of direct expression, through the action of its constitutive elements, line and color, on our sensibility, which sets off a nervous shock that arouses emotions and produces states of mind.

We go astray when we regard art as a mere plastic game, when we neglect its function of interpreting reality. The language of images must not be confused with the language of words, must not be turned into a mere duplication of it. The two do not designate the same kind of reality, nor do they designate reality by the same means. The language of images belongs to an area of inner life that is distinct from that of ideas, which give substance to words; and even if the two languages happen to deal with the same reality, they approach it from different angles. The image performs a psychological function that it alone can perform, for it expresses elements of the psyche that would not be accessible without it; moreover it serves as outlet for tensions that could not be released by any other means.

This question will be dealt with at greater length in a later chapter; it is mentioned here in an attempt to dispel certain misunderstandings that might arise from this definition of art. The definition is sound, however, in that art does enable the artist to express for himself his inner aspirations, as well as to disclose them to others, to communicate to others the hidden riches, felt or created, in which he wishes them to share.

THE TEMPTATION OF FORMALISM. Nature furnishes the language of art with its vocabulary, and the artist's soul gives it its substance; but, as in the case of any language, there arises the problem of its form. It has to communicate *something*, but it must do it in a *certain way!* Merely to observe the rules and conventions of the established syntax would amount to staying within the realm of utilitarianism. To achieve art, form as well as content must be given a quality sufficient to invest them with value in the eyes of others. Goethe warns us:

> *Just because you have composed a verse in a language already formed*
> *Which versifies and thinks for you, do you think you are a poet?*

To confuse the beauty of a language with its correctness, that is, conformity with current rules and conventions, is the eternal error of academism. The language of images becomes an art if its forms convey a quality, and if, in addition, this quality is the product of creation. The same is true of verbal expression when it achieves the level of poetry. Then it serves a higher purpose than utilitarian communication; the form, the harmonious arrangement of syllables, the rhythm with which they succeed one another, their stresses and pauses, aim essentially at conveying a certain quality. The aim of art is the same, and plastic form is in it what prosody is in poetry.

As in the case of poetry, there arises inevitably the question of a pure and disinterested art. Since art begins where the mechanisms of technology leave off, since it is not a means put at the service of some other activity but an end in itself, there is a temptation to go to extremes. Poetry is a language of words, in which the communication of meaning and the correctness of form have a place only as they contribute to the perfection of the whole; this perfection is its sole justification. Similarly, art is a language of images, which treats a subject and observes rules of execution only as a means toward discovering beauty; this ambition and purpose is what makes it art.

Why then, it has been asked, should we not reduce the utilitarian element in painting to an absolute minimum, since it is only a pretext, and make art its own justification, allow it simply to seek its own consummation? Mathematics is to be envied, says Valéry, for having long since become independent of any goal other than knowledge of itself, which it attains abstractly, through the development and exercise of its own technique.[1] Thus our refined culture has given rise to the idea of a pure art, that is, an abstract art, counterpart of pure poetry.

Since the poet does his utmost to bring out the music which is inherent in words, apart from their meanings, cannot these words be assembled for the sake of their music alone? If in the most beautiful examples of classical verse the music coincides with the meaning, why not cut the moorings, relieve the balloon of its ballast, set it free? If this can be done, what is to prevent painting from pursuing a similarly bold course? With the lines and colors for which the landscape was the pretext, Gauguin improvised a symphony that also merely *coincided* with its figurative content. Would it not be tempting to set this music completely free, to give full rein to its possibilities? It is as a result of such questions that abstract art made its appearance.

This may be the sin of the absolute. Because art, in order to constitute a vocabulary for itself, had to reproduce reality, the nineteenth century imagined that all its other functions could be dispensed with. Because art achieves beauty through harmonious combinations of plastic elements, the twentieth century imagines that art will find its supreme consummation in the exclusive pursuit of beauty.

Let us be wary of men possessed of a single idea. Such an idea gives us a glimpse of the truth, and we need such glimpses to come close to it; but many ideas are needed in order to encompass and conquer the truth. The single idea, while it may be correct at the outset, goes astray as it branches out, losing contact with the initial truth which forms its root, till it seems to be blossoming in the void. We are not superior to life. Let us question it humbly; it is wrong to interrupt it the moment we have grasped one, a single one, of its truths; it has many more to give us, and we have much more to learn from it.

We have questioned life, and so far it has disclosed to us three essential possibilities inherent in painting—the representation of external reality, which is its pretext; the autonomous development of the means of representation, which is its activity; the evocation of inner reality, which is its goal. Three doors lie open before us. Before drawing our conclusions, we must enter each one in succession and see where it leads us.

[1] Paul Valéry, *Les divers essais sur L. de Vinci*, p. 136.

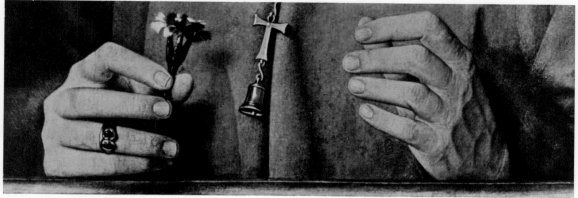

Realism tends to the trompe-l'œil.

91. - *VAN EYCK*. MAN WITH A PINK (detail). Museum, Berlin

CHAPTER TWO

THE VICISSITUDES OF REALISM

*Beauty is everywhere, but it
reveals itself only to love.*
Emile Mâle

THE conception of art as an imitation of reality is utterly false; yet we are
forced to recognize the greatness of art's achievement in the conquest of
reality, of natural appearance—in rendering the shock of beauty we experience before things, in wresting from time the priceless moment that would
otherwise slip away with the ticking of the clock.

Painters, however, have always preferred to keep nature at a distance; it was not
until about a century and a half ago that they began to work from life, to set up
their easels before their actual subjects.[1] Hitherto they had preferred to work in the
seclusion of their studios with models who were more compliant; or they went out

---

[1] We may recall here a conversation between Corot and Renoir, as the latter reported it to Vollard (*Renoir*,
p. 136): "One day I was lucky enough to find him alone; I told him that I found it hard to work out of
doors.—The fact is, he replied, that out of doors one can never be sure of what one is doing; one must
always go over one's work later in the studio." This did not prevent Corot from rendering nature with a
truth that no Impressionist has ever equaled.

103

into the world and observed, made notes, then, returning home, sought to break the spell of the sensations they had absorbed, to regain their self-possession and an awareness of their own powers and of the work to be composed.

The Impressionists, coming at a time when naturalism was in the final stages of development, were almost the only ones to paint outdoors. And yet... "Claude Monet painted from nature, but for no more than ten minutes at a time," Bonnard related to Angèle Lamotte in 1943.[1] "He did not want to give things an opportunity to get hold of him." And Bonnard, that grandson of Impressionism, confessed: "I tried to paint accurately, scrupulously, I let myself become engrossed in details.... The presence of the object, of the motif, is very embarrassing to the painter while he is painting." At such moments, he said, he had to resort to a "very personal system of defense"; and that was why, Bonnard added, "I paint alone in my studio, I do everything in my studio."

What is the source of the danger? Bonnard answers this question. "The starting point of a painting," he says, "is an idea." Delacroix used almost the same words when he wrote in his diary: "The model ... appropriates everything to itself, leaving nothing to the painter.... Therefore it is far more important for the artist to pay attention to the ideal he carries within himself," that is, to his "intentions," his "imagination," to that which he seeks in nature as well as in art,[2] to what attracts him there. This was also Bonnard's opinion: "It is through being captivated by an object, and conceiving an idea for a painting of it, that the painter achieves universality. This original fascination not only determines the choice of the motif, it gives the painting its distinct quality. If the fascination, the original impetus evaporates, there remains only the motif, the object, which invades and dominates the painter. From that moment on the painting is no longer his own."

What must the painter do to avoid this danger? He must follow the example of Cézanne, Bonnard tells us. "Cézanne when confronting his motif had a clear idea of what he wanted to do, and took from nature only what was relevant to this idea ... only those elements that fitted his conception."

Bonnard, whose work to the very end was a hymn of love to nature, to woman, to flowers, to light, to life, is an admirable lesson for us. It seems that no artist has more completely abandoned himself to reality, had greater confidence in it; and yet Bonnard keeps his distance from it.

The problem of realism has always been a disturbing one for artists, who have never looked on reality with the blind acceptance with which the public views it. Reality for the artist is but a starting point, not the goal; it provides a foundation of experience, a frame of reference; it is the pedestal on which the work is built, sometimes even the springboard from which the artist takes off into other realms, occasionally very far away, so far that he forgets where his impulse originated: then the sensations provided by the eye no longer serve as a model, but merely as an assortment of colored forms which he uses arbitrarily, having entered the path of abstract art.

Thus we come back to the question: *Should* art imitate nature? Or can it turn its

---

[1] *Verve*, v. V, Nos. 17–18.

[2] *Journal*, II, p. 87 (Champrosay, October 12, 1853). Thirty-five years later, Emile Bernard, a friend of Gauguin's, voiced the same conviction somewhat more ponderously: "Since the idea takes its form from things stored up in the imagination, one must paint not with the object before one's eyes, but from the reproduction of it in one's imagination, where it has been stored, where its form has been preserved."

back on nature and set out in quest of the pure creations of the mind and of sensibility? Theoreticians, as always, find it easy to take sides in this debate, but we shall not try here to settle the question. Experience alone can provide an answer, historical experience, which tells us what art actually has been in the course of centuries, and what man has wanted art to be. We might even call this a phenomenology of art, if that fashionable term were not so barbarous. The fundamental problem of realism, of the part it plays and should play, can be formulated and solved only in terms of such a retrospective inquiry.

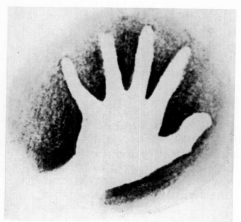

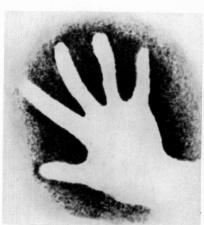

Art was born of man's need to leave his mark on things.

92. - PREHISTORIC IMPRINTS OF HANDS. Castillo (Spain). Drawings copied by the Abbé Breuil

1. THE SEARCH FOR ORIGINS: PREHISTORY

LET us go back to the very sources of art, to prehistoric man, who first experienced and gave evidence of the need to create something, though he was not aware that it was art. Where was he led by this instinct still uncontaminated by theoretical principles? Was his solution a simple one, primitive though it is? The dogmatists who, eager to confirm their thesis, expect it to be simple will be disappointed.

THE INFANCY OF ART. The first stammering attempts at art seem to have been born of accident. At least so the keen analyses of the greatest French prehistorian, the Abbé Breuil, indicate,[1] and psychology does not contradict his findings. Psychology is well aware that the imagination never creates *ex nihilo*. It

[1] In addition to his classic works on the subject, he discussed the question in a number of valuable articles and communications (cf. his communication to the Académie des Inscriptions et Belles-Lettres, 1905; to the *Revue Philosophique*, 1906; " Les Origines de l'Art" in *Journal de Psychologie*, 1925, pp. 289 ff.; and "Les Origines de l'Art décoratif," *ibid.*, 1926, pp. 364 ff.).

always requires, initially, a contribution from outside, which it develops gradually; and occasionally the initial element is so completely transformed that it is difficult to discover its source.

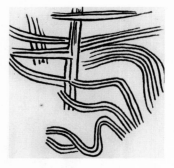

Sometimes prehistoric man let his fingers trace random marks in the clay.

93. - FINGER TRACINGS. Hornos de la Peña (Spain). Copied by the Abbé Breuil

Prehistoric man, like the still extant savages in the Americas and Australia, felt a need to put his mark on things. The Abbé Breuil likens this instinct to the one which drives the child to leave his traces wherever he can: he scribbles formless lines with a crayon or a pencil on white surfaces; he makes finger drawings on the sand of a beach; he dips his hand in the mud, and then applies it to a wall; he lies spread-eagled in the snow to leave the imprint of his body is the soft mass. The adult is probably seeking a similar obscure gratification when he inscribes his name on a monument he happens to pass. Such projections of the self indicate that art has its origins in a basic human drive.

The cave dweller who applied his hand to a wall (e.g., at Gargas in the Hautes-Pyrénées, at Pech-Merle in the Lot, at Castillo or Altamira in Spain, and in many other widely scattered places) was not behaving any differently. The prints he left are the oldest manifestations of prehistoric man, "stratigraphically prior to the simplest outline drawings.... Ringed with red, and later with black lines, those hand prints go back to the archaic Aurignacian,"[1] that

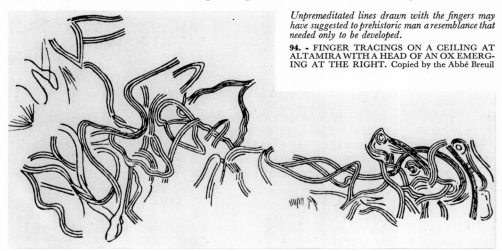

Unpremeditated lines drawn with the fingers may have suggested to prehistoric man a resemblance that needed only to be developed.

94. - FINGER TRACINGS ON A CEILING AT ALTAMIRA WITH A HEAD OF AN OX EMERGING AT THE RIGHT. Copied by the Abbé Breuil

is, to the very beginnings of artistic activity. The hand was sometimes applied directly to the wall, sometimes to an area clearly distinguished, by its color, from the surrounding space (figure 92).

[1] Bandi and Maringer, *L'Art préhistorique*, p. 98.

Similar marks, made by present-day primitives, have been discovered on rocks in Australia and in California. While more than 150 such imprints were found at Gargas, 64 hands in red have been recorded at Coolsalwin, and 38, in white, red, or yellow, at Coonbaralba. The Australian tribe of Worora at Port George also makes imprints of feet. In some cases, the Paleolithics let their fingers wander over the soft damp silt covering the walls of their caves; occasionally they dipped their fingers in paint, often a light yellow ocher, which they probably used as make-up, and traced parallel or diverging wavy lines. There are numerous examples in Spanish Cantabria (Hornos de la Peña, La Pileta) and also in southwestern France (Gargas, Cabrerets in the Lot, La Croze in the Dordogne, etc.). These tracings, however, seem to belong to a later stage, when the purely mechanical imprint began to yield to rudimentary design (figure 93).

The random shapes of stone needed only slight improvements to give birth to the art of sculpture.

95. - THE STONE OF PREDMOST IN THE SHAPE OF A MAMMOTH (45⅝ × 37¾"). Collection Kriz, Brno

FIRST ATTEMPTS AT LIKENESS. Then, in those random wavering lines there arrives the extraordinary moment of the birth of art: crude, tentative figures, mere outlines, but figures nonetheless, appear, somewhat the way knots form spontaneously in a tangle of string. On the ceiling of the right-hand gallery at Altamira we find the head, surprising in its likeness to life, of a *Bos primigenius* emerging from the interwoven tracings; at Baume-Latrone in the Gard, elephants and a snake take shape. When, with a brush or a sharp flint, the primitives begin to try reproducing these felicitous accidents of the finger tracings, figurative art comes into being (figure 94).

The higher a living being climbs on the ladder of consciousness, the more he tends to organize his elementary sense perceptions, and to interpret them. A similarity between two objects suggests at once the possibility of generalizing, of devising categories; in short, the intellectual act comes into being. The most highly evolved animal, the ape, is capable not only of ascertaining similarities between things but also of producing similarities, by mimicking. Man inevitably went further with this. He was able to produce likenesses of animals by merely developing certain suggestions contained in natural objects he came upon; eventually he discovered that he could do without such accidental suggestions, that he could create *ex nihilo*, as it were.

In mountain regions, rocks or peaks are often called by names such as the Chamois, the Bear, or the Old Woman, for the animal or person the particular rocky profile or silhouette suggests. Such improvising of names continues to this day: guides tell us that in the Pyrenees there is a cliff which bears a resemblance to the face of Napoleon III! Most of us have fancied, at one time or another, that we saw outlines of strange animals in the shapes of drifting clouds. Leonardo da Vinci says that clouds and old walls inspired him with beautiful and varied designs, and that the illusory shapes he saw there, though often imperfect in their details, displayed a kind of perfection in their movement and action. He also refers to "the sound of bells in whose clanging you discover every name and word you can imagine."[1] A chance spot can evoke, and hence represent, almost anything. Modern psychology is aware of this fact, and makes use of it in the well-known Rorschach test, in which the associations touched off by ink blots are made the basis for clinical diagnosis.

The *Bos primigenius* of Altamira moves us deeply: in this assimilation of a line into the tracing of a head we can catch the first faint intimations of art being born.... But this discovery may itself have been the result of many thousands of years of development. To perceive, in a jumble of lines, the factitious appearance we call a contour requires a great capacity for abstraction; and it requires daring to make this figment of the mind stand for so many qualities of the object it represents—form, volume, mass, substance, color, and above all the natural appearance as it is continually changing in time.

Clearly, art could not have emerged at the moment man did: the ability to extract such an instantaneous image from the continuously unfolding pattern of life, to conceive it as generalized, as typical, and on top of that to transform it into an arbitrary arrangement of lines, required a high degree of maturity and a conscious

---

[1] MS. 2038 Bib. Nat. fol. 22, v. The whole passage deserves to be quoted: "If you look at any walls spotted with various stains or with a mixture of different kinds of stones, and if you are about to invent some scene, you will be able to see in it a resemblance to various different landscapes adorned with mountains, rivers, rocks, trees, plains, wide valleys, and various groups of hills. You will also be able to see diverse combats and figures in quick movement, and strange expressions of faces, and outlandish costumes, and an infinite number of things which you can then reduce into separate and well-conceived forms" (*Notebooks*, II, 250).

Although Leonardo is often quoted on this subject, there are many other testimonies, some little known. Ch. Monselet, in his *Recollections*, relates (p. 213) that on a visit to a friend at Pierry, in Champagne, he was shown a mantelpiece done by Cazotte: "There, I saw something unusual and truly fantastic, in the artistic sense of the word. First it was a kind of jumble, chaos; then, looking more closely, lines appeared, forms took shape; in the end one distinguished a whole world created by a marvelous fantasy. The slightest whims of the marble, its specks, its veins had been made use of by an imaginative pencil; the smallest hints had been followed up, completed, extended with wonderful skill. It was like the things one sees in clouds: endless cavalcades, fairylike landscapes, plains, valleys, mountains, torrents; then also interlocked bodies, inverted torsos, bold foreshortenings, a witch riding on a broomstick and nymphs dancing executed in one stroke." Monselet adds some keen reflections on this "pencil seized with vertigo," Jacques Cazotte's pencil profiting from and transforming the irregularities of marble; in this work, he sees "a unique album, which opens to us some of the secrets of his temperament, his dreams, his deliriums." But let us not anticipate here our analysis of the psychology of art, to which we shall return later.

Odilon Redon, too, recalled (in *A soi-même*, p. 11): "My father often told me: 'Look at these clouds; do you discern in them, as I do, changing forms?' And then he showed me, in the restless sky, apparitions of bizarre, chimerical, and marvelous beings."

use of human faculties. This decisive step, which seems so natural to us, actually marks a great conquest.

It is therefore probable that the ability to create a likeness first came to man in an area where near-identity could be achieved and grasped without a special effort of mental adaptation, where the acrobatic trick of reducing the three dimensions of reality to the two dimensions of a surface was not required—in short, in sculpture. Sculptures appeared in the earliest periods; witness the so-called "Venus" figures, which date from the Aurignacian epoch. The natural shapes of stones suggested animal shapes, and such stones could easily be made to resemble animals.

The Predmost stone (Kriz Collection, at Brno), which was discovered in 1926, and dates from the Aurignacian or Solutrean epoch, is a rare example of such a conferring of the appearance of nature upon an object that suggests it. In size and shape the stone resembles a small-scale mammoth. The hand that picked it up was seized with an impulse to accentuate, to heighten this likeness. Tools were used for the purpose, as can be seen from the indentations that emphasize or define the modeling of the head, the shoulder, the tail, and that denote the long fur with which mammoths are so frequently shown by prehistoric artists. The stone is a permanent monument to the creative impulse, which chose likeness as the goal of human will and skill (figure 95).

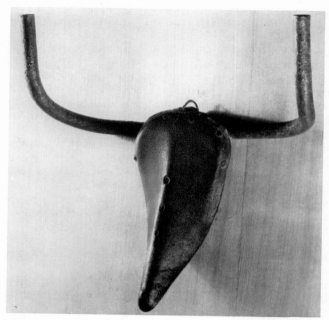

Photo Chevojon

Even today's art, however unrealistic it may be, sometimes exploits the accidental appearance of non-art objects.

96. - *PICASSO.* BUCRANIUM. Composed of a bicycle seat and handlebars. Galerie Louise Leiris, Paris

These artificial forms imitating reality have a close connection with the natural forms that suggest them—a connection that remains unbroken. The great headless bear, modeled in clay, of the Montespan grotto, once had a real head; an actual bear's skull was found between the statue's paws where it had fallen. In this example, the umbilical cord tying fiction to truth has not yet been cut. (Are not the collages used by the Cubists in some of their early works simply a new version of the same combination of object and image?) At Commarque, the procedure is reversed: an engraved head completes and gives meaning to the relief on the wall, which suggests the body of a horse.

TOWARD ABSTRACTION.   Everything in these earliest attempts at art speaks the language of realism; is evidence of an effort toward realism. To be sure, there is also an attempt to simplify the too-great complexity of nature; but we may regard this as really a concession by the artist, who does not as yet feel himself skilled enough to render so much complication. But the attempt also reflects another concern of art: to show significant forms.

That the primitive artist was able to conceive forms is demonstrated by the abstract designs he produced as decorations. Prehistoric man, motivated as in other instances by a need to leave his imprint on things, engraved designs on objects made of bones of animals he had devoured, in order to claim them as his own.

Apparently these designs, too, have an accidental origin: according to students of prehistory, they probably started with the marks left on the bones by the tools which removed the flesh and scraped them clean. The human mind did the rest: having observed these markings, it sought to improve them, to fashion them in accordance with its desires. Such desires may be termed aesthetic, no matter what entered into them later. What do they aim at? Obviously, no longer at resemblance, but rather at something new—ornamentation.

Prehistoric man was not satisfied with the unformed, involuntary marks left by his impatient, disorderly activity; he wished subconsciously to transform them in such a way that they might give him pleasure when he looked at them, i.e., that they might gratify certain inner needs. It is tempting to specify these needs—to say that they were the source of the aesthetic impulse.

The most elusive idea with which man has to deal, the most impossible to assimilate, is certainly that of the unlimited, the infinite; yet he is confronted with it at every step. Man, by nature, is *one:* his body is an organism—i.e., a single entity composed of many elements joined together in a common existence—which cannot live if it is broken up. His inner life is founded on the consciousness that resides in the self, and everything that he becomes aware of in the life around him is referred to this self. Man can focus his attention and consciousness upon only one object at a time, and in order to apprehend multiplicity, he must invent or discover some means of classifying the elements of reality. Just as the hand needs a strap in order to hold together a bundle of sticks, so the mind requires some collective term, some general notion, under which the separate elements may be subsumed; or else it must have the power of logically connecting the different elements. Failing either of these solutions, the mind loses its way in the maze that confronts it.

A word in common usage often becomes even more expressive when we go back to its etymological origins. This is true of "comprehend," from *cum-prehendere,* to gather together. Thus, faced with the multiform reality which threatens to overwhelm him, to dissipate his energies, to dissolve his being, man sets himself to weaving a net which, though its meshes will encompass the widest possible range of objects, can nevertheless be gathered together and held in the grasp of one hand.

The human intellect dreams always of finding a definitive formula, a single principle, that will explain reality by reducing it to some kind of unity. This tendency, so evident in the history of thought, also governs artistic decoration, which seeks to replace the incoherent and haphazard with order and clarity. To this end it is necessary to isolate certain simple elements, which may be repeated or combined in a way easy to grasp, yet producing an appearance of complexity and richness.

Ornamental art derives from the primitive effort to organize accidental hatchings.

97. - *Left to right:* ENGRAVED BONE. Predmost, Museum, Brno; ENGRAVED BONE of Laugerie-Basse (reindeer horn), recto and verso; ENGRAVED BONE. Le Placard (Charente); A CHISEL DECORATED ON FOUR SIDES. Saint-Marcel (Indre), Museum, Saint-Germain-en-Laye

THE LAW OF DIVERSITY IN UNITY.   On the dry bone of a reindeer prehistoric man sees certain scratches—put there accidentally—that go in all directions. In this form they are alien to him; they do not respond to his nature or his expectations. To make them conform to his needs, he must impose an order upon them which his mind can grasp and respond to.

The first technique he uses is repetition: he makes other scratches on the bone, seeking to establish an identity, that is to say, a parallel, with the marks already there. What was complexity thus becomes mere repetition.

At this point, however, he meets with resistance from his sensibility, which, having a closer connection with life than the intellect has, rebels against monotony, which threatens it with starvation. The problem any artist, however primitive, has to solve is that of achieving a unifying principle while at the same time preserving an appearance of diversity, for diversity in itself lends a richness to sensory impressions. The search for diversity leads to an important discovery: that of symmetry. It may well have been suggested to man by his own body, which is essentially a unit, and yet is double, for the right half is like the left half, only inverted. I have referred indirectly, above, to the "dialectics of contradiction," so indispensable a part of intellectual development. Symmetry plays a part similar to this in art: by setting up an opposition within the unit, it makes diversity possible.

Symmetry is introduced into the scratches, or hatching, on the bone when the two lines meet at one end, forming a V, or when they intersect at the center, forming an X. These elementary solutions to prehistoric man's need for diversity were discovered very early. In the Upper Mousterian period, even before art, in the full sense of the word, had made its appearance, the scratches on bone became regular, as can be seen in objects found at La Ferrassie, or La Quina.

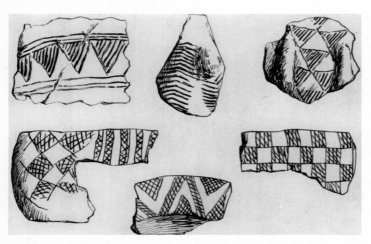

Neolithic pottery merely systematized the themes previously developed in Paleolithic times.

98. - CHECKERED PATTERNS ON NEOLITHIC JARS.
Camp de Chassey (Saône-et-Loire)

It was not long before such marks were being arranged in decorative patterns. One of the Predmost bones at the Brno Museum displays a pattern of parallel lines that seek to attain variety by changes of direction; one side has Vs with their wings spread wide. A sculptured mammoth found at Vogelhard (Württemberg) provides an instance of figurative art combined with decoration: it is ornamented with a regular line of Xs. An engraved bone from Laugerie-Basse (Dordogne) is particularly helpful in demonstrating the logical evolution of these elementary patterns. Two Vs not only produce an X when one is inverted and the points touch; they also produce the lozenge pattern, when the open ends of the two triangles are joined, thus giving rise to the first closed geometric figure. The fact that the center of the lozenge is marked by a dot, on the bone, shows that prehistoric man was aware of this. The principle of repetition having been arrived at, the Vs are placed one next to another, forming more complex serrated patterns. The earliest ornamental motifs were thus formulated; this particular one was to remain in use, handed down from one civilization to another (figure 97).

New patterns, making use of repetition and symmetry in ever more refined combinations, are devised; at the same time, regularity gains in assurance and its standards are raised. Small masterpieces are produced—for instance, a chisel ornamented on all four sides (figure 97) in which parallelism and symmetry, repetition and alternation, are all used to achieve a skilful counterpoint.

Thus the impulse arose to create an art other than figurative, an art of pure form. Alongside the embryo of realism we find the embryo of plasticism—and occasionally, as in the mammoth of Vogelhard, the two are present simultaneously.

It is worth noting that in this new art the straight line is used almost exclusively. Not that the curve is entirely lacking; on some exceptional finds, such as the sculptured rods of Lespugue or the engraved bones of Espélugues near Lourdes, it is the only line used. But even on the rare occasions on which it was used, it posed certain problems. The straight line—abstract, like its definition: the shortest distance between two points—is suited to intellectual creations, but the curve, dynamic, more complex, suggests life, living forms. It was only gradually assimilated by the human mind, and the human hand mastered its regular forms only after a long struggle. It stands halfway between the spontaneity of nature and the abstract formulas of thought.

It is not surprising that when man, in the following epoch, the Neolithic, made his first efforts at ceramics whose surfaces called naturally for ornamentation, he confined himself for a long time to perfecting and refining his earliest decorative themes: the parallels, herringbones, lozenges, and serrated patterns led to the even more regular square, which was repeated in a checkerboard pattern (figure 98).

An art completely abstract in its essence[1] is thus as old as realistic art; it can claim equal rights and an equally impressive pedigree. We are obliged to recognize that there are two innate tendencies in man, and that art depends on both of them. The opposition which the modern era has established between the two is artificial as well as pointless.

REALISM AND ABSTRACTION JOIN FORCES. Though the facts seem to justify the assertion, often repeated, that abstraction belongs to the field of ornamentation and hence should stay there, the argument behind this is false. Decorative art is the result of the artist's putting his imprint on an object, natural or artificial, which serves a utilitarian purpose; we have pure art when the object's sole purpose is to assert its own quality.

Were the geometric patterns of prehistory confined to ornamentation? Ignoring, for the time being, the converse question of whether realistic representations of animals were used for a practical purpose (in this case, that of magic, which also provided an occasion for art), it is possible to find objects, dating from the earliest epochs of prehistory, in which realistic representation is inseparable from plastic construction. Such an example is provided by noting the so-called Aurignacian "Venuses."

Several of these statuettes, which were probably used in connection with fertility

---

[1] Some writers maintain that decorative art resulted from excessive stylization of animal forms. This is a completely unfounded hypothesis. It is true that animal forms, as they became progressively more schematic, were used, along with the geometric patterns, as ornamentation. But they were not the source of the abstract designs; primitive man's repertoire of geometric forms was complete and in use long before realistic art began to evolve toward schematization. The hypothesis in question violates both chronology and psychology.

As early as the Aurignacian epoch, man was capable both of grasping the features of reality and achieving a plastic construction which recall modern developments.

99. - *At left and center:* THE LESPUGUE VENUS. Musée de l'Homme, Paris
At right: BRANCUSI. MADEMOISELLE N.C. 1928

rites, are masterpieces, particularly those of Willendorf and Lespugue. They were found at Mezin and at Kiev in the Ukraine, at Predmost in Moravia, at Savignano near Modena, at Menton on the Franco-Italian border, at Sireuil in the Dordogne—in short, throughout the area covered by the civilization of the Ice Age. Examples have been found as far south as Malta, and north as far as Irkutsk, in Siberia.

The statuettes are a unique combination of the figurative and the abstract. They are figurative in the sense that they aim at a faithful representation of the female anatomy, by stressing the most concrete details, all of which relate to sexual attraction; the thighs and breasts are exaggeratedly heavy, the pubic triangle prominent. At the same time the statuettes are pronouncedly abstract in design, the earliest rules of ornamentation—repetition and symmetry—providing the key to their forms. The *Venus* of Lespugue, particularly, clearly discloses the artist's intention to reduce everything to circular forms, which we find in the head, the shoulders, the breasts, the pelvis, the thighs, etc. The figure seems to consist wholly of variations on the curve. It can be exactly enclosed in a lozenge, for it is symmetrical both vertically (as is the human body) and horizontally—the top half being approximately identical with the bottom half. Moreover, the sculptor seems to have aimed at a shape similar to that of a spindle, convex at the center, suggesting that the human brain even at that early date aspired toward geometric perfection. Has even Zadkine or Brancusi gone further than this Aurignacian sculptor toward assimilating the outside world to the laws governing the structure of the mind (figure 99)?

As for the woman engraved on the bone of a mammoth found at Predmost, she joyfully renounces all reference to natural appearance; here, perhaps for the first time, a dimly sensed plasticism takes over completely. Straight lines and curves alternate in an intricate pattern; not only are repetition, by means of parallel lines, and symmetry made full use of, but—a considerable innovation—the geometric forms which are the artist's only means of representing reality are interrelated and *harmonized*. The strongly emphasized breasts are pear-shaped; the triangular head is set between the shoulders, but its sides are curved to match the curve of the breasts; similarly, the lines suggesting the arms are curved, also following the contour of the breasts. The artist was obviously motivated by a vague notion that unity must prevail among the forms; and his work is not unlike that of the

The prehistoric artist's interpretations are sometimes no less bold than the most recent ones.

100. - *Above: PICASSO.* WOMAN BEFORE A MIRROR. 1932. Museum of Modern Art, New York

101. - *At left:* ENGRAVED VENUS OF PREDMOST (Moravia)

Cubists, particularly certain canvases by Picasso (figures 100 and 101).

REALISM ALTERNATES WITH AB-STRACTION. Realism and abstraction, as we have seen, exist simultaneously at the very outset; and they remain inseparable in the subsequent evolution, as we read it from the data provided by prehistory.

The chosen field of realism in those early epochs was the representation of animals; but this realism is neither constant nor uniform. At first, the animal figures are purely intellectual simplifications; gradually they come to approximate natural appearance, only to succumb, soon afterward, to the eternal temptation of geometry. The earliest figurations display a decidedly abstract character, or, if you will, they owe as much to intellectual interpretation as to visual observation.

Is this so surprising? Children go through the same stages. Their first attempts to copy nature are completely arbitrary; they represent a simplified idea rather than an actual impression of an object. In other words, their drawings reflect what they have learned rather than what is there to be observed. This is perfectly normal. Those who express surprise at the fact that children do not draw "what they see" are merely displaying the realistic bias which is so solidly rooted in the Western mind.

Child psychologists have discovered that at eighteen to twenty months of age a child begins to "scrawl," producing purposive scribbles. At the age of about three, those scribbles begin to be imitative, but the figure of man consists of a circle and two sticks. The period of haphazard scrawls is over, however. At the age of four,

Photo Flammarion

Moving toward realism, prehistoric man in the Aurignacian epoch began, like the child, with most characteristic aspects. Thus he drew the horns in frontal view on a body drawn in profile.

102. - ENGRAVED BISON OF LA GRÈZE
(plaster cast)

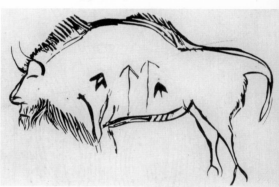

Photo Flammarion

In the Magdalenian period, the rendering is more exact. Note the horns now drawn in profile, and the marks of the arrows corresponding to the magical operation.

103. - THE BISON OF NIAUX. Wall painting in black and red

Photo Flammarion

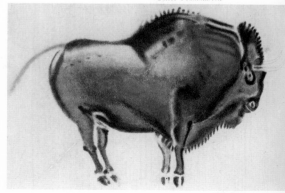

At Altamira, modeling of the forms was added to the contour drawing.

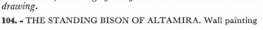
104. - THE STANDING BISON OF ALTAMIRA. Wall painting

two dots are placed inside the circle to suggest eyes; according to Dix, "it is only at this age that the idea of comparing the model with the drawing arises" and (according to Burk) "interest in the object as it is actually seen begins to develop." Nevertheless, the child at that age enters on "the great period of schematism," which lasts until he is perhaps eight, and this schematism, for fifty per cent of children, "is complicated by symbolism," as has been established by Bühler. Not before the age of six is a concern for imitative likeness manifested: then "the figure of the man is complete, though the limbs are still badly articulated." This objective feeling for lines and forms develops gradually till, at the age of eight or nine, "visual realism makes it appearance . . . and schematism is definitely transcended." Shortly afterward "the symbol yields to reality," and perspective rendering of space becomes a major concern.[1]

Will not the foregoing do as a brief sketch of the evolution of art itself, at its beginnings, from the simple motor projection to the representation of reality, first in simplified form, then gradually coming to resemble its model? The child at first brutally imposes his sense of unity. Having only a few simple elements —the circle, the dot, the "stick"—to work with, he confines his representations to these; the introduction of a second circle (one for the torso as well as the head) marks an important step forward. And as the child's repertoire of forms grows richer and his skill greater, he discovers that he can use these to convey not only his ideas but his perceptions.

In the same way, man, more ready to follow his own inclinations than to adjust himself to the world around him, having transformed his own gesture into a hand print on the wall, next forces what he sees into the mold of what he conceives. The earliest animal tracings, such as the bison of La Grèze (Dordogne) (figure 102), unquestionably from an Aurignacian stratum, are merely a continuous outline, depicting the simplest features and eliminating all the visual accidents that might not fit into this general structure. The same is true of the wall of Pair-non-Pair.

Proust in describing the supercivilized Impressionist painter Elstir referred to his effort "to divest himself of intellectual concepts in the face of reality," to paint what he *saw* rather than what he *knew*. The superprimitive does exactly the opposite: he finds it more convenient to show the idea he has of his model than the forms he actually perceives. For instance, the horns of the bison are shown spread out on the plane of the wall, as they "are," rather than in perspective, as they appear to the eye; and the outline of the animal has only two legs, the other two, which should be partly visible in the background, not being shown; and so on.

Later, the draftsman, more confident of his powers, is able to make his forms more flexible, without, however, losing sight of his conception. As the Magdalenian period begins, his drawings are still clear and intelligible, but they are less stiff. The rigid contour is varied; the bare outline is enriched by the rendering of the body mass, its coloring, by details suggesting the fur, a pricked-up ear, the finely articulated joint of the leg. Now the representations begin to convey the

[1] The above observations and quotations are taken from a study by Pierre Naville, "Characteristics of the development of drawing in different age groups, according to various authors," in *Le Dessin chez l'Enfant*, Paris, 1951, pp. 35 ff.

artist's impressions, skillfully rendered. The half-closed angry, stupid eye of the bison of Niaux, expressed by an energetic stroke, is quite unlike the gentle, attentive, malicious eye of the mammoth of Bernifal. Soon the patch of color within the outline begins to be modulated to suggest volume; and occasionally,

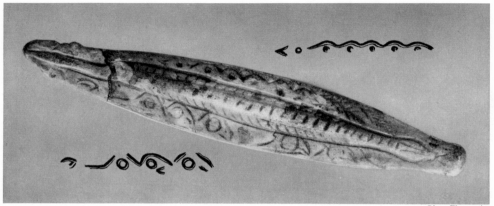

Photo Flammarion

Having achieved realism, art rapidly developed toward schematism. In the Lortet bone we see a band of birds' heads change into a scalloped line.

105. - THE SNAKE OF LORTET. Museum, Saint-Germain-en-Laye. (The design motif is reproduced on the margin of the photograph)

as at Altamira, the artist exploits the protruding contour of the rock on which he paints in order to strengthen his effects (figures 103 and 104).

TRANSITION FROM REALISM TO ABSTRACTION. Realism reaches its height; then the geometric tendency asserts itself. Every language, as it is perfected—or, more accurately, as those who use it master it more completely— tends to become more concise, to require less effort in order to be understood. The explanatory refinements that the language, in its early stages, had struggled to achieve become superfluous; an allusion is now sufficient; a well-trained memory fills in the gaps. Further, every group tends to exclude those who do not share its conventions, to admit only initiates. Thus various kinds of jargon, like the slang used by students, come into use. Slang words that gain general acceptance are soon replaced with new words.

Similarly, in any society, the language of images evolves toward the artificial and symbolic. Eschewing explanations, emphasizing the schematic and the conventional, it eventually becomes a system of written signs. Thus it came about that the late Paleolithic age, which followed the Magdalenian, with its naturalism, marked a rapid decline in imitation.

The Abbé Breuil has strikingly shown how the head of an animal, used as decoration on a particular object, gradually loses its early representational qualities, and becomes purely ornamental. Bit by bit it is simplified, stripped down, until, a mere complex of formal elements, it at last becomes part of a continuous band of ornamentation.

This was obviously the case with a cylindrical rod from La Madeleine, in which we may observe the transition from the expressive Magdalenian profile to a combination of two simple lines. On a bone from Lortet (Museum of Saint-Germain) is an engraving of a snake; the engraver added a border of birds' heads on each side. On one side, the birds, with their open beak and round eyes, are clearly identifiable as such; on the other side the series of heads becomes a single wavy line, and the eyes have been reduced to dots, marking the crest of each wave. In other words, the original drawing has been geometrized; more than that, the draftsman, realizing his opportunity, has boldly elaborated upon his theme (figure 105).

It is noteworthy, moreover, that this "wavy" motif should have been suggested by the central subject, the reptile engraved along the axis of the bone, which communicated its own sinuous rhythm to the subjects along the sides. This presupposes on the part of the artist a highly developed plastic sense, almost an overt awareness of plastic reality. Thus, another aspect of artistic creation besides simplification has contributed to the final result.

The shift to abbreviated form, foreshadowed at the end of the Paleolithic period, produced extraordinary results on the Iberian Peninsula during the Neolithic. We have seen earlier the way in which reality is reduced to a species of shorthand, so that the drawings on the pebbles of Mas d'Azil[1] were mistaken for an alphabet (see p. 31, figure 23).

Thus everything suggests that man, equipped with the simple forms he had constructed and codified into geometry, first tried to assimilate reality to these forms, when representing it; then he sought to make the forms themselves more flexible and to assimilate them to the outside world, the infinite diversity of which was alien to his sparse and vigorous concepts; in the end, having captured reality, he sought only to make it his prey, to take it into his den, to digest and reduce it to the same simple forms, congenial to his mind, which had served as his point of departure.

The prehistoric is not the only age in which we see this pattern of evolution. Marthe Oulié[2] has pointed out three successive stages in Aegean art, which she calls the period of unskilled schematization, the period of naturalism, and the period of stylization. The process is identical with the one described above. Is it not the very process of human life?

The diehards of realism, of course, maintain that the two "abstract" stages, the first and the last, correspond to the primitivism of childhood and the attribution of old age, while the middle, or realistic, stage indicates full maturity. But in actual fact, we have two different orders superimposed one on top of the other. It is true that the initial schematism coincides with and may reflect an inadequacy of skill and that the terminal schematism may indicate decline in power. But, while the artist practices realism after he has transcended the poverty of his abstract forms, he also transcends realism when he rises to an awareness of his plastic freedom: who would deny that the Aurignacian Venuses are among the greatest achievement of prehistoric art? Abstract schematism is not a value in itself, but it becomes one when it is combined with plastic inventiveness (figures 106 and 107).

[1] Evolution proceeded at a more rapid pace north of the Pyrenees, for the pebbles of Mas d'Azil belong to the late Paleolithic.

[2] Marthe Oulié, *Les Animaux dans la Crète préhellénique*, Paris, 1926.

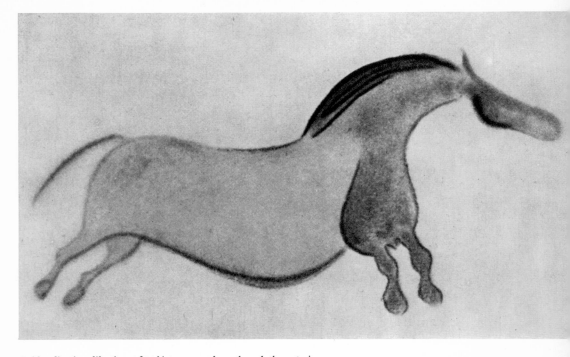

Bold stylizations like those of prehistory recur down through the centuries.
106. - PREHISTORIC HORSE, as copied by the Abbé Breuil. Aurignacian black horse on the right wall of the left gallery at Le Portel. Length, 37³/₈″

We may repeat here the basic truth, that a particular aesthetic approach has no value in itself: everything depends on the uses to which it is put, on the quality achieved with its help. Beauty is never the product of a doctrine.

IS THERE SUCH A THING AS PREHISTORIC REALISM? It is not, however, its realism that makes Magdalenian art great. We may even ask whether it is realistic at all. It seems to us that it is because we judge it by our own standards, but the men of that epoch were very remote from such judgments. A study of prehistory has given us sufficient insight into the mentality of these men, and into the aims their artists pursued, to convince us that they were not very concerned with reproducing reality—any more than they were with creating works of art.

To be sure, in carrying out the task, very different from that of art, which was assigned to him, a prehistoric artist experienced intense pleasure—a pleasure that was essentially aesthetic, though he did not realize this, for though it aroused his sensibility, his understanding still lay dormant. He certainly did not practice realism for the sake of a pleasure he did not understand (nor did he know why he was partial to a certain arrangement of lines). He was merely fulfilling a function with which he had been entrusted by the community. The fact that his represen-

107. - HORSE FROM A PERSIAN MINIATURE (detail). School of Bahzad. 1487

tations of animals were strikingly true to nature does not imply that the public he knew favored realism. In fact, these images were not made to be exhibited. As many writers have pointed out, they were done in almost inaccessible places, often in subterranean galleries enveloped in a darkness that could scarcely be pierced by the primitive means of lighting. Some of the drawings at Altamira are situated almost three hundred yards from the entrance to the caves, and the paintings at Niaux are about eight hundred yards from the entrance.

We cannot assume that the images were deliberately made inaccessible in order to keep them in reserve for special occasions. For we find that they are often superimposed one on another, several layers deep, and that no effort was made to preserve them. What we come on today is often merely a disorderly tangle of lines, and specialists have had to display extraordinary patience to find their way in these mazes. The works were neither visible nor legible.

The actual significance of the images has, however, been fully established. The primitive mind was magical, and took refuge in the idea that the part is equivalent to the whole. Sorcerers of our own time still believe (or pretend to believe) that by doing something to the hair or fingernails of a certain person, this person himself can be affected. In the same way, the appearance of a thing is a part of it, and by capturing this appearance one can gain power over the thing itself. Even in our day, many primitive people refuse to be photographed, out of fear. The ancient Egyptians believed that they could secure a man's comforts in the afterlife by placing near his tomb the effigies of persons and objects that formerly provided him with the same comforts.

This idea of the magic "double" is the basis of prehistoric art. The spells cast on the painting or the sculpture of an animal were believed to influence the fate of the animal itself. Frobenius, in his *History of African Civilization*, relates certain observations he made on a trip to Africa as proof that such spells were still being practiced as late as 1905. Prehistoric representations of animals often show the marks of arrows or spears, confirming that these works served as instruments of "destructive magic"; other signs point just as surely to their use in a complementary "fertility magic," for game had to reproduce abundantly in order to be hunted and killed in sufficient quantities (figure 103).

That Magdalenian realism does not reflect an artistic need is also suggested by the fact that it was practiced only in relation to animals, i.e., only for practical purposes. The human figures that are occasionally found lack any representational characteristics.

Furthermore, unlike the nineteenth-century variety, prehistoric realism had no

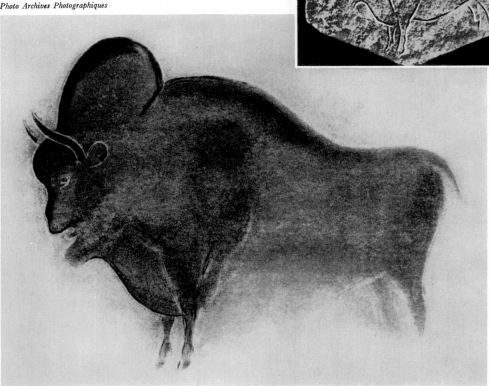

The prehistoric artist did not work from nature, but from accepted models, some of which have been found.

108. - BISON OF LA GENIÈRE (Ain). Engraving on stone

109. - PAINTED BISON AT FONT-DE-GAUME (Dordogne). Museum, Saint-Germain-en-Laye

Photo Archives Photographiques

Photo Flammarion

The prehistoric artist's occasional inability to finish his drawing proves that he was copying a model.

110. - BELLOWING DEER OF LIMEUIL.
Museum, Saint-Germain-en-Laye

connection with direct observation. Prehistoric man, who began the debate with which this chapter opened, did not work from nature. He never envisaged a single, specific animal. For magic cannot be effective if its workings are confined to one particular animal, which may not, after all, be encountered during the hunt; the spells cast upon the image must be aimed at the species as a whole, in order to be efficacious. Thus the object, to the prehistoric artist, is an abstract concept—of the mammoth, for example, or the bear—the form of which implies a tendency toward generalizations.

The same tendency is revealed by the execution. Magdalenian man may be a realist, but he is so in the manner of certain highly skilled draftsmen, such as Toulouse-Lautrec. The visual impression, the play of varicolored spots an object presents to the eye, is replaced arbitrarily by a contour, indicated by an accentuated line that is highly significant, in that it intelligently sums up important features. A complex work of synthesis is required to produce such an expressive structure, however instinctively it is executed. The term "realism" cannot be used here in the sense of submission to visual data, but rather as indicating an effort at intellectual assimilation and graphic transformation. The mind produces a type that is based on sensory experience; but when the artist's work is completed he has long since integrated and transcended the observations that were his point of departure.

PREHISTORIC ACADEMISM. Prehistoric art was, then, necessarily an art of convention: that is to say, its images were types that were arrived at gradually, over generations, though the process was marked now and then by dazzling discoveries, flashes of genius. When a given type seemed to have achieved perfection, it acquired prestige and became fixed, its form being carefully preserved and passed on from one generation to the next.

We may even say that prehistoric realism was a kind of academism, in the nonpejorative sense of that term. Certain pebbles fashioned in a prehistoric workshop seem to have been "exported" to far-off places to serve as models. The animals we see at Altamira and Font-de-Gaume, despite their seeming diversity, all conform to a limited number of types. One of the bisons at Font-de-Gaume, shown facing to the left, occurs elsewhere in the same cave in almost identical form, except it now faces to the right; and at Altamira a few slight changes were all that was required to transform a charging bison, his head down, into a running bison, his head back.

There is even more convincing evidence. In 1926 a pebble was found at La Genière (Ain) bearing a drawing of the bison of Font-de-Gaume, which is in the Dordogne; and an almost exact replica of the same beast may be seen at Altamira, that is, near Santander! Obviously, prehistoric artists formed something like schools, each with its repertoire of drawings, which were the products of a long process of evolution rather than of spontaneous impressions, and the formulas for these drawings served as models for local artists. Proof of this was provided by the drawing of a bellowing stag at Limeuil;[1] the artist, having misplaced the model he was copying from, found it impossible to rectify his drawing, and did not finish his figure (figures 108, 109, and 110).

I have dealt at some length with prehistoric art because it casts a great deal of light on the origin of the artistic sense. We may draw several conclusions from it; the representational and the abstract tendencies appear together at the outset, and proceed hand in hand; sometimes they are combined, sometimes they alternate. Realism reaches its high point in the Magdalenian epoch, but even then art is not merely a docile copy of nature: the part played by the mind, which transforms, organizes, and legislates, is as great as that played by the senses, which observe.

Thus, while resemblance to nature cannot be an impediment to the highest art, as some would maintain today, it is not a natural, spontaneous requirement either, since it has its roots in magic practices. The testimony of prehistory does not fully settle this question; at all events we must guard against oversimplification. The Aurignacian Venuses, in which representation and abstraction are strikingly balanced, are an instructive example of prehistoric art.

2. WESTERN TRADITION
FROM ANTIQUITY TO THE MIDDLE AGES

IT is to the West, the center of realism, that we must address ourselves if we are to grasp the purposes and significance of this form of art. To subjugate reality—"to make ourselves the masters and possessors of nature, as it were," as Descartes put it—has been the constant effort of the civilization that began with the Greeks.

GREEK AESTHETICS: MIMESIS. Is not imitation the basis of any aesthetics? Imitation strives to get at the facts by means of the senses, making an exact inventory of them through the medium of the eye, and avoiding the distortions resulting from preconceived ideas or false beliefs; and it strives to organize the

---

[1] Pijoan, *Summa Artis*, VI, p. 72.

data thus collected according to the laws of reason, thus increasing our mastery over them. Our senses, too, enable us to establish a relationship—perhaps an even closer one—with the outside world, but our tradition accepts it only with reservations and restraint. Order imposed by the senses remains personal in character, whereas the intellect transcends the individual, attaining universality. Such were the beliefs set forth by the Greeks, which have been adhered to by all civilizations that derive in any degree from theirs. Our sense perceptions were regarded by the Greeks as inseparable from our rational judgments, since the former serve as the basis for the latter, and the latter serve to verify the former.

We cannot, therefore, speak of realism in its proper sense, in this connection; for realism admits only the evidence of the senses, and dismisses the judgments of the intellect. Greek art contains elements of realism, but it also transcends it. We must not forget that the dominant Greek philosophy, that of Plato, relegates the material world which we grasp through our senses to the realm of non-Being, μή ὄν, and relies on reason as the means of attaining the only authentic reality, the Ideas. Concrete reality, as we conceive of it today, is, for this philosophy, valid only to the extent to which it is transformed by the mind and made to resemble immaterial Being. "The beautiful has no sensory forms," we read in the *Symposium*. For this reason Plato thinks that the beautiful can be grasped more easily through some abstract figure, such as may be constructed with a ruler and compass, than through the deceptive images of art.[1] This would seem to justify abstract art, which indeed invokes Plato as its authority.

Greek art did not follow Plato all the way, but it was nonetheless marked by his ideas. Even when it lent a sympathetic ear to Gorgias' doctrine of total illusion or Aristotle's theory of imitation, it never lapsed into pure naturalism.[2] In the visual world, it was always devoted to form, because form reflects the mind and its organizing powers; and to measure and proportion, because these bring into the material world an echo of that eternal beauty, mentioned in the *Symposium*, "which neither comes to be nor perishes, which never appears in the guise of corporeal beauty ... nor exists in any substance, such as an animal, or the earth, or sky, or any other thing; but existing in itself, by itself, with itself, in the eternity of its unique form, while all the multitude of beautiful things partake of it."

[1] And yet, as we have noted before, Plato accepts mimesis (μίμησις) in art, i.e., imitation, resemblance. Is this not a contradiction? Not if we distinguish between art and beauty, that is, between the image and the Idea, and if we keep in mind that Plato professed hostility to and occasionally contempt for art and works of art precisely because they can never coincide with absolute, essential beauty, which is "not infected with the flesh and color of humanity, and ever so much more of mortal trash" (*Symposium*, 212A). For Plato, art is only a diversion, and often a source of corruption. It is the task of art to reproduce the illusory shadows of the cave, vain fancies like "those seen in mirrors." The artist is condemned precisely because he can reproduce only appearances. This aspect of the Platonic aesthetics has been excellently expounded by Schuhl.

[2] The following passage from Emile Boutroux's *Etudes sur l'Histoire de la Philosophie* (p. 186), which accurately characterizes this realism which, even for Aristotle, remained tempered by thought, will spare us from going into the subject at greater length: "With Plato, Aristotle defines the essence of art as imitation. Art results from man's propensity to imitate and the pleasure he derives from it. What man imitates (that is, nature, according to Aristotle) is not merely the external appearance, but the internal ideal essence of the things of nature. Art can represent things as they are or as they should be. The representation is the more beautiful the greater the degree to which the artist has succeeded in completing, by following nature's own intention, the work nature necessarily leaves imperfect." This is what I call "ideal realism."

Greek art never separates the work's physical resemblance to the model from "the resemblance that is obtained through the idea of the beautiful" and that can be grasped only by the mind.

Any Greek masterpiece is evidence of this. The *Doryphorus* by Polyclitus of Argos might seem to be a statue faithfully representing the body of an athlete; but we are obliged to see in it an application of the first theoretical treatise on sculpture, the *Canon*, which the creator of this work gave to Greece. According to Polyclitus, beauty, the supreme goal of the artist, is "the symmetry of all the parts of the body, the relations of these parts among each other and between each of them and the whole."

The Greeks consciously applied the principles that had been applied instinctively long before, in the Lespugue *Venus*, for example. Greek civilization made these principles the goal of art; and it gave them a strict formulation in the proportions on which it based its concept of harmony. The senses might be gratified by an exact reproduction of natural appearance, but the mind found its gratification in a more precise awareness of the beautiful, formulated in mathematical terms. Once again, total realism proved unattainable (figures 111 and 112).

And once again we are reminded of the dangers of oversimplification. In Greece, the growth of naturalism heralded weariness and decline, while in the prehistoric age these things apparently came with the growth of abstraction. No one, indeed, will maintain that Greek art after the fifth century remained at the level it had previously attained. From that moment on, Greek aesthetic theory tended toward naturalism, toward the rendering of appearances and of expressions under the aegis of Aristotelian philosophy.

Under the Roman civilization, more materialistic, this development was accelerated: the Romans imitated the Greeks faithfully and narrowly, or, when they struck out for themselves, they produced literal imitations of nature.

THE BEGINNINGS OF IMAGERY: OUTLINES. Although only a few specimens of the painting of antiquity have survived, it is possible to obtain an idea of how it tackled the problem of realism in the course of its development. Apart from the vases, what is there left of Greek painting? What a pity that we cannot see the fifth-century examples which, according to engravings made long ago, still existed in Paestum during the Renaissance. Ceramics, and certain Etruscan funerary decorations, afford some insight into the efforts the Greeks made in this field to reproduce what they saw, while retaining mastery over it by dominating it intellectually. Here, to a greater extent even than in their sculpture, the Greeks moved away from the sensory illusion, for painting, by requiring forms to be transposed onto a flat surface, fosters a departure from the model, indeed makes it necessary. In painting, the image, of its own accord so to speak, assumes a position halfway between what is perceived and the means by which it is transcribed.

This means, extremely simple in the beginning, is the line. Prehistoric art already knew how to make use of it. The Greeks had an explanation for how it originated: Pliny the Elder relates (*Natural History*, xxxv, 151) that the daughter of the potter Boutades of Corinth, *capta amore juvenis* (taken with love for a young man) who was about to depart, conceived the idea of keeping an image of the loved one, since she could not keep him.

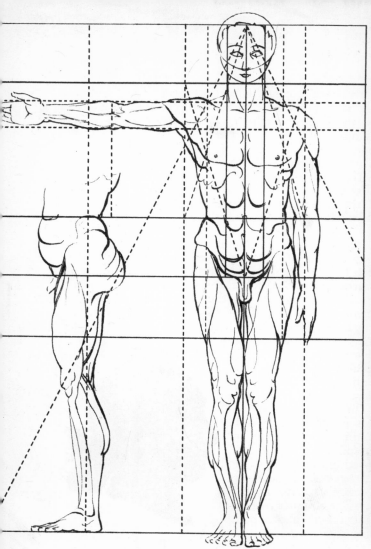

Photo Anderson-Giraudon

Greek art, seemingly realistic, is just as much based on calculated proportions.

111. - PROPORTIONS OF THE BODY ACCORDING TO THE
GOLDEN SECTION

112. - *POLYCLITUS.* DORYPHORUS

This legend expresses one of the purposes of realism, perhaps the most valid one: the will to replace fragile memory with an appearance fixed in permanent form by art. But does this not imply the preservation also of the emotion of the moment, which gave it its quality? Thus realism is once again transcended, this time by the need to express the inner life.

It is also transcended by plastic requirements, born of necessity. For the fact is that the young girl in the legend is at a loss. How will she obtain the image she wants? Nature has to make the first move and suggest the artifice by which the object will be entrapped: this body, this face are already inscribed on the wall in the form of a shadow. Everything that evades capture—the contours of the body as they are enlivened by the reflections of lamplight or swallowed up by the night, its multiple reliefs—is reduced, on the smooth wall, to a black area defined by an outline. The young girl now will need only to secure a piece of charcoal and to trace with her unskillful fingers the boundary between light and shadow, the *line* that this boundary suggests—*umbram . . . in pariete liniis circumscripsit* (she circumscribed with lines the shadow on the wall). The young man will move, the shadow will glide away, change, vanish. But the next day both he and his shadow will be the prisoners of the line that has captured them. Thus the line formulated the convention by means of which the artist dominates the reality that presses in upon him from all sides.

The legend is not far from the truth. Leonardo da Vinci says that the first painting was merely a line traced around the shadow of a man, cast by the sun on a wall. For a long time, and particularly during the sixth century, painters used this technique of the cast shadow as a means of effecting automatically that transformation of reality into plastic form which is so difficult to conceive.[1] Pliny the Elder assures us that the technique was used by the ancient Egyptians: *umbra hominis liniis circumducta* (the shadow of a man circumscribed by lines), and as late as the eighteenth **century** the so-called physionotracer, which was so fashionable, was merely a mechanical version of this method (figure 113).

The method, to be sure, captures only the profile. But that need not be a handicap: the profile will simply be compelled to express more than it can do by its own resources, be more than the faithful record of the boundaries of a form. What it cannot say, it will suggest. By becoming more adroit, more flexible, it will overcome its own nature, and a day will come when it will be capable of suggesting everything that it is not—volume, consistency, movement, and even —almost—light. The Greek ceramists have accustomed us to this magic: the best of the silhouettes they traced with a flowing arabesque satisfy—thanks to their intensity—the threefold requirement stated in the opening pages of this book as that which a complete work of art must meet—they evoke reality, convey **plastic** harmony and have the power to communicate the artist's emotion (figure 114).

According to legend, contour began with the tracing of a shadow cast on a wall. In the eighteenth century the "physionotracer" mechanically copied profiles like this.

113. - DRAWING MADE WITH "PHYSIONOTRACER." Eighteenth century

It would be easy to show that color too can be endowed with the same multiple powers. Matisse, keeping strictly to the picture plane, compels color to render everything that is alien to its nature—light, space, and even what he calls "expression."

THE CONQUEST OF DEPTH.   For the time being, however, we are discussing only realism. Line, which from prehistoric times appeared in conjunction with color,

[1] This was proved by Edmond Pottier (*Recueil Edmond Pottier*, 1937, pp. 262 ff).

was increasingly called upon to render effects outside its own inherent potentialities. Here begins the career of the *trompe-l'œil*: the effort to produce an illusion of depth on a flat surface.

To begin with, line must suggest volume. Even in our time, Pierre Bonnard has stated: "To represent on a flat surface masses that are situated in space: this is the problem of drawing." The Greeks faced this same problem. They invented techniques of modeling and even foreshortening. Xenocrates, referring to Pausias, who had represented an ox, said, using almost the same terms as Bonnard, that he "displayed great skill in representing depth on a flat surface and in using foreshortening." Several examples of this skill have come down to us by way of the Romans.

An unspoken convention required that the most prominent part of a form, the part nearest to the observer's eye, should be conspicuously displayed, i.e., in full light; those parts which recede from the eye are left in shadow. The progressive intensification of shadow will suggest to the mind the idea of a surface relief. Thus an imaginary depth came to be invented, within which masses are made to advance or recede (figure 115).

The Magdalenian artist of Altamira, who used the raised places on a rocky ceiling as a means of

Confronted with the problem of representing volumes on a surface, the Greek vase painters employed only line.

114. - SINGER WITH CITHARA. From a red-figured vase. First half of fifth century. Boston Museum of Fine Arts

Rendering of relief by shading and modeling was added to contour.

115. - IXION CONDEMNED TO THE WHEEL. House of the Vettii, Pompeii

lending a dimension of reality to his bisons, had noticed that the effect could be enhanced by lightening the color on the protruding areas. Similarly, at Font-de-Gaume, the color is applied more lightly, even showing the bare wall, at the places representing protuberances.[1] Thousands of years later Leonardo was still enthusiastic about the power painting has of showing a body in relief against a flat surface. And he also was to remark that "painting seems a thing miraculous, making things intangible appear tangible, presenting in relief things which are flat, in distance things near at hand" (*Notebooks*, 1, *op. cit.*, II, p. 230).

[1] This method is the opposite of that of surface relief, by which the painters of antiquity made the shadow, rather than the light, progressively more intense (figures 104 and 115).

CHRISTIANITY AND THE CRISIS OF REALISM. Down to the end of antiquity, Western realism, strengthened in the course of the previous centuries, made concessions only to the pursuit of plastic harmony. With the infiltration of Eastern ideas, however, realism was confronted with the alien demand for spiritual expression. At first it succumbed under the attack, then gradually regained its hold. Its initial defeat had been prepared by the Asiatic cults that were spread by the Roman legions.

Christianity was to shake realism to its foundations, by its conception of the spiritual life. But Christianity was not alone in this: those who spoke in the name of Plato, the Neoplatonists of the third century and their master Plotinus, also reacted against the domination of the senses, against the cult of the visible and the tangible, and strove to go beyond sensory reality. "The arts are not confined to the imitation of objects presented to our eyes," says Plotinus (*Enneads*, VI, "On the Beautiful"); they should "sever those objects from their material form, and seek beauty in proportions." Nothing in this goes beyond the Greeks' ideas of art and their "idealized realism." But suddenly, carrying Plato's concept of the Ideas to its ultimate conclusion, under a new, no doubt Eastern, impulse, the Neoplatonists took a new tack.[1] The artist's goal, Plotinus proclaimed, is "neither the figure, nor color, nor a visible dimension." In this we see the triad of art completed: the Soul has come to take its place alongside Reality and Plastic Form. The work of art will now have the task of suggesting the soul, by communicating it to the viewer; the eye will have to be reinforced by the "inner vision"—indeed, it will have to give way to it.

Christianity exerted all its force in the same direction. For the first time, the uncontested rule of the senses combined with reason suffered an eclipse. Reality changed sides. It no longer resided in what was seen. Analyzing medieval Christian thought, Etienne Gilson writes: "Nature is not what it seems to be; it is the symbol and sign of a deeper reality.... It heralds or signifies something else," this something else being God. In this respect the Middle Ages confirmed St. Augustine, who, in the fourth century, had

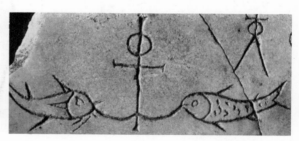

Early Christian art reflected a crisis of realism, which yielded to symbolism.

116. - SYMBOL OF THE FISH. Early Christian art

implicitly condemned the very principles of ancient art when he said: "We must turn our minds away from corporeal images."

Early Christian art marked a radical departure from Western realism. This attitude was dictated by the need for secrecy as well as by the new spirituality. The

---

[1] The fact that Plotinus was influenced by Eastern thought is well established. His disciple Porphyrius relates in his *Life of Plotinus* (ch. III): "He came to master philosophy so completely that he sought to acquaint himself directly with the philosophy practiced by the Persians and the philosophy honored by the Indians." (Cf. Olivier Lacombe, *Note sur Plotin et la pensée indienne*, École Pratique des Hautes Études, Sciences religieuses, Annuaire 1950–51, pp. 3ff.)

paintings in the catacombs no longer reproduce natural appearance; the objects represented are now symbols, which serve to divert the mind from the physical world to hidden meanings. There are "corporeal images"—fishes, dolphins, doves, or lambs—but each is merely an arrow pointing to or suggesting something invisible. The directness of realism has yielded to the indirectness of symbolism, and the image is but a way station which one passes by instead of dwelling upon. It comes close to the hieroglyph.

The example of the fish is most striking. Here the symbol has a double meaning. The figure of the fish suggests its name, ἰχθύς, which in turn is a reference to the Lord, for it is an acrostic formed from the initial letters of "Jesus Christ, son of the Redeeming God," Ἰησοῦς χριστός θεοῦ υἱὸς σωτήρ (figure 116).

As late as the middle of the twelfth century, Suger, the illustrious Abbot of Saint-Denis, testified to the permanence of this trend toward the symbolic— although he was one of the moving spirits of Gothic art, which marked a renascence of realism—when he said: *"Mens hebes ad verum per materialia surgit":* to attend to the tangible, material realities, which are the objects of realism, is evidence only of the weakness of the spirit; we must use these things, rather, as stepping-stones in our ascent to the supreme Truth, which is beyond the reality of the senses and even of the intellect. The visual world has no reality save as a sign of and a way of access to the Invisible.

BYZANTINE SPIRITUALITY.   The tradition inaugurated by Plotinus, which had such a profound influence on St. Augustine, had a long life. Prior to the Romanesque period, it nourished Byzantine art, which, if only for geographical reasons, is closely linked with Eastern art.

To be sure, the Church, particularly after the fifth and sixth centuries, favored pictorial representations of Biblical history rather than the symbols used by the early Christians. Even so, the violent iconoclastic reaction of the ninth century came close to purging religious art of all its representational elements, as happened in Moslem civilization at about the same time. Although the paintings and mosaics of that period often told a story, they were not realistic, for the narrative was intended only as a framework for the "message" the work conveyed. Early in the fifth century St. Nilus, writing to a high official of the Empire, ordered him to see to it that "those who do not know their letters and cannot read the Scriptures remember, when looking at pictures, the noble actions of those who faithfully served the true God and be encouraged to imitate their conduct." This art, which, however far removed from realism, at least aims at representing something, does not do so out of an aesthetic conviction; it conceives of itself merely as a convenient means of attaining a religious end. It remains faithful to Plotinus' revealing injunction: "to open the eyes of the soul by closing those of the body."

This is why Byzantine art is not bound by natural appearance. Perfectly adapted to the requirements of its surface, instead of impressing the viewer with its skillful command of illusion, it exploits its materials—brilliant mosaics, glittering gold —fully, in order to overwhelm the soul with the splendor of light. This light, immaterial and yet visible, acts powerfully on our optical nerves, producing a fascination that is almost hypnotic, which is designed to lead the viewer directly into the miraculous Presence. The artist, following a path opposed to that of realism, has recourse to the material world only as a means to inducing the kind of contemplation in which the beholder sees "what is not a spectacle, but a form of vision, ecstasy," and which, according to the *Enneads*, is the goal of art. Such works appeal to the emotions rather than to the eye, seeking to project the soul upward into "an intimate union, not with the statue but with the Godhead itself..." (figure 117).[1]

The mystics have always regarded light as the closest physical approximation to the Godhead; the later use, in the West, of stained-glass windows was occasioned by this religious significance of light. The stained-glass window transfigures reality rather than showing it; it gives to objects a radiance, makes them seem devoid of substance and inconceivably luminous, as though they belonged to another world. The stained-glass window takes the place of the mosaic in northern countries where the light is not strong enough merely to be reflected, as in mosaics, but must be fully conserved by being allowed to pass directly through the glass.

Photo Anderson-Giraudon

Byzantine art treated natural appearance with the greatest freedom, striving primarily to represent ideas, while also evoking a spiritual force from light playing on golds.

117. - DOME, PALATINE CHAPEL, Palermo

REDISCOVERY OF NATURE. Not until the end of the twelfth century did the West rediscover its orginal bent. It was then that a trend toward the reconquest of reality began—a trend which asserted itself in Gothic art, and which, with the Renaissance, re-established its connection with the tradition of antiquity, and was taken over by the Platonists. Realism experienced a brief period of triumph between the moment when it overcame medieval spirituality on the one hand and when it was subordinated to the quest for ideal beauty, on the other. It recovered its force when the concept

[1] André Grabar has shown, with remarkable insight, to what extent the philosophy of Plotinus not only influenced Christian thought but accounts for certain of the features of Byzantine art that from our instinctively realistic point of view have often been regarded as anomalous ("Plotin et les Origines de l'Esthétique médiévale," *Cahiers archéologiques*, I, 1935, pp. 15 ff.).

118. - ROMANESQUE CAPITAL. From the cloister of the Abbaye de la Daurade, Toulouse. Musée des Augustins

of nature came back into its own, and when natural appearance was once again valued for its own sake, for then the artist was tempted, once more, to try to reproduce that appearance.

The revival of Aristotelian philosophy by Arab commentators paved the way for this reversal. There was a reawakening of the belief that the only reality accessible to us is the one revealed to us by our senses, "the extensive and sensory forms," which we can touch and see. This belief accounted for the popularity of nominalism, a philosophy which regarded general ideas or abstractions as mere artifices of the mind, denoting nothing more solid than the words in which they are expressed, or the sound made by these words: *flatus vocis*.

The turn toward realism was irresistible; even the most unflinching opponents of Aristotelianism, the Franciscans, in effect contributed to the triumph of the movement. St. Francis, to be sure, teaches only love of God, but we are to love Him in His creatures, and His world: "Praise to Thee, O Lord, for sister Earth, our mother, who ... produces various fruits and colored flowers and the grass!" The Franciscans of Oxford sought to base knowledge in experience, sensory experience. Only then, says the greatest of them, Roger Bacon, "is the mind convinced, and at rest in the presence of truth." Except for divine revelation, no proposition can be regarded as certain *(nullus sermo potest certificare)*, "unless it derives from experience."

In the field of art, this was the period in which the Gothic sculptor renounced

134

Between Romanesque and Gothic art, realism reasserted itself.
119. - GOTHIC CAPITAL. Nave of Reims Cathedral. Thirteenth century

the radical stylizations of his Romanesque predecessors, and shook off Eastern influences. He carved in stone accurate likenesses of divine or sacred figures, reproducing folds in the drapery and ringlets in the beards. He studied plants in order to be able to render exactly a strawberry leaf or the tendril of a vine; these plant motifs, shown in a natural-seeming disorder, alternate with figures of animals and birds, also represented naturalistically, which replace the terrifying imaginary monsters inherited from far-off Asia (figures 118 and 119).

It was with pride that the architect Villard de Honnecourt wrote next to the drawing of a lion in his famous album: "*Et bien saciez que cils lions fu contrefais al vif.*" This new preoccupation, so characteristic of the thirteenth century, was shared even by Jean de Meung, whose *Roman de la Rose* dates from the end of that same century. In the second part, speaking of the artist, he says:

> *A genouz est devant nature ...*
> *Qui d'ensuivre la moult s'efforce*
> ***Et la contrefait comme singes.***
> (*On his knees before nature ...*
> *Doing his utmost to follow it,*
> *Like a monkey, he mimics it.*)

In both these quotations the word *contrefaire* ("to sham, to imitate") appears with a significant emphasis.

Painting, too, set for itself the goal of being the "mirror of the world," *speculum mundi*, the title used, significantly, by Vincent de Beauvais in the same century. This was the major concern of the illumination done in the north, which advanced with great strides toward fifteenth-century naturalism; it was also the concern of Italian painting. The latter, which stayed closer to classical sources, paved the way for a new rapprochement between the senses and the intellect; reflecting the positivist spirit of the rising middle class, it submitted more readily to the fascinations of visual appearance.

ITALY AND INTELLECTUAL TRUTH. Italy, where Byzantium had implanted an art obedient to the conventions of idealism, found it more difficult to shake off the Eastern influence; but, inspired by the classical example, it rapidly passed—once again —through the same stages as antiquity.

The Italian eye repossessed the visual world. The painters learned from antique examples the transcriptive possibilities of line, and they soon equaled the Greek ceramists in its use. Simone Martini's subtle arabesques render the silhouette of the Virgin, the soft texture of her drapery, and the gracefulness and tenderness of her pose (figure 120).

Photo Anderson

Beginning its reconquest of reality, Italian art rediscovered the importance of contours and lines.

120. - *SIMONE MARTINI.* ANNUNCIATION (center section). Uffizi Gallery, Florence

Continuing their reconquest of reality, the Italian painters coped next with the problem of volume. Once again modeling produced the illusion of solidity for the eye and even for the sense of touch: Berenson speaks of "tactile values." Giotto and Masaccio mark the victorious stages of this effort (figure 121).

The Italians did not confine themselves to producing forms that stood out in relief; they created a space in depth. Their solution was perspective, a network of imaginary lines converging at a vanishing point. Perspective was one of the most amazing achievements of the Mediterranean mind in its attempts to bring about a union between the senses and reason. It is based on both the sensory illusion and on intellectual laws, logical and calculable, which impose upon space, by nature diffuse, a central and unifying point. It is not surprising that for the Italians perspective was more than a technical device—it was a noble science which afforded the mind the perfect pleasures of a superior sort of game. According to Vasari,

Photo Anderson

Between Giotto and Masaccio, modeling was rediscovered.

121. - *MASACCIO.* **THE TRIBUTE MONEY** (detail).
Church of the Carmine, Florence

Uccello "devoted himself exclusively to the solution of difficult and **quite** impossible problems of perspective.... These studies engrossed him and made him eccentric to the point where he locked himself up in his house for weeks and months on end, refusing to see anyone." The garrulous chronicler reports that Uccello often worked till daybreak on the arduous constructions that held him spellbound, and that when his wife, whom he neglected for these abstract pleasures, protested, calling him to join her in the conjugal bed, he would answer from his study: "Ah, what a sweet thing is perspective!"

Thus, the intellectual elaboration of form went hand in hand with the rebirth of realism. The revival of Greek thought was given a powerful impetus by the arrival of numerous Byzantine scholars seeking refuge in Italy after the Turks captured Constantinople in 1453. Once again Plato ruled supreme; his philosophy was the object of a real cult, whose high priest was Marsilio Ficino, with the Platonic Academy of Florence serving as its College of Cardinals. The few remaining adherents of Aristotle, whose stronghold was the University of Padua, were routed. Ideal beauty was reinstated and was the aesthetic standard until the nineteenth century.

THE FLEMISH BOURGEOISIE AND THE RENDERING OF MATERIALS. In the north, however, realism held undisputed sway, bringing to fruition the trend begun by the Gothic art of the thirteenth century, and carried over into painting through the mediation of the miniaturist's art. It is well known that Van Eyck was greatly influenced by the Turin *Book of Hours.* The social factor played an important part in this determined swing toward realism. It is the form of art favored by the classes least affected by culture, which is primarily a scale of established values, and those most remote from the aristocracy, which seeks quality, whether based on convention or not.

122. - *GIOTTO.* ST. FRANCIS RECEIVING THE STIGMATA
(detail). The Louvre, Paris

The class which has always evidenced the most pronounced down-to-earth tastes is the bourgeoisie. Consisting as it does of entrepreneurs conscious of the material value of the products they handle, trained in the practices of measuring, weighing, evaluating, this class, more than any other, makes a specialty of concrete appraisal. Its envy and hatred of the aristocracy has often induced it to denounce and ridicule the ideal values cherished by the latter class (though in later periods, having acceded to power, it has begun partly to emulate the aristocracy). This class recognizes neither ideas nor words, only marketable values.

There can be no doubt that the gradual rise, from the twelfth century on, of the bourgeoisie contributed to the restoration in the West of the direct sense of material reality, which had characterized the harshly positivist Romans. Gradually undermining the position of the feudal lords, whom it ridiculed in the *Roman de Renard*, wresting from them their rights and privileges, and supplanting them altogether in the Duchy of Burgundy, which in the fifteenth century was the trade center of the West, the bourgeoisie caused art to develop in a direction parallel to its own interests. In the fourteenth century, says Paul Fierens,[1] "people gradually moved away from medieval mysticism; they began to show a passionate interest in the actual properties of things, in nature, in the spectacle of the world, and in likenesses of bodies and faces." It was, of course, in this same Duchy of Burgundy, in Flanders, grown prosperous thanks to its cloth merchants, that realism reached its full development, though colored still by the religious spirit inherited from the Middle Ages.

Italian realism represents primarily those features of objects that can be encompassed by the eye—that is, their intelligible elements: the contour, an abstraction by means of which the eye delimits what it sees, and the form, an abstraction by means of which the eye conceives of the objects in space. Flemish realism

[1] Paul Fierens, *Le fantastique dans l' Art Flamand*, Brussels, 1947, p. 21.

138

introduces a new kind of vision, based on the exact rendering of the very substances of which the objects are composed. In a painting by Giotto, the substance of a fabric cannot be distinguished by the eye from that of a chair: only the structure, modeling, and color are shown. By contrast, Van Eyck asks first of all what the objects are made of; he discriminates among them, makes them specific: the stone is granite or marble, the fabric is cloth, linen or muslin. However strong his constructive instinct, he is equally intoxicated by reality, its inextricable tangles, its abundance—by that other microcosmic infinity which is revealed to us by the limitless particularity of the detail (figures 122 and 123).

Just as every invention appears at the right moment, in response to a demand, so too with every new technique. The appearance of a particular technique—namely that of oil painting—makes it possible to gratify a demand for precision that previously had gone begging. The principle of this technique had been known before

Two treatments of the same subject—one by an Italian (opposite page), the other by a Flemish artist—show the intellectualism of the former and the realism of the latter.

123. - *JAN VAN EYCK.* ST. FRANCIS RECEIVING THE STIGMATA. Museum, Turin

Photo Alinari

but had not been applied. Opaque distemper and fresco painting can show only coloring. Oils make it possible to reproduce all the effects of light playing on shapes, and thus to make visible the matter composing them. In impasto, oil can render opaque and reflecting substances; it is sufficiently thick to lend itself to the whims of the brush, to become at will smooth or rough, calm or agitated. Glazed, it can be used to render translucent materials, from which the rays of light do not recoil, but which they penetrate and in which they are refracted. Thus the full range of qualities perceivable by the eye can be shown. The totality of visual experience surrenders unconditionally.

In dealing with the problem of space, the north tended to disparage the linear and dogmatic method of Italian perspective, which it found too abstract, and to favor the recording of all the tiny nuances produced by variations in distance. Atmospheric perspective replaced geometric perspective; the "matter" of space, as it were, was reproduced, rather than its form (figure 66).

A passive, receptive kind of realism asserted itself increasingly, in the north; it differed from the active realism of the Italians, which did not confine itself to recording natural appearance, but aimed at grasping the structure of the world, discovering its laws and re-creating them in accordance with its own requirements. Then, at a certain point, the religious fervor that had caused this northern realism to outdo itself

in the earlier painters began to diminish, to dwindle. The northern bourgeoisie in the seventeenth century, severed through Protestantism from the emotional and lyrical elements that Catholicism had preserved in its forms of worship, was led to prize only the skill of visual recording; indeed, it was unable to appreciate the genius of the artists who had transcended that approach and, misunderstanding and sometimes ignoring Rembrandt, Hals, Vermeer, and Ruisdael, it preferred mediocre artists, whose objectivity was as flawless as it was unimaginative (figure 124).

Flemish realism, which by the nineteenth century had become banal, was justified in the fifteenth by its intensity.

124. - *At left: VAN STRY.*
CONVERSATION AT THE INN. 1825

125. - *Opposite page: JAN VAN EYCK.*
GIOVANNI ARNOLFINI AND HIS WIFE. National Gallery, London

THE EPIC OF REALISM.   It may be asked, however, why the stubborn effort to reduce painting to the truthful rendering of natural appearance, an effort that continued from the fifteenth to the seventeenth century, from Van Eyck to Vermeer, produced masterpieces whose qualities are recognized even by our time, which is dedicated to completely different goals. And why does this realism seem to us odious in the nineteenth century, in Meissonier, for example? The answer is that in the latter case the painter contents himself with displaying his dreary skill, that he has abdicated from his role as creator and become only a docile reflector of what he sees. In its great periods, realism is active and creative; it is a *means of expression* by virtue of its passionate interest in the spectacle of things; it communicates an emotion, which had lost a great deal of its intensity by the seventeenth century, but which in the fifteenth was of almost lyrical power (figures 54 and 125).

The great adventure of the West was the assault launched upon the outside world, the convergence of all human effort toward a single goal: mastery over nature. The conquest of nature has not yet been completed. It was for this purpose that the West sent its ships out upon the seas and discovered unknown continents, and that it explored, through the intellect, the structure of the cosmos. During the Middle Ages the total submission of the individual to God had considerably weakened the human drive toward power over nature. In the fifteenth century, however, man began to recover his impetus and greed: from then on, whatever faith in God he still preserved, he relied first of all upon himself, upon the resources of his intelligence and industry, of his science. Nature ceased to be primarily the Creation, the admirable image and likeness of God; it became a field of action for man to test himself upon.

The artist, carried away by the same excitement, tried to seize with his eyes that which men everywhere now tried avidly to grasp. He too, in his own way, set out to conquer the world, passionately seeking to fathom the secret of its appearances in order to reproduce them. Just as prehistoric realism gained, from its use as magic, an impetus that gave it greater importance, so fifteenth-century realism was enhanced by the exalted ambition it shared—an ambition that makes this epoch a crucial one in history.

Similarly, in the nineteenth century, there existed alongside the barren official realism, as servile toward the model it represented as toward the predecessors it imitated, another realism, Impressionism, which shared in the feverish drive of contemporary science. Impressionism took on an affirmative active quality, displayed a will to create, in contrast to the barren imitative realism whose negative virtues delighted the debased public taste.

3. THE MODERN ERA:
FULFILLMENT AND DEATH OF REALISM

THE subjugation of reality was not complete: further battles were still to be fought. But are not form, space, and material qualities all that painting can hope to reproduce? The answer is yes, if our knowledge comes as much from the hand as from the eye. Would, then, consistency and mass—the so-called "tactile values"

IV - HOLBEIN
JANE SEYMOUR (portion). 1536
Kunsthistorisches Museum, Vienna

Photo Draeger

—not be the essential elements of truthful representation? Courbet said: "I paint only what I see"; others would as soon say: "I paint only what I touch."

TRUTH FOR THE MIND AND TRUTH FOR THE EYE. Wölfflin has made the very subtle point that the opposition between the tactile and the visual is the touchstone of truth, as it were, for the Classical mind, whereas the Baroque mind is infatuated with the elusive. He has keenly and eloquently analyzed the differences between the tactile image and the visual image, between the taste for "things as they are" and for "things as they seem to be."

The great historian has shown that the duality corresponds to two successive phases through which art has passed. "The tracing out of a figure with an evenly clear line has still an element of physical grasping. The operation which the eye performs resembles the operation of the hand which feels along the body, and the modeling which repeats reality in the gradation of light also appeals to the sense of touch. A painterly representation, on the other hand, excludes this analogy. It has its roots only in the eye and appeals only to the eye." When the latter mode of representation triumphed, it resulted in "the most decisive revolution which art history knows."[1]

Wölfflin is inclined to see in this change a surrender of realism to subjectivity. It is true that the relinquishment of the sense of touch as a reliable source of verification resulted in the progressive abandonment of strict adherence to the object and the increase of free and undisciplined interpretation. But this was a consequence, and moreover an unforeseen one, not the cause of the decline of realism.

The artist originally took this direction—away from the tactile—in order to perfect, to extend his realism. He did not suspect that it would in the end lead to the ruin of the very realism whose resources he had thought to increase. In fact, he destroyed realism in the act of trying to enhance it.

The occurrence is so important that it must be examined in some detail. The moment realism attempted to free itself from its bondage to the tactile, it had necessarily to take flight, to lose contact with the solid ground, as it were; and in the end it evaporated into mere clouds and light, as was the case with Impressionism.

The descendants of the Greeks and Romans, basing themselves almost exclusively on the data of sensory experience and on intellectual constructs, suspecting the emotions as a source of obscurity and confusion,[2] were led inevitably to seek support in measurable elements—in the surface circumscribed by the outline, in the form assumed by the masses, in the substance which is an indication of their density and weight, their presence in the material world. For the function of the senses is to explore "extension," or space; the intellect, as Bergson showed long ago, completely adjusts itself to this, and follows the senses: we think in spatial terms, and our language makes use of spatial metaphors to denote nonmaterial realities.[3] An art based on sense data combined with reason was led perforce to define everything in terms of discernible form. Beyond this lay the realm of the vague and the unverifiable.

[1] Heinrich Wölfflin, *Principles of Art History*, tr. M. D. Hottinger, Henry Holt & Co., New York, 1932, p. 21.

[2] Even Aristotle, who recognizes that art has the capacity of expressing and "purging" the passions, declares that it "*orders* the sensibility at the same time as it affects it."

[3] For instance, as Bergson says in *La Pensée et le Mouvant*, "the terms denoting time are borrowed from the language of space. When we summon time, it is space that answers" (p. 12).

As early as the fifteenth century, realistic effects of light were being used.

126. - *UNKNOWN MASTER.* SUNRISE. From "The Heart Seized with Love." Livre du Roi René. Albertina, Vienna

Realism, having gained a solid foothold, conceived the ambition of venturing into this uncertain realm and of creating the means for exploring it. Once again, art was merely following a path parallel to that taken by the human mind. Science, too, had at first been based exclusively on spatial realities: it had measured bodies, studied their structures, their interrelations, their interactions, the mechanical action of masses, the chemical reactions of the substances of which they were composed.

Then, spurred on by the realization of its gaps and inadequacies, it gradually extended its sphere to include immaterial, imponderable forces; it became evident that physics must take into account not only the matter of which bodies are composed, but also the invisible forces at work upon them. What a moving and significant moment it was when Leonardo first subjected a substance like water, with its elusive eddies, to the simultaneous attention of his eye and his mind.

The human mind succeeded in accounting for light, attraction, electricity; it formulated the concept of pure energy. Then came the day when modern science was tempted to reduce matter, formerly sacrosanct, to a mere aspect of energy, to regard its basic unit, the electron, as nothing more than "a semblance... the localization of that energy in a very small segment of space."[1] The sixteenth century, as it ended, had not yet reached this point, but it had entered upon the path leading to it.

[1] Augustin Boutaric in *Le Tableau du XXe siècle: Les Sciences*, Paris, 1933, p. 372.

Venetian art could render the subtlest nuances of light.

127. - *TITIAN.* Landscape detail from THE VIRGIN WITH CHILD. Pinakothek, Munich

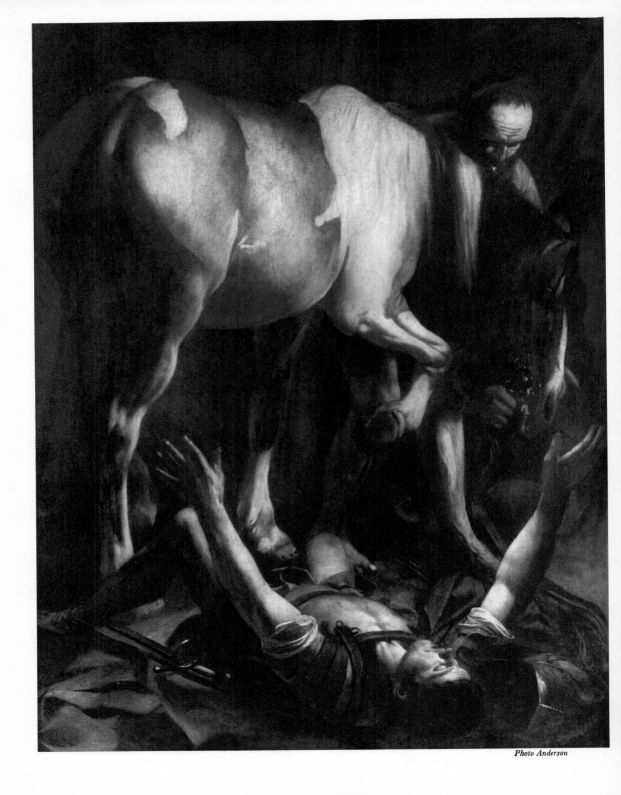

THE CONQUEST OF LIGHT. Up to that time painting had looked upon light as a space in which forms become visible; light itself had remained neutral and anonymous, a transparent receptacle almost as theoretical as the ether of the physicists, a medium. And yet light has a life of its own, its own variations and irregularities; it manifests itself. One day the artist discovered that at such moments it becomes individual, particular; it is real in the same way as that which it enables us to see.

The northerners, thanks to their training and the subtlety of their eyes, had been aware of this fact as early as the fifteenth century. Under their influence, the Venetians began to record, with that sensuality which distinguishes their art from that of the rest of Italy, the palpitations of daylight, showing how dawn and dusk colored and inflected the rays of light. An unknown master, the genius who illustrated the manuscript of *Cœur d'Amour épris* for King René, had previously depicted the variations of light and shadow at different times of day in a series of marvelous masterpieces. From Van Eyck and Memling, through Conrad Witz, to Bellini, painters were increasingly concerned with the effects of light (figures 126 and 127).

At the end of the sixteenth century, however, Caravaggio brought about a revolution whose consequences were incalculable. He was one of the first painters clearly to realize the biased quality of the Classical vision, confined as it was to solid forms and their architecture; he became weary of it, almost hated it. He felt that light was not merely a complementary but also an antagonistic element, and that it could be used as a weapon against the primacy of idealized forms. With the help of light, he thought, he could undermine the Classical doctrine of art. For light, unless it is conceived merely as a subordinate element, the medium within which the forms are seen, can manifest itself only by altering the appearance of the forms. Every solid body, every object in Italian art had a well-defined "normal" aspect, which ended up by becoming conventional. But a ray of light, if the artist directs it properly, can completely change this anticipated aspect, by illuminating small islands that emerge from a sea of shadow, by absorbing some of the darkness and thus affecting even areas of the painting it does not touch. It can have the effect of a cataclysm which descends upon a continent whose configuration is known to us from maps, submerging familiar salients at will, and thrusting into prominence formerly neutral planes. Light transforms, in the literal sense of the term. Like a hardened trooper turned loose upon a conquered city, it works havoc, cutting up the object, amputating, torturing, raping it (figure 128).

The discovery of these effects of light marked a turning point in art. The traditional union between sensory data and the rules of the mind—the foundation of Mediterranean art—no longer prevailed. The new school brutally repudiated the intellect in order to exalt the senses. For the predecessors of Caravaggio, form expressed both what the painter knew about a given object and what he perceived of it according to the variable conditions of vision. But Caravaggio is concerned only with what the eye happens to perceive, depending on the light. A leg may appear as a stump, and a skull as a quarter moon, if it has been so decreed by the accident of their momentary exposure to light.

Caravaggio used light with searching effect, violating the customary appearance of forms.
128. - *CARAVAGGIO.* THE CONVERSION OF ST. PAUL. Santa Maria del Popolo, Rome

In this new kind of vision, the painter, while refusing to alter his perception of natural appearance to fit preconceived ideas, nevertheless asserts his right to stress some aspects at the expense of others. Idealized reality is submerged head over heels in naturalism. But this is not to imply that Caravaggio was any partisan of passive visual recording. Far from it! He endows light, the instrument of his violence, with an intensity which serves his aggressive purposes. Hard, implacable, this light builds a new art on the ruins of the mental laziness that characterizes all academic art. Has there ever been a more "biased" art? The conflict the painter sets up among the visual elements reflects the powerful, irresistible brutality of his appetites and of his will, of his passionate and vehement spirit.

As a result of this development, light came to be part of the domain of painting. Caravaggio had countless disciples throughout Europe. Some merely imitated him; others, such as Tournier and Georges de La Tour in France, used his new technique as a means of expressing the inner life, of introducing poetry into painting. They confirmed what had been known since Leonardo, and what Rembrandt was to demonstrate in his works of genius: the fact that the shadow can serve not only to instill new life into desiccated intellectualized patterns, but also to open an intangible domain where the spirit loves to soar.

Claude Lorrain, in the seventeenth century, made use of this latest conquest of realism to achieve one of those lofty syntheses of Truth, Beauty, and Poetry in which art reaches perfection. He depicts the changing light of day in all its variations of intensity and color, from sunrise to sunset; at the same time he uses these rays traversing space as the instruments of a converging perspective, achieving extraordinary effects of depth, and subjecting all of space to the same logical order that governs the receding lines of the architectural elements. This combination of truth and harmony issues in a song of splendor and sadness: the splendor speaks to the mind of the Classical rule of reason; the sadness whispers to the heart of the irreversible flight of the moment, intense in its precariousness. Claude's painting is a language which comes from the soul and goes to the soul. Until the dawn of Impressionism, painting seemed unable to go further in its dialogue with light, which had now become its creature.

THE CONQUEST OF LIFE. Had the conqueror overrun all the territory accessible to him? By its conquest of light, painting had gone beyond the realm of material form, but not beyond space, to which it continued to be confined. Now, however, it was to undertake something almost impossible: this art which is of the surface, of the extended plane, was to go against the laws of its nature by attempting to penetrate the incommensurable—the realm of time, duration.

For a long while it had been thought that painting must never represent anything without first freezing it into immobility. Such a restriction, based no doubt on the fact that painted figures remain stationary, is most arbitrary; it imposes on the living world a permanence that it does not have, by virtue of a convention designed merely to make it easier to focus upon the object. A marksman improves his aim by shooting first at a fixed target, and later at a movable target; however, one day he is bound to confront the unpredictable actions of living things.

In the real world, physical appearances seem to exist only in order to record

Bruegel began to add life, which he suggested by the successive phases of a single movement, in this case that of falling down.

129. - *PIETER BRUEGEL.* THE BLIND LEADING THE BLIND. Museum, Naples

impact upon objects of forces which are constantly manifesting themselves, struggling, blossoming, or dying out as the moments run their course. Was the striving of art to reproduce reality to be confined to collecting the husks which the forces of the real world leave behind them in their inexorable course? Was painting never to confront that which is at the very heart of reality, its justification, so to speak?

The seventeenth century did succeed in confronting it, thanks to those northerners whose sense of reality was less fettered by preconceived intellectual ideas than that of the Mediterranean artists. In the sixteenth century Bruegel, like Patinir, had minimized the importance of forms by placing them within vast panoramas, in which the swarming objects appear as in a cloud of dust. In such works the painter revealed the general activity of which the swirling forms were a sign, as the movement of debris strewn on the placid surface of a pond is a sign of the currents stirring underneath.

The greater attention paid, in the north, to the landscape rather than to the human form, which is the source of measure and order, had prepared the eye for the teeming or swarming effect, as shown in the foliage, for example, of these canvases. Is not the thickly foliaged tree an example of the statistical "law of large numbers," in which the eye makes no attempt to analyze the constitutive elements, retaining only an impression of the general features?

Bruegel went further. In *The Blind Leading the Blind*, in the Naples Museum, he developed a germ contained in the technique of the primitives, who had juxtaposed in one picture the successive stages of a single event. Bruegel showed the phases of a single movement, that of falling, which is accelerated as it is passed along from

Bruegel was even able to suggest speed by his use of violently converging lines, a procedure followed by contemporary painters.

130. - *BRUEGEL.* UNFAITHFUL SHEPHERD. John G. Johnson Collection, Philadelphia

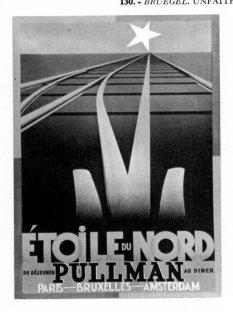

one figure to the next, from left to right. He even anticipated the rendering of speed in the dizzying frenzy of the elements churned by the storm in his *Shipwreck*, in Vienna, or in the fright of the *Unfaithful Shepherd*, in Philadelphia, where the furrows are projected toward the horizon, skimming the field which also seems to be in motion, following the curvature of the earth (figures 129, 130, 132). Not until the twentieth century was such a mad flight depicted again, in Cassandre's poster *L'Étoile du Nord* (figure 131). An art that had remained static from time immemorial began to give way to dynamism. No longer was it confined to the instantaneous view of arrested motion; now it could suggest that motion as it unfolded.[1]

[1] It is only fair, however, to note that prehistoric art had anticipated this possibility too, in the rock paintings in the Iberian Levant and South Africa.

131. - *CASSANDRE.* Poster for the "Étoile du Nord." 1927

150

The intensity of the artist's feeling is recorded by brush strokes more effectively than by drawing.

132. - *BRUEGEL.* SHIPWRECK (detail).
Kunsthistorisches Museum, Vienna

133. - *RUBENS.* THE KERMESSE (detail).
The Louvre, Paris

Rubens went further than Bruegel. Inspired by Michelangelo and Tintoretto, the founders of Italian Baroque painting, he instilled mobility into the very elements of pictorial art. Hitherto, line had been merely the expression of a contour striving to achieve fixed perfection. Rubens retained only the undulating rhythm, the perpetual caprice of line, using it to record movements and gestures, both

However, with Rubens, line drawing begins to convey movement.

134. - *RUBENS.* Nude, study for ADORATION OF THE MAGI. 1610. Cabinet des Dessins, The Louvre, Paris

By means of composition Michelangelo represents bodies floating in an imaginary space.
135. - *MICHELANGELO.* GOD SEPARATING THE WATERS. Sistine Chapel, Rome

of the model represented and of the painter's hand. He did this consciously. In one of his letters, criticizing "the ignorant or even the learned painters who do not know the distinction between matter and form,"[1] whose figures have an indefinable quality of hardness and completeness, who "represent only marble statues painted in various colors," he says that a painting "absolutely requires," in moderation, "places which change according to the figure's diverse movements, and which, because of the suppleness of the skin, are sometimes smooth and taut, and sometimes creased and heavy"[2] (figures 133 and 134).

Pigment was a far more suitable medium for recording such movements than line alone. Here, too, Bruegel was a pioneer, particularly in his *Shipwreck*. And Rubens made his brushwork the record of the creative act, the graphic testimony of its force and passion.

The composition of painting, too, became dynamic. Formerly it had been a structure composed of lines, and depending on lines; now the lines swept it up in their motion; they became lines of energy, the products of various forces, like the currents in the ocean, rushing headlong across the canvas, their speed and rhythm perceptible. To be sure, the picture did not move, would never move; but the eye resting upon it was carried along in a series of movements which compelled the vision to be animated. And the imagination, swept along after the

[1] This phrase strikingly confirms my observation, above, as to the antagonism between form and matter which divides Italy from the north.

[2] "The Imitation of Statues." De Piles was the first to translate this text, written in Latin, in his *Cours de peinture par principes*, Paris, 1708, p. 139.

gaze, hurried panting, all but dazzled, having become the plaything of forces which had been communicated to it and whose inherent impulses had developed through it. Painting had conquered life, adding another domain to those it had previously wrested from reality (figures 135 and 136).

THE MIDDLE CLASSES REINSTATE REALISM. In Italy, the middle classes had early evolved toward a patrician and princely culture; in France, after the uncertain period ending with Richelieu, they were once again kept down by the aristocracy, which was closely allied with the monarchy. As a result, realism, despite the spectacular advances made by Caravaggio and his followers, was gradually pushed back, and came under the dominance of Ideal Beauty. Only the north and, in the seventeenth century, only Protestant Holland, continued firmly to adhere to the realistic foundations of art, although there were a number of "Romanist" deviations.

Beginning with the eighteenth century, the rumbles of a new movement became

In Tintoretto, the composition has become a crisscross of lines flying off in all directions.
136. - *TINTORETTO.* THE LIFE OF ST. CATHERINE. Accademia, Venice

Photo Alinari

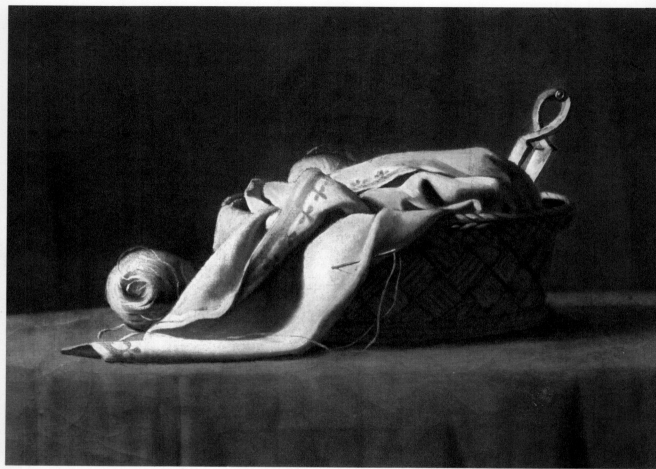

In the eighteenth century, realism reappears, due to the interest of the rising middle class. Many a surprising detail in David is reminiscent of Chardin.

137. - *JACQUES LOUIS DAVID.* Enlarged detail of basket from THE RETURN OF BRUTUS. 1789. The Louvre, Paris

audible. In Italy, particularly in Venice, there appeared an anecdotal genre painting, which stemmed from the work of the Lombard "painters of reality."[1] In France a bourgeois school carried on the tradition of the French "painters of reality," who, early in the seventeenth century, had achieved their most significant expression with the Le Nains. This neo-realism, which in Chardin rises to the heights of an *intimiste* poetry, owed much to the Dutch school; but in France it was inspired by a rising social class seeking to express in it both its physical aspect and its soul. That was why, at least in the works of Chardin, it surpassed its Dutch model, for which imitation was now only an indolent exercising of an acquired skill. This shows, once again, that realism creates positive values only if it expresses a real passion and enthusiasm.

[1] An exhibition devoted to them was held in Milan in 1953.

This renascence, moreover, had deeper causes; it reflected a view of the world that was transfiguring contemporary thought. The new philosophy, too, sought to throw off the conventions by which it had been shackled since the Renaissance, when the Platonists had come to dominate thought with an idealism that had gradually become infected by dogmatism; it, too, strove to find once again a limited but positive basis in sensory experience. Locke had restored all its original weight to the assertion, *Nihil est in intellectu quod non prius fuerit in sensu* (Nothing is in the mind which has not first been in the senses). In France, the Encyclopedists championed this pre-eminence of sensation proclaimed by Condillac, reviving the thirteenth-century nominalist theory according to which ideas are consequences, not causes. Experimental science, also prefigured in the thirteenth century (which had coined the term *scientia experimentalis*), advanced irresistibly. The theory of innate ideas, so favorable to an idealistic art, was discredited, eliminated. The phenomena that had accompanied the emergence of the middle classes recurred at a time when they were about to triumph over their old adversary, the aristocracy, the inheritor of feudal tradition.

The discovery of the art treasures of antiquity, which began in 1748 with the excavation of the city buried by Vesuvius, and the instinctive need to invoke Roman and republican virtues the better to denounce the degenerate upper classes, were superficially a setback to this development, giving rise to a Neo-Classical art. But this revival of antiquity was a deceptive one. Instinct spoke out more loudly than the refurbished theories of Ideal Beauty which came back into fashion. For David is actually a realist in disguise, as is clearly shown by his portraits, in which he freely expresses his true bent. He could not resist the temptation to including a most prosaic sewing box in his *Return of Brutus* (figure 137).

Just as David ended by losing his way between the doctrine of idealism, to which opportunistic considerations gave rise, and his own instinctive realism, which he repressed or made artificial, so all the official (i.e., bourgeois) painting of the nineteenth century gave evidence both of a loyalty to some intangible Ideal Beauty and an irresistible craving for the most down-to-earth and most platitudinous naturalism. The offspring of this monstrous marriage was a hybrid—a conventional realism which "retouched" its servile reality with an affectation of purity. The fate of this school came to rest in the hands of Meissonier and Bouguereau.

IMPRESSIONISM DISCOVERS OPTICAL TRUTH. Writers on French politics often distinguish between *le pays réel* and *le pays officiel* (the real France and the official France); a similar distinction might be applied to painting in the nineteenth century. Alongside the official realism, another kind of realism asserted itself, in answer to an inner need, i.e., the new positive (and even positivist) conception of reality that was developing out of the revelations of experimental science. In addition, discoveries were being made in the field of optics which had a more direct bearing on painting.

I have referred repeatedly to the distinction between passive, barren realism and active, inspired realism. The difference between the two once again manifested itself toward the end of the nineteenth century. Once again, the trend that won out was the one inspired by a creative enthusiasm, which endows with a poetic significance the images the artist believes to be faithful transcriptions of reality.

138. - *MONET.* THE THAMES WITH HOUSES OF PARLIAMENT
IN LONDON. 1871. Collection Lord Astor of Hever, London

*Concerned with optical rather than conventional truth, Monet was
gradually led to abandon in turn the elements of form, volume, and matter.*
139. - *MONET.* THE THAMES WITH HOUSES OF PARLIAMENT.
1901-2

Photo Durand-Rue

Even before Impressionism,
in the mid-nineteenth century,
when Auguste Comte's positivism was creating a stir in the
intellectual world (the philosopher's major works were published between 1830 and 1854),
naturalism had taken the lead
with Courbet. The work of the
painter of Ornans is characterized by a pictorial intoxication,
born of the happy union
between the artist's sensuality
and an aesthetic doctrine that
provided it with adequate

140. - *MONET.* LONDON, WATERLOO BRIDGE. 1903. Ordrupgaard Collection, Copenhagen

In the Impressionist mirage, density and mass have become endlessly changing fictions.

141. - *MONET.* LONDON, WATERLOO BRIDGE. 1903

substance; this intoxication was enough to transfigure realism by making it lyrical.

The old realism was now doomed. After the invention of photography it could no longer be considered an adventure, an exciting possibility. The representation of the visible was now in the public domain, instead of being, as before, the exclusive privilege of the artist. Realism was a calamity when it became a manifestation of purely mechanical skill; with the advent of the camera, realism became impossible. Automatism precludes art.

It was then that Impressionism, making a sudden leap, broke out of this stultifying situation. For science, inexorably pursuing its researches, had condemned the appearances with which the eye had been contented, disclosing them to be a mixture of illusions and conventions. Vision was now defined as the perception by the retina of luminous spots varying in intensity and color. These luminous variations could not be reproduced by photography. This opened a virgin territory to art, and made possible a new incarnation of realism, in which it recovered its freshness and purity, and in which the painter was given the opportunity of enriching his art with a new lyricism.

Thus, after all, realism continued its progress. Starting with contours defining forms that appeared solid and heavy, it had gradually abandoned these in order to pursue intangibles. From the tactile it had passed to the visual, from the material to the immaterial. The lighting effects used by Caravaggio had caused the forms to seem distorted; reflected light, discovered by Veronese and Rubens and cultivated by Delacroix, had vanquished the so-called "local tones," which were another source of the appearance of solidity.

Now the pursuit of pure luminous energy carried on by the Impressionists was to dissolve matter itself. Disintegrated, scattered into myriad bursts of color, matter was sacrificed on the altar of vibrant light. The fixed concepts that made it possible to conceive and to envisage a permanent reality were abandoned in order to conquer the two elements most resistant to painting—movement, and its consequence, duration. The painter, mindful that moments never return and can never be recovered, set out to reconstruct the successive sensations that comprise such moments. Monet's series of haystacks, cathedrals, etc., were the consummation of this dream of representing time. The illusionism of depth was followed by the illusionism of time.

But the fate of this campaign was similar to that of certain colonial expeditions. The army keeps advancing, subjugating new territories and organizing them as they yield; but as it continues its advance, the territory it has left behind returns to its original condition, and gradually banishes the traces left by the conquerors. In striving to annex the whole of reality, Impressionism succeeded in grasping the most inaccessible elements only at the price of losing the accessible ones.

Look at the *Thames with Houses of Parliament* in the Astor Collection, which Monet painted during his first visit to London in 1871; then compare it with his later *Thames with Houses of Parliament*, done during his visit of 1901-2. You will see, as though it were taking place before your very eyes, the gradual dissolution of the landmarks of form, mass, consistency. Where does the water end, in the second of these paintings, and where does the sky begin; what serves as the support for the stone of the building, and where is it situated? The vertical and horizontal axes which are still stressed in the first painting, and the clearly defined areas of color that give form to the objects, have yielded in the second to a molecular dance of fog oscillating between two luminous poles, the sun and its reflection in the river (figures 138 and 139).

Another comparison is even more instructive, if such a thing is possible. Look at the two views of *Waterloo Bridge*. Not only does Monet minimize stable values in favor of impalpable ones, but, paradoxically, he even replaces the former with the latter. In the first of these two landscapes, density of substance fulfills our expectation, for it gives the impression of solidity to the massive stone arches under which the water glides. But in the other it is the hollows that are emphasized; the space between the arches takes on solidity while the stone becomes no more than evanescent light. The most firmly established *notions* become reversible at will—and endlessly (figures 140 and 141).

And now, a final confrontation: on the one hand, a church at Gréville, as seen by Millet, and, on the other, the church at Vétheuil, as seen by Monet. The first is a solid block, and our eye grasps its mass, clearly drawn, emphasized by shadows, and its substance, rough stone, its texture distinct from that of the earth and the grass. What is the second but a bemused condensation of light above a surface that reflects it, a mist of colored particles that makes the head swim, as one has never known it to do before, on looking at it—a mist scarcely distinguishable from the mirage of its reflection in the riffled water? Painting has at last captured the very essence of reality—it is like the colored powder that a butterfly leaves on your fingers when you touch it. But the butterfly itself has slipped away (figures 142 and 144).

EXHAUSTION OF REALISM.   At the end of its insatiable and impossible quest realism burned itself out, destroyed itself. Impressionism, by throwing overboard the ballast of material data, weakened the ties with the object; and a non-representational realism is a contradiction in terms. Now it was borne back onto the flood of multiplicity, always in motion, always transforming itself; it was cast adrift from the moorings of certainty on which the senses allied with reason had depended. The new school, by removing visual data from the realm of common consent, by offering it up to the implacable and personal analysis of the individual artist, opened the door to subjective variations, for each organism perceives the same external datum in a different way. Who then could decide where sensory diversity ends and emotional diversity begins? How could the painter respect the uncertain boundary separating the two?

In striving to transcend itself, realism overshot its mark and sent art off on another tack, that of the free interpretation of reality—an interpretation determined by the artist's temperament, and soon by his whim. Will history ever be able to draw the line between Impressionism and Fauvism? Bonnard, for example, can be claimed by both schools—by the first, as a continuator, and by the second, as a precursor.

Furthermore, in subjecting to its corrosive analytic technique elements which had previously adhered solidly together, by severing contour from form, form from color, and color from light, Impressionism threw man back into the chaos from which he had emerged by dint of hard work. This danger was apparent to Cézanne, who strove to reintroduce into these purely chromatic images the time-honored

Striving to capture reality, Impressionism destroys it, reducing it to a haze of color.

144. - *MONET.* VÉTHEUIL. AUTUMN AFTERNOON. 1901

elements that painting had thrown overboard in its impatient search for purity—
form, construction, composition (figure 143).

    These elements, once part of the bedrock of painting, which held them together
and disciplined them, had now become dissociated, free to follow their individual
destinies. Impressionism showed that it was possible to operate with pure color
without taking the trouble to render the matter to which the color is bound, without
forcing it to stay within the limits of a mass, i.e., a modeled surface, or a contour. It
is not surprising then that the next generation, that of Gauguin and particularly the
Nabis, proceeded to use color for its own sake, and line for its own sake. The way
had been paved for Cubism, and the abstract art which followed it.

Nineteenth-century realism still faithfully translated what we perceive of things—their contours, structure. It took Cézanne to reconstruct their essential truth.

142. - *Opposite page, above: MILLET.* CHURCH AT GRÉVILLE. 1871. The Louvre, Paris

143. - *Opposite page, below: CÉZANNE.* VILLAGE OF GARDANNE (detail). c. 1885. Brooklyn Museum, New York

Impressionism, the sorcerer's apprentice, had broken up the fusion of elements that had made realism possible; then in pursuit of its goal it went beyond realism. This paved the way for the opposite tendency and led to nonrepresentational art.

THE SIGNIFICANCE OF REALISM. Reproduction of visible reality, whether we are viewing it at its origins or tracing its evolution in Western painting, is never the actual goal of art. It can be a prerequisite, but only as a means to an end which transcends realism. Apart from the extra-artistic functions assigned to it by magic and religion, realism has always been justified only by the emotion to which it gave expression. Left to its own resources, to being a discipline for its own sake, it collapses.

Occasionally realism was inspired by a wish to preserve an emotional state by recording the spectacle that had nourished it; occasionally, by a need to give an apparent external validity to confused feelings seeking to understand themselves. But in every case realism was no more than a support for art.

Man has often used realism as a method of securing mastery over the external world. It is the intensity or the quality of this ambition toward mastery that measures the value of realistic painting; the moment the ambition is absent, the moment realism becomes merely a technique of painting, it is indefensible and outside the domain of art.

It was, once again, Wölfflin who observed rightly (*op. cit.*, p. 264): "It would be foolish to suppose that an artist has ever been able to confront nature without preconceived ideas. His conception ... is far more important than anything he may owe to direct observation.... The idea of observing nature is vain unless we know under what forms nature is to be observed." To the forms, we may add the feelings, the state of mind.

In short, it is not realism itself that has validity, but the human concern it expresses and projects onto the object which fascinates it, and which it removes thereby from objective neutrality, from the indifferent status of crude fact; but the moment it does this, the object no longer conforms to its definition. In other words, realism is justified only as an instrument of expression, by which it negates its own purpose. Indeed, the artist soon realizes that in order to gratify his passion to reproduce what he sees, he must make it his own, assimilate it, bring it into conformity with his expectation, however diffident the latter may be; and in doing so he adds, changes, interprets, ceases to be a realist. He discovers that what interested and attracted him was less the object that he thought he was reproducing than the image he was going to give of it. After that he cannot help asking what distinguishes this image from its model, what makes it more satisfactory than the model. Even if the image does come finally to resemble the model, it will nevertheless be made up of elements that differ greatly from it—of lines, colors, textures—but which are made to serve that resemblance. Is it not then in these elements that the secret of the new value the object takes on, in being reproduced, resides? For after all it is they that created the value in the first place.

At this point a new adventure begins: the one upon which painting embarked in turning toward the possibilities afforded by these means. Here begins the adventure of plastic form.

145. - *VAN GOGH.* Greatly enlarged detail of the pigment texture. Self-Portrait. 1890. The Louvre, Paris

CHAPTER THREE

PAINTING IN SEARCH OF ITSELF

A painting is an original combination of lines and tones which assert their own value.

Degas

THE realistic painter is confronted at the outset with an obvious fact, and it is the major difficulty he has to overcome: if, when the work is completed, he has managed to convey the illusion that his canvas is identical with the model which it portrays, he will have done so only by overcoming a fundamental difference between what he sees and the means at his disposal to reproduce it. We have mentioned this difference before: the luminous impressions that strike his retina, which his mind interprets as objects situated in space, have absolutely no relation to the flat, two-dimensional surface on which he executes his representation of them—save the relation he will himself establish.

163

1. PLASTIC FORM

At first glance, line and color seem to serve only as agents of the process through which they are transformed into an image—the image of something they are not. Yet nothing can prevent line and color from having their own existence, nothing can stop a line from being a line, and a color a color; nothing can prevent the artist from realizing this, and from reflecting at some point on the peculiar nature of the instruments so familiar to his hand.

WHEN THE MEANS BECOME THE ENDS. It is a law of nature that each thing tends to fulfill its potentialities—a law that applies, more particularly, to the instruments invented by man, and that has its effect upon the purposes for which they were invented.

In the formula, "to persevere in one's being," philosophy has given expression to this law, which governs every organism on earth, from the moment of its creation, no matter how humble its purpose. In life, every force, from the moment at which it comes into being and acquires the power to act, seems to strive to assimilate everything around it to its own existence. Every movement made by this force with the object of reaching a certain goal becomes circular: instead of following the path that would lead to the goal, the force describes a circle, with itself as the center around which the action revolves.

Our old, refined civilization, as has often been said, is threatened from all sides by the revolt of its instruments. They all seem unconsciously to be striving to free themselves from their proper functions and to live their own lives, to devote themselves exclusively to their own development. It is as though the original purpose for which these instruments were created were only the pretext for their present drive toward expansion.

The machine, which man invented as a means of increasing his possibilities of action, has gradually revised the world to its own specifications; now man adapts himself to the machine, acquiring new characteristics which make him more capable of serving this new force. And, as happened at the end of the Roman Empire, the institutions designed to carry out the functions of the state tend to develop into autonomous powers which obstruct the activities they were designed to further.

In the nineteenth century, the individual came to assume exaggerated importance; in the end he challenged the community and asserted himself to its disadvantage. Literature and art, which are the individual's chosen fields of action, seemed to have become wrecking concerns, bent upon the destruction of rules that had been worked out for the good of all. To be sure, we are now witnessing a reaction, often brutal and excessive, on the part of the newer societies, which strive to check the individual and force him to submit to the general interest, which he betrays without stopping to think that he himself will perish with the group whose good he undermines.

Realism has followed the course of the other instruments of civilization. It, too, is a means become an end; what began as a technique at the service of magic, is now an artifice cultivated for its own sake.

In prehistoric and Egyptian art, line is not merely a means of representation; it is also a delight to the eye.
146. - PROFILE OF ONE OF THE RAMSESES, PORTRAYED AS OSIRIS. Twentieth dynasty.
Sketch for a tomb painting. The Louvre, Paris

The resources used by the artist—line, color, pictorial media—have in turn become rebellious. At first they sought only to serve their purpose, i.e., the pursuit of resemblance, as best they could. But later, though they still appeared to be docile, they began to demand that the forces of which they were the instruments should be sacrificed to them. They demanded to be diverted from their purpose, which had become an extrinsic one; they wanted now to pursue only the improvement of their own quality. And what can we call this intrinsic quality, except beauty?

Physics teaches us that energy required to propel a moving body will be transformed if the body encounters an obstacle that prevents it from continuing in motion: it becomes heat, and this, on reaching a certain degree of intensity, becomes light. In the same way, the means of art, when they no longer serve realism, begin to pursue their own refinement. That refinement is the province of plastic form.

165

Hogarth was so struck by the harmony of the line known as the S curve that he devoted a treatise to it.

147. - *HOGARTH.* THE ANALYSIS OF BEAUTY. Bibliothèque Nationale, Paris

DRAWING: PHYSICAL RESOURCES.   It is possible to show that one by one the means used by the painter to the end of creating an imitation of reality have become the tools of aesthetic research.

First, the linear element. Originally, it was the net by which the apprentice realist sought to capture his prey. But even in the prehistoric bison of Altamira, in the Egyptian bearer of sacrifices, in the athletes on Greek vases, line, which seemed to have been created only for a limited, practical purpose, had begun to serve the purposes of pleasure as well. In the same way, walking is supposed to serve a purpose, that of moving us from place to place; but steps taken along a path by a dancer no longer have anything in common with the practical purpose of walking: the dancer's steps are taken only to display the rhythm of the movements, and their harmony—to create beauty (figure 146).

Gradually art discovered the pleasures afforded by line—physical pleasures as well as intellectual pleasures, and sometimes both.

Physical pleasure, to begin with. To take cognizance of a line the eye must follow it; in other words, the eye transforms the line into movement, or rather, re-creates the movement of the hand that traced it originally. This retracting is done not only by the eyes but by the mind, which, in order to comprehend the line, re-experiences it mentally.

Images, like ideas, can become active forces. We relive mentally the action of which the line is the written record; we anticipate that action with our muscles.[1] The spectator at athletic contests, if he concentrates fully on the sights before him, can sometimes scarcely keep his own muscles from attempting to reproduce the contestants' motions; he mimics them in spite of himself.

The same applies to lines. Some of them are angular, and disorganized; if we were to execute them with our muscles, we would have to make painful, laborious motions, which would result in a series of uncoordinated contractions and relaxations. Such lines suggest toil and fatigue. They create an obscure discomfort which anticipates, as it were, such unpleasant sensations. But there are also smooth, curved lines, which would afford relaxation, even play, to the muscles that executed them; drawing such lines would be a kind of dance, to return to our earlier example. The flowing arabesque, with its effortless curves that carry us along, is essentially such a line.

For this reason the S line has always enjoyed a curious popularity. Lomazzo and Félibien recognized this fact. Dupuy de Grez, in his *Traité sur la Peinture*, published in 1699, refers to the "Lomasse" rule which gives preference to "figures that curve like the flame which always curves as it rises" (quoted by A. Fontaine, *Doctrines d'art en France*, p. 91). De Grez is merely repeating, in less imaginative terms, what Ch. A. Dufresnoy recommends in his *Art de Peindre*:

Photo Flammarion

No artists have used line-play with greater refinement than the Japanese in their prints.

148. - *HARUNOBU*. TWO LADIES WALKING IN THE AUTUMN WIND IN A GRASSY FIELD. Musée Guimet, Paris

---

[1] According to Jung, "the arms and hands of an individual are never completely motionless when he is awake, but are perpetually subject to almost imperceptible vibrations. Prayer and Lehmann, among others, have shown that these movements are largely determined by predominant mental images" (*Occult Phenomena*). This passage is quoted in Hélène Kiener's book on the musician Marie Jaëll; since the turn of the century she has been studying the incipient muscular responses which are suggested by lines (Bibliothèque d'Esthétique, Flammarion, Paris, 1952).

167

Que les contours tracés avec grâce et souplesse,
Coulent comme la flamme en ondes s'élevant,
Ou le serpent qui rampe et glisse en circulant.

Let contours traced with grace and flexibility flow like the flame rising in waves,
or the snake that crawls and slithers as it winds along.

Hogarth thought that he had discovered in the S line the secret of harmony, and
devoted a treatise, *The Analysis of Beauty*, to it. He inscribed this line on his palette
in his self-portrait. He distinguished two varieties: the wavy line, which he calls
the line of beauty, and the serpentine line, which he calls the line of gracefulness.
"The eye is singularly diverted in following these lines, with their spirals," he
writes, "as well as their concavities and convexities which offer themselves alter-
nately to our vision" (figure 147). Hogarth also had an inkling of the reason for
the pleasurable sensation this line gives. Speaking of the ornament that the English
call "the stick and ribbon," he analyzes its attraction: "Its seductive movement
gives me the same sensation I have sometimes experienced watching a dance in a
village."

The curve is pleasurable in itself, by virtue of its continuous and effortless tran-
sitions. Ingres said: "To achieve beautiful form, one must not use harsh or angular
modeling; the modeling must be rounded and without apparent inner detail." What
will be the result if the initial curve, which corresponds to the most natural swing
of the arm, is completed by an inverse curve, as effortless as the first, which is
complementary to it, and supports it? The key to this secret was known by the
Japanese print-makers as well as by Ingres and Toulouse-Lautrec; the speed and
rhythm of the curves in their works vary according to the artist's temperament,
but all of them belong to the same general type. Suzuki Harunobu's print, *Two
Ladies Walking* (figure 148), is only a dazzling variation on the same theme.
Here reality is merely an instrument serving to display the lines; it has been reduced
to a pretext, the roles have been reversed. The wind plays with the ladies' ample
drapery, enabling the artist to vary his arabesques; the sash responds to its breath,
and the billowing robe describes the famous S line. If further proof of the draftsman's deliberate intention is needed, it is provided by the line of the ground, which,
though stationary, is drawn in the same vigorous arabesque.

The basic principles discovered by the prehistoric artist are still vital, still being
developed; repetition, which answers a deep need of the mind, is used more than
ever, as a means of imposing order on multiplicity. The hems of the robes in the
Japanese print repeat the same contour, forming a kind of frieze of S lines. At the
same time we are witnessing a deeper realization of the interrelationship and harmony of forms which was first demonstrated in the Lespugue Venus. The wavy line,
which was in that instance the plastic principle on which the composition as a whole
was constructed, now appears in countless paraphrases reflecting all the possibilities
of dimension, extension, and concentration that can be executed without violating
the unity of the form.

DRAWING: INTELLECTUAL RESOURCES.   Line can also provide pleasure
of an intellectual nature. There are lines so logical, so directly comprehensible, that
they suggest the most perfect geometric formations, those which, because of their

clarity and simplicity, are most gratifying to the mind. Clarity and simplicity are always instinctively resorted to by the human mind in its efforts to make the world accessible, by reducing it to the unity that is inherent in human nature.

We want to assimilate the outside world; to this end we reduce it to forms, each of which delimits a compact area lifted out of the primal chaos. These forms, for the mind, are ideas, and for the eye they are the simple geometric figures. The effort to construct ideas runs parallel to that of devising ideas.

That the effort is spontaneous is best proved by the devices which memory uses to grasp and retain the natural appearance of an object: details are summed up and unified in a simple diagram, and this diagram is further simplified by being reduced to an elementary geometric figure. Villard de Honnecourt's famous *Album* of the thirteenth century is a striking illustration of this procedure. This architect, whose realistic aspirations—characteristic of his era—are clearly shown in his drawing of a lion (mentioned previously), nevertheless records the subjects he encountered most frequently in the form of familiar geometric figures. He uses triangles, squares, and crosses in making diagrams to show the essential outlines of models which he might otherwise have forgotten, because of their complexity. Significantly, the forms of these models from life fit in very well with the abstract architectural forms he also recorded in his notebook, which for their part are purely intellectual creations (figure 149).

Let us make no mistake: what we have here is not yet plastic or aesthetic exploration, as we find it in Dürer, but a practical, utilitarian device resorted to by a man who tries to practice his profession as best he can. It all the more convincingly illustrates the spontaneous, organic need of the mind to simplify or, as Emile Bernard said six centuries later, in 1888, "to rediscover in geometry all the typical forms of objects." This need, when extended into the search for enjoyment, ends by producing plastic

Photo Bibliothèque Nationale, Paris

In the thirteenth century, Villard de Honnecourt set down, for purposes of simplification, geometric diagrams of the human form.

149. - Page from Villard de Honnecourt's sketchbook. Bibliothèque Nationale, Paris

harmonies. These harmonies have their origin in the effort to discover the structural principle of a certain figure, its essential form divested of the multiple details with which nature has clothed it.

Looking at Paolo Uccello's great mural in the cathedral at Florence, representing the *condottiere* John Hawkwood (Giovanni Acuto), we might be tempted to think it primarily a masterpiece of realistic illusion. By using only the resources of a monochrome painting the artist has produced the perfect illusion of an equestrian statue standing with its pedestal against the wall, in the manner of a funerary monument. One could easily be taken in by such realistic virtuosity (figure 150).

But the preliminary sketch has been preserved, and there can be no doubt as to the actual intentions of the artist. This sketch is only a line drawing; there is no trace of modeling, which so readily simulates depth: all we have is an outline clearly circumscribing the figure against a dark background. Paolo's deepest preoccupations are disclosed in the refined combination of curves, full and firm, which testify to the use of the compass—the varying curves of the rump, the belly, the neck of the horse, which are enlivened by several complementary curves delineating the sinuous contour of the "line of beauty."

In this case, however, the S line no longer suggests the free arabesque: it has the harsh precision of geometry. In it, we are no longer following the work of the hand, but rather the work of the mind in quest of certainty; it communicates to us a serene feeling of ease (figure 151).

A considerable effort is required to take in a simple cross section of a tree trunk. It is impossible to conceive of a law from which this outline, with all its irregularities, could be derived. The mind, tired in advance, gives up the attempt. By contrast, a circle suggests repose, it seems unalterable and definitive; the outline of the tree trunk seems merely a distortion of a circle. We speak of the concentric rings appearing in the cross section of a tree trunk as "roughly circular," while a perfect circle is that with an absolutely regular circumference.

The closer a form approximates the simple designs of geometry, the more it suggests the power of the mind to apprehend reality. While it is difficult to draw a completely regular curve by free hand, the simple mechanical device of making a straight line drawn outward from a central point serve as a radius will produce a most perfect curve, the circle. The circle, the square, and the triangle provide the basis of pictorial compositions, because each of them derives from an easily graspable principle. The layman is often hardly aware of the extent to which these figures impose their structures on the painter's mind. We may recall what Pierre, then the director of the Academy, said in chiding David for his *Brutus:* "What gave you the idea that you could make a composition without using the pyramidal line?"

According to Emile Bernard, we tend instinctively to form "a diagram of any sight before our eyes." In what is only a colored vibration we proceed first to discern lines; then we arrange these lines as a "geometric architecture." The infinitely varied forms we perceive are replaced with a limited number of intellectual constructs.

Our repertory of these constructs, however, is not fixed once and for all; slowly it evolves. It is not the same today as it was earlier. I mention this fact in passing, because of its considerable implications. For many centuries the basic geometric figures were those arrived at with the help of "compass, ruler, and square," in Plato's listing. These instruments were developed by an agrarian civilization; geometry arose out of the dividing up of the land. It is only in the past two centuries that this type of civilization, which goes back to the Neolithic, has begun to be threatened.

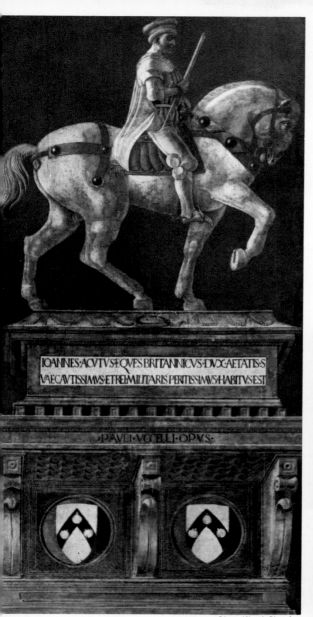

IOANNES·ACVTVS·EQVES·BRITANNICVS·DVX·AETATIS·S
VAE·CAVTISSIMVS·ET·REI·MILITARIS·PERITISSIMVS·HABITVS·EST

·PAVLI·VCCELLI·OPVS·

*At first sight, Uccello's painting looks like a straightfor-
ward illusion, but the preliminary drawing discloses that
it is based on intricate geometric calculations.*

150. - *At left: PAOLO UCCELLO.*
SIR JOHN HAWKWOOD. Fresco in Florence Cathedral

151. - *Below: PAOLO UCCELLO.*
SIR JOHN HAWKWOOD. Drawing. Uffizi Gallery,
Florence

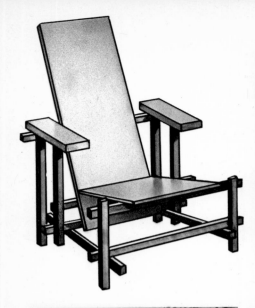

Photo Vandor

The basic forms which the artist uses vary with the civilization. Recently, we have shifted from elementary geometric figures to dynamic curves.

152. - *Above, at left:* Chair in painted wood, 1917

Above, right: HERBIN. VEINING

At right: KOLL. Chair

At left: NADELMAN. MAN IN THE OPEN AIR. 1915. Museum of Modern Art, New York

172

The present machine age has brought about a profound change. The use of graphs, based on the analytical geometry invented by Descartes and the descriptive geometry invented by Monge, the need to calculate resistance, the growing importance of aerodynamics—these factors have made the modern eye familiar with the conic sections, particularly the ellipse, the hyperbola, and the parabola. The attentive observer will easily detect the influence of these constructs on modern art and design, from painting to furniture or ceramics; he will see to what extent these curves tend to supplant designs based primarily on the triangle, square, and circle, which until recently were dominant (figure 152).

FORM OUT OF CHAOS. By its emphasis upon symmetry and repetition, prehistoric art suggests how strong from the outset was the need to grasp a figure not merely by perceiving its appearance but by understanding the principle by which it was possible to re-create it intellectually. The human mind likes to start with the elementary and to make it progressively more complicated, without, however, losing the thread of the initial unity, until the supreme triumph of a complexity seemingly equal to the very chaos of nature is achieved.

Leonardo da Vinci succeeded in portraying such complexity. The foliage he painted on the vault of the Sala dell'asse in the Castello Sforzesco at Milan has the appearance of luxuriant vegetation. One has to be forewarned in viewing this immense tangle; one discovers, on close scrutiny, that it has a rational key, and actually follows the contours of a homogeneous and intelligible figure. If one mentally removes the branches and their offshoots, one finds an interlocking design with thousands of twists and turns, the result of an initial formula multiplied a staggering number of times. This design resembles the geometric labyrinths, entirely abstract by virtue of their mathematical structure, which are the hieroglyphs of the artist's projected "Leonardian Academy" (figures 295 and 296).[1]

Here, perhaps more than in his most famous works, Leonardo brought over into reality the most stubborn dream that man has pursued, in art as in so many other activities: the dream of bridging the gap between the unity of an intellectual principle and the seemingly irreducible multiplicity of nature. All of Leonardo's works reflect, in varying degrees, this temptation of the mind: each of his paintings suggests to the sensibility an impenetrable mystery, which embodies the very opposite of intellectual clarity. And yet Leonardo knew that such a mystery was the result of a perfectly lucid operation, carried to its ultimate conclusions by his own will. It is not surprising that every work he created both fascinates and irritates its students.

Leonardo was carrying on the line of thought begun by the Greeks, who delighted in geometry and found their favorite expression in it. They dreamed of discovering in geometry the intelligible principle of everything complex. Thus Plato proves the excellence of the five regular solids, which were called thereafter the five Platonic bodies. In the *Timaeus* he celebrates the dodecahedron, whose twelve facets are the three-dimensional amplification of the pentagon. Carried away by his enthusiasm, he even sees in it the mathematical symbol of cosmic harmony. "God used it to compose the master plan of the universe." God, as conceived by Plato, had merely

[1] Six engravings of this type have come down to us; according to Richter, they interested Dürer to such an extent that he copied them.

applied on a cosmic scale the device that Leonardo was to use later to create his canopy of foliage!

From antiquity on, form became the primary problem of art; and for a long time aesthetics was to be only the study of beautiful form. Etymology, which often casts light on the secret thoughts of a people, reveals this identification of beauty with form. The word "ugly" in Greek is ἄσχημος, i.e., ἄνευ σχήματος, "without form." Madame Krestkovsky has shown that the same connection can be discovered in English, German, and Russian.

When the dream of antiquity was revived by the Renaissance, form regained its ascendancy; art set out to discover rational principles for itself and in the end fixed on pure mathematics as a way of accounting for the most various and most unexpected embodiments of beauty. In 1492 Piero della Francesca wrote his treatise *De quinque corporibus*, in which he developed Plato's geometric discoveries. From this treatise Fra Luca Pacioli drew the essence of his *De divina proportione*, published in 1505. The year before he, too, had written a *Treatise on Regular Polygons and Polyhedrons*, which, as the title indicates, was based on Plato's ideas. I have mentioned previously the interest displayed in this work by Leonardo, who undertook to illustrate it, and by Dürer (p. 84).

That the basic principle of art was now sought in a mathematical proportion rather than a geometric figure means merely that a new stage had been reached in the path toward abstraction. The study of proportions, i.e., ratios expressed in simple formulas, which cover the largest possible number of terms, reflects once again the striving to reproduce the multiplicity of natural appearance according to some single intelligible principle. The same people—Plato in antiquity and Piero and Luca Pacioli during the Renaissance—led the way in the new turn taken by these explorations.

Pacioli's treatise *De divina proportione* deals with the "golden section," which has been so much discussed, and to which modern art has upon occasion assigned an important place. As we have seen, it had also been revived in the thirteenth century, an age which gave the impetus to several developments of the present time.

How can we account for the popularity of the golden section? It most adequately serves as a means of reconciling a single and simple intellectual principle with consequences which in their variety come as close as possible to the bewildering complexity of the cosmos. Now, a proportion is the expression of an equation between two ratios; hence it must have at least three terms. What is so marvelous about the golden section is that it has only two terms. For we obtain it by dividing a line into two segments, in such a way that the longer part is to the whole as the shorter part is to the longer.

This property of the golden section can serve as the basis for an indefinite number of inferences. By means of it a solid and easily accessible bridge has been erected between the unity of the mind and the infinite complexity of nature, which the mind aspires to reduce to its own measure. Any proportion is welcome to the mind, for it suggests a basis on which disparate elements may be unified. But the golden section seems endowed with an almost miraculous power, which the senses in some way perceive and delight in. It is perfectly clear, exceptionally homogeneous as a principle, and there is no limit to the progression that follows from it.

Thus line, which originally was put at the service of the representation of reality, in the end irresistibly carries art to the extreme opposite of reality: into the abstract reaches of geometry, and even those of pure mathematics.

AESTHETICS OF MASS. It would be possible to show that every means used by the artist to represent reality undergoes a similar transformation if it is developed for its own sake, for the sake of its own beauty, and hence becomes an end in itself.

From showing contour, painting passed on to rendering mass. The means, however, remained the same; they were merely extended into an additional dimension. Representations of mass appeal to the sense of touch, suggesting to the hand the physical motion which models the forms. We say of an object that we "caress it with our eyes." The mind also delights in such representations, and what we have said about the line also applies to mass. We have seen that Plato connects the pentagon, a flat figure, with the dodecahedron, a solid. The same problems arise, the same rules apply to both, only a third dimension is added.

Plato was the first to define mass independently of nature, as both a linear and a three-dimensional form. In the *Philebus* he says: "What I call here beauty of form is not that which is commonly called by this name; I refer not to the beauty of living things or to representations of them, but to something rectilinear and circular and surfaces and solids composed of straight lines and circles by means of the compass, the ruler, and the square. For these forms, unlike the others, are not beautiful only under certain conditions, they are always beautiful in themselves."[1] It was these forms that Paolo Uccello aimed at when he plotted the curves outlining his equestrian figure; Piero della Francesca also had them in mind when constructing the planes of his figures. He sought not only to define these masses clearly, so as to provide the pleasure of understanding; he also sought to make them perfect, so as to give the pleasure of harmony. To transform, by an effort of mind, the data of the outside world is to bring these data into conformity with the mind (figure 153).

The same effort is made by Fouquet, whose disturbing similarities to Piero were noted by Henri Focillon. In his *Virgin*, in the Antwerp Museum, he geometrizes the relief of each part; without exceeding the bounds of plausibility (which no one in his time would have dared to violate), he comes close to depicting the prototypal forms conceived by the intellect, eliminating everything accidental, and preserving only the essence. The heads of both figures and the Virgin's breasts suggest spheres; the arms, cylinders. These abstract shapes are affirmed in the solid objects—as, for example, those appearing on the back of the throne—which adapt themselves most readily to the design; they are a fixed reminder of the themes which are developed in the human figures. Thus the bodies themselves are transformed into structure of the mind (figure 154).

The similarities between Fouquet and Piero della Francesca may be accounted for by the fact that in the fifteenth century the entire Latin world rediscovered the

[1] In the same spirit, which testifies to the persistence of certain human preoccupations, Maurice Denis says in *Theories* (p. 9): "The depth of our emotion is accounted for by the fact that these lines and colors are beautiful in themselves, and divine in their beauty."

Photo Anderson

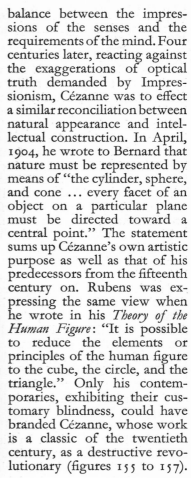

Photo Flammarion

balance between the impressions of the senses and the requirements of the mind. Four centuries later, reacting against the exaggerations of optical truth demanded by Impressionism, Cézanne was to effect a similar reconciliation between natural appearance and intellectual construction. In April, 1904, he wrote to Bernard that nature must be represented by means of "the cylinder, sphere, and cone ... every facet of an object on a particular plane must be directed toward a central point." The statement sums up Cézanne's own artistic purpose as well as that of his predecessors from the fifteenth century on. Rubens was expressing the same view when he wrote in his *Theory of the Human Figure*: "It is possible to reduce the elements or principles of the human figure to the cube, the circle, and the triangle." Only his contemporaries, exhibiting their customary blindness, could have branded Cézanne, whose work is a classic of the twentieth century, as a destructive revolutionary (figures 155 to 157).

What others had done for line, Piero, Fouquet, and De La Tour did for volume, developing idealized features from natural appearance.

153. - *Above:* PIERO DELLA FRANCESCA. THE RETINUE OF THE QUEEN OF SHEBA. Detail from the LEGEND OF THE CROSS. Church of San Francesco, Arezzo

154. - *At left:* JEAN FOUQUET. VIRGIN AND CHILD (detail). Museum of Fine Arts, Antwerp

155. - *Opposite page:* GEORGES DE LA TOUR. THE NEWBORN BABY (detail). Museum, Rennes

176

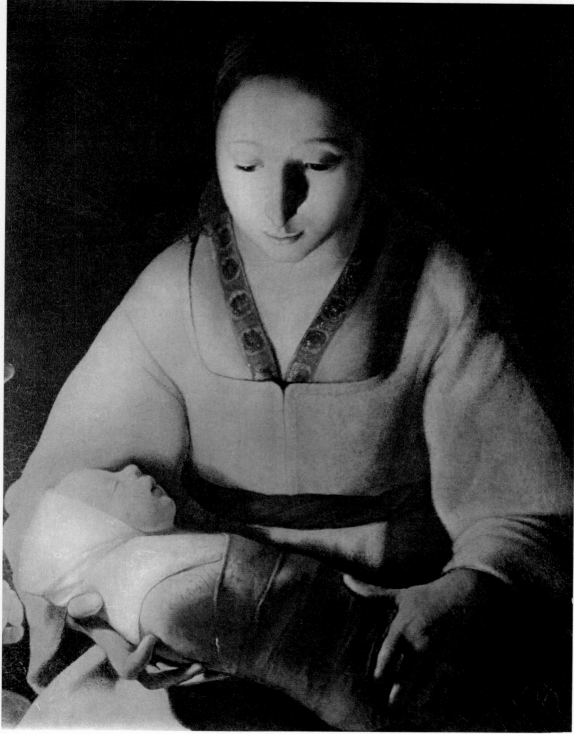

Prehistoric man, in particular the Aurignacian sculptor, attempted to reduce reality to its basic elements through the taming of the mind; but he was obviously motivated by instinct, for he was striving to defend himself against the confusion resulting from the excessive complexity of the outside world.

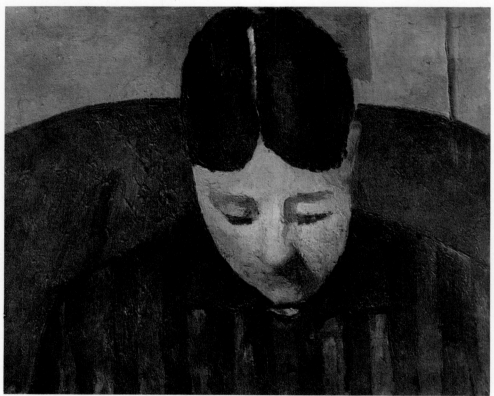

Cézanne maintained that the human form could be reduced to the cylinder, the sphere, and the cone.
156. - *CÉZANNE.* MADAME CÉZANNE, WITH BOWED HEAD. 1870-72. Private collection

THE BEGINNINGS OF THE ORGANIZATION OF PICTORIAL SPACE. The organization of the space within which the forms are disposed, its subjection to the rules of geometry, involves a problem similar to prehistoric man's, though at a higher level of abstraction. We have become too accustomed to this organization to suspect the difficulties that had to be overcome in achieving it.

A long time was required, thousands of years of artistic experience; the problem was not clearly formulated until its solution became a basic social need.

When, in the Neolithic times, the stage of agriculture succeeded that of hunting, and when, following the end of the glacial period, the newer civilizations came to be concentrated in the valleys of the great rivers—the Nile, the Tigris, the Euphrates,

178

and the Indus, the future territories of great empires—the conditions of human existence underwent a complete change. In these relatively small areas it became necessary to divide the land; the surveyor made his appearance. Man was confronted with a new problem: space was no longer merely the field of his activity, but a reality which it was necessary to organize, that is to say, first of all to master intellectually. The human mind addressed itself to a hitherto unknown task, which had suddenly become vital: the definition, measurement, and division of space in accordance with general and incontestable rules. The science of geometry, "the measurement of the earth" ($\gamma\varepsilon\omega$-$\mu\varepsilon\tau\varrho\acute{\iota}\alpha$), was born, and with it a new concern, connected with this new power.

Added to the problem of partitioning the land, of fixing boundaries in accordance with easily graspable rules, was the problem of irrigation. Water, which was scarce, had to be drained from the rivers by means of a network of canals conveying it to the various points at which it was needed. It was thus that the primitive peasant became familiar both with the regular figures by which his fields were delimited and those traced by the water channels.

It would have been surprising if this new development had not affected art. Henceforth art, too, strove to organize space. Prehistoric man had tackled these problems in only a summary way, incising ornamental designs on the surface of objects in daily use; the figures he used might be called "protogeometric," for they only remotely foreshadowed the coherence they were one day to achieve.

The art of ceramics, which came into being with the age of agriculture, registered a tremendous advance in this respect: the regular lines traced on pottery were inte-

Photo Flammarion

Long before the modern painter, art discovered how human motions could be rendered by geometric forms.

157. - *BRACELLI* (1584-1609). Engraving from *Caprices.*
Bibliothèque Nationale, Paris

grated into over-all compositions; which were divided into sections. Borders and checkered patterns made their appearance; the art of sectioning eventually gave rise to the metope.

A parallel development took place in the realm of figurative art. The earlier efforts to simplify contours and to adapt them to the limited possibilities afforded by the design and the means of execution were now abetted by attempts to order the total space treated by the artist. There is a striking difference between rock paintings—for instance, those belonging to Iberian prehistory, with their figures scattered at random like a handful of seed—and the earliest Egyptian paintings.

The prehistoric hunter placed his figures haphazardly; it took the discovery of agriculture to teach the artist to organize his surfaces.

158. - FRESCO AT ALPERA (Province of Albacete). Rock painting. Eastern Spain

159. - THE SO-CALLED "FLAG" MOSAIC. ROYAL TOMB OF UR. Beginning of third millennium B.C.
British Museum, London

An even more striking contrast may be seen between the latter and Egyptian prehistoric paintings such as those discovered by Winkler in the deserts along the Nile (*Rock Engravings of Southern Upper Egypt*, London, 1938–39), or the tomb frescoes of Hierakonpolis, dating from the period directly preceding the first dynasty, which for the most part have not been preserved. In none of these early works do we find the slightest trace of a total and ordered vision of space.

But the moment we enter history, what a transformation! We find the same space divided by means of parallel lines, and the figures arrayed like soldiers obedient to the orders of the intellect. The contours of these figures have lost the intuitive, almost impressionistic quality which led us, earlier, to compare the Paleolithic style with that of Toulouse-Lautrec; they are now coherent and regular, unambiguously announcing the birth of geometry.

Simultaneously, the geometric treatment of mass, which had been brilliantly anticipated in the Aurignacian Venuses, reaches new heights, revealing the artist

Egypt was first to achieve an intellectual grasp of volume.   *Greece refined geometrical form with calculated proportions.*

160. - SO-CALLED "SPARE" HEAD. Limestone. Fourth dynasty. c. 2600 B.C. Museum, Cairo

161. - HEAD OF A YOUTH, FROM THE ACROPOLIS. Museum of the Acropolis, Athens

Photo André Vigneau   *Photo Atlantis*

as in command of a logic of simplification and combination. The marvelous and too-little known "spare" heads, as they are called, epitomize, though their purpose is obscure, the sovereign power of mind over the forms of reality, which submit without resistance to its law (figure 160). The Mesopotamian masterpieces of the same period embody similar principles, confirming the fact that this artistic stage is parallel to and reflects a stage of social development.

It remained only, thereafter, for Greece to contribute the basic idea of geometric form, as well as the subtler idea of mathematical ratios and proportions, thus achieving a formula that has greater capacity for nuance and is more flexible. The Greeks were able more accurately to approximate natural appearance, and at the same time to give greater leeway to the mind in imposing its own laws upon the forms (figure 161).

At that moment the classical Mediterranean ideal took shape, overcoming the contradiction between reality as it appears to our senses and the harmonies that we delight in conceiving. This subtle balance prevailed, till it was upset by a tidal wave from the East upon which Christianity was borne in, and

Iberian sketches of living things were gradually transformed into a kind of shorthand.

162. - *Above:* SIMPLIFIED DEER. Tajo de Las Figuras. Laguna de la Janda, Cádiz

163. - *Center:* SCHEMATIZED DEER AND HUNTER. Nuestra Señora del Castillo, Almadén. (Drawing by the Abbé Breuil)

164. - *Below:* DEER REDUCED TO SIGNS. Specimens from Southern Andalusia, grouped by the Abbé Breuil

182

PLASTIC FORM

Vigorous movement in art emerges in the prehistoric Iberian Levant...

165. - BAND OF WARRIORS. Cueva del Val del Charco del Agua Amarga (Teruel). Painting of the Iberian Levant (J. Cabré)

which was to bury the Western world under an alluvial stratum alien to its own geology.

ENTER LIFE. Classical Mediterranean civilization had always been surrounded by cultures that did not share its taste for realism. The art developed during the Bronze Age and later during the Iron Age had come down to these cultures free of any Greco-Latin influence, and contacts between it and Classical art remained rare and superficial. The very different tradition in these surrounding cultures can be credited with having made a contribution to art: whereas in our Western tradition it is the forms of nature that are the object of simplifying and ordering thought, in this other tradition nature provided not so much formal suggestions as the impetus of its life, its dynamism. Reality was perceived not in terms of linear contours which immobilized it forever within set boundaries, but in its movements; and it was rendered by what we have called "lines of energy" as opposed to "lines of form."

...it finds an amazingly close echo in the rock paintings of South Africa.

166. - RUNNING FIGURES. Rock painting. Basutoland, South Africa

In Irish miniatures the abstraction of dynamic forms was carried almost to the point of visual confusion.

167. - IRISH MINIATURE. Book of Durrow. Trinity College, Dublin. About 700 A.D.

Prehistoric art, which unquestionably contains the germ of all future developments of art, provides us with the earliest examples of lines of energy. The art of the Iberian Levant, though partly deriving from Magdalenian art, which evolved in the northern Pyrenees and the Cantabrian mountains, and which for this reason is called Franco-Cantabrian, took an entirely different direction from it. Like the prehistoric paintings of Africa—to which, incidentally, it seems related—it contributed an animated vision, concerned with the motile and even teeming condition of living creatures, men and animals. Little interested in defining forms by contours, as was done by the Magdalenians, the Iberian artists preferred to represent them by splotches of color which captured their fleeting quality.

In an amazing advance, this style of art spread not only to North Africa but as far as the southern tip of that continent; we find examples of it among the Bushmen in Southern Rhodesia, where it was still being practiced at the dawn of our own era. The obsession with movement was so strong in this art that it led to deformations, the limbs being stretched in the direction in which they are bending their efforts (figures 165 and 166).

In the stylization at which it ultimately arrived, both in North Africa and Spain, this art preserved the same tendency, thus ending in a mode quite unlike that which marks the end of Magdalenian art. Instead of moving toward an ever more pronounced geometrization, it ends in a kind of condensed notation, a real stenography, which totally ignores regularity, symmetry, and rational method and produces purely graphic art reminiscent of written characters. The formula of vitalist aesthetics, that proposed by Guyau, "art as concentrated life," might be applied to this early work (figures 23 and 162 to 164).

The art of the nomads, which obviously owes nothing to these prehistoric works, displays the same dynamic features, indicating a major concern with representing movement and elaborating upon the turbulent lines it suggests.

Thus, among the varieties of art that give a free interpretation to the data of nature, two large categories may be distinguished. One is the product particularly of agricultural and sedentary civilizations, at periods when they depart from realism and aim at imposing on forms a definite and fixed geometrical order. The other, the product of cultures of hunters and nomads, for whom life means constant movement, shifting from place to place, is typified by simplifications and contractions which suggest a coiled spring about to be released.

This contrast may be supplemented by another. The straight line, the embodiment of rigidity and fixity, prevails in the stylizations of the first category, while the curve, which records living reality more directly, is preferred by the latter. Motivated by a need for the release of inner tension, the masterpieces of jewelry produced by the nomadic art of the steppes most often represent not single animals but groups of figures struggling together, tangled in knots like intertwined snakes. Here the line, instead of immobilizing the form, conveying it toward a perfection beyond time and giving it an eternal aspect, is a complicated trajectory, extraordinarily and endlessly mobile, sometimes constricted and sometimes relaxed and soaring freely.

The offshoots of this trend, so alien to Mediterranean Classicism, are found in the Scandinavian interlacings and, to an even greater extent, in Irish illuminations,[1] where it manifests itself in interminable linear fantasies (figure 167).

This form of plastic abstraction discloses a profoundly different spirit from the other: the Celtic line, instead of keeping to the finiteness of the form and the fixity of the contour, seems to suggest the infinite. Ireland, which had little contact with Greco-Latin art and distorted the slight influences it did receive, has given us in its miniatures the ultimate expression of nomadic and seminomadic civilizations, whose fundamental feature is their instability. Is it not significant that Arab culture, spurred on, moreover, by religious scruples, should often in its art have prohibited the representation of figures, to give free rein to the abstract and dynamic graphic tendencies of its wandering peoples?

THE EMERGENCE OF ABSTRACT ART. It may be that nomads are naturally less inclined to be absorbed in the contemplation of nature than are sedentary populations. After the Neolithic age—that is, after the third millennium B.C.—the art of the steppes spread throughout Central Asia; passing through Mongolia and Siberia, it was to link China with Europe. The first to carry it westward were the Huns; then, in the Classical era, the Scythians came in contact with

---

[1] The use of the term "Irish" is contested today by some scholars who maintain that almost all these masterpieces were created in the monastery workshops of Northumberland in northeastern England. Needless to say, even so they reflect the genius of ancient Eire.

the Greeks in Crimea; later, a short time before the Christian era, it was brought in by the Sarmatians, whose tendencies were even more rigorously geometric; finally there was the great mingling of peoples following the invasions of the barbarians, and the raids of the Scandinavians.

All this led to the spread of an art in which reality was as responsive to the injunctions of form as molten metal is to the mold into which it is poured. From Luristan, with its bronzes, in the south, to the Chinese borders in the east, to the Vikings, with their interlacings in the north, and to the Celts of Ireland, with theirs in the west, this art marks the triumph of plastic imagination over the resistance offered to it by the picturesque disorder of reality.

The Siberian gold ornaments show to what extent the animalistic realism inherited from the Assyrians by way of Persia had been transformed. Human invention, with its abstract combinations, has subjected the data of nature to its dissolving and reorganizing powers.

The spread of this art of dynamic abstraction, both in space and through the centuries, can be observed by following the undulating motif of the double dragon,[1] which forms an S, from the art of the Ordos,

[1] Cf. Edouard Salin, "Les Influences Asiatiques et le haut Moyen Age," in *Amour de l'Art*, July-August, 1936, pp. 240–45.

Photo Flammarion

The S form was brought from China to the Pyrenees, first by nomads, and later by the barbarian invasions.

168. - *At left, above:* ORDOS KNIFE. Musée Cernuschi, Paris

169. - *At left:* BUCKLE. Museum, Narbonne

In Merovingian buckles, the dragon motif was soon transformed into a purely decorative theme.

170. - *At right, above:* BUCKLE OF BOUROGNE, with vestiges of animal feet and head. Seventh century

171. - *At right:* BUCKLE OF LÉZÉVILLE, entirely geometrical. Eighth century

The evolution starting from Greek realism in Celtic coins can also be observed at the other end of the Mediterranean world, at the approaches to India. The progressive stylization and abstraction can be followed step by step.

172. - *Above, left to right:* COINS OF PEROZ (457-483), TAROMANA (490-514), and GADHYA, *from countries east of Persia* (c. 750)

173. - *At right:* EVOLUTION OF THE HEAD, STARTING WITH ANCIENT COINS FROM GAUL (Coins of the Volsci Tectosagi.) Cabinet des Médailles, Bibliothèque Nationale, Paris

at the bend of the Yellow River on the frontiers of China, down to its penetration into the ancient Roman Empire on the buckles of the belts, the fibulas, of the Merovingians. As the motif develops, the linear elements devour all the rest, till all that remains of the dragon is a summary evocation of its head at each of its extremities; in the Irish illumination the same dragon's head marks the end of the interminably involuted line, when it is at last willing to come to a stop. Finally, in the eighth century, on the eve of the emergence of Romanesque art, this last survival of the initial realistic datum, which was still discernible in the seventh century, is eliminated from the motif, and becomes a free linear improvisation, looping and interlacing (figures 168 to 171).

This completes the cycle. Carried away by the importunities of the lines, which he first used to define the silhouette of an animal, the artist becomes reconciled to the geometric forms suggested by his model. The realistic motif has been entirely assimilated to the means of plastic expression, which absorbed it entirely, fed on it, and then forgot it in order to pursue its own ends, and inevitably to draw those purely abstract conclusions which delight the mind.

We witness the same process in the transformation of the naturalistic motifs on Greek coins in the imitation of them in Gaul, in which the models are invariably "dissolved," and replaced with an arrangement of unrecognizable elements. Gallic coins and Irish miniatures have a common Celtic origin. Some writers have diagnosed the propensity for abstraction which they have in common as a "racial" trait. This is doubtful, however. Even though this phenomenon occurs only in certain human groups, and, generally speaking, among those which did not take part in Mediterranean civilization—and which this civilization referred to as "barbarians"—it is nevertheless universal in scope. We have seen it in prehistoric art; and we see it here once again (figure 173).

We also see it at the other extreme of the Classical world, where that world merges with the East. Those inclined to see the dissolution of

187

figures as "Celtic" will find instances of a similar dissolution east of Iran, in Afghanistan, in Gandhara, and in other places where, several centuries later, models deriving from Greek coins were similarly transformed. In this case the process did not result in clearly discernible geometric forms, but in signs, in abbreviations tending toward the dot and the line and complex linear constructions; and these, once again, end by becoming a rudimentary form of writing which serves as an excuse for creating this subtle plastic counterpoint.[1] Thus the Greek aesthetics based on the harmonization of reality is submerged and dies on entering foreign territory, both in the East and in the West (figure 172).

Total abstraction, therefore, is not a caprice of our era, as some people think. It reflects a deep tendency that manifested itself in the art of the past. The champions of modern art may well justify it not merely through dogma but by pointing to its historical antecedents. They may also point to other arts, observing that in music the basic elements, i.e., sounds, are combined and elaborated with no restrictions save those imposed by aesthetics. The composer is not required to reproduce or imitate the noises the ear perceives in nature; if he does occasionally do so, it is only in a spirit of playfulness or virtuosity. Thus music is the prototype of an art that lives solely through its means: its only aim is to accomplish its own form and to evoke or provoke emotion. It is concerned only with problems of sonorous perfection or suggestive power, which find their counterparts, in the realm of painting, in those of plastic quality and evocative intensity.

[1] Our thanks to Mr. Hamelin for making this information, and the accompanying reproductions, available to us.

174. - GOURO MASK. Ivory Coast. Collection O. Le Corneur

Photo Flammarion

Modern art, encouraged by the example of music, has tried to isolate these elements and liberate them from all alien concerns, such as that of copying nature. Thus, on exclusively logical grounds, purely abstract painting came to be championed. Henceforth, beauty, like Mallarmé's Herodias, has the right to exclaim proudly: *"Oui, c'est pour moi, pour moi, que je fleuris déserte!"* ("Yes, it is for myself, for my sake alone, that I am flowering in the wilderness!")

DIVERSITY OF ABSTRACT ART. But we must guard against absolute judgments. In the past, as today, the elaboration of plastic form produced amazingly varied results, the range of which we must consider in order to avoid confusing one kind of solution with another, in present-day art as well as in that of the past.

Sometimes reality is bullied into submitting to basically geometric organization, the space being divided into planes or masses whose arrangement is conceived as a new order and as a harmony. This architectural and static tendency first manifested itself in the Aurignacian Venuses, and it has, in our own day, led to Cubism. The tendency was first seen in modern times in the use made of African masks by Vlaminck and Derain, when they shared a studio at Pont de Chatou (figure 174). But the perfection sought by such geometric arrangements presupposes their being unchanged by time, and thus being outside life. Life, however, also has a right to inspire human creation and the style in which it is executed. And the assertion of this right leads to the replacement of static geometric arrangements by more dynamic ones.

This dynamic tendency may be confined simply to the forms, which continue to serve

As a first step toward abstraction, matter is reduced to basic shapes; in this, our time has rediscovered Negro art.

175. - *MODIGLIANI.* SCULPTURE

Photo Archives Photographiques

as the basis for plastic creation but are given a new appearance and order. This was the course pursued by the Baroque. It was also the direction taken by the so-called Art Nouveau, inspired by plant life, the rhythms of which, however, are too lackadaisical for our rapid age. The same tendency is shown in the influence of geometry on recent constructions, not by architects but by engineers, who make use of dynamic curves to solve the problems of energy and speed.

Occasionally the surge of life manifests itself, not in forms and masses, but simply in the line that registers the movement of the artist's hand, its impulses and intentions. A whole new art is in process of developing out of this trend, using primarily lines and slashes or touches of color. The trend was seen first in the prehistoric age, in the Iberian-African area; it prevailed in Chinese painting, which cannot be separated from calligraphy and the stroke of the brush; it accounts for the interlacings and sinuosities of Irish illumination and Viking ornamentation, as well as the swirling motifs of Polynesia; in our time it has inspired the flashing effusions of André Masson, or of such more recent abstract painters as Hartung, Soulages, Mathieu, and Michaux (figure 176).

Whether the artist seeks to divide his space into

By successive eliminations, modern art has moved from abstraction to "concrete" painting, which confines itself to dynamic linear expression and the vigorous presence of the raw materials of art.

176. - HARTUNG. February, 1955

Raoul Dufy

Deauville

V - DUFY

THE RACE COURSE AT DEAUVILLE (portion)

Collection Paul Pétridès, Paris

Photo Draeger

planes or masses, or sees it primarily as a medium for depicting explosive energies by means of lines and color touches, he is always concerned solely with the plastic aspect of his art; he thinks of it above all as a construction. But that is not all there is to it. After discarding nature in favor of forms that can be detached from it or created out of it, art has come to discard forms in favor of the materials of which they are composed, and, in the case of painting, in favor of the pictorial substance, the paint itself. The modern school, with its radical and extremist

solutions, has helped to bring this factor, which is often insufficiently distinguished from the others, into prominence. Along with the painters of abstract form, we now have —within abstract art—the painters of the *formless;* their work is sometimes given the seemingly contradictory name of "concrete art" or "raw art." Such painting aims at liberating the artist from the habitual notions of form and from the obligation to represent nature, and compels him to obtain his effects from the very materials he uses.

Some artists have resorted to this style primarily as a way of being provocative, humor playing an important part in this (e.g. Dubuffet); others have displayed true creative inspiration, for instance, Hosiasson in his latest manner (figure 177), Riopelle, Vieira da Silva, and Wols, who significantly entitled one of his canvases *Grande Pâte* (which might be translated as "The Big Impasto"). Pursuing this quasi-alchemical

Photo Marc Vaux

177. - *HOSIASSON.*
PAINTING. 1955

exploration of matter, Baskine created a painting-sculpture which could be entitled *The Mercurial Philosopher's Stone*.

Here again, our contemporaries are so bent on analyzing the ultimate nature of painting that they are often carried away by their theories rather than justified by them. The fact is that no theory can account for all the forces that combine to produce the creative act. I am convinced that what is needed, instead, is as complete an understanding as possible of the complex motives that operate whenever man acts.

At all events, modern art, by carrying its solutions to the extreme, has contributed to our understanding of the inner resources of painting, which might otherwise have remained insufficiently defined. Thus we are led to take up not only the problem of plastic form, but that of pictorial form, which is often confused with it.

2. THE PICTORIAL ELEMENT

PAINTING shares with sculpture and architecture the distinction of being a plastic art, in so far as it attempts to solve the essential problem of those arts— the construction of forms. But the moment painting asserts its individuality, its own nature, it breaks away from those other arts and turns toward life and movement, employing resources of its own. Then the line ceases to be merely a contour bound to a specific mass, and becomes a mobile outline that winds freely in and out, suggesting the living movements of the artist's hand; the colored paste is used not merely to fill in the previously drawn silhouette but to display the charms of hue and nuance and the felicitous impulses of the brush; it becomes a record of the movements by means of which the work was executed. All this distinguishes painting from the other arts, opening up to it a world of new possibilities, to which the principal keys are the pigment, the brushwork, and the color.

A NEW RESOURCE: OIL PAINT.   In the earliest techniques the paint was only a very thin coating of color, used to fill in the contours of forms and to show their reliefs by various degrees of light and dark. Everything was subordinated to the achievement of effects of roundness and relief (figure 178).

When oil paint came into use it marked the birth of the pictorial. What had been merely a colored coating spread relatively evenly now became a substance of varying thickness, which could be modeled by brush and palette knife.

In the early fresco and distemper paintings the liquid vehicle (water, various glues, sizes) with which the colored pigment was mixed had deprived the paint of body. Only when wax (which, however, the painters of antiquity seem to have used less often than some writers believe) is used does the paint have the consistency of a paste. Moreover, the brushwork cannot be seen if the paint is absorbed, "drunk up," by the surface to which it is applied, as was the case with fresco and, to a lesser extent, with distemper painting.

The older painting techniques resulted in smooth and even effects.

178. - *SCHOOL OF FONTAINEBLEAU.* Sixteenth century. GABRIELLE D'ESTRÉE (detail). The Louvre, Paris

179. - A mural painting. Pompeii. Museum, Naples

The painters of antiquity and at the close of the Middle Ages, who did not yet use oils, nonetheless achieved brushwork effects of pictorial handwriting with their materials...

180. - *HIERONYMUS BOSCH.* TEMPTATION OF ST. ANTHONY (detail). Museum, Lisbon

To be sure, there have been exceptions. From antiquity on, artists have occasionally succeeded, by the skillful placing of clearly defined accents, in endowing their works with a vigor and even vehemence that we are tempted to call "modern"; such works appear from time to time throughout the centuries (figures 179 and 180). However that may be, it is undeniable that the technique of painting with oils actually began a new era in the fifteenth century. When this thick but malleable paste, which can form heavy coatings as well as thin and transparent ones, came into the hands of painters, they did not at once realize all its potentialities. At first they confined themselves to using its infinite resources to create a closer imitation of reality. They even went so far as to conceal every trace of their own execution, in the painting, in order not to divert the viewer's attention from the realistic illusion that was their goal. For this reason they laid on the paint as evenly as possible, keeping it to an almost constant thickness and letting the brush strokes be completely absorbed into the fine glaze (figure 181).

At a certain point, however, painters became aware of the specific properties of their medium, of its personality, as it were. This was bound to happen; an actor capable of mimicking the individuality of others cannot keep, at a given moment, from revealing his own. As we have seen, every means tends to become an end in itself. The new medium, after being used to further the cause of the imitation of reality, began to be used to further its own independence. Painters proceeded to exploit the specific properties of oil paints—the fluidity, density, the

...on the other hand, oil paintings on occasion present as even and neutral a surface as enamel.

181. - *Opposite page: VAN DER WEYDEN.* THE LAST JUDGMENT (detail). Hospital, Beaune

182. - *At left: VELAZQUEZ.* THE CHRIST IN THE HOUSE OF MARY AND MARTHA (detail). c. 1619. National Gallery, London

Various kinds of brush strokes, from those that model to those that only suggest, can be observed in the different works by a single painter, for instance, Velázquez.

183. - *At right: VELAZQUEZ.* THE MAIDS OF HONOR (detail of the Infanta Margarita). 1656. The Prado, Madrid

Photo Anderson-Giraudon

Photo Moreno

blandness or vehemence with which they could be endowed. In music, each instrument has its own sound, its own pitch, inflections of its own which serve to enrich the score. While art was engrossed in its concern with exact likeness, the resources of the execution and the beauties of the medium were only adjuncts, which were not allowed to interfere with the main pursuit. But now the degree of independence achieved by the medium was to increase progressively.

THE PIGMENT ACHIEVES INDEPENDENCE. The evolution of painting parallels that of language. In the latter, at first, everything has to be spelled out, no word can be omitted lest the meaning be lost; but at a certain point expressions that have become habitual begin to be anticipated by the memory, and these no longer have to be said. Similarly, in painting, the trained eye will grasp the meaning of condensations of form, abridgments, and even mere allusions. As a result the painter, instead of methodically and completely expounding his subjects, painstakingly following each contour with his lines, showing each mass by his modeling, could from a certain moment on confine himself to making typical and striking suggestions.

In everyday life we do not need to examine a given object in detail in order to identify it; a few characteristic impressions are sufficient. In the same way painting came to confine itself to touches or patches of color which we are able to recognize as objects. But the less explicit painting becomes, the more precise it must be in what it does say. It finds such precision, as regards form, in a characteristic configuration; as regards values, in a well-chosen relationship between lights and darks; as regards color, in chromatic effects that strike the eye with a certain freshness. The eye will be satisfied if only the essential features of an object are rendered. This gives the artist the freedom to use according to his own wishes the technical resources available to him.

196

Impressionism merely carried to its logical extreme a movement that had begun much earlier, aimed at freeing the painter from his servitude to visual reality; the only tribute the Impressionist painter is required to pay to natural appearance is in the veracity of the touch of color. He was thus enabled to escape from his long servitude to the intellectual or tactile notions of contour, form, modeling, and so on.

In this respect the greatest precursor of Impressionism was certainly Velázquez, who in the course of his own career made the transition from the traditional rendering of reality to the optical impression. Around 1619, for instance, executing a head for his *Christ in the House of Martha*, he meticulously defines the silhouette by a continuous stroke, and the mass by intricate gradations of shadows superimposed on the flesh tones. In 1656, in his portrait of the Infanta in *The Maids of Honor*, the color has become extraordinarily refined: it now does everything; every part of the skin in this face is rendered in its specific tonality, and we marvel at the number of variations, often unexpected and hitherto unnoticed ones. But this precision in conveying the quality of the color frees the artist from suggesting any other qualities. He has expressed the essential: why should he add the superfluous data that might be provided, in a more theoretical and less evocative way, by drawing or modeling? This would lead to redundancy (figures 182 and 183).

In his reliance on the judgments of his own eye, Velázquez occasionally defies our strongest expectations. Examine the head of his *Reclining Venus* (National Gallery, London) at close quarters. You will discover that the artist has laid on the paint most thickly where actually there is a void, the mere brightness of the luminous air, and that the flesh of the figure, where it is given prominence by the bones, is rendered by a gossamer wash, a mere metaphor of color (figure 184).

The painter is now aware of having mastered his own language, including its vocabulary and grammar. Into this language he translates reality, but this time his version is not a literal one; for, while that would be exact, it would be much less effective than an elegant transcription which brings a fresh vitality to the beauties of the original. Moreover he realizes that greater intensity can be achieved by conciseness, just as a single phrase of Tacitus is often more striking than a long disquisition (figure 194).

The Venetians were the first to discover that continuous gradations of values could be dispensed with. A few apt notations induce the eye—without the eye consciously realizing it—to supply whatever has been omitted. It would be extremely instructive to compare a fourteenth-century head—which a disciple of Giotto had modeled

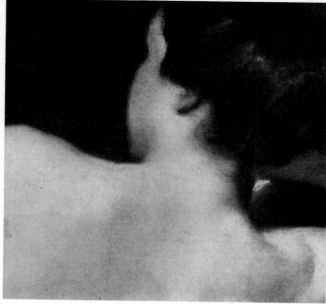

Photo Anderson

Brush strokes may be so free with respect to reality as to seem to contradict its fullnesses and its hollows.

184. - *VELAZQUEZ.* RECLINING VENUS (detail). National Gallery, London meticulously and, one might say, spherically, in accordance with the conventions still followed by certain Renaissance masters—with a face by Titian, in which distinct and separate touches of color mark the essentials of the relief. Each of these touches is rendered individually by a stroke of the brush, which thus recovers its freedom of expression.

The vehement Tintoretto boldly confines himself to a few brush strokes, which, seen at close quarters, are as distinct one from another on the canvas as clouds drifting in space separated by zones of air; and yet, when we look at the picture from a distance, everything falls into place, according to the scale of values, and we see only a marvelously modeled surface which has the tangibility of a compact mass that we might caress with our hands (figures 185 and 186).

PIGMENT AND BRUSHWORK.   Thus liberated from its servitude to visual reality, the paint can now be used to reveal its own qualities as well as those of the brushwork.

Pigment plays a double role. At a distance, when the spots of color merge on the retina, giving the mind free rein to reconstruct them, the viewer only perceives an illusion of reality; when he comes closer to savor the nature of his enjoyment, he

At the height of the Renaissance, the blended technique of a Florentine is contrasted with the discontinuous brushing of a Venetian.

185. - *TINTORETTO.* Head of an old man. Detail from THE CRUCIFIXION. 1565. Scuola San Rocco. Venice

186. - *BRONZINO.* Head of "Time." Detail from VENUS, CUPID, FOLLY, AND TIME. c. 1545. National Gallery, London

enters a new realm, the realm of painting proper.

The helmet in Rembrandt's *Man with a Gilt Helmet* (a portrait of the artist's brother) will arouse the enthusiasm of the layman for its wonderful rendering of the gleaming metal and the intricate jeweler's chasings. At close quarters, however, the illusion is dispelled; the pigment asserts itself to the exclusion of everything else. We marvel at the richness of its possibilities. Here it is smooth and slick like enamel, an effect which had been discovered by the primitives; there, twisted and contorted like flowing lava, it eddies, spurts, seethes. We can gaze at it endlessly, as at the thousand shapes assumed by foaming waves or a crackling fire. It holds us spellbound, as we are held on the banks of a stream that is sometimes clear as crystal, sometimes seething with currents; as we are held,

Photo Gaston Bernard

Photo Walter Steinkopf

From a distance, the material of a Rembrandt painting is identical with the object represented; close up, it becomes a substance which has been made fascinating, unknown.

187. - *Above:* REMBRANDT. MAN WITH A GILT HELMET. Museum, Berlin

188. - *At right:* ENLARGED DETAIL OF THE TEXTURE OF THE HELMET

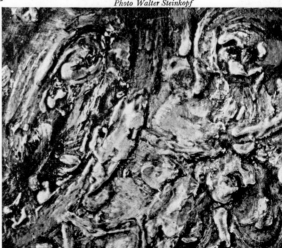

in winter, before a fireplace, watching the leaping flames and sparks flying up from the collapsing, ruddy logs (figures 187 and 188).

It is regrettable that Bachelard, who analyzed so marvelously the poetry imagery of the elements, should have neglected painting, this Protean medium that is capable of taking the form of everything outside it and at the same time of arousing pleasures which belong to it alone. Who has not lingered in front of a Chardin,

199

A magnified detail of a Chardin brings out its eleborate texture.

189. *CHARDIN.* SAYING GRACE (detail). The Louvre, Paris

forgetting the pipe, the kitchen pot, or the blue chest shown in the painting, to marvel at the paint itself, which intoxicates the eye? The eye, too, develops appetites and learns what will gratify them; it becomes fond of the oily, thick substance which, as with ancient ceramics, cracks in the fullness of time, like a good wine that mellows with age. The pictorial substance is hard and enduring as a mineral, it is supple and pulpy as a plant, as alive and sensual as flesh (figures 189 and 193).

It is alive, yes, for it has received its impetus from the human hand, which leaves its imprint. It is not merely matter, it is frozen motion, a motion that is a thought. The hand remains in it thanks to the brushwork, which can be emphasized now that the touch of color has recovered its autonomy.

The lover of athletic contests does not attend them merely in order to learn the results of the competition. He follows the spectacle with attention because he enjoys the manner in which a certain athlete wins. Watching a fencing match, he almost forgets it is a competition and becomes engrossed in the swift, precise, and elegant motions of the duelists with their foils. The same is true of painting, in which the competition is between the artist and nature. It is important that the artist be able to strike his target; if he could not do so he would be merely parodying virtuosity. But the motions by which he achieves such a result are as valuable in themselves as the final thrust of the *torero* is for the *aficionado*. This thrust may be merely correct or extremely skillful; it may be dazzling or deeply moving.

If the artist does not deliberately remove his traces (as did a certain archbishop, who, according to Saint-Simon, had his gardeners remove the footprints he left behind him when walking, so infatuated was he with the perfection of his paths), the brush strokes serve as a faithful and legible record of the creative act, testifying to its quality, certainty, facility, intensity, power of renewal, passion—one is tempted to say, its spirit. It bestows the permanence that the work itself possesses on that momentary flash of creativity (figures 190 to 193).

At this point we have gone beyond the problem of plastic form, and come close to that of expression. For the pigment is twofold by nature: through its substance, it partakes of the spatial composition of the picture, and the effects that can be drawn from it; through the brushwork with which it is applied, it casts light on the artist and on what he reveals of himself in his work.

THE MAGIC OF THE HANDLING. An infinite variety of techniques prevailed from the eighteenth century on, after the painter had won the right not to adhere strictly to his model. While mediocre artists, those lacking in personality, were unable to turn this new freedom to account, exceptional talents joyfully took possession of the new means of expansion.

To the casual glance, a portrait by Frans Hals may appear indistinguishable from one by Verspronck with respect to the pose, the general appearance, and even the model; but the trained eye will at once perceive, in the painted surface of the Hals, an animation, a secret sparkle, a kind of fermentation indicative of intense vitality. Seen at close quarters, the forms, the features so submissive to their real models in the other painting, break apart, explode, become transformed into active forces. The pictorial space is traversed by a continuous crackle of brush strokes, coming together and dispersing.

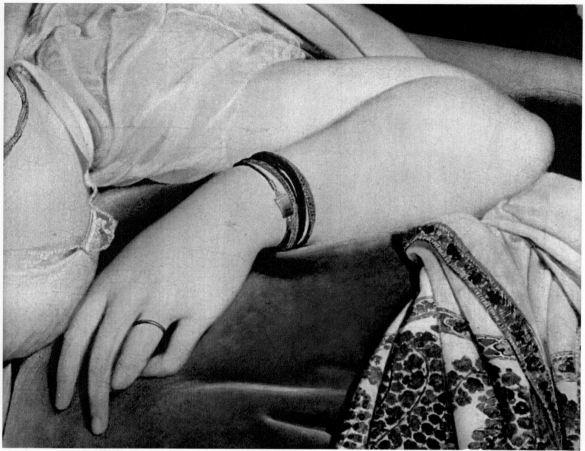

Photo Laboratory of The Louvre, Paris

*The great masters provide us with an infinite variety of treatments
—smooth, granular, nervous, and so on....*

190. - *INGRES.* Left hand of MADAME RIVIÈRE. The Louvre,
Paris

The marvelous thing about this violent
eruption of paint, which might have resulted in
incoherence, is that in the end it is always
organized; with an infallibility which is the
mark of the great painter, the paint never
interferes with the final suggestion but rein-
forces it with an unsuspected throb of life.

I have just referred to fencing; we have an
example of it here. The brush strokes evoke a
flashing wrist, infinitely flexible, producing a

191. - *VERMEER.* YOUNG WOMAN IN BLUE (detail). Museum,
Dresden

Photo Alinari-Giraudon

192. - *FRANS HALS.* The hand of a regent in GOVERNORS OF THE OLD MEN'S HOME. Frans Hals Museum, Haarlem

scintillation of accents that are never wasted; each one hits its target, achieving the intended visual shock. Unlike his predecessors, who attempted to copy exactly the slightest inflection of reality, Hals, wallowing in his freedom, leaves the purely optical reconstruction of it until the moment it is perceived by the viewer (figure 192).

We are thus confronted once again with the problem of life in painting, no longer from the point of view of its faithful representation, but from that of the aesthetic pleasures it may procure for us. As I have noted, movements are no

193. - *CHARDIN.* SAYING GRACE (detail).
The Louvre, Paris

longer merely *represented*; they are now an integral part of the painting itself, of its structure (cf. pp. 148 ff.).

Art historians have shown little concern with what I call the "pace" of a painting. This idea may seem paradoxical. And yet it is self-evident in the works; speed is perceptible in accents or lack of accents, in the gentleness or vehemence of the brushwork. There are paintings as motionless as stagnant water, limpid pools of reflected light, which nothing threatens to disturb. There are others in which the caresses of the brush create an animation as subtle as a suppressed sigh. Still others crack at the seams like the ground when shaken by temblors. And there are paintings that heave or seethe like streams in which strong currents create eddies and whirlpools and spend themselves upon rocks.

The pace of a painting is inseparable from its rhythm. Hals, Rubens, and Fragonard are among the swiftest painters, but Hals is impetuous, imperious, abrupt; the powerful Rubens is like a tidal wave sweeping everything before it; Fragonard, more nervous, surges, foams, and, also like a wave, ends in a similar flourish.

Each of these painter's movements, so different one from another, communicates itself to the viewer, and by their effortlessness and perfection contribute to the pleasure given by the painting.

COLOR IS FINALLY RECOGNIZED.   And what about color? It, too, had been the servant of realism, contributing to the identification of the objects represented as well as indicating light. But color, too, can be detached from the surfaces it helps to define, and within the contours of which, working in close conjunction with the modeling, it was formerly confined. Impressionism taught it to do without these surfaces, to animate the whole composition through its own resources. And Dufy's brush even went further, taking malicious pleasure in disposing his hues in such a way that they no longer remain within the boundaries of the objects (plate V).

Actually, color is the element in painting most independent of realism. The unsophisticated regard color as an embellishment, granting it the right to all the vagaries and caprices that are denied to form and its instrument, line. For a long time one spoke of "correct" drawing, or "honest" drawing, whereas color was permitted the license of reverie and imagination.

This is accounted for by the fact that our sensory knowledge of reality is based on the experience of space; and intellectual concepts are also based on spatial analogies, as Bergson has shown. Our physical grasp of reality grows weaker as we leave the realm in which things are apprehended through their form and enter that in which they are perceived according to intensity and quality. "Clear and distinct" ideas are formed only by analogy to separations in space. Pure sensibility, on the other hand, is blurred; it consists of nothing but time.

For this reason, in rendering nature, painting sought support primarily from that which reminds the eye of its experience of space and, by the same token, links vision with touch. All else was not "reliable," and was distrusted. While form and mass can be measured, expressed in dimensions or proportions, and governed by them, color, unless it is confined within forms, can be appreciated as color only by the sensibility.

The closer we get to modern art, the less does the painter disguise his treatment. This Monet might almost have been painted by Matisse.

**194. - *MONET.* Vase of flowers. Detail from PORTRAIT OF MADAME GAUDIBERT. 1868. The Louvre, Paris

Because color does not easily submit to the rule of the senses allied with reason, because it tends rather to be governed by impressions, classical painting used it only with caution, and only as a means of ornamenting and strengthening the forms. Significantly, the writers of antiquity condemn it, rejecting it contemptuously as a crude pleasure of the barbarians. Pliny says proudly: "With only four colors, Apelles and others executed immortal works. Today, when India sends us the mud of its rivers, the bodies of its elephants and dragons, masterpieces are no longer created." It would be difficult to find a clearer indication that Mediterranean civilization regarded fondness for color as something alien to it, something Eastern. Similarly, Vitruvius writes: "Today only one thing is appreciated: brilliance of color. The painter's science is ignored." And Lucian observes: "A spectacle fit for the eyes of a barbarian.... The barbarians have less regard for what is beautiful than for what is rich." And he castigates them for their failure to appreciate "art, beauty, just proportions, and elegance of form."[1]

COLOR AND MUSIC.   Tolerated but kept within bounds by both realistic and "plastic" painting, color was in the end assigned to an uncertain realm not clearly belonging to the spatial arts, and which through a vague analogy is associated with music. Of this, language once again provides irrefutable evidence, by its frequent association of music and color. We speak of the "scale" of color values, of "loud" colors and "muted" colors, and the term "tone" applies both to color and music. We also speak of "colorful" music, of "dull" sounds, etc.

It is not surprising, then, that painters were soon granted the right to choose and mix colors at will, without reference to their disposition in nature. It was considered permissible that colors be arranged in such a way as to give pleasure to the eye, in other words, that they form harmonies (another musical term!). Later, it was discovered that colors could provide not only physical enjoyment but also an emotional gratification, an affective resonance (once again, as in music).

Color takes us into a purely sensory world to an even greater extent, in a way, than music; for the scale of sounds, as well as their organization into melodies, harmonies, and counterpoints, can be formulated with mathematical precision and subjected to rules. Color, despite numerous attempts to subject it to such measurements, has so far proved resistant to any system. It cannot be expressed as a formal proportion or a chord. Only a subjective appreciation can approach it.

Abhorred by "rationalists" who admit it only as an embellishment, color delights the "sensualists," to whom it opens out the magic universe of painting. This is the gist of the conflict between Ingres and Delacroix, a conflict that goes back to the Renaissance, to when the classical Mediterranean conception was revived and opposed to medieval conceptions. "Color adds ornament to painting," said Ingres, "but it is only painting's handmaiden." Whereas Delacroix noted down in his *Journal* (III, p. 391) certain thoughts that had come to him: "Colors are the music of the eyes; they combine like sounds.... Certain color harmonies produce sensations that even music cannot achieve."

The nineteenth-century painters, Delacroix in particular, realized these irrational

---

[1] These characteristic passages are quoted by Lionello Venturi, in his *History of Art Criticism* (French edition, Brussels, 1938, p. 66).

powers of color. In a famous passage the great Romantic painter says: "Who speaks of art speaks of poetry. There is no art without a poetic purpose. The pleasure provided by a painting is entirely different from that provided by a literary work. There is a kind of emotion peculiar to painting; nothing in literature gives an idea of it. There is an impression resulting from a certain arrangement of colors, light, shade, etc., which might be called the music of a picture. Even before you know what the picture represents—as when you enter a cathedral and are too far from a painting to see what its subject is—often you are captivated by this magic harmony." And although Delacroix goes on to say: "Occasionally the lines by themselves have this power because of their grandiose quality," color remains for him the principal medium (*Oeuvres littéraires*, I, p. 63).

Baudelaire, who certainly owed a great deal of his insight to the conversations he had had about art with Delacroix, discusses the same subject, in describing *The Entry of the Crusaders into Constantinople*. "It must be noted—and this is very important—that even seen at a remove too great to permit the subject to be identified, let alone analyzed, a painting by Delacroix leaves on the mind a rich impression, joyful or melancholy. It is as if the painting, like a sorcerer or a mesmerist, imposed its will from a distance. This singular phenomenon is due to the artist's mastery of color, the perfect accord among the tones, and the harmony (arrived at in advance in the painter's mind) between color and subject. It is as though this color ... were thinking for itself, independently of the objects it clothes. The admirable relations among his colors frequently make one dream of harmonies and melodies, and the impression left by his paintings is often almost musical."[1]

Thus we see that color acts directly on the sensibility, independently of all intelligible meaning. Color is no longer regarded as a mere adjunct of the drawing but as an autonomous factor in the art of painting, one which may be compared, in its effects, with music (plate VI).

COLOR AND EXPRESSION.   Color is the quintessence of the pictorial, just as form is the quintessence of the plastic. But color sweeps us along on the path we are following, which leads from the objectivity of realism to what will be the terminus of our journey of exploration, the subjectivity of expression, till we find ourselves in an entirely different country.

To be sure, line and volume, too, became detached from that reality which they had at first merely striven to reproduce exactly; an art arose that combined and har-

---

[1] It is interesting to note that Charles Blanc, who knew Delacroix, expressed similar ideas in a study published in *Le Temps* (May 6, 1881) when the paintings in the library of the Chamber of Deputies were being restored. He too may have been influenced by his conversations with the master: "Before knowing anything about the subject of the painting, the pantomime of the figures, the various roles they play, we anticipate the emotion we will feel, in such a way that if the picture were upside down it would still produce the intended impression, or at least would arouse the first intimations of it in the mind, like one of those preludes that prepare us for a solemn or light, a sad or triumphant melody, a funeral march or a gay tune."

The idea continued to be influential. We find it expressed by Matisse: "A work must carry its full significance within itself and impose it on the viewer before he knows its subject. When I see Giotto's fresco in Padua, I do not ask myself what particular scene from the life of Christ I have before me; rather, I grasp immediately the emotion it suggests, for it is in the lines, in the composition, in the color, and the title will merely confirm my impression." Matisse, however, makes the question a broader one, referring not merely to the expressive power of color but to that of the painting as a whole.

monized these two elements; but their suggestive, expressive powers were more restricted than those of color.

Color too had contributed to the rendering of natural appearance, though in a more subsidiary capacity; it had leagued itself with line and volume to organize the pictorial space, and had lent itself to the same plastic combinations.

The painter is well aware of the fact that colors are subject to a grammar of their own. They attract or repel one another; a balance of colors requires that the dominant tones should not remain isolated, that they should be echoed; and the optimum effect is achieved when the relaxation induced by a variety of colors helps us appreciate the unity of the whole. We recognize in this certain principles of plastic relations, which apply not only to color but also to line and to volume. An art which devoted itself to these relations more intensively than any other has done—i.e., Cubism (and its more uncompromising descendant, abstract art)—realized perfectly the interdependence of the two elements: the most accomplished works of Cubism are refined structures in which both form and color play a part, and are so closely involved with each other that often we cannot tell which of the two has the major role.

However, it is not in the plastic realm that color finds its true homeland, to which it summons us imperiously, and in which it deploys fully its most magical powers: this realm is that of the psyche.

To enter this realm now would require us to move directly from this chapter dealing with plastic considerations into a discussion of the expressive powers and the inner significance of painting. But the time has not yet come for that. We have still to study the crowning achievement of painting, the co-ordination of all the elements considered so far with a view to securing their full effectiveness. They must all be gathered into a single structure, in which they will reinforce one another, creating a foundation for the work which comes into being only after these elements are integrated into a single organism. Lessing once said (*Laocoön*, ch. xx) that plastic beauty results from the harmony of all the parts of a work that can be encompassed by a single glance. We may add that, at a deeper level, it results from the harmonious organization of its powers.

195. - *VERONESE.* CHRIST IN THE HOUSE OF LEVI. Accademia, Venice

CHAPTER FOUR

PAINTING IN SEARCH OF ITSELF: COMPOSITION AND TOTAL EFFECT

To give real existence to things which have re-
mained at the stage of intention in nature.

Goethe

THE visible elements of which a painting is composed—the lines and forms, medium and color—have gradually emerged; but the painting becomes an independent entity, unlike any other, only when these elements are integrated into a whole. This primary goal of artistic creation can be achieved only by means of the composition. Only then can we speak of the painting as a work of art, only then can it perform its vital function—that of revealing the secret of its invisible elements.

THE WORK OF ART CONCEIVED OF AS AN ORGANISM. It is doubtless to the credit of our era that it has realized more fully than any other that a work of art must not merely demonstrate the artist's skill or illustrate the application of an

209

Whereas in his study from nature Corot unified his painting solely by harmonizing the values...
196. - *COROT.* BRIDGE AT NARNI. Sketch. The Louvre, Paris

aesthetic doctrine, but must also *be*—that it must exist as an original entity, something that has never existed before and that has no existence outside itself.

The work of art is a "creation" not merely because it reveals new aesthetic or plastic values, but because, once it has been completed, it has the character of a little universe of its own. Each work of art involves a fresh and total act of creation, which is as likely to fail as to succeed.

Therein lies the danger of what the Germans call *Kunstwissenschaft*, "the science of art." In attempting to account for the work of art—to determine the historical and psychological laws that govern it—we are prone to forget that it also exists as an independent entity. To be sure, it is the fruit of a complex process of gestation; but a fruit must ripen and fall from the tree that has produced it and nourished it, before it can be truly savored and consumed, that is, before it can fulfill its destiny as far as we are concerned. A knowledge of botany does not help us to taste the fruit; we must bite into it.

"The science of art" tells us everything about this fruit except how it tastes; we can learn this only from experience. This is not to say that such a science serves no purpose. Every pleasure is enhanced by knowledge; but intellectual knowledge is significant in this case only if it extends the boundaries of sensory experience without

...on the canvas which he sent to the Salon he achieved unity by a balance of lines and masses that obliged him to introduce imaginary elements.

197. - *COROT*. BRIDGE AT NARNI. National Gallery of Canada

supplanting it; for only through the latter can we truly comprehend the nature of the thing before us.

This fruit must have a fertile soil from which the tree that bears it can extract the nourishment it requires; it must have a climate in which it can thrive; but above all it must have an inner core, something exclusively its own, around which the pulp, the flesh, the skin that sanctifies it as an isolated entity, will gradually form. All else is mere preparation, and leads to failure unless this *result* is achieved.

The problem was stated with particular clarity by Henri Focillon in his *Life of Forms in Art* (English translation, Wittenborn, Schultz, Inc., New York, 1948, pp. 2 f.); "How best can we define something that lies so far beyond the reach of time and yet is subjected to time? Is this prodigy merely a simple phenomenon of cultural activity in a chapter of general history? Or is it something added to our universe—an entirely new universe, with its own laws, materials, and development, with its own physics, chemistry, and biology, with its own engendering of a separate humanity?... In other words, a work of art is not the outline or the graph of art as an activity; it is art itself. It does not design art; it creates it. Art is made up, not of the artist's intentions, but of works of art. The most voluminous collection of commentaries and memoirs, written by artists whose understanding of the problems of form is fully equaled by their understanding of words, could never replace the meanest work of art. In order to exist at all, a work of art must be tangible. It must renounce thought, must become dimensional, must both measure and qualify space. It is in this very turning outward that its inmost principle resides. It lies under our eyes and under our hands as a kind of extrusion upon a world which has nothing whatsoever in common with it save the pretext of the image in the so-called 'arts' of imitation.''

The work of art comes into existence only at the moment when it is self-sufficient, when explanations are no longer needed to justify it, but only to comment on it, to define its true scope. To achieve such self-sufficiency, it must be an organism, that is to say, a living unit composed of diverse elements brought together to fulfill a common function. This living homogeneity can be proved only by the impossibility of severing any part from the whole or even of altering any part without affecting the whole.

The painting achieves unity through the composition, and the composition is valid only if it brings about this indissoluble solidarity, not only among all the visible elements, but also among all the invisible elements that nourish the life of a painting. It results, in other words, from a convergence of the plastic with the intellectual, the sensory warp with the mental woof, the many and inextricably interwoven threads which constitute the mysterious fabric of the work of art.

Any artist who is unaware of this will fail dramatically. Charles Delaberge, the early nineteenth-century landscapist admired so much by the young Théodore Rousseau, is a case in point. His precocious gifts justified the highest expectations. Everything was within his reach, but he fell under the spell of reality and his own capacity for reproducing it: the thousand little details of the outside world, brought to life solely by his skill in capturing them, proliferated endlessly under his eye and brush; the tide of them kept mounting, breaking the artificial boundaries of which every work of art is comprised, and at last submerged the painter himself. "To give substance to a tone,'' Delaberge said, "to strengthen a harmony, thousands of forms of vegetation and myriads of beings must be conjured up from the earth. You will see later ... when you come to love life to the point of losing your mind, how gratifying it is to look into the very souls of the infusoria.''

It is this submission of the artist to external reality, which dissipates the energies he must seek to control and bring together, that Delacroix warned so passionately against when he said that the artist must above all be able to make sacrifices. On April 16, 1846, he wrote to Champrosay: "Only the greatest artists are capable of endowing their works with the utmost possible unity, so that the details not only do not work against it, but are absolutely indispensable to it.''[1]

---

[1] *Oeuvres littéraires*, I, p. 110. Diderot, in his "Salon of 1763,'' had made the same point in trying to justify the technique of Loutherbourg, Casanova, and Chardin, who bewildered him somewhat by their inclusiveness. "Nothing is more difficult,'' he says, "than to combine this meticulousness, this concern for detail, with what is called 'the broad manner.' If the brush strokes are discrete and must be perceived separately, *the effect of a whole is lost*. What artistry is required to avoid this pitfall!''

A great critic of the next century, Théophile Gautier, in his *Histoire du Romantisme* (p. 215), observed of Delacroix, possibly recalling his conversations with him: "Everything is held together, everything is connected, forming a magical whole, no part of which can be removed or displaced without causing the edifice to collapse.'' Gautier praised the Romantic master for a quality he found also in Rembrandt: "this profound, indissoluble unity.''

This point is of the greatest importance. The gradual labor which, beginning with an idea, a sketch, a trial version, eventuates in the work, must aim at unity and solidity at each of the levels of artistic creation. At the level of realism it must sort out and bring into harmony all the details taken from nature; at the level of plastic form, it must unify the visible elements that comprise the structure of the painting; at the poetic level, it must integrate the spiritual elements that permeate it. Finally—and this is the crowning achievement—all the resources utilized at each of the three levels must be made to work together in such a way that only a single entity, the painting itself, emerges at the end.

This labor of fashioning the final unity carries with it a danger, however. If the unity it results in is too imperious, the painting as a whole will be impoverished. Unity must be attained by a seeming contradiction: through the development of a richness found only in diversity. Montesquieu made, on this subject, a profound observation, which may provide us with a key to the art of composition: "Things we see one after another must have variety; those we take in at a single glance must have symmetry."

The artist must not only provide the music for each of his instruments to play; he must rigorously subject each one to the direction of the conductor, who makes all the separate voices of the orchestral instruments combine into a single voice, a single song rising out of the harmony of all of them. The trained ear will be able to distinguish the melody played by each instrument, and to appreciate its timbre and sonority, at the same time never losing its awareness of the total impression produced by them all. Thus, once again, we see art attempting to forge a bond between contradictories: between the striving for unity, on the one hand, and for the boundless, on the other.

COMPOSITION THROUGH FORM. Nothing is more instructive for an understanding of composition than to follow a painting from the preliminary sketch —made directly from life and which the artist uses as his point of departure—to the finished work, in which he fuses together the contradictory elements in the sketch by means of his intelligence and sensibility.

The two versions of the *Bridge at Narni* are a familiar example. In the study, Corot, with marvelous skill, transforms his initial impression of the landscape before his eyes into a jewel of luminosity, in which the effect is achieved unconsciously, and yet how subtly, by the spontaneous harmonizing of the tonal values, by the sustained quality of the emotion, by the magic of light. The finished painting, which was exhibited at the Salon of 1827, is governed by more intellectual and more conscious concerns (figures 196 and 197).

Without doubt, we will prefer the first version, in which the unity is achieved miraculously, by purely instinctive means; but we find it easier to understand the mechanisms operating in the second. In it, in accordance with the teachings of the academy, Corot aims primarily at a well-calculated balance of lines and masses. He chooses as his guiding plastic theme a form suggested by his subject matter: the projection of the river bank on the right, which describes a parabola. The other bank lends itself to the development of this theme, in fact, already hints at it: it will suffice to place a tall tree there, whose shape prolongs the curve of the bank. Thus, like ripples in a pool that keep being repeated in wider and wider circles, a sequence of similar and interrelated motifs runs from one end of the painting to the other. Along the left bank a road, imagined by the artist, begins to describe a third curve, still broader, which is echoed symmetrically by the clump of trees.

At this point Corot becomes aware of the fact that a too rigid unity threatens to become mechanical. To avoid such a result, he turns the road he has invented toward the lower left-hand corner of the painting, thus forming a counter-curve, the reverse of the one that might have been expected, but still in keeping with the general spirit of the composition: it creates an element of surprise.

Frequently the plastic organization of a painting is based not on an element borrowed from nature but on the pictorial space itself. There are countless examples of this. The figure of the Virgin in the *Virgin and Child* by the Master of Moulins is placed at the center of a luminous circle, which, being set within the rectangle inscribed by the frame, raises a problem analogous to the one the architect has to solve when he sets a cupola upon the square formed by its supporting walls. He seeks to effect the transition from one shape to the other by means of pendentives and squinches, and the stone obeys his command. The painter, however, is compelled to perform such an operation on an image taken from nature, which resists him. He therefore adapts his design to it. The angels hovering over the Madonna can, thanks to their suspended position and their fluttering wings, serve as a plausible means of effecting the transition between the circle within which the central figure is placed and the rectangular outline of the frame. The color helps in achieving

Photo Giraudon

When the Master of Moulins tackles the problem of a circular composition inserted into a rectangular space...

198. - *MASTER OF MOULINS.* **THE VIRGIN AND CHILD** (detail)

214

this: it encloses the Virgin within successive circles, in the various hues of the rainbow, which grow fainter as they move outward (figures 198 and 199).

The illusionistic effect of depth created by perspective can be used, in the composition, in conjunction with pictorial surface. The lines of perspective may serve to create the illusion of distance, seeming as they do to lead inward toward the horizon; while, on the picture surface, they buttress the plastic structure. Illusionistic effects and composition, instead of being at cross purposes, will then work in collaboration. The most famous example of such co-operation is Leonardo da Vinci's *Last Supper*: the vanishing point coincides with the principal subject, the head of Christ; thus the lines of the rafters can be seen both as an inverted pyramid with the head at the apex, and as parallels converging upon the vanishing point in an imaginary distance (figures 208 and 209).

Veronese, in his *Christ in the House of Levi*, carries this duality to its ultimate extreme. He introduces two balustrades which are seemingly in the picture plane, but which at the same time form diagonals leading toward the center at which the lines of perspective meet. Such refinements in the construction result in an impression of perfection, hence of beauty (figure 195).

Photo Alinari

...he faces and solves it in the same way as the Byzantine architects decorate a dome on a square base.

199. - DOME OF THE MARTORANA. Palermo. 1143

COMPOSITION THROUGH MOVEMENT.   Any given element of the painting, whether representational or purely formal, can provide a basis for its organization. The general structure may be dynamic or static; the lines on which it is based do not have to be those which define forms, but may equally well be those which indicate the direction of the forces suggested by the action represented.

Rubens' *Allegory of War* is an example of a dynamic composition. It is animated by a single impetuous movement, which begins at the left, with the gesture of the woman attempting to hold back the warrior but helplessly dragged in his wake.

It is continued in the surge forward of the same male figure, propelled by Discord,

Rubens is fond of compositions which run from one side to the other of his canvas.
200. - *RUBENS.* ALLEGORY OF WAR. Pitti Palace, Florence

whose outstretched arms extend the line of the woman's arm. Then, to avoid the danger of excessive regularity, the artist gives the basic movement a twist upward, toward the right-hand corner, so that the total effect is that of an epic upheaval, a cry of protest rising to the sky.

Rubens' wealth of invention does not stop there. As he often does, he repeats and gives emphasis to this lateral thrust with another, along a different trajectory. The axes of the figures in the painting progress from the vertical to the horizontal, the movement being that of a collapsing fan, similar to what we have seen in Bruegel (figure 129). In the Rubens, the pivot of this movement is in the lower left-hand corner, at the base of the vertical column. The allegorical figure whose raised arms express despair begins the trend away from the perpendicular, which becomes more marked in the nude female figure and the warrior who is breaking away from her. His raised arm, holding the shield, establishes the diagonal, and the furious figure of Discord all but bisects the superior angle. The clouds of smoke and the group of terrified mothers approach the horizontal, along which is extended the prone figure at the lower right. While the first movement ends in an epic thrust upward, the second movement ends in the fall downward, evoking death (figure 200).

We have said that the line that comes closest to embodying life is the curve. Rubens often bases his compositions on curves—but never on fixed, closed curves that suggest the monotonously circular, which is merely camouflaged immobility

216

("the center of the wheel where speed is slumbering," Cocteau has said). His curves are open and irregular, of the kind that can be expressed by geometrical progressions such as the spiral, sign of an infinitely

201. - *At right:* *RUBENS.* VIRGIN WITH ANGELS. The Louvre, Paris

Occasionally Rubens based his compositions on movement swirling through the picture space like a tornado.

202. - *Below:* *RUBENS.* BATTLE OF THE AMAZONS.
Pinakothek, Munich

Photo Braun

Photo Flammarion

It is the dramatic play of lights and shadows that creates expressive effects in the works of Rembrandt.
203. - *REMBRANDT.* DESCENT FROM THE CROSS BY TORCHLIGHT. Etching

ERROR

218

expanding form. A notable example is his *Virgin with Angels* in the Louvre. There, the Virgin's breast is the generating point of a curve that broadens continuously, passing through the body of the Child Jesus, is drawn up past the cherubs holding the crown, then, gathering force, goes swirling through the clusters of infants and runs off the canvas into space at the upper left-hand corner. According to legend, the Milky Way was thus formed in outer space, from a drop of the precious liquid that spurted from Juno's breast; and Rubens treated this subject in another painting, where the curve suggests the path of a comet. Here the curve, uncoiling like a spring, suggests the swirling of nebulae, of worlds in the process of formation (figure 201).

His *Battle of the Amazons*, too, displays looping curves in the frenzied rotating movement that surges across the canvas. The arch of the bridge seems to be there only to remind us of the fixed, geometric form the curve would assume if it consented

Photo Bulloz

Rubens was fond of diagonal arrangements because of their instability. Here the diagonal emphasizes the effects of weight conveyed by the muscular efforts of the figures.

204. - *RUBENS.* THE RAISING OF THE CROSS. Sketch for the ceiling of the Jesuit center at Antwerp. The Louvre, Paris

to return to immobility. All the more powerful, by contrast, is the sight of the charging horses, carried forward by the very imbalance of their rearing positions, whose tilt is repeated across the canvas, preparing the way for the fall, the violent collapse at the right, where the wave, having spent its force, curls over and recedes in its own foam! The whole painting is swept along in the wake of this movement, which refuses to surrender to the perfection of the circle, with its eternal beginning-again, which keeps breaking out of it, as in the centrifugal thrust of the horse at the right, which has unseated its rider.

Rubens' rich genius, however, also owed much to Italian classical sources; and, faithful to the principle of unity in diversity, he discreetly suggests a vertical axis, which in another kind of composition might have served as the pivot for a fixed structure as well as for a symmetrical arrangement. Here, by merely hinting at such a point, he emphasizes all the more strongly the irregularity of this mad swirling. At the center of the bridge is the body of a slain combatant, whose arm, hanging down, interrupts the curve of the structure, as it interrupts, by its silence, the tumult of battle. This is no mere anecdotal detail, as some might think; its perfectly central and vertical position, its straightness, are a reminder to us that no matter how madly a pendulum may swing, it has its fixed point. It was by instinct, no doubt, rather than by cold calculation, that Rubens, this master of composition, placed at the heart of his work the small contrast which provides a point of repose and emphasizes the dynamic character of the whole (figure 202).

Life is more than crude energy released in action. The visible world extends into the invisible, and finds its echo in spiritual meanings. Movement, much more than form, is evocative. Rubens again provides us with an example, in his *Raising of the Cross*, a study for which is in the Louvre. The cross is shown at the moment when its rigid line describes a diagonal across the painting—a type of composition often found in Rubens. Though the diagonal is a straight line, it is unstable, its raised end being weighed down, suggesting the possibility of falling and thus returning to the horizontal: it is a Baroque form par excellence. This formal consideration is closely linked with another, psychological one. The weight of the beam is stressed by the muscular effort being made by the executioners, who are straining their legs, torsos, and arms to lift the resistant mass, and thus emphasizing its movement away from the horizontal. The body of Jesus is luminous against the black sky, whose darkness adds still more to the weight of the cross. The impression received by the eye is that the true burden, too heavy for the human powers striving to lift it, is in the immobility of the crucified Christ, who alone can dispel the massive darkness (figure 204).

A gratuitous literary observation? Not in the least! The forms and colors impress themselves on our sensibility as directly as a seal. The explanation is not a conjecture as to what we might feel, but a confirmation of what we do feel, in spite of ourselves. We are as powerless to resist the suggestion as the bell is to refuse to vibrate the instant it is struck by its clapper.

COMPOSITION THROUGH LIGHT. In *The Raising of the Cross*, the effect of light is inseparable from that of line. Can light, too, serve as the basis for the composition?

If Rubens is the master of life, Rembrandt is the master of light. His *Descent from the Cross* provides us with an example of this.

Everything in this engraving is ordered according to the distribution of the light. From the pitch dark of the background emerges a long, flowing white shape, the shroud, containing the sagging, livid corpse. The vertical line of the cross, the slightly inclined ladder, and the line of the shroud, which is extended along the leg of the man receiving the body of Christ, are in the same fanlike arrangement referred to above, the pivot in this case being situated at the top, at the upper left. The diagonal outlined by the lights forms the external vector of this fan; it then traces exactly the edge of the hillock, beyond which the shadows begin, and leads finally to a second luminous area, where it comes to rest—the horizontal of another shroud on a stretcher waiting for the dead Christ (figure 203).

The balance between these two major concentrations of light, set against a background made homogeneous by the constant and evenly matched play of light and shadow, constitutes both the unity and the diversity of the engraving. The light replaces—or rather becomes—the lines, the forms, and the movements.

Once again, by virtue of the reversible quality of all great works, the visible world is echoed by the invisible and a significance results which is completely contained in the optical impression. To express it in words, we have merely to describe this impression. In the midst of the conflict between the hope suggested

Van Gogh's picture space is organized by the brush strokes which deepen the perspective and send the clouds scudding across the sky.

205. - *VAN GOGH*. FIELD UNDER A STORMY SKY. Collection V.W. van Gogh, Laren

Photo Vizzavona

by the light, and the horror conjured up by the darkness, the body of Christ sliding helplessly down the winding sheet proclaims: "It is finished." Nothing remains save the inextinguishable glow of this light which dispels the dark. Into this glow a hand reaches up, ready to receive the head of Christ; it is as eloquent as the hand of a drowning man rising for the last time above the water.

Thus, in every work of genius, the three constitutive elements of painting— realism, plastic form, expression—are held together, merged, welded into a whole; and it is through the composition that the artist brings about this merger, by virtue of which the work comes into being. The term "composer" would long since have been applied to painters as well as to musicians if the public at large had not been obsessed with a confused notion of realism, to which it adheres stubbornly and which makes it turn a deaf ear to interpretation.

It would be possible to show in detail how each of the other elements in the painting can collaborate in its composition. For instance: the brushwork is inscribed movement, a scattering of arrows indicating a direction; it can thereby serve as a means of emphasizing a contour or a form, i.e., of organizing the pictorial space. Every Van Gogh provides irrefutable proof of this (figure 205).

And as for color, by virtue of its double allegiance to the realm of nuance, of modulation, and that of forms, it lends itself with equal ease to sensory, musical combinations and to intellectual, architectural ones. According to his temperament and the occasion, the artist uses color in the former or the latter way, giving his works a unity based either on emotion or on logic. There are masters of harmony, and there are masters of counterpoint.

The latter is the particular province of the Classical painters, who carefully calculate repetitions and echoes of tones, the order and balance of patches of color, the alternation of warm accents with cold. Ghirlandaio's *Virgin and Child with Sts. Dominic, Michael, John the Baptist, and John the Evangelist*, in the Munich Pinakothek, is constructed like a fugue: its theme is a joining of blue and red; its countertheme repeats this in blue-gray and copper; the sphere, behind the Virgin, picks up the two themes in a stretto, with the blue and red wings of the cherubs, and the copper and blue-gray of the two circles. The robes of the angels in the upper corners repeat the colors of the outside and inside of the cloak worn by the saint kneeling at the lower right. And the counterpoint of colors appears again where the two diagonal lines of construction intersect, at the center of the circles which surround the Virgin and Child. The intellect delights in this exact science (plate VII).

Velázquez, conversely, is a master of harmony. His *Infanta Maria Margarita* is only a variation on the basic chord of rose and silver, which has a piercing voluptuous quality, hitherto undreamed of. The variations he achieves on it are dazzling, and the unity of the painting imprints itself on our hearts rather than on our minds, by virtue of its unique resonance and the delightful emotions it arouses (plate VIII).

It is not necessary, however, to go through all the instruments of the orchestra; our main purpose is to define the result achieved by their collaboration.

COMPOSITION: CLASSICAL AND BAROQUE. At each stage of this survey certain fundamental truths become plain—truths which we glimpsed at the outset,

but which become richer with each reappearance. In studying composition, we have stressed the fact that two major groups, the Classical painters and the Baroque painters, divide the history of art between them.

The former are concerned exclusively with static formulations that emphasize the permanent aspects of the work, and pass over in silence everything that might suggest the feeling of mobility, of possible development, i.e., of transformation; they base themselves primarily on form, and banish everything threatening to disturb it, to plunge it back into the original chaos from which it was rescued by the work of the intellect.

The second group take the opposite course, striving to catch the intoxication of life, the continuous and inexorable movement that creates time and is created by time. Form, for these painters, is a barrier that man has erected to stop this flow, to nullify it, to prevent it from disturbing and destroying the structures he builds. The Baroque artists are bent on taking advantage of this life force, reveling in its headlong pace and at the same time subjecting it to their discipline. Of this rushing life they demand intensity, which serves to enhance their own; but they also impose on it their own lucidity, so that they may guide and direct it at will. Occasionally relaxing, however, they let themselves be swept away on its intoxicating tide.

But both groups—the infantry, as it were, of the followers of plastic form, with its compact and clear-cut units, and the passionate cavalry of the devotees of vital movement—take orders from the superior strategy of composition, which mobilizes all the resources of art to attain the final goal.

This divergency of means coupled with an identity in guiding principles may be illustrated by a comparison between a master of Classicism, Raphael, and a master of Romanticism (one incarnation of the Baroque), Delacroix—a comparison which will reveal a superficial contrast and a fundamental similarity.

CLASSICAL UNITY.   The art of Raphael without doubt reached its height in the Vatican fresco of the *Disputà*. The perfect illusion of space in depth is achieved here by means that are in complete accord with the demands of plastic form (figures 206 and 207).

The wall on which this great fresco is painted is topped by the regular curve of the vaulted ceiling. For this reason, in the lower part of the painting, which rests on a rectilinear base, depth is suggested by an arrangement of straight lines, converging in perspective; in the upper part, it is suggested in a different way: the semicircular edges bend inward from the vertical plane of the wall and establish a horizontal plane—the "bench" of clouds on which are seated the celestial witnesses of the scene, the patriarchs, prophets, etc.

The composition as a whole carries out this basic design. At the bottom, it ranges the crowd of earthly figures about on the ground; at the top, it takes its cue from the curve of the rim, which seems to be centered upon the half-circle surrounding Christ, the Virgin, and St. John. And this circular form gives rise to the smaller circles that join in with the earth—first the circle with the dove of the Holy Spirit; then the still smaller circle surrounding the Holy Sacrament, which is placed at the very center of this symphony.

In Raphael's large frescoes the composition is conceived as a harmonious and intelligible whole.

206. - *Above: RAPHAEL.* DISPUTA. Vatican

207. - *At left:* Diagram of the composition

Though of minimal compass, the Holy Sacrament becomes the prime reality in the painting, that which serves both as the center of organization and as the center of interest. Indeed, it is toward it that the whole human, earthly world tends physically by the perspective lines clearly marked in the pattern of the floor, of which it is the vanishing point and the point of concentration; morally, by the common aspiration which makes it the focal point of all the looks and gestures.

224

The Disputà develops a theme formulated by Leonardo da Vinci in his Last Supper, where all the lines, by their convergence, and the geometric figures, by their symmetry, lead the eye to the Christ.

208. - *Above: LEONARDO DA VINCI.* THE LAST SUPPER. Church of Santa Maria delle Grazie, Milan

209. - *At left:* Diagram of the composition

The same circle serves also as the focal point of the divine world. The vast dome of light behind the figure of Christ seems to extract from its substance, like the amber globule which contains all the aromatic juices of the tree, the sphere in which the dove of the Holy Spirit is contained, and from which as a final distillation flows the Eucharistic Host. The three successive circles are inscribed into a large V whose point is at the center of the Host; one of the wings of this V even follows the line of the staff held by St. John.

Thus, in a marvelously legible visual language, the quintessence of the divine substance and the surge of earthly matter toward it are conjoined, in the end, at a single, almost abstract point, the throbbing heart of the immense fresco.

A similar compositional device had been used earlier by Leonardo in his *Last Supper*. In this fresco the figure of Christ is situated at the intersection of the vertical axis of symmetry and the horizontal axis of the table, under the central window, the only one with an arc above it, Christ being at the center of this arc.

Here, as in Raphael's painting, Christ is placed at the vanishing point where all the lines of perspective meet, and is the focus of the passionate and humanly varied attention of the Apostles. Here, too, physical realities, plastic conceptions, and deeply felt emotions are miraculously joined in the work (figures 208 and 209). It might be—and actually has been—thought that Raphael merely elaborated upon the magnificent conception of the earlier master. But he added an important feature, deliberately introducing what seems to be a compositional flaw, a break in the unity of the work: he split the composition into two parts, confining the celestial figures to the upper section and the earthly figures to the lower, and separating the two by a blank space, which ought to keep them apart. But it is precisely at this point that he brilliantly asserts his mastery, by connecting the two separate realms by means of a link, which is tenuous in appearance but actually essential. The Eucharistic Host bridges the gulf, or rather occupies it, and serves to effect a miraculous convergence of the two incommensurable worlds. The history of art records no other work in which the resources of painting are so perfectly organized and so completely at the command of the artist's intention.

ROMANTIC UNITY: THE WORK IN PROGRESS.   Delacroix's studies for his *Battle of Nancy* provide us with an example of the various stages in a Romantic artist's method of composition. Here, too, the subject is not a mere pretext, an unimportant anecdote, but the central core around which the work is organized.

In their hasty reaction against the errors of the past, our contemporaries think it necessary to do away with the subject, which is actually a major resource of art. To be sure, it must be condemned when the artist uses it as a substitute for plastic and pictorial values. But when it is the seed around which the whole work is formed organically; when it has been chosen as embodying a state of mind which the artist wants to express; when, above all, after it is chosen it becomes no longer a narrative but an image, the artist, in order to define this image more clearly, being concerned only with the forms and colors that will serve as the appropriate outer garment of his thought—then the subject need no longer be defended or justified: it is an essential means of pictorial creation. A liability when it is nothing but a fabrication of the mind, it is restored to its full significance when it serves to "crystallize," i.e., to give settled and definite form to the sensations, emotions, and ideas that constitute the work.

This is precisely the function the subject has for Delacroix. If the Romantic artist is one who renounces the pursuit of serenity, permanence, and perfection behind the veil of transience, if he is on the contrary one who glories in life itself, in all its frenzied, intense, and precarious movement, then Delacroix is a Romantic. How intoxicated he is by the spectacle of human force confronted with death and about to be annihilated by it! He experiences a similar excitement in imagining voluptuous young women threatened by slaughter, as he portrayed them in his *Scio, Sardanapalus, Crusaders*—in each case, we witness a dialogue between intensity and precariousness.

Nor is the subject of his *Battle of Nancy* merely an anecdote he ran across in some book, and then paraphrased with his brush. It is an echo, suddenly arising out of history, of the painter's own obsessions, as follows: Duke Charles the Bold has

Delacroix sketches the general theme of the painting he plans, indicating the expressive motions of his figures, but even at this early stage he seeks to formulate the main outlines of the structure.

210, 211, 212. - *DELACROIX.* Three studies for THE BATTLE OF NANCY. Collection Clément-Carpeaux, Paris

attained the height of his power; on the foundations laid down by his predecessors, he has erected what will soon be the greatest nation of the West; he is on the verge of vanquishing his rivals and achieving his proud ambition. One battle, however, one blow of a lance, is to prove sufficient to abolish all this, to relegate him, a corpse abandoned with many others to the chilly night and the wolves, to the anonymity of oblivion.

Delacroix begins with realistic elements, seeking documentation that will give verisimilitude to what at this point is nothing but a dream. On a page of his sketch-book he draws the outline of the battlefield, the softly surging hills on the horizon, the silhouette of a chapel in the distance. In a few hasty strokes he sketches in the cavalry charging the enemy forces (figure 210).

Other sketches (which, like this one, were once the property of the great sculptor Carpeaux) gradually develop his theme. A few strokes in watercolor re-create the atmosphere of this fatal hour. The approaching night darkens a sky already suffused with storm clouds (figure 211). Step by step, the scene which is to be the focal point of the drama takes shape. An ordinary horseman chosen to be the instrument of fate unseats the Duke by a blow of his lance. The sketch shows the two figures, armed centaurs, one leaning forward to deliver the death blow, the other about to succumb to it. This page of the sketchbook contains all these elements, but they are still scattered; they have still to be brought together in a suggestive arrangement.

Before tackling this problem, Delacroix makes some important changes in the principal group. In the preceding sketch, he drew the attacking horse in the most natural, most classical position: its forelegs stiffened for the sudden stop, its head and gaze turned toward its adversary. Now, in a new sketch, the horse has its head thrown back, as though the victorious animal were shying away from its triumph. The effect is quite different and singularly suggestive: it shows the unconscious fear that assails the animal at the moment it is carrying out the implacable decree of fate. It no longer dares to look, as though stricken by panic, and the horror of the drama becomes palpable (figure 212).

This is no doubt a deliberate effect, fully realized by Delacroix; but at the same time, the changes work a considerable improvement in terms of plastic form. In the original position the expressive quality of the parallel between the line of the lance and the braced legs of the mount was dissipated by the different direction of the legs of the horseman, one of which, the right, was hidden. In the later sketch, the blow aimed at the Duke is emphasized by the multiplication of lines all leading in a single direction, all the contradictory or attenuating elements having been eliminated. Delacroix has simultaneously strengthened both the plastic form and the expression.

Now finally he makes a study on canvas of the composition as a whole. The victorious army is advancing from the right, charging the Burgundians, who are shown scattering under the impact and disappearing across the plain. And what of the principal group? A Classical artist would have placed it at the center of the composition. But Delacroix knows that the conquerors' irresistible drive sweeps everything before it, carrying the whole composition along with it. The protagonists of the drama are therefore moved to the left, a shift which embodies the dynamic force of the action (figure 213).

ROMANTIC UNITY: THE FINISHED WORK.   Let us now examine the painting, begun in 1831, as it was exhibited three years later at the Salon (figure 214). The composition has now found its definitive form. The victorious army, its horses and men, press forward, impatient, forming a solid moving mass, bristling with lances and oriflammes which bow before the wind of victory, like the masts of a ship. This moving mass is wedge-shaped, tapering off gradually, and its sharp point, like that of an arrow, makes contact with the opposing mass, a blurred black mist partly hidden by a rise in the ground, and already dissolving in rout. Like debris left on the shore as the tide recedes, the wounded are shown crawling away, or giving up the struggle and surrendering to death. But they too are held firmly in check by the artist; they form a kind of triangle whose apex points toward the place where the two armies meet.

The immense plain serves as a backdrop for this tumultuous scene. The earth, indifferent to the struggle, seems to slumber, silent beneath the snow. All the horizontal and incidental lines of the plain are smoothed out, as are those of the somber, drifting clouds in the livid sky. Everything in this background is blurred, without light or color, a soft downy blanket thrown like a shroud over this macabre turmoil. Nothing, not even the banners, rises above the line of the horizon, which hovers over all the agitation of men, and extinguishes it. Both the human and the natural elements—the former violent and the latter impassive—in the painting tend equally toward death, and proclaim it.

The deafening noise of battle and the silence of the landscape somehow cancel each other out, and our awakened senses wait for a cry of murder. And, sure enough, one breaks forth, struck like a spark from this human tension, and cleaving the silence of nature. At the exact place where all the lines converge, to which our attention has been covertly drawn—at the point of contact, that is, between the two triangles formed by the armies—a warrior in armor, implacable as an archangel, rises up in the foreground. His right arm, which holds the lance, is drawn backward; twisting in his saddle and twisting his horse, he is like a spring about to be released. His bent head, his fixed stare indicate, precede, the motion still to come.

We are compelled to follow the direction of this head, this gaze, this rigid lance with its point thrust forward as the snake darts forth its lethal tongue. And there, staring at his assailant with dilated pupils, slipping on his steed which desperately holds its ground, slipping into the mire that will engulf him, slipping into the lower left-hand corner toward which the whole composition pushes him, slipping into death, Duke Charles the Bold is waiting. He is waiting for this loaded moment, already detonated by the spark of the lance, to go off. Disheveled, howling with rage, all but ejected from the painting, he is no more than a presence about to withdraw, no more than a hand clinging convulsively to life the instant before it is swallowed up by the abyss.

Significantly, it is at the extreme left of the painting that Delacroix has placed his doomed hero. The left is the "sinister," the maleficent side. The artist instinctively perceived obscure symbolic relations that modern psychology is only beginning to understand.

The composition is as rigorous as Raphael's: no matter where the eye enters, it is led irresistibly to the point of intersection, from which the blow will be struck.

In the oil study, Delacroix has not yet fully mastered the vehement disorder of his composition nor the picturesque details.

213. - *DELACROIX*. DEATH OF CHARLES THE BOLD AT THE BATTLE OF NANCY. Sketch. 1828. Carlsberg Foundation, Copenhagen

In Raphael's fresco all the lines led to the Host. In Delacroix's painting the tension results from the deliberate imbalance; in Raphael's the immutable serenity is born of a positive symmetry. The logic of plastic form is the same, though the spirit in which it is applied differs.

INSPIRATION AND CONSCIOUS CONTROL. The effect in this case may have been the result of the infallible instinct of sensibility; but lucid intelligence may have played an equal or superior part—who can tell? And no matter! In the soul of a great artist all the resources of art contribute to the result, each in its own manner, according to the circumstances, and the artist's temperament and individual gifts. He may say, for instance, with Odilon Redon that his gifts have led him to the dream: "I have experienced the torments of the imagination and the surprises it gave me when I used my pencil; but I have directed and guided these surprises in accordance with the organic laws of art, which I know and feel, for the sole purpose of arousing in the viewer, through a sudden appeal, every suggestion, every enticement of the unknown, within the capacities of thought" (*À soi-même*, 1922, p. 27).

The slow maturation of the work is marked by countless discoveries, the product

In the final version Delacroix, sacrificing details to the unity of the whole, intensifies the expression and creates a thoroughly disciplined composition.

214. - *DELACROIX*. DEATH OF CHARLES THE BOLD AT THE BATTLE OF NANCY. Begun in 1831, exhibited at the Salon in 1834. Museum, Nancy

of intuition as well as reflection. The initial enthusiasm, the inspired impulse, no doubt play a predominant part in the first sketch; in the finished work they have certainly yielded to deliberate thought, which controls and combines. It is easy for us to see the effect of the latter, for the painting differs from the first sketch in several respects. The elements spontaneously generated by inspiration have been evaluated and given their final well-calculated form. What sparkled and flashed in the sketch here appears in its proper light.

In painting, ideas must be expressed only plastically; everything that might have the effect of deliberate calculation, that might appear to be thought rather than seen must be unflinchingly eliminated. It is impressive to see the clarity with which Delacroix applies this principle. In his initial sketch, motivated by a concern for realism, he included a chapel with a bell tower; a chapel is indeed recorded in the documents of the time. Perhaps the painter intended to use it to create some gloomy effect, some allusion to the bells' ringing the knell of defeat. But he felt that such an effect would be too "literary," and removed the chapel from the final work. By the same act he strengthened the visual effect, to which the chapel had been an obstruction—the unrelieved horizontality of the plain, with the horizon cutting across the canvas, pressing down upon the scene like a leveling slab, putting the finger of silence on its tumultuous din.

At the same time, the arrangement of the groups, the discipline which they obey, enhances the expression. The clash of the two armies and the advance of the conquering force are indicated in the convergence of almost straight lines. Similarly, the lance, the fateful weapon, which in the sketch could hardly be distinguished from the neck of the defeated horse, now stands out clearly against the snow.

Thus everything—subject, line, color, movement, light—contributes to the unique effect, which is summed up in the sensory shock we receive. And this profound and gloomy harmony, this lugubrious fanfare that Baudelaire described as "a stifled sigh of Weber," has at once the poignant beauty of nature, the solemn beauty of lines and tones, and finally the beauty of a state of mind that is re-created in ourselves, as an echo of Delacroix's very soul.

There can be no doubt that all this was perfectly understood by the man who put it so well, in his *Journal*, in 1840: "If, to a composition which is interesting for its subject, you add an arrangement of lines that enhances the impression, chiaroscuro that is striking to the imagination, a color suited to its general char- acter, you have solved at the same time a more difficult problem, that of adapting a harmony and its combinations to a single song...." His clarity of mind was such that he perceived that Romanticism and Classicism join together in the pursuit of unity, out of which the work is born. And it is understandable that he should have striven to transcend the notions of Romanticism that prevailed in his time, and to speak in behalf of a broader conception of Classicism. He voiced one of the most fundamental laws of painting when he wrote in his *Journal* toward the end of his life, on January 13, 1857: "I should gladly call Classical all regular works, those which gratify the mind not only by accurate or grandiose or stimulating representations of feelings and things, but also by logic, order, and unity, in short, by all those qualities which enhance the impression through the achievement of simplicity."

FROM THE VISIBLE TO THE INVISIBLE. In these two works, produced by masters so dissimilar and representing in themselves the traditional opposition between Classicism and Romanticism, complete success implies the same phenom- enon: the plastic form toward which the artist bends all his efforts is fulfilled in the composition, but it is at the same time transcended by it. For, though it is impossible to establish where one leaves off and the other begins, the intellectual feat that results in the architecture of lines and color is also a work of sensibility, aimed at communicating an inner experience.

As the work of art takes shape and is perfected, it asserts itself as a plastic organ- ization—but at the same time as a manifestation of life. As it evolves into an independent, autonomous reality, it becomes more intimately linked with the artist; as he creates it, he detaches it from himself, but in its new existence it remains a permanent testimony to its creator. A testimony for his own use, perhaps, for it is not impossible that in order to understand himself better he needed to contem- plate this projection, as on a screen, of the forces stirring in the depths of his soul.

Therein lies the essential mystery of the work of art, which eludes all logic, with its avidity for simplifying formulas. Only through metaphor may this seeming contradiction be understood: the work of art is like the drop of resin extruded from a tree—a distillation of the tree's juices, its sap, which till then had been diffused through it.

The problem of the duality between plastic form and expression is solved the moment it is raised. Content *or* form? Certainly not! Content *and* form. It is the significance of which the work is the bearer that calls for, imperiously demands, form, in order to become perceivable; and conversely, form draws its intensity, its life, even, from the significance it conveys.

To ignore the one at the expense of the other is to set at odds two things that cannot even be viewed separately. Form achieves its true density only if the work's inner drive is made manifest; vice versa, the content of the work cannot be communicated, and hence cannot be effective—cannot even truly come into being— unless it is given form. Otherwise, we have imbalance, failure, miscarriage. The exclusive, sectarian emphasis on form is one of the aspects of an excessive concern with technical problems and strict definitions, which today stands in the way of a broad conception of culture.

As we have seen, a work of art which is merely a representation of nature does not deserve the name; but a work which is nothing but an exercise in plastic form is an empty shell. The nineteenth and the twentieth centuries may be indicted before the court of history for two different, and converse, crimes—the former for having succumbed to the temptation of realism, the latter, to the temptation of form. For both realism and form can be justified, in the work, only through their connection with the soul of a creative artist.

It would be just as great an error to believe that the artist's soul, with all it contributes, is a sufficient justification for the work of art. The work of art is not merely an echo of the soul. To be sure, it is always nourished by the spirit of an individual or a society; but it will not fulfill its task, which is that of embodying this spirit, unless it gains independence from it.

In the last analysis, art is essentially a mode of expression. The term "mode of expression" implies the thing that is expressed as well as the way of expressing it. There is a saying that the way of giving is more important than the gift; still, you cannot have a way of giving unless you have something to give. Art is a language. From a purely visual standpoint, it is certainly true to say that a work of art is a more or less complex form; similarly, we may say that a word, from a purely auditory standpoint, is a sequence of sounds. And, without doubt, poetry achieves many of its most marvelous effects by means of combinations of sounds. Must we, for that reason, deny the part played by the meanings? Actually, there is no conflict between the two, nor is choice necessary: the work of art effects the integrated and homogeneous union of the content with the container, just as when a certain number of elements are exposed to high temperatures new substances are produced which are more than the mere sum of their components. This is perhaps the true miracle of artistic creation.

Therefore, even though the work of art appears to our eyes as a form, and as nothing but a form, we perceive it to be charged with a double meaning. The first meaning is plastic, and produces an emotion born of the visual impression; the second, by virtue of its being a necessary extension of the first, is human; and in relation to this human meaning, the work appears only as a *sign*. This sign manifests a presence—a presence comprised of society as well as the individual, of durable as well as transitory elements, and, in the case of works of genius, even of eternal elements.

The composition, which makes for the superior unity of the painting, demonstrates all the complexity and indissolubility of the relationships constituting it. In the painting, the inner life of the artist is joined with a plastic entity; the former is externalized through the mediation of the latter, and the latter borrows breath that animates it from the former. Nature supplies the raw material for both, which they in turn process in order to manifest themselves adequately to the viewer.

Toward the end of his long career Emile Mâle confided to the readers of his *Religious Art at the End of the Medieval Era:* "In the last analysis, the least important line has a spiritual essence: the fold of a drapery, the contour of a figure, the play of lights and shadows can reveal the sensibility of an epoch as clearly as can the subject of a painting. Whatever the problem the art historian attempts to solve, he always encounters the spirit."

So we must at last confront this problem of communication, the starting point for the artist, the terminal point for the viewer. For, when all is said, this is perhaps the supreme justification for the magic which is painting: to give substance to a state of mind through the mediation of a plastic harmony. We have still to inquire how this miracle can be effected.

Lines are eloquent: horizontals suggest eternity.

215. - TEMPLE OF GURNAH. Engraving from Jelloys and Devilliers, DESCRIPTION DE L'ÉGYPTE

CHAPTER FIVE

THE LANGUAGE OF THE SPIRIT: THE POWER OF IMAGES

What we feel can be expressed only in terms of an image having some reference to external reality.
Henri Wallon

LANGUAGE cannot come close to conveying the totality of our inner life; we all know how much of it is left unspoken. Words, the labels we attach to ideas, were designed to promote understanding among men. Since this is their very function, it is natural that they should denote only what men have in common, what they already know; words suggest these things to each of us by means of conventional and common designations. As Hobbes put it, words are used by men as signs, each of which has the power of arousing, in the mind of the person to whom it is addressed, a thought relating to some concept already familiar to both the speaker and the listener. "The words of the tribe," as Mallarmé calls them, have no other function, unless we are capable of giving them new and "purer" meanings.

To perform their function, words have to eliminate from the ideas they signify all the emotional and individual components, all the nebulous aura of sensibility that is an integral part of our inner experience, and preserve only the central core, which is very small but has the advantage of being firm and clear. This core refers to a limited and verifiable experience—the sensory datum or the general idea abstracted from it.

1. THE PROBLEM OF LANGUAGE

L ANGUAGE, like the intellect, has been forced to confine itself to the realm of the objective in order to secure a firm ground for its development. It was able to retain at best only such subjective elements as can be caught within the rigid net of rational thought. Language can speak of love and of pain, but it expresses only a small part of those emotions as we experience them in the depths of ourselves.

INADEQUACY OF WORDS. Take such a simple word as "tree." Those who use it imagine they are denoting the same *thing*. This may be so, but how widely the reflection of this particular thing differs in the shifting mirror of each individual soul! For primitive man or the man of early epochs, the tree was a deity, the soul of an ancestor or the spirit of the woods, whose mysterious presence was sensed behind the visible bark. What is it for our contemporaries? It can be a number of things, depending on what kind of contemporaries we have in mind. For the vacationer, it denotes relaxation and rest; for the painter, light playing through foliage of various greens; for the musician, the singing breath of the wind in the branches or the modulated notes of a bird, and the business man sees in it a potential source of salable timber. Moreover there are countless species of trees, and no single tree within a species is exactly like any other.[1]

It was necessary to eliminate all of a thing's individual qualities and particularities in order to make it possible for people to communicate regarding it. By making the notion of the thing progressively more general and more abstract, a fixed point was at last reached in the perpetual flux, an entity that was bare and soulless, but solid—the *idea* of the tree, with the word serving as its garment. The intellect, pruning, weeding out the tangled mass of sensations and emotions, simplifying the original datum, discovered the basis of communication.

[1] A Chinese fable, quoted by Claude Roy in *Comprendre* (September, 1953), poetically expresses the same truth. "A monk, a robber, a painter, a miser, and a sage were traveling together. One night they found shelter in a grotto. 'Can you conceive of a place more suitable for a hermitage?' said the monk. 'What an ideal hiding place for outlaws,' said the robber. The painter observed: 'What a magnificent subject for the brush—these rocks and the shadows cast by the torch!' The miser said: 'I cannot think of a better place for hiding a treasure.' The sage, having listened to the four others, merely said: 'What a beautiful grotto!'" Language is the sage.

The shock of being deprived of these qualities was so severe that human ingenuity has always done its utmost to endow words with the power of expressing more than bare facts or abstract ideas, to instill into them the unique fragrance of the reality from which they were extracted, to make them communicate, as Proust wrote to Princess Bibesco, "a quality of the vision, a revelation of the particular universe each of us sees and no one else can see."

With this end in view, language resorted to images in order to *suggest* things rather than to *denote* or *define* them; thus it escaped from itself to enter the domain of poetry, to become an art. For art is that medium thanks to which the ineffable does not have to remain imprisoned in the secret places of each individual life. Poetry and art are based on images; and images possess the power of penetrating into the individual soul and extracting from it and communicating to others its secret treasures, which hitherto had belonged exclusively to the sensibility of that individual. This does not pretend to be a final definition of the function and goal of art; art is a phenomenon far more complex and vast than this indicates. But it is true that to the extent to which art is poetry, the expression of the inner life is one of the things of which it is capable.

ART AND THE INNER SECRET. "Each of us," says Musset, "carries within himself an unknown world which is born and dies in silence." In order to experience this world and to dwell within it, a man must plunge himself into a state of concentration which isolates him from others and makes him unable to communicate with them. The problems this involves and the anguish it creates were felt with particular keenness in the nineteenth century, when the cultivation of the individual soul reached its apogee in Romanticism. At the age of twenty-six, Delacroix wrote in his *Journal* (1, entry of April 26, 1824): "Nature has erected a barrier between my soul and that of my closest friend."

Art and poetry are indispensable not only as a means of penetrating the secret places of the human spirit, "the real and incommunicable part of ourselves," as Proust calls them. For the ineffable is not merely the property of the individual, as the Romantics believed; it can also be experienced by a human group, a social or religious community, and still remain beyond the reach of language. This happens when it falls not within the realm of the intelligible but within that of pure sensibility or of the unconscious, which was discovered only about a century ago.

It might be objected that the unconscious is a realm inferior to that of ideas, and that its contents need only be raised to the level of consciousness. But there is a realm which transcends ideas, and which cannot be reduced to their level without becoming impoverished and distorted—the realm of the spiritual. While the overrationalistic minds of our fathers overlooked the unconscious and its right to expression, our own, still imbued with materialist values, find it difficult to believe that the world of the spirit is not on a par with the intellectual world, and even superior to it. For it is in the realm of the spiritual that the peaks of our inner life are situated—those peaks from which we glimpse regions inaccessible to thought, as the highest reaches of the stratosphere are inaccessible to the airplane.

Allegory treats images as an abstract language, each figure representing an idea.

216. - *N. BERTIN*. ALLEGORY OF THE PROSPERITY OF FRANCE

Now, the realms of the unconscious and of the spirit, where the inner life of the individual and of society is nourished, are doomed to exist in silence because of the inadequacy of ordinary language, unless they are liberated and made manifest through art and its images. Only art—or its sister, poetry—can rescue them from this silence, by translating them into signs. This is why art has always been the chosen language both of religious revelation and individual avowals, of all that lies beyond the sensory and rational knowledge that falls within the normal province of the word. Malraux says: "A museum of religions—an odd designation—would be at best a collection of sacred texts, but we can understand faith, as we can understand love, only by experiencing it." For religion, he goes on to say, "is based on states of mind.... And the salient fact remains that the Sumerian statues speak to us, even though the echo aroused by the universe in the soul of a Sumerian priest has ceased forever, even though an account of the religions of Sumeria and Egypt says nothing to us." Religions, expressions of faith, are "hymns of which only great art, through its transformations, has preserved the music" (André Malraux, *Musée imaginaire de la sculpture*, p. 58).

SELF-EXPRESSION. Two languages, so to speak complementary to each other, are available to man. One externalizes what he experiences, explaining it with the help of ideas and relations of ideas; the other embodies, with the help of images, what he feels more or less dimly. The first language requires objective clarity, i.e., reduction to a common denominator; the second is permeated with subjectivity, striving to preserve the irreducible quality, the richness and the nuance of the initial emotion.

Both require, first of all, that we circumscribe a portion of our inner life, in order to concentrate our attention upon it and to understand it; and secondly, that we give it a form—the form in which it will be communicated. The second stage involves a projection into the physical world, the domain common to all men. This amounts to a real transmutation: what was at first only felt is changed into an idea, then into words. This is the way the first language, that of the intellect, works. The language of emotions follows a parallel course. First, images, more or less distinct, are aroused in the mind; these are then given material form through a special representation.

The two languages differ in scope. The idea-word, as we have seen, achieves maximum objectivity by neutralizing the sensory elements; however, something of their quality is retained thanks to the adjective, the epithet, and the capacity words have of creating evocative mental images by means of associations. The image, however, belongs in the realm of art—a direct, nonreflective projection of the inner life, unexpurgated, unfiltered, it is charged with an almost infinite content, powerful and imprecise.

The idea-word is enriched, recharged with the sensibility of which it was at first stripped; and as it is able to call up images, it rises to the level of poetry. Conversely, the image is impoverished when it becomes intellectu-

The symbol, an image projected by the unconscious, is illogical but emotionally suggestive

217. - ODILON REDON. THE BUDDHA

alized. The idea-word, by resorting to suggestion, acquires a radiance that increases its scope; whereas the image, when it strips itself down in order to compete with the idea, loses some of its emotional force. Like a battery which, having lost its charge, can no longer produce sparks and becomes a mere box, an image that aims only at rendering ideas loses the source of its power. This is evident when we compare the symbol with the allegory. The symbol, spontaneous, irrational, has indefinable and unlimited significance; the allegory, which merely embodies an idea, is no better than a halting word, less precise than a written text, and incapable of speaking to the unconscious (figures 216 and 217).

There is evidence that language at first consisted solely of images. Only gradually did it achieve the bareness required for abstraction. Similarly, when writing made its appearance, the process of differentiation was slow. Consisting first of simple figures, scarcely differing from those of art, writing moved away from these as it came closer to making use of abstract signs. We have already described this development, which led from the pictogram, ideogram, and hieroglyph to syllabic and finally to alphabetical script.

THE WESTERN ATTITUDE. This development, which was determined by purely practical needs, was not without its effect on art in societies bent primarily on increasing their material power. For this reason the West concentrated on the development of the intellectual resources of art, which were regarded as more reliable, more controllable, and more manipulable, at the expense of the spiritual. Western art has evolved under the constant threat of losing its emotional values, in its concern with registering tangible data, those most effectively controllable by the intellect or the senses. Out of this concern arose its great temptation, realism. Time and again the West has succumbed to it.

The more or less openly acknowledged dream of Western aesthetics is to be in a position to explain art, to give an objective estimation of a painting, either by comparing it literally with the model it represents or by showing that it is an application of a particular theory or, better still, of a mathematical proportion. Nevertheless, beauty and taste have always been the standard, and, whether

Greek art does not seek to make statements or to arouse emotions; it aims solely at harmony.

218. - HESTIA (so-called VESTA GIUSTINIANI). Municipal Museum, Rome

Photo Alinari

the theorists liked it or not, purely qualitative appreciation was not eliminated.

The Greeks, who were the first in the West to try to arrive at a clear conception of art, strove to reduce it to sensory and intellectual data. Their philosophers hesitated between the requirements of verisimilitude and those of harmony based on a canon. As a result, Greek art tended to be shorn of its powers of suggestion, which were allied with the life of the senses, readmitting them only in its decline, when it began to succumb to Eastern influence. Ernst Robert Curtius has observed justly that Greek art was "nonpredicative," i.e., it did not aim at the expression of ideas. More than that: it did not undertake to communicate states of mind, unless we can call that condition of emotional indifference which is a mark of inner peace a state of mind. Such a condition seeks neither to express nor to suggest. It is only what its visual appearance shows it to be (figure 218).

Why, then, is Greek art one of the greatest, one of the most sublime, the art which some regard as the highest ideal? Because, both in imitating nature and in striving for measure and proportion, it aims only at quality; and quality is something that may be experienced, but not proved. Thus the full powers of what can be perceived only by the senses were restored

Photo Flammarion

For the Chinese artist, the landscape expresses reverie and meditation, often embodied in the minuscule figure of the hermit.

219. - *KU CHAN YU.* LANDSCAPE. Formerly Collection Dubosc. Musée Guimet, Paris to art. But with the advent of Roman art, when the keen sense of quality gave way before the demands of the imitative principle, leading to naturalism, or the principle of formal correctness, leading to academism, Western art suffered its first defeat at the hands of the forces lying in wait for it. From that time forth it has been under a double threat.

THE EASTERN ATTITUDE. The East has preserved a much greater instinct for sensory values than has the West. This is not to imply that the Indian thinkers are less lucid than our own. Just as they evolved a psychology that is far more flexible than the one that prevailed in the West as late as the nineteenth century, so, like the Chinese, they were able to lay the foundations of an aesthetics at an early period. It must be acknowledged that this aesthetics gives us amazing insights into the nature of art.

For Indian thought, the inner life is made up essentially of tendencies, or rather latencies, *vâsanâs*, which lie ready to be awakened into action. Mircea Eliade has pointed out "the profundity of the psychological analyses of Patanjali and his commentators. Long before psychoanalysis, Yoga revealed the importance of the subconscious."[1]

These latent tendencies, which are nourished by unconscious memories whose content is revealed when the tendencies become actualized, "determine the specific character of each individual." Moreover these dormant qualities "strive to emerge into the daylight, to become conscious." They are a seething caldron of possibilities, of capacities seeking to project themselves, to become effective. But to be actualized they must enter the physical universe, hence they must assume a form preceivable by the senses or by the intellect.

No other psychological theory gives us a better account of art. Art is the assuming of form, the donning of clothes, as it were, in order to gain admission to the physical world—it is the process of creating an image that will embody obscure forces. By means of art these forces make their way into and take their place in the visible world.

Diffused vapor can be transformed into water and thence into ice, thus acquiring tangible substance; the same substance can be made to reassume its liquid or gaseous state. In a similar way the artist's sensibility acquires physical substance when it is transmuted into images. Henceforth perceivable by others, it waits for the viewer who will restore it, within himself, to its original condition as a state of mind.

Another basic difference between Western and Eastern art will be clear from this. While the West is primarily concerned with the specific form of the work

[1] Mircea Eliade, *Techniques du Yoga*, 1948, p. 64. The quotations that follow are also taken from this work' which contains a keen analysis of Indian thought. The latter has been the object of equally penetrating studies by Masson-Oursel and Jean Herbert.

Byzantine art expresses spiritual rather than material realities.

220. - CHRIST PANTOCRATOR. Mosaic. Apse of the cathedral, Monreale. Late twelfth century

and its quality—that is to say, the state which it assumes—the East regards this as only a passing phase, a means by which one soul communicates to another its intensity, by revealing the unique and irreplaceable savor it has discovered in things. Kuo Hsi, a landscape artist who lived in the eleventh century, said: "An artist should identify himself with the landscape and observe it until its profound meaning is revealed to him." His task, then, is to reveal this meaning to others (figure 219).

The West has periodically held a similar view: for the first time toward the end of antiquity, under the influence of the East, as is evidenced by the theories of Plotinus (cf. pp. 131 ff.). The same view triumphed again in the nineteenth century, and Eastern thought, particularly Indian, which became known through the works of Burnouf, once again contributed to this development.

The West has therefore been familiar with both attitudes toward art, and has, in fact, fluctuated between the two. At times, clinging to its Classical tradition, it has set for itself the task of creating forms that reflect the union of reality with intellect, with ideal truth; at other times, its primary purpose has been to communicate the artist's inner experience to the viewer. In the latter periods it has succeeded in outwitting "the law of incommunication," as Emerson calls it, which led Baudelaire to write: "The unbridgeable gulf caused by lack of communication remains unbridgeable" (*Mon cœur mis à nu*, LV). Baudelaire was speaking of love: he would not have said this about art, which he regarded as a means of overcoming the obstacle, as did Delacroix, who wrote: "Painting is but a bridge connecting the painter's mind with the viewer's.... The chief source of interest lies in the soul, and is irresistibly communicated to the viewer's soul" (*Journal*, III, p. 48, entry of January 25, 1857). Hugo, too, speaks of "a ray that moves from soul to soul" (*Les Contemplations*), and Rimbaud almost echoed the phrase. And elsewhere Delacroix describes painting as "a silent power that speaks only to the soul... a mysterious language."

THE EXPLICIT AND THE IMPLICIT. "I don't understand what this painting means!" is an objection frequently encountered. The fact is that painting does have meaning, but that meaning can only be felt, not understood, and it cannot be explained.

Ordinary spoken or written language breaks the complex and fluid stuff of life down into a few well-defined chemical elements, and tells us how to combine these and use them. But the other language, that of images, does not elucidate, does not supply us with an inventory of familiar elements; nor does it give us theoretical formulas that would enable us to reconstruct in our own minds, as in a test tube, the ideas presented to us. It aims rather at preserving, as completely as possible, a particular fragrance, savor, presence. It tosses this sumptuous gift at our feet; it is up to us to bend down and take it, and to breathe our life into it. Painting does not explain: it *is*, and shows what it is; it is up to us to experience it, through its capacity for being communicated.

Incorrigible Westerners that we are, we believe only in meanings that can be expressed by clear and distinct ideas. But there are meanings that are communicated in the way a motionless string can be set to vibrating in unison with another vibrating string. There are, in short, implicit as well as explicit meanings. And though there is no clear-cut line of demarcation between the two, which complement each other and are always somewhat associated one with the other, the implicit meaning is the true province of art. To look for explicit meaning in art is thus a fundamental error, based on a total misunderstanding of the medium.

It is easy to see why calligraphy in China was considered an art, like painting: in addition to its literal meaning, the written character evoked a sensory "aura" (cf. pp. 31 ff.). Typography eliminated this aura in the West; but it persists in handwriting, for obvious reasons. Our latent tendencies, our natural impulses are communicated to the living hand, imposing on it a particular rhythm, or "spirit." The conveying of this sensory aura was cultivated in China and raised to the level of an art; in the West it is involuntary. But the intuitive, suggestive language that has, in the West, been driven out of everyday life, to make room for the language of abstraction, has, by way of compensation, taken refuge in aesthetic creation. Even there it has been threatened by the explicit, which, having invaded even the realm of painting, has introduced into it realistic description, the narrative subject, the intellectual allegory. The image itself is threatened with being reduced to a mere ideogram, to be deciphered by means of a key which can be memorized.

This accounts for the conflict, mentioned above, between Ingres and Delacroix. "To know how to draw," for Ingres, is to master and to be able perfectly to reproduce a set of recognized forms. For Delacroix, it is to invest the line with an electrical quality that "induces" a similar current in the viewer. This is, by definition, to abandon the conventional forms, which Classical art strove merely to reproduce perfectly. Suggestion is effective, for the expressive artist, only by virtue of its force and its divergence from established conventions.

There is no meeting ground between these two systems of aesthetics. Explicit language can only be based on the known, on bringing what is known to perfection, and implicit language only on the revelation of the unknown, of that which has not yet been experienced.

Take, for example, a Delacroix drawing, his sketch for *Liberty Leading the People*. It contains explicit elements: it depicts a recognizable figure, that of a draped female body, in a pose that we interpret, on the basis of the one bent knee and the position of the other leg, as that of someone trying to climb. The rigidity of the raised arm suggests the gesture of brandishing. All this could have been shown by any other equally competent artist. Delacroix's own contribution lies in implicit elements in the drawing, those which communicate to us his particular vibration, his rhythm. The dynamism of the line, the speed with which it appears to have been drawn, its nervousness leave an indelible impression upon us, awakening in us the emotions that brought the work into being (figures 221 and 222).

It seems obvious that in societies whose populations are largely illiterate, the language of images must do double duty, i.e., be both explicit and implicit. This language then becomes what has been called "the Bible of the poor." It serves to convey the content of the sacred texts, which would otherwise be accessible only to those who can read, and at the same time, through its power of suggestion, to produce the necessary exaltation in the faithful, to put them in a "state of grace" (figure 220).

It is therefore not surprising that medieval art, whether Byzantine, Romanesque, or Gothic, should have pursued this double aim, to an extent that varied with the nation and the period. Nor is it surprising in our own age, when the printed page and photography have taken over the explicit tasks of art, that art should have become more adept at communicating feeling or producing purely aesthetic pleasure.

In our "objective" civilization the artist can avail himself, in his drawing, of an expressive language reflecting his individual sensibility.

221. - *DELACROIX.* Study for LIBERTY LEADING THE PEOPLE. The Louvre, Paris

Photo Giraudon

2. DIRECT SUGGESTION

Now that we have distinguished sufficiently between the language of suggestion and the language of the intellect, which we have been taught to look upon as the only real and reliable one; and now that we have seen what a preponderant part the former plays in painting; we shall proceed to analyze the means by which it operates, and the methods by which it arouses in us the desired effects. In other words, we shall ask how the painting is transformed into a spiritual condenser, as it were, and how it communicates its charge to us.

222. - DELACROIX. Study for MEDEA. Pen drawing. Musée Bonnat, Bayonne

TO RE-CREATE REALITY. The painting is an image. Now, every image is taken from the outside world, either directly, by literal imitation, or indirectly, after being altered, transformed. Everything is to be found in nature, at least potentially. But the things we find there are neutral, devoid of human significance, at the mercy of chance and the operation of physical laws. It is up to man to "popularize" these objects, which are still unformed, like stones before they are quarried. Man must be the architect, he must select each stone, extract it from its setting, give it form, integrate it into a construction, and endow it with function and meaning.

At this stage anything is possible; everything is still *only* a possibility. The artist must discover reality, must "find" it in the sense in which St. Helena "found" the Holy Cross. She did not create it, since it had been buried in the ground, unbeknown to man; but she extracted it from the earth in order to restore it to man, for him to worship. The painter follows a similar course. He observes the presence of things, at least of certain things in nature. The mere fact that he directs his attention, and hence ours, to these things, that he extracts them from the limbo of the outside world, makes them inseparable from him, and hence an expression of himself. He is determined in his choice of objects by a dimly felt kinship between himself and certain things, which makes him look toward them, desire them.

If we examine the objects he has thus selected from nature and brought over into his works, we notice that certain ones recur constantly, indicating a particular

223. - *REMBRANDT.* LANDSCAPE WITH MOUNTAIN AND RUINS. 1650. Gemäldegalerie, Cassel

preference. We also discover that however different from one another they may have been originally, they now display a similarity which justifies their being grouped together in a painting. This common factor is the key to what we might call the artist's "constant."

Thus, bit by bit, the artist reveals himself, as a magnetized piece of metal reveals its difference from other metal by its capacity to attract iron. Everything he includes in his works is, strictly speaking, a function of an X, an unknown quantity which remains to be perceived, and which is his own sensibility.

Proust, in *The Captive*, has shown that this is also true of the novelist. After pointing out that Thomas Hardy's novels are characterized by a "stonemason's geometry," he says: "I cannot summarize the greatest writers like this in a moment's talk, but you would see in Stendhal a certain sense of altitude combining with the life of the spirit: the lofty place in which Julien Sorel is imprisoned, the tower on the summit of which Fabrice is confined, the belfry in which the Abbé Blanès pores over his astrology and from which Fabrice has such a magnificent bird's-eye view. You told me that you had seen some of Vermeer's pictures; you must have realized that they are fragments of an identical world, that it is always, however great the genius with which they have been re-created, the same table, the same carpet, the same woman, the same novel and unique beauty, an enigma, at that epoch in which nothing resembles or explains it, if we seem to find similarities in subjects but isolate the peculiar impression that is produced by the color. Well, then, this novel beauty remains identical in all Dostoevsky's works...." (Translated by C. K. Scott Moncrieff, Random House, New York.)

Proust does not shrink from using the term "monotony" when discussing the works of Vinteuil, his imaginary composer. He speaks of the "insistence" with which the composer groups together diverse sensations, the sum of which nevertheless suggests to Proust "the perfumed silkiness of a geranium," which is not "a material explanation" of Vinteuil's music, "but the profound equivalent, the unknown and highly colored festival ... the mode in which he 'heard' the universe

The similarity of the sites represented by Rembrandt and Ruisdael emphasizes the differing poetic qualities of these artists.

224. - *JACOB RUISDAEL.* BURST OF SUNLIGHT. The Louvre, Paris

Photo Archives Photographiques

and projected it far beyond himself." He thus conveyed "this unknown quality of a unique world which no other composer had ever made us see."

Similarly, the mere presence of certain objects in a painting, however realistic it may appear to be, permits inferences to be made as to the nature of the artist's sensibility: the universe he creates with elements he has taken from nature is the visible likeness of that sensibility. Under the hands of the painter, the world becomes a piece of material, which he cuts according to his own pattern, transforming the pieces into a garment for his own soul, his only concern that they fit it properly. Henri Focillon is one of those who clearly realized the importance of such choices: "Just as every artist defines the image of man according to certain preferences," he writes in his posthumous book on Piero della Francesca (p. 133), "so that the greatest among them may be regarded as creators of a humanity that is their own, that belongs to them, so every artist selects, evaluates, and combines, from the appearance the world presents, certain elements that are characteristic of him, of his creation, of his universe."

IDENTITY AND DIVERSITY.   Some paintings, however, are completely passive, reflecting nature as mechanically as a mirror, but these are rare. Such paintings, the only ones that fulfill the theoretical requirements of realism, merely reproduce the inner vacuity of the men who painted them.

Every painting has a certain *character*. It can have it by virtue of reflecting the personality of its creator, as in the cases described by Proust and Focillon. Or it may acquire such a character through its creator's reflecting unconsciously the habitual patterns of his period, or even of the atelier in which he has been trained. Often a painter acquires a certain visual vocabulary without actively sharing in the choices that determined this vocabulary, merely assimilating them passively. For this reason, one of the historian's tasks is to distinguish, in a given work, between the elements that reflect the artist's own personality and those that reflect his period; moreover, the more one knows of the period, the more accurately it is possible to define the painter's contribution. The originality of an artist is measured by the degree to which he departs both from the data provided by nature and from the elements which his period supplies to him, so to speak ready-made.

The view of nature contained in the Dutch landscape paintings of the seventeenth century was determined by the natural features of the artist's country as well as by the prevailing ideas of the time. And yet the greatest of these painters produced widely differing variations on their basic theme. A landscape by Rembrandt in the Cassel museum and Ruisdael's famous *Burst of Sunlight* in the Louvre seem to have been constructed according to the same pattern. Both works are views of the northern plain spread out beneath the sky, on which the attention is focused more than on the plain, because on this moving stage a drama of light and clouds is perpetually taking place (figures 223 and 224).

Moreover, this countryside, so distinctive in itself, is treated in both paintings in a spirit common to all schools of the period. We recognize in this treatment an emphasis that is typically Protestant and northern. The silent expanse of the plain suggests man's feeling of insignificance in the face of overwhelming forces. We also detect in both a discreet hint of Italian influence in the handling of forms, in the tendency to organize the space by means of lines indicating roads and rivers. The two works are also strikingly similar in their arrangement of the various elements of the scene.

Having so many features in common would seem to point to a similar effect. But in fact the landscapes revealed in the two paintings are as different as if they were situated on different planets. In the Rembrandt nature is a presence; the pictorial space is filled with masses of light and shadow in violent tumult; a surge of lyricism floods, submerges, engulfs reality. In the Ruisdael the impression is one of absence and void, of solitude and silence scarcely disturbed by the flowing river, the drifting clouds, and

Photo Marc Vaux
"The externalization of my desires is written in images," says Van Dongen.
225. - *VAN DONGEN.* IN THE CLOUDS

the minuscule figure of a man on horseback. The landscape is a vast inducement to contemplation and reverie.

We might say, using the terms referred to above, that while the explicit elements in these works are identical, the implicit ones are completely different. Looking at the two paintings, we realize the limitations of the famous theory of Taine, who dared to assert that the work of art is formed by the general spiritual climate and by the customs of its time. All unilateral definitions of art run the risk of similar errors.

CHOOSING AMONG REALISTIC ELEMENTS.   We may say, then, that even if each element of the painting is in itself realistic, the sum of such elements constitutes a system of images. Quite apart from the interpretation given to them, the manner in which the objects are selected, repeated, and grouped is an index of the artist's habits and obsessions. The habits reveal the spirit of the time, the obsessions the spirit of the individual.

We may also now define more precisely the part visible reality plays in the painting. We think we are seeing it reproduced, and, strictly speaking, external reality is all we can see; but it reflects so exactly a particular sensibility that what we actually perceive is this sensibility. The perspicacious eye will try to discern this sensibility rather than dwell upon the lifeless material that serves to embody it. The sensibility is like an organ not shown by the X-rays, an organ into which the radiologist injects a substance that makes it opaque, thus giving it a material and visible quality it lacked.

The choice the artist makes among the elements of reality often directly indicates the goal he seeks to attain. Charles Baudouin, in his *Psychoanalysis of Art*, has emphasized the fact that art often has the character of an inhibited action. The forces that determine a man's inner life are always pressing for self-realization, striving for gratification. If for some reason they are inhibited in this aim, they content themselves with a substitute gratification, which may take the form of an appearance, an image.

The image seems to play, for the modern age, the part of the "double" or "shadow" that it played in prehistoric magic and in Egyptian religion, but for us it is a moral "double." Needless to say, desires cannot be fully known unless they are personally experienced; it is, however, possible to re-create them imaginatively if their objects are clearly designated. The artist defines his sensibility through those elements in the world that attract it, thus revealing it as clearly as another might reveal his through his actions. The painter Van Dongen confessed: "The externalization of my desires is written in images.... I like things that are brilliant, precious tones that sparkle, fabrics that gleam, beautiful women who arouse sexual desires.... Painting gives me a more complete grasp of all this." It would be difficult to speak more clearly and frankly (figure 225).

The example of Toulouse-Lautrec is even more instructive. Occasionally he is described merely as a keen observer of contemporary ways of life, and of the very Parisian, somewhat decadent milieu which he frequented. Was he, then, a realist, an anecdotal artist? Such an opinion might be refuted on the basis solely of his artistic powers, his ability to render not only physical appearance but also moral character in a distinctive linear style, laconic and precise. However, we do not admire his line for its formal beauty alone; it conveys, with equal intensity, both the model it represents and the man who traced it. The artist is present in it, in his totality. His arabesque cracks like a whip and lays a burning welt upon our memory. Flexible and imperious, flashing and biting, it strikes its target with the swiftness and infallibility of a fencing foil. Graphology discerns a man's character in the involuntary features of his handwriting. How much more revealing is the work of the graphic artist who puts everything he has and is into his lines!

History informs us that the painter was indeed the man whom these lines reveal. Henri de Toulouse-Lautrec-Monfa was a descendant of the illustrious Counts of Toulouse, the last scion of a family of dashing warriors and aristocrats. His father was an anachronism, wedded to his horse, a belated follower of the traditional sport

Toulouse-Lautrec, with his dwarf's legs, was obsessed in his art, from his youth, with the horse's swift and nervous movements.

226. - Photograph of Toulouse-Lautrec

Photo Flammarion

227. - *Above: TOULOUSE-LAUTREC.* COUNT TOULOUSE-LAUTREC DRIVING HIS STAGECOACH AT NICE. 1881. Petit Palais, Paris

228. - *Below: TOULOUSE-LAUTREC.* AT THE CIRCUS: JOCKEY. 1899

of falconry, who asserted his individuality with arrogance and contempt. He was once seen in the Bois de Boulogne milking an Arab mare for his picnic breakfast; at another time he pitched his tent in front of the Cathedral of Albi, his ancestral domain.

His son might have gratified the inclinations that were his by birth, but which are out of place in our era, by engaging in horseback riding, hunting, violent physical exercise, and public eccentricities. But in 1878, at the age of fourteen, he broke a leg, and a year later, his other leg. The rest of his life he spent as a cripple. The accidents stunted his growth, and he was grotesque in appearance (figure 226).

Here we have a classic case of inhibited action, of energy in need of an outlet. It found this outlet in drawing. As the blind man develops an extraordinarily keen sense of hearing, so the crippled Lautrec developed his talent for draftsmanship to the point of virtuosity, and he put into his sharp, incisive, swift lines all the impatience throbbing in his wrist.

His character, which is so clearly visible in his lines—as well as in his swift and even brushwork—is also indicated by his choice of subjects. In his life he could exhaust himself only by means of drink and sensuality, and keeping late hours; all other physical activities were denied him. Therefore he indulged in them through the images he created.

From boyhood on, he sketched horses galloping on the Promenade des Anglais in Nice. Later, when he began to devote himself to the pleasures of night life in Paris, he was attracted, like a moth to a flame, to dancers, acrobats, and the circus, where once again he saw horses lashed into frenzy by whips, as well as the spangled tutus of the dancing girls. During the weeks he was hospitalized as a result of a breakdown, it was the circus that occupied his memory and imagination (figures 227 and 228).

Is it not revelatory that this partial cripple dreamed only of horsemen and of legs? How taut and precise is the musculature of the legs of Miss Ida Heath (figure 229). Is it not revelatory that he was one of the first to become interested in bicycling, and that he did several posters on this subject (figure 230)? His art thus became indeed an "imaginary life," in which, through his ability to visualize and his skill in drawing, he was able to depict all the physical pursuits that were barred to him in actual life. His friend Thadée Natanson clearly realized this. "Whereas always and everywhere he wanted only to live," he writes (*Mon Toulouse-Lautrec*, p. 47), "he was doomed to be able only to watch. Muscular perfection he prized more highly than any other."

Needless to say, his paintings contain other elements, such as the sensual subjects, the prostitutes, the bordellos, that reflect his way of life; but these, too, we recognize as projections of obsessive desires he could not gratify in real life, and hence sought to gratify vicariously in art.

Another relevant example of this is Maria Blanchard, a hunchback who, deprived of the normal gratifications of womanhood, devoted her paintings, which were influenced by Cubism, to a passionate portrayal of childhood and motherhood (figure 346).

"We have no cause to look at any object in life," says Mallarmé, "except as it represents one of our own interior states: the complex of features which it shares with our inwardness elevates it into a symbol."

In both his subjects (dance, sports, etc.) and his linear forms Toulouse-Lautrec is dynamic through and through.

229. - *At left:* *TOULOUSE-LAUTREC.* MISS IDA HEATH. Lithograph. 1896. Bibliothèque Nationale, Paris

Photo Flammarion

230. - *At right:* *TOULOUSE-LAUTREC.* Poster for "La Chaîne Simpson." 1896. Bibliothèque Nationale, Paris. The bicyclist behind the trainers is the contemporary champion Constant Huret

255

RECASTING REALITY.   If the part played by the artist's inner compulsions is so evident even in an art whose avowed purpose is the recording of reality, how much more evident will it be when the artist's imagination comes into its own! The work will no longer be subject to the demand that it be "truthful"; it will suffice if it is plausible.

In other words, the artist will have complete freedom of choice. No longer will he have to take his subjects ready-made from nature. Taking a further step toward his goal of dissolving natural appearance, he will set aside certain elements which we might call "preferential," and use them exclusively for the construction of an

Everything in Ruisdael suggests the passing of time—drifting clouds, fleeting lights and shadows, flowing water, wheat swaying in the wind.

231. - *JACOB RUISDAEL*. HAARLEM SEEN FROM THE DUNES. Private collection

unknown world—a world of which he alone, in the depths of his own being, divines the existence.

Every element in this world is taken from nature, true enough, but the whole, designed to fit the artist's inclinations and intentions, is a fresh creation, a composite which reveals to us a quality previously unknown. The superficial viewer may be deceived by its appearance of normality, and conclude that the painter has actually seen what he is showing us. But if he looks more closely, he will perceive what Proust called "the unknown quality of a unique world."

Proust, incidentally, who denied that he was a realist, though he may seem to be one, has brilliantly analyzed the emergence of such new worlds. It is difficult to resist the pleasure of quoting him at length: "Style is for the writer, as for the painter, a question, not of technique, but of vision. It is the revelation—impossible by direct and conscious means—of the qualitative differences in the way the world appears to us, differences which, but for art, would remain the eternal secret of each of us. Only by art can we get outside ourselves, know what another sees of his universe, which is not the same as ours, and the different views of which would otherwise have remained as unknown to us as those there may be on the moon. Thanks to art, instead of seeing only one world, our own, we see it under multiple forms, and as many as there are original artists, just so many worlds have we at our disposal, differing more widely from one another than those that roll through infinite space, and years after the glowing center from which they emanated has been extinguished, be it called Rembrandt or Vermeer,

Photo Giraudon

Ruisdael's figures are most often shown walking along endless roads.

232. - *RUISDAEL.* THE BUSH (detail).
The Louvre, Paris

they continue to send us their own rays of light" (*The Past Recaptured*, translated by F. A. Blossom, Random House, New York, p. 1013).

How does the artist achieve this? Once again, let Proust tell us: "Artistic genius in its reactions is like those extremely high temperatures which have the power to disintegrate combinations of atoms which they proceed to combine afresh in a diametrically opposite order, following another type" (*Within a Budding Grove*, translated by C. K. Scott Moncrieff, Random House, New York, p. 647).

In such cases we are witnessing, often

233. - *At left:* Photograph of the Jewish Cemetery in the village of Ouderkerk, near Amsterdam

Photo Rijksmuseum, Amsterdam

without suspecting it, a genuine transformation of reality by the artist, though each element of this reality, taken separately, is truthfully reproduced. No wonder that artists who can do this are held to be strict realists. Jacob Ruisdael is a case in point. Each of his canvases seems to open a window, almost at random, on the Dutch landscape of his time. But when we become familiar with his works, comparing them with one another, and going deeper into his world, we inevitably notice the recurrence of certain details and themes, indicating the presence of certain constant

234. - *RUISDAEL*. THE JEWISH CEMETERY. Drawing from nature. Teyler's Museum, Haarlem

factors. These constants form the invisible texture of Ruisdael's soul: he has arranged the visible world according to them in order to reveal that soul to us. If we look for the recurrent elements in his paintings, we are soon able to distinguish the inward strain of which they are the visible manifestation.

Thus we discover that Ruisdael's art emphasizes, occasionally with obsessive insistence, all that is transient, ephemeral, in nature—the foaming and seething flow of streams, the drifting of clouds, the violent winds that sweep across the plain,

235. - *RUISDAEL*. THE JEWISH CEMETERY. Detroit Institute of Art

The transmutation effected by Ruisdael's imagination can be followed step by step beginning with the tombstones of the Jewish cemetery near Amsterdam. First he drew them accurately, and then he combined them with his favorite themes. A Romanesque church actually stood in the background. The ruin and the hill on which it is situated, however, are products of the painter's romantic imagination.

236. - *RUISDAEL*. THE JEWISH CEMETERY Gemäldegalerie, Dresden

bending trees, shaking bushes, skimming over the fields of wheat like a wave that passes from one stalk to the next, swift and pale as a ray of light. Moving at a slower but steadier pace are the roads, their uneven ruts bearing witness to the feet of the men who have walked on them. Yes, here comes one of those men, a horseman wrapped in his cloak to protect himself from the cold, or a peasant striding heavily, leaning on his stick. The plodding traveler seems to be nibbling at space; he penetrates into it (figure 232). Indeed in most cases they are seen from the back, about to disappear in the background.

Gradually there emerges a feeling of inexorability, of the futility of the movements of living beings, as they pass lightly over the surface of things. One hears in the mind a silent voice, which seems to be saying with Ecclesiastes: "One generation passeth away, and another generation cometh; but the earth abideth for ever.... All the rivers run into the sea; yet the sea is not full; unto the place from whence the rivers come, thither they return again ... and, behold, all is vanity and vexation of spirit." But the light and shadow racing across the surface of the plain, do they not say as much, like Macbeth's, "Life's but a walking shadow..." (figure 231)?

Our interest is awakened: this thankless earth, out of which Ruisdael constructs his pictorial space, is alive with biblical images. The more he lets himself be carried away by his self-invented fantasies, the more insistent they become. We begin to recognize them: here are the road, the clouds, flowing water, the dead tree; here is the vanity of man's eternal pursuit of an unknown goal, just over the horizon, which he will never reach. Ruisdael, realistic? No more than a dream is! He has borrowed his vocabulary from nature, but he uses it according to the rules of his own personal syntax, arranging his words, so to speak, in order to make them express the meaning he wants to express.

The Jewish Cemetery, one of his paintings, we know with certainty does not correspond to reality, for the site it represents is still in existence. He painted this subject twice; the two large canvases are among his most important works. We have, moreover, some preliminary sketches for them, done from life, showing the isolated tombs, surrounded by shrubbery, just as they can be seen today, a few miles from Amsterdam (figures 233 and 234).

The details of the actual appearance of this place, which had stimulated Ruisdael's imagination, he combined with other elements, which nature had supplied to him at other times, and which had struck him by their affinities with his own sensibility. He summoned all these things, as if for a sentimental reunion of everything he loved (figures 235 and 236). Here is the foaming torrent leaping over rocks; the dead tree—first erect, then cut down, and slowly decaying in the water; the somber cloud whose architectural mass drifts across the sky, obscuring the light. The tombs themselves aroused images familiar to Ruisdael, who often meditated on the Bible, and he gives free rein to his melancholy.

Through this deeply religious man, a Mennonite, lonely, misunderstood, who had turned away from the pursuit of earthly fame, the vast stretches of the Dutch landscape acquire meaning. They become a symbol of transience, a place where nothing endures, in which man, an insignificant insect, is carried along by his fate toward the goal of all his insectlike activities—death.

Thus the artist's choice of elements from reality is determined by his inner life; he fixes only upon those things which confirm the meaning he intends, which is expressed with seeming realism but actually reflects a bias. The elements supplied by reality are not arranged according to the accidental order of nature, but according to purely moral affinities, a system of associations governed by the imagination. The viewer is at least as aware of the purely pyschological links that hold these elements together as he is of the objects represented, and becomes concerned only with the silent dialogue that takes place among them.

TRANSMUTING REALITY. In the works we have examined so far, natural appearances have been preserved: reality might appear unchanged to the casual observer. In the same way a tree may be consumed and transformed by a flash of lightning and the bark remain intact.

But more radical transformations can be brought about in the painter's crucible. His brushwork was the first of his instruments to reveal its alchemical powers, and these were not discovered straight away. Deep-rooted prejudices as to the neutrality and "the finish" of the execution had to be overcome before the brush took its rightful place as a means of expression. As late as the fifteenth century its mode was still impassive; but then it began to grow lively, and to display a talent for mimicry. All over Europe the technique of brushwork was developed into an interpretive art of its own. Only Holland, under the sway of middle-class conventions of realism, remained faithful to the pictorial neutrality displayed by the primitives, till as late as the seventeenth century. However, the greatest Dutch master, Rembrandt, had given an extraordinary impetus to this new freedom— which was, incidentally, one of the reasons he was discredited in his lifetime.

Everyone knows that a person's inner tendencies are reflected in his physiognomy, and in his attitudes, in his slightest muscular movements, to such a point that if we want to imitate another person's ways, we can succeed only by dint of a compromise which adopts those ways and makes them conform to our own. This is true to an even greater extent of pictorial transpositions, which involve countless movements by the artist in drawing his lines or placing his spots of color. Each of these elements will bear his mark, all the more clearly if he possesses a strong personality. We leave the mark of our character even on our handwriting, though our hand seeks to follow a pre-established pattern. Needless to say, such marks will be far more striking in drawings and paintings, where the artist is under no such constraint.

Rouault says: "Art is an admirable outlet ... but it has its difficult aspects. Many people boast of their ability to analyze a man's character on the basis of his handwriting, but only a few take the trouble to study a beautiful or controversial painting. It is true, though, that it is easier to make prognostications on the basis of handwriting than to give a sensible evaluation of a work of art" (*La Renaissance*, X–XII, 1937). A few years later the painter of the *Miserere* put his finger on the real reason for the expressiveness of so-called "pictorial handwriting": "Whether we like it or not, and no matter how clever jugglers or magicians we believe ourselves to be ... the work of our art is an unwitting disclosure of our true nature; or else it is merely a paler reflection of another reflection, a mediocre work, though occasionally successful" (*Le Point*, VIII–X, p. 32).

The appearances that the artist thinks he is reproducing are thus permeated with a character they did not originally have; the artist injects this character into them without realizing that he is doing so, by means both of his original perception of them and of his treatment. We recognize a vintage by the flavor of the wine; the expert seeks to discern the special "flavor" imparted to everything a given artist treats. This "flavor" or "manner" may degenerate into mannerism if it becomes conscious, and is deliberately cultivated and practiced. Then art yields to artifice, which begins at the point where mechanics takes the place of creation.

In the case of the true artist, however, the individual character of the creative act is so involuntary that even if he tries to produce an exact copy of another's work, he inevitably marks it with his own imprint, with what pedants might call "the personal factor." Indefinable and yet unmistakable, this factor is implicit in the artist's way of perceiving as well as of painting, in his eye as well as in his hand: it is implicit in his very nature.

Photo Flammarion

237. - *JAN VAN SCOREL*. PORTRAIT OF PARACELSUS.
The Louvre, Paris

In the Museum of Fine Arts in Brussels there is a copy which Rubens executed in 1615 of a portrait of Paracelsus, now attributed to Jan van Scorel, which is in the Louvre. We know that the original was at that time in Antwerp, in C. van der Geest's gallery, where Rubens was doubtless able to study it. Seemingly he copied every detail of the original, and yet the one version is as different from the other as the two different centuries in which they were produced. The firm, pure, slightly inflexible vision and execution characteristic of the sixteenth-century portrait has yielded to the living fluidity of the seventeenth century—has yielded, above all, to Rubens, for no one contributed more than he toward the emergence of the new manner. This pulsating blood, this sensual vibration, this disguised irregularity that undermines the form, liberating the malleability of the flesh, the airy lightness of the hair, the softness of the fur cap, the movement of the clouds, the radiance of the color—all this intensity and warmth are living testimony to the presence of the great Antwerp master (figures 237 and 238).

When one of our contemporaries, Bernard Buffet, set out to emulate Courbet in his powerful, voluptuous *Sleeping Women*, he produced a painting from which Courbet's rich sensuality is absent. The opulent Second Empire interior has become a sordid hotel room; the bed linen is now of doubtful cleanliness; the jewels have turned into cheap baubles, the women's well-brushed hair into a disheveled mass. The clandestine atmosphere of the older painting has become suspect; and the rounded forms have become angular. The earlier painter's immense appetite for flesh and matter has been transformed into a bitter awareness of human misery. The silvery succulent trout has become the herring of the poor. Nothing has been changed, save the essential, imponderable element that is the artist's own presence underneath the surface (figures 239 and 240).

Photo Bruckmann

Even when he makes a copy of another artist, Rubens cannot help imprinting his own personality on the painting.

238. - *RUBENS.* PORTRAIT OF PARACELSUS. Museum of Fine Arts, Brussels

3. INDIRECT SUGGESTION

LITTLE by little an invisible presence has insinuated itself among the visible elements. It is not yet openly acknowledged. But how can a man holding a ball of clay in his hands prevent himself from communicating his own warmth to it? And if he suddenly feels it softening, becoming responsive and malleable,

239. - *COURBET*. SLEEPING WOMEN. Petit Palais, Paris

will he not be tempted to mold it, to put his imprint upon it, and even to fashion it in the image and likeness of his dreams? The artist at a certain point is no longer able to confine himself to recording the echoes of his inmost nature, which he finds in the external world, and which help him to become aware of that nature. Taking another step forward, he at last gives precedence to this inner world which he feels so strongly alive within him.

He then tries to express, to make tangible, the obscure impulses that stir within him. But they are nothing but impulses; how can he give them material form? They are like the ray of light, which is no more than a stream of energy with its own direction and intensity, and in a certain sense its own color and form; but none of these qualities become perceivable unless the ray strikes a solid surface which stops it and fixes it, a screen which will suddenly arrest its course and receive its imprint. Nature, with the range of images it offers, in the same way gives substance to things that hitherto were mere possibilities.

H. G. Wells's invisible man could be perceived only through the disturbances he created in the physical world, or by his donning clothes, which gave him a form that was visible. In much the same way, the artist's soul manifests itself only through

An artist can impose his own vision, even when copying the identical subject.

240. - *BERNARD BUFFET.* SLEEPING WOMEN. 1955. Collection M. Maurice Garnier

the transformations it effects in the established order of reality, or through the images in which it clothes itself, and which become its living outer shell.

ALCHEMY OF THE IMAGINATION.   At this point the imagination comes on the stage. Imagination has been defined as "the faculty of combining images into pictures, which imitate the effect of nature but do not represent anything actually in existence." How does it operate?

To the intellect, every object is neutral; it merely corresponds to its intelligible definition. To the sensibility, however, every object is "qualified," endowed with a force that attracts or repels, with a unique flavor which sensibility alone can identify, and which arouses associations with everything that seems to possess a similar flavor. Each thing remains linked with the sensation that it provoked and that is preserved in memory; as a result it becomes expressive.

In this way a bond is formed between the external world, the objective realm of things, and the inner world, the subjective realm of sensations and feelings; the two

265

are separate only in theory, for actually the former leads directly into the latter. This fact is borne out by language: the same adjectives are applied to physical realities as to states of mind. Terms such as "bitter," "brisk," "dull," or "warm," to mention only a few, testify to the unity of that which is within us and that which is without.

Delacroix, the first great theorist of the imagination, pointed out that there is no such thing as objective reality for the artist, that the moment he perceives an object he invests it with an emotional charge. "The fact counts for nothing, since it is transitory. Only the idea remains; actually the fact exists only through the idea, for it is the idea that gives it color, that, indeed, becomes conscious of it by coloring it in its own way according to the inclination of the moment."

This coloration acquires a permanent existence through memory, which integrates it into the totality of past experience in a way similar to that by which the imagination projects it into future creation: "Why do our past pleasures appear to the imagination as infinitely more vivid than in fact they were?... Because the mind, recalling the emotions of the heart, acts in the same way as does the creative faculty when it makes use of these emotions to animate the real world and to extract images from it. It composes, i.e., it idealizes and chooses" (*Oeuvres littéraires*, 1, p. 114).

The imagination draws upon recollections of the visible world, of which the memory has an immense store, consisting of signs whose meaning is common to all men; but it has still to combine these signs in a way that will suggest a meaning that is only latent in the soul. Having observed external objects, Delacroix says (*Journal*, III, p. 222, entry of March 1, 1859), "having made them its own, as it were," and having retained only those elements from them that have significance for the mind and the heart, the imagination begins its work of creation. "What we call 'creation' in great artists is but a way, distinctive with each one, of seeing, combining, and reproducing nature." This work of creation continues through the stage of execution: "The work of idealization goes on almost without my being aware of it, even when I am copying a composition that has already taken shape. The new version is always different and comes closer to a necessary ideal" (*Journal*, II, p. 87, entry of October 12, 1853). In the last analysis, "the true painter is the one in whom the imagination speaks before everything else," and speaks in order to make known "the microcosm that man carries within him" (*Journal*, II, p. 374, entry of September 11, 1855).

As Baudelaire summed up the painter's position: "Delacroix starts with the principle that a painting must above all reproduce the innermost thought of the artist, who dominates his model as the creator dominates his creation."

THE IDEAL ACCORDING TO DELACROIX AND TO INGRES. This "innermost thought" is what Delacroix calls "the ideal." He uses this term in a somewhat special sense. The ideal for him is not, as it was for Plato, a supreme and nameless perfection, something that transcends all particularities. On the contrary, it reflects the artist's own peculiar idea of the world, his own way of thinking and feeling. What Delacroix calls "idealization" is the subconscious process by which the elements the painter receives from the outside world, which carry with them the illusion of objectivity, are permeated by his own sensibility, and dominated by it, thanks to memory, and above all thanks to the imagination. The ideal in this sense, without which "there is no such thing as a painter, or a drawing, or color," has nothing in common with "the borrowed ideal" which imitators "learn at school and which is enough to make him loathe his models" (*Correspondence*, II, p. 388; letter to Léon Peisse, July 15, 1849). Nor has it anything in common with "the shared ideal which nature may supply" (*Journal*, II, p. 87, entry of October 12, 1853). Neither to copy fixed types nor to copy reality, but to give rein to one's own individual imagination—such is the path as this great painter clearly defines it.

These two irreconcilable definitions of the term "ideal," which for Ingres denotes a principle of perfection, unique and yet common to all, and for Delacroix the most intimate manifestation of an individual's emotions, reflect the conflict between

"What is called Creation in Great Artists is but an individual way of seeing, co-ordinating and rendering nature' (Delacroix).

241. - *CLAUDE LORRAIN*. SEAPORT: THE EMBARKATION OF THE QUEEN OF SHEBA. National Gallery, London

Photo Anderson

the drives toward the plastic and toward expressiveness, which too many theoreticians of art regard as mutually exclusive (figures 242 and 243).

Delacroix cannot resist the pleasure of ridiculing the ideas of his adversaries, thus helping us to distinguish their ideas from his own: "that much-vaunted beauty that some see in the curved line and others in the straight line—all of them stubbornly refusing to see it anywhere except in lines.... They refuse to see proportions, harmony, except as contained in lines... and the compass alone is their arbiter" (letter to Léon Peisse, *op. cit.*). But in reality "it is far more important for the artist to come closer to the ideal he carries within him—his own, individual ideal" (*Journal*, ii, p. 87, entry of October 12, 1853).

Modern art has been entirely won over to this doctrine, transmitted to it by way of the Symbolists and Gauguin. Formulating the platform of the new school, in a famous article in the *Mercure de France*, Albert Aurier merely paraphrased Delacroix: "The work will be idealist," he said, "for its sole ideal will be to express the idea; and it will be symbolist because it will express this idea through forms."

In attempting to communicate his inmost thoughts by means of images taken from the external world, the painter is implying that there are "correspondences" between the two, to use Baudelaire's term. He is introducing us into a more complex realm, that of a true, spontaneous symbolism. In it what we see is closely connected with what we feel, the former being expressive of the latter. Through symbolism the work of art can become the repository of the most valuable spiritual goods. The explicator has a right to look for these treasures and to bring them to light without being reproached for indulging in "literary interpretations"—provided he present the evidence for them solely in terms of form and color. Barrès saw this clearly: "We never exaggerate in finding endless riches of meaning in the works of geniuses. Eternally striving, they have no explicit understanding of the ideas that inspire them.... But whether they are aware of it or not, the beautiful forms and the moving colors they have studied so profoundly have an intense spiritual significance" (*Le Mystère en pleine lumière*, p. 115).

It is, however, possible to offer a more concrete explanation for the expressive power which every great artist wields to such noble effect.

COLOR AND ITS MAGIC.   Whereas our examination of plastic form required first an analysis of the problems of line and form, our examination of expression demands that color be given priority. There is no color that does not have its emotional connotations.

Red may serve as an example. It is associated with ardor, intensity. It predominates in the work of those painters whom we regard as the major interpreters of life, its splendor and energy, its sensual flowering—in Rubens, Fragonard, Renoir (plate IX). What inner necessity led them each to choose red as the basis of their harmonies? Empirical minds will insist that this is merely accidental. Well, then, let them study the question from a purely physical point of view.

We have now learned that red is biologically related to the stimulation of energy.

The Classical painter's ideal is supreme perfection divorced from all particularity.

242. - *Opposite page: RAPHAEL.* GRANDUCA MADONNA (detail). Pitti Palace, Florence

We know the effect it has on the bull, whose fury it kindles; more recently it has been discovered to have a stimulating effect on procreation in animals. Professor Jacques Benoit has shown that light can be used to hasten the puberty stage in ducks, by increasing the rate of glandular activities. "It is light, not the heat that may accompany light," he writes, "that produces the above-mentioned effects. Ultra-violet, blue, violet, yellow, and infra-red rays are inactive. But orange and red rays are very active."

While colored light does have a certain effect on the retina, the eye is not indispensable for provoking what has been termed the "hypophysio-sexual reflex." Professor Benoit was able to ascertain "a penetration of visible rays of great wave length, active red rays, to the inside of the head, through the skin, the fleshy covering, and the skull itself, as far as the hypothalamic region of the brain" (*Journal de Physiologie*, 42, pp. 537–41). Thus a color can exercise a direct, almost mechanical effect on the nerve centers, and hence on emotional life.

What is true of an animal, whose reactions are determined largely by instincts and by physiological reflexes, does not necessarily apply to the more complex human organism, in which consciousness plays a preponderant role. But here, too, the symbolic value of red is evident. The general significance of a color emerges only gradually, through countless individual experiences of it, but unconsciously it remains associated with the impressions left on our sensibility by particular substances that have that color. Thus, obviously, our ideas of red are linked with our feelings about blood, the sign of life as well as of wounds, brutality, cruelty.

These associations were formed in prehistory. The presence of red pigment on bones or of powdered hematite in receptacles placed inside tombs dating from the earliest epochs (Mousterian), the traces of red pigment on some of the Aurignacian Venuses (Willendorf, Laussel) indicate that Neanderthal man and his successors had already begun to use color for the magic purpose of preserving life and its properties.

The same is true of other colors. Their traditional and curiously consistent symbolical use merely serves to verify and make systematic the associations originally established between them and the elements of nature of which they seemed to be manifestations. Blue denotes the sky or water, green thriving vegetation, yellow fire and light. There is no need to resort to esoteric sources to account for such associations. It will surprise no one to learn that the planet Mars is orange and red, Venus light green, Jupiter blue and purple; or that the robes of Jesus during his ministry on earth and the cloak of the Virgin Mary were azure-blue, and so on.

The expressive colors of light and of the sky will always be associated with the ideas of purity, chastity, divine wisdom. This symbolism has such profound and universal roots that it is identical, except for a few variations, in all places and all periods. For instance, in Africa, the Ewe regard blue and white as the colors favored by God, and so these colors are worn by their priests. Blue and white, and blue and yellow, also suggest the association of the celestial and the luminous. Vermeer, the painter of purity, instinctively chose the latter combination as his favorite harmony.[1]

---

[1] May I, in order to avoid a long explanation, refer the reader to my essay "The Poetics of Vermeer" and to *Vermeer* by A. B. de Vries, Paris, 1948 pp. 109 ff.

IX - RUBENS
ANGELICA AND THE HERMIT. c. 1625
Kunsthistorisches Museum, Vienna

RENOIR
ODALISQUE ON A SOFA
Collection Katia Granoff, Paris

Photos Draeger

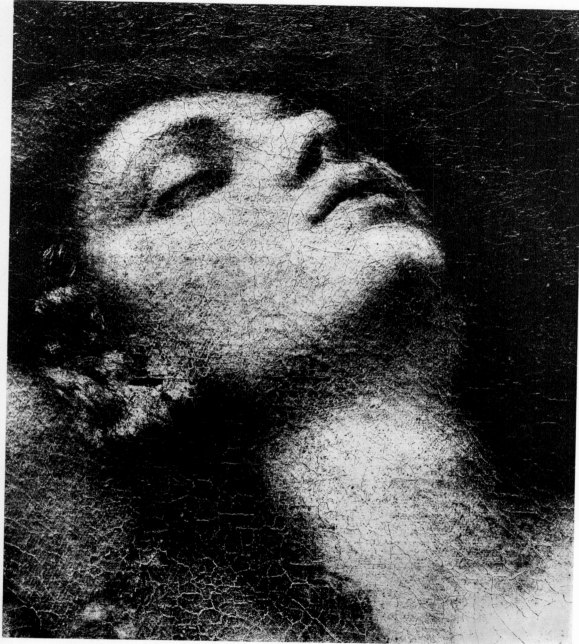

The impassioned painter's ideal is conformity with his innermost feelings.

243. - *CORREGGIO.* ANTIOPE (detail). The Louvre, Paris

Similarly, we may mention the well-known preponderance of yellow in Van Gogh's palette. Emile Bernard, a friend of his, writes: "Yellow, the color denoting divine light, had a great attraction for him" (*Van Gogh raconté...*, p. 183). Van Gogh was obsessed with such problems. "I don't know whether anyone before me has dealt with the suggestiveness of certain colors," he wrote to Théo. He was not far wrong: an awareness of the evocative powers of color dates only from the nineteenth century; and the credit for having formulated it in his writings goes, once again, to Delacroix.

COLOR AND THE SYMBOLIST THEORY. The man who said of painting that it arouses feelings that words can express only vaguely, knew that this magic power resided largely in color; unlike the line, the forms, the subject-matter, all of which, as we have seen, appeal primarily to the intellect, color has no significance for the mind, but speaks eloquently to the sensibility. With color it is impossible to compensate for a deficiency in feeling through some intellectual device: color can only be felt. Therefore it is the favorite messenger of the artist's soul, an arrow with brilliant feathers darting directly to the viewer's heart and implanting itself in it.

In an entry in his diary dated June 6, 1851, Delacroix, referring to the Le Sueur canvases in the Louvre, wrote: "I hold that color is a far more mysterious and perhaps more powerful force than it is commonly believed to be; it operates, as it were, without our being aware of it." Today we say that it acts upon our unconscious. Half a century after Delacroix, Paul Gauguin, whose thinking owes a great deal to the earlier painter, continued this analysis in a letter of March, 1899, to Fontainas: "Color, which is a vibration, as music is, can express that which is the most creative and at the same time the least definable thing in nature: its inner force."

Gauguin, of course, was anticipating what present-day science has proved. We have already mentioned Professor Benoit's studies of the physiological effects of the color red on animals. Felix Deutsch has shown that colors have certain biological effects on the organism, particularly on the vascular reflexes; the emotional excitation shown by variations in blood pressure and pulse, he says, is produced by mental associations; and these superficial associations dredge up deeper memories which account for the emotions experienced at the sight of colors. Thus science confirms something that art revealed long ago, and that Delacroix was alluding to when he noted in his diary, on January 2, 1853, that color "enhanced the effect of the picture by stimulating the imagination."

After Delacroix, the Symbolists gradually became more aware of the secret relationships that are generated by the vibrations of the optic nerve. As early as 1885, Gauguin, writing to Schuffenecker from Copenhagen on January 14, tried to clarify a theory that was beginning to take shape for him: "At times it seems to me that I am mad, and yet, the longer I lie awake in my bed at night, thinking, the more I believe I am right. Philosophers have been reflecting for a long time on the phenomena which seem to us to be supernatural, and which we nevertheless can feel. It is all there, in this word 'feel.'" To feel something without being able to account for it, Gauguin says, is a characteristic of great artists, "people in whom the feeling takes shape ahead of the thought."

244. - French School of the seventeenth century. VENUS AND AENEAS. Private collection

Whereas a composition rising to the right suggests action and warmth, one descending to the left suggests nostalgic reverie.

245. - *WATTEAU.* EMBARKATION FOR CYTHERA. The Louvre, Paris

Photo Flammarion

Mantegna's vision creates a universe which seems carved out on flint and marble.
246. - *MANTEGNA*. THE AGONY IN THE GARDEN. Museum, Tours

With a proud awareness of attacking an unsolved if not an unsolvable problem, Gauguin points out that our sensations are more revealing than is generally admitted: "Each of our five senses is directly connected with the brain, conveying countless numbers of things which no amount of education can do away with. I conclude from this that there are noble lines, deceptive lines, etc. The straight line suggests the infinite, the curve suggests limits.... Colors are still more expressive, though there are fewer of them than lines, by virtue of their power to affect the eye. There are noble tones, and vulgar tones; quiet harmonies, and harmonies that excite by their boldness. After all, graphology tells us that some handwritings indicate sincerity, others deceit; why should not ... lines and colors reveal the degree of greatness of an artist?... The more I think about it, the more I am inclined to believe that the inner life can be translated into a medium quite different from literature; we shall see who is right." In Raphael's paintings, he goes on to say, "there are harmonies of line that we never become aware of, for they are the veiled expression of the innermost thoughts of a man." It would seem that Gauguin was the first to conceive of this new interpretation of art and its effects.

Van Gogh, who admired Delacroix and was for a time strongly influenced by Gauguin, concerned himself with the same problems, and also attempted to elucidate them. He was particularly interested in color, continually referring to it in his letters to Théo, most often toward the end of 1888 when he was at Arles, saying once that the study of color was no less absorbing to him than his "financial difficulties." He wished to discover the secret of color's magical properties: "To express love by a joining of two complementary tones, by blending them and contrasting them, and by the mysterious vibrations of related tones. To express thought by the radiance of a light tone on a dark background. To express hope by a star, the warmth of one's being by the glow of the setting sun" (Letter 531). Again, a few days later—on September 8—he writes: "I sought to express the terrible human passions with red and green," and adds: "What we have then is not true color, as judged by the standards of realism of the *trompe-l'œil*, but color suggestive of an emotion, an ardent temperament."

Poussin always seems to be molding flexible and compact masses of earth and foliage.
247. - POUSSIN. LANDSCAPE WITH SNAKE (detail). National Gallery, London

Baudelaire, with whom Delacroix discussed his ideas, had made similar observations earlier. He regarded red and green as the basis for the harmonies used by the Romantic master:

> *... lac de sang hanté des mauvais anges,*
> *Ombragé par un bois de sapins toujours vert.*

(Lake of blood, haunted by demons, in the shade of a pinewood that is always green.)

Analyzing this poem in his "Exhibition of 1855," Baudelaire said that the "lake of blood" was intended to suggest "red," and the pines "green, the complement of red." For it might be said, he added, "that this kind of painting, like a sorcerer or a hypnotist, produces its effects from a distance. This singular phenomenon is made possible by the skill of the colorist, by the perfect blending of the tones, and the harmony (established in advance in the painter's mind) between color and subject. It seems that the color ... has, as it were, a mind of its own, independent of the objects it clothes. Moreover, these admirable blendings of color often make one dream of harmony and melody, and the impression one gets from these paintings is often a musical one."

To be sure, Delacroix was not the first to create such an impression. The greatest of his predecessors had used color in order to manifest their inmost feelings. But Delacroix, with his keen mind, had a clear understanding of the powers that these predecessors had used only instinctively, and thanks to him painters became aware of the potentialities of their art.

SYMBOLISM OF LINE AND OF SPACE.   Color, as we have seen, is eminently suitable for direct communication with the soul in the language of emotions. But line, although its principal task is to give intelligibility to form, is not devoid of suggestive powers. Gauguin had a glimpse of these powers.

Here, once again, everything follows from our earliest impressions. From childhood on we are aware of the contrast between matter, which is subject to the law of gravity, and air, which seems to defy this law. Nonmaterial things, i.e., those which have neither volume nor weight, seem to be associated with the life of the spirit, which thus comes to be seen as opposed to heaviness. Everything that rises, that tends to be vertical, seems to indicate a liberation from the physical world, a movement upward, a striving toward divine realities. God is instinctively located in heaven, while the powers of evil are relegated to the depths of the earth. "High" and "low" are commonly used metaphorically. Because of its soaring forms, Gothic art seems the very embodiment of a mystical force.

The triangle, by means of which a rational relation is established between these two opposing directions, has come to be regarded as a symbol of balance and reason. It was the figure preferred by the Greeks, who gave its form to the pediments of their temples, and by the Renaissance artists, who used it as their favorite compositional schema.

With the horizontal, this striving upward ceases; it is the position assumed by the lifeless body. Egyptian art, in which this direction predominates, suggests to us the permanence and immutability of death (figure 215).

Photo Flammarion

248. - *FRAGONARD.* PASTORAL SCENE. Collection Robert de Rothschild

As seen by Fragonard, nature in its entirety seems transformed into splashing waves and swirling vapors.

249. - *FRAGONARD.* BATHING WOMEN (detail). The Louvre, Paris

Photo Laboratory of The Louvre, Paris

The same kind of observations could be made about every linear form—the circle, for example, which is the image of perfection. It would be possible to formulate an entire symbolism around the significance of colors and forms, of space and directions within space—but such a possibility deserves to be studied in detail. We would have to apply the same method as has been used above, starting from primordial and atavistic human experiences which determined the symbolic significances of these elements once and for all. In the previously quoted letter to Schuffenecker, Gauguin, once more evidencing an amazing understanding of these aspects of art, writes: "From the point of view of literal truth, there is no such thing as right and left; but to our sense of things, lines running to the right advance, and lines moving to the left retreat. The right hand strikes, the left hand is the one used for defense."

This statement might serve as a preface to the whole symbolism of space which modern psychology is investigating, and on which Max Pulver has cast a great deal of light. The right hand, which is the active hand for the vast majority of people, is beneficent; the left, because of its ineffectuality, is maleficent, as we have noted previously. The interpretation of handwriting has taught us a new sense of space. For Western man, strokes of writing that incline to the right are expressive of the future, whereas strokes inclining to the left indicate the past. The psychoanalytic interpretation of the role of the father and the mother in the development of the child lends further richness to this spatial symbolism. The mother, from whom the child slowly detaches itself, in order to attain independence, symbolizes the past and the leftward direction, while the father, model for the child's ambition to grow, to become a man, symbolizes the future, which is associated with the rightward direction. We cannot do more here than briefly to indicate the direction taken by these investigations.

Why does the *Embarkation for Cythera*, which should evoke a promise of happiness, suggest such melancholy, such nostalgia? The island is a mirage, and the bark of hope can never reach it. The procession of lovers is shown drifting leftward and, apart from a certain vivacity in leave-taking, slopes off like a drooping garland of flowers (figure 245). In Guido Reni's triumphant *Aurora*, in the irresistibly joyous *Kermesse*, in the *Raft of the Medusa*, with the tense attitudes assumed by the castaways at the sight of their rescuers, and in the little-known canvas *Venus and Aeneas*, showing Aeneas looking worshipfully at the goddess, the movement rises toward the right (figure 244).

SYMBOLISM OF MATTER. Our images of water, air, earth, and stone also reflect our earliest experiences; they too are charged with emotional meaning, each suggesting a particular quality that repels or attracts. Bachelard has shown, in a series of masterful studies, the intimate associations that can be established between our interior states and the principal forms of matter. It is to be regretted that he has not applied his perspicacity to painting.[1]

The ancient belief that each individual had his own particular element, in astrology,

---

[1] However, in a study of H. de Waroquier, he does observe: "There is a great deal of evidence to show that a fully developed imagination deals not only with colors and forms, but also with matter and its elementary properties."

just as he had his own color, gem, and planet, was merely a crystallization of a profound experience. It would be easy to show that every painter, provided he has a strongly defined personality, assigns a preponderant, sometimes almost an exclusive, place in his universe to some special aspect of nature. In this he resembles the poet. How revealing is Baudelaire's concern with barren materials:

> *J'avais banni de ces spectacles*
> *Le végétal irrégulier*
> *Et, peintre fier de mon génie,*
> *Je savourais dans mon tableau*
> *L'enivrante monotonie*
> *Du métal, du marbre et de l'eau....*
>
> (Le Rêve Parisien)

> (I banished from these displays
> The irregular plant
> And, painter proud of my genius,
> I savored, in my picture,
> The intoxicating monotony
> Of metal, marble, and water.)

He would even freeze water:

> *En des cataractes pesantes*
> *Comme des rideaux de cristal ...*
> (Into heavy cataracts
> Like crystal curtains.)

The Italian painters of the fifteenth century, particularly those of the School of Ferrara, some of the Venetians, and Mantegna, reveal their desire for precision by their obsession with stone. Mantegna lovingly carves its prisms and facets and makes it the essential stuff of the world: fluted cliffs, sharp rocks, grottoes with stone walls, pebbles along roads fill his landscapes with their clear-cut forms. All of nature seems to imitate stone: the armor, the fabrics, even human flesh seem to share in this universal petrification. Waldemar George's description of the painters of the *Forces Nouvelles* as suggesting "a world of quartz and granite from which no flower grows" can even more aptly be applied to the works of Mantegna (figure 246).

Poussin, on the other hand, is obviously preoccupied with earth. It is known that he always made clay models of his characters. This native of Normandy, when in Rome, was asked to choose the most beautiful souvenir of antiquity he could see, to be preserved in a museum. He picked up, according to Bellori, "a bit of earth mixed with bits of lime, some fragments of porphyry, and marble dust, saying, 'Here, take this to your museum, and tell them that this is ancient Rome.'" Poussin's figures seem to be an integral part of the soil. Built like peasants, with powerful hands, their feet firmly placed on the ground, brown as clay, they seem to be the products of the soil whose rich texture is lovingly rendered by the painter (figure 247).

Occasionally, as in the *Landscape* at Chantilly, he paints with earthy greediness the nude bodies of women scattered about on the lush grass. His last large canvas was *The Four Seasons*, a celebration of rustic labors, and indeed his entire art might be described as a great ode to rural life.

In the works of Fragonard matter is seen in a more fluid state.[1]

The whole world seems transformed into air and water in drawings such as *Fountains* and *Firecrackers*, in *Festival at Saint-Cloud* with its fountains, in *Festival at Rambouillet* (Gulbenkian Collection) with its swirling streamers, in *Beggar's Dream*, *Danaë*, *Opportunity*, and many others. The nude bodies of his bathers wallow with delight in the water they splash and spatter. He gives a fluid or vaporous appearance to the other kingdoms of nature as well, the mineral and the vegetable. In *Pastoral Scene* (Rothschild Collec-

Photo H. G. L.

250. - *TENIERS THE YOUNGER*. AUTUMN. National Gallery, London

tion) the sheaves of wheat are metamorphosed into a surging wave; the powerful oak trees of his *Renaud and Armide* turn and twist like leaping flames. In his *Pot au lait renversé* (Cognacq-Jay Museum) he seems intent on vaporizing all of matter in order to make it more amenable to the flights of his imagination (figures 248 and 249).

The intellect is drawn into this game, adding its inferences, often artificial, to these instinctual data of which it is vaguely aware. Thus we see the emergence of a symbolism of numbers, the result of a complex process, which is, however, somewhat controversial. By contrast, the symbols prescribed by our sensibility are firmly rooted in our nature; they do not permit of any arbitrary interpretations so long as they are not the object of gratuitous games of the intellect. They even provide us with a hint of certain universal laws, which account for their turning up in the most diverse civilizations, widely separated from one another in time and space. They have their origin in human nature and its primordial experience of life. It is only the attempt to rationalize and to systematize them that introduces an element of uncertainty and arbitrariness into this eternal symbolism.

[1] Lucien Rudrauf, in his essay "Material and Formal Imagination in Fragonard" (in *Cahiers techniques de l'Art*, Strasbourg, 1947), has treated this subject with great penetration. I dealt with it in a lecture, "The Evolution of Matter in Painting," given shortly after the end of the war.

The proportions an artist gives spontaneously to his figures reflect his personality—trivial, aristocratic, mystical, and so on.

251. - *VAN DYCK.* THE ABBÉ SCAGLIA.
Museum of Fine Arts, Antwerp

252. - *EL GRECO.* ST. JOHN THE BAPTIST.
M. H. De Young Memorial Museum, San Francisco

SYMBOLISM OF THE HUMAN FIGURE.   When the elements available to the painter begin to be organized, when figures begin to emerge, painting has developed still another means of playing on our emotions. The very proportions the painter gives his figures express a distinctive, though unconscious, attitude toward man.

Teniers, jovial and down-to-earth, portrays dwarfs with big heads on short necks, wizened and shriveled like their lives spent in sordid occupations and petty amusements (figure 250). Caravaggio, whose art is a vehement protest against the idealistic conventions of the Renaissance, paints strong men, with powerful limbs and tanned complexions, their faces furrowed by the storms and brutalities of life. With him, the pictorial world, hitherto reserved for heroes and gods, is invaded by "boors." Van Dyck, on the other hand, who tends spontaneously to lighten the burden of matter, makes his figures elongated, with thin and flexible silhouettes, with a cultivated, patrician look (figure 251). The figures of the mystical El Greco are consumed by a hope of escaping from the earth: they seem to soar toward the sky (figure 252).

Thus, the human body, too, can speak the language of forms. It is the source of many other associations. Each of its parts is linked with a particular activity: the

Caravaggio emphasizes the most "material" parts of the human body, particularly the feet.

Photo H. G. L.

253. - *CARAVAGGIO.* ST. MATTHEW AND THE ANGEL. Museum, Berlin. (Destroyed in 1945)

face and the hands reflect the nobility of the mind, while the feet, which support the body and are the humble means of its balance and movement, suggest vulgarity. It is not surprising, therefore, that the refined Van Dyck should focus the light, in his portraits, on the faces and fingers, while Caravaggio stresses the massive hands and the legs. The latter's figures display their feet grimy with dust and covered with calluses in the foreground of his religious paintings, for instance the *Madonna of the Pilgrims* at the Church of St. Augustine in Rome, and the *St. Matthew and the Angel*, which was destroyed in the Berlin Museum in 1945. Caravaggio's contemporaries were shocked by the importance he gave to the feet in the latter painting, and he was ordered to paint a new version of it, on the grounds that he had represented a saint "uncouthly showing his feet" (figure 253). According to Bellori, his *Virgin and Child Crushing a Snake* met a similar rejection, because "the scene was portrayed in a lowly manner." Significantly, this expression "lowly" denotes both a moral idea and a physical position, the "low" position which cast discredit on the feet that Caravaggio dared to flaunt as a challenge.

Even though the painter's mission is to express the ineffable, he has means of universal significance at his disposal. He will combine them, arrange them, strengthen them, and vary them through their reciprocal action, mixing them as he does the paints on his palette, in order to place the exact visage of his soul before our eyes. Through the combined action of the various sensory shocks, which he orchestrates with a sure instinct, he reveals his inner world, which cannot be expressed through ideas.

PAINTING BECOMES CONSCIOUS OF ITSELF. It took a very long time, however, for the artist to become aware of the powers inherent in the language of painting. For centuries, at least in the West, he regarded himself merely as an illustrator, whose task it was to translate into images what was expressed just as well, if not better, by words. He could conceive of nothing beyond this task; nor could his public. What stood in the way of progress was the eternal question, alluded to at the beginning of this chapter: "What does a painting say?"

The question was answered by Baudelaire, who, speaking of music, wrote in his "Opium Eater": "Many ask what are the positive ideas contained in sounds; they forget, or rather they do not know, that music, which in this is related to poetry, represents feelings rather than ideas; to be sure, it suggests ideas, but does not contain them in itself."

Our culture, dominated first by the Scholastic rationalism of the Middle Ages, and later by the Cartesian rationalism of the classical period, found it very hard to understand that certain things cannot be expressed by ideas, and that it is even possible to express things that are not ideas. But the most profound psychologists had a glimpse of this truth. St. Thomas Aquinas says that our "cognitive faculties" seek not merely "what is the truth" but that, in the ideal state of contemplation, a kind of sympathy is awakened in them because they find in the truth their own reflection. This implies that our images do not merely represent and identify things, but that there is a kind of sympathy between them and the things, so that the latter can be made to reflect our inner states.

But it was not until the nineteenth century that the German philosophers developed an approach less committed to rational forms of thought and admitting intuitive perceptions, which made it possible to bring to light the human ability to respond emotionally to images. Eventually a complete theory was developed, accounting for the traffic that exists between our inner life and the outside world. This is the theory of *Einfühlung*, to which we shall return later (cf. p. 430).

Photo Giraudon

254. - *POUSSIN.* THE MARRIAGE OF THETIS AND PELEUS BEFORE POLYPHEMUS PLAYING THE FLUTE
Museum, Dublin

In France, the Romantics took a similar direction. For instance, to use a little-known example: in his *Manuel Roret du peintre et du sculpteur*, published in 1833, and widely read by artists, L. C. Arsenne, whose work is now completely forgotten, wrote: "Man reproduces himself in his work. Man, in reflecting the world, also reflects his own individuality, his personality: he reflects himself."

Thus, step by step, there came into being the new idea that the artist's or the poet's soul could borrow from things their visible appearance and make of it the expressive garment for his own sensibility, all the while believing that he was merely perceiving and bringing to light a secret presence hidden in the world.

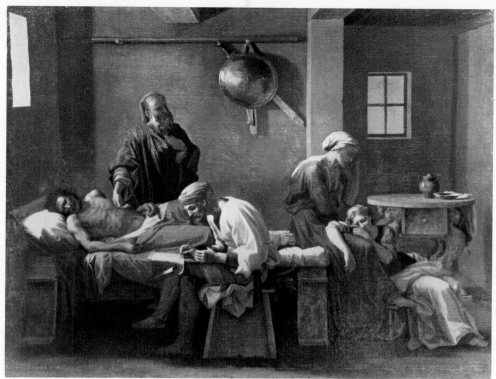

255. - *POUSSIN.* THE LAST WILL OF EUDAMIDAS. Royal Museum of Fine Art, Copenhagen

In his "theory of modes" Poussin explains how all the elements of a painting—subject, composition, rhythms, and color— must be harmonized in a single over-all impression.

256. - *POUSSIN.* LANDSCAPE WITH THREE MONKS. Formerly Collection Prince Paul of Yugoslavia

REPRESENTATION; SUGGESTION. While philosophers were obliged to formulate this elusive idea, the artist—at least the great artist—has always known it intuitively. What is it that the Venetians, Giorgione, Titian, do, if not to constrain natural appearance to serve as the medium through which their inner life is expressed? It was, however, the great French Classical artist, Nicolas Poussin, who first attempted to introduce some logical order into this obscure region of art.

Poussin's aesthetic views, formulated in his own rough language, seem to have been singularly broad in scope. He was apparently aware of the fact that art aimed at both plastic beauty and expressive intensity. He strove to give his own painting the most finished and most harmonious form, to make it an "object of delight"; but he strove at the same time to endow it with "the power to arouse diverse passions in the souls of the viewers." His academic explicators have stressed only the logic and the formal perfection of his art, the only aspect of it they are capable of noticing; they have overlooked its suggestive force, although the great painter was explicitly concerned with this.

In the famous letter written to Chanteloup on November 24, 1647, Poussin pointed out that in treating a subject, he tried "not only *to represent* various passions in the faces and figures, but also *to stimulate and arouse* the same passions in the soul of the viewer." In distinguishing so clearly between the two aims, representation and suggestion, he was, through the understanding he showed of the psychology of art, well in advance of his time. Moreover, he did not believe that he was departing from the lessons of antiquity in concerning himself with the suggestive powers of art as well as with formal beauty; for he observed that in Greece and in Rome, "the best poets" did not confine themselves in their verses to the pursuit of formal perfection, were not concerned only with rhythms and cadences; they also applied themselves with great skill "to fitting the words to the line, and to suiting their meters to the meanings of what was said." In other words, they too aimed at arousing a certain emotional state in their listeners. Take Vergil, Poussin says: "He arranges the sounds of his lines with such skill that he seems to be bringing before our eyes the very things he speaks about; when he refers to love he skillfully selects sweet and most graceful words, pleasing to the ear; and when he refers to warlike deeds or describes a naval battle or a disaster at sea, he chooses harsh, jarring words, so that when we hear them pronounced, we are filled with terror."

The painter proceeds in the same way. Instead of words, he uses images; instead of verbal rhythms, he uses drawing and composition; instead of sonorities and stresses, he uses colors. It is up to him to choose the proper means, and to make them "conform to the nature of the subject." Delacroix admired nothing more than this "conformity" and this "expression."

POUSSIN AND THE THEORY OF MODES. It would seem, then, that Poussin had a clear idea of that about which others before him had had only brilliant intuitions. Continuing his analysis of the artist's means and his aims, he developed his theory of "modes." Each subject should be treated in a style and spirit that accords with the artist's intention. For himself, he says, the subject "does not always sing in the

same key"; he "varies his manner according to the subject." In each case he works out "a certain specific and firm manner or arrangement, within which the thing preserves its own entity." And he says: "It is in this that the whole art of painting consists."

The sensory elements of the painting, which the mind perceives in the subject itself, are like a musical theme which the artist develops by all the means available to him—drawing, color, composition, the selection of suitable details and objects. Everything converges upon this theme, the heart of the painting, and points to it. But this alone is not enough: in addition, the general organization of the painting and its elements must contribute to its suggestive power. Delacroix says that Poussin "accorded to each object only the degree of interest required by that object."

Now it is clear that for Poussin, the major element, the dominant factor on which his sytem of expression is based, is the landscape. He was brought up in the country, in close proximity to nature, to which he was drawn moreover by his meditative and solitary temperament, and it was nature that he chose as his favorite theme, as his means of arousing emotion. In his paintings, the human myth is joined with the scene that expresses it.

In his *Phocion*, the corpse and those who bear it are all but lost in the impassive serenity and harsh brilliance of the light, the trees, the objects. *Métamorphose des plantes*, that apotheosis of the flower, unfolds against a background of the garden, with its trellis and overflowing fountains, with huge clouds marking the course of the sun. In each of his works, both the subject and the pictorial resources, which he plays upon as upon the keyboard of a musical instrument, are focused on the emotional impression he seeks to arouse in the viewer (figure 255).

The Marriage of Thetis and Peleus (figure 254) rises like a song. The harmonious color combines splendid reds and blues, an orchestral background for the surge of joy that echoes the rhythm of the sea. The composition is not architectural in the usual Italian manner, but is marked by a series of sudden movements that rise upward only to lapse away gently, like the curves of a garland. The whole painting is a melody, a dance tune, that seems to be coming straight from the pipe held by Polyphemus, and that suggests the waves of the sea.

Landscape with Three Monks (figure 256), on the other hand, conveys only silence and solitude. Where *The Marriage of Thetis and Peleus* reminds us of Titian, this painting recalls Ruisdael. The figures are minuscule; they are dwarfed by the wild valley, and it is only thanks to the skillfully organized lines of composition that they are not dissolved altogether in the landscape. These lines are drawn rigidly: the tree is vertical, the surface of the water horizontal, and the diagonal of the ground at the right descends sharply. Everything is in harmony with the austere greens and the subdued light, producing a solemn resonance.

Poussin even divined the relationship between painting and music; and in this, too, he was inspired by antiquity. The Greeks knew that words do not merely denote ideas, but that they can acquire the power of arousing emotional states by means of sounds, harmonies, and rhythms. They distinguished seven modes, the Dorian, Phrygian, Lydian, etc., each suitable for arousing a specific inner state. Poussin, who is often regarded as the most rationalistic of all painters, sought to make his art take in a territory that previously had been reserved to music.

However, though Poussin saw these new possibilities in painting, he applied them only to the treatment of traditional themes, which the intellect had become accustomed to formulating. That, no doubt, is why he is a Classical painter. The glimpses he gives into the life of the soul do not contain any human enigmas; he does not even suspect their presence or possibility. With him, painting became aware of its capacity for rendering the invisible; it was left to others to discover that it could also penetrate the unknown.

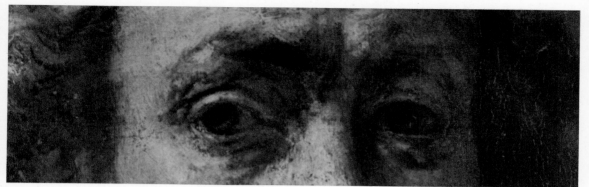

Painting, like the eyes, is the window of the soul.

257. - *REMBRANDT*. PORTRAIT OF THE AGED ARTIST BEFORE HIS EASEL (detail). 1660. The Louvre, Paris

CHAPTER SIX

THE LANGUAGE OF THE SPIRIT: THE INNER WORLD

*Paintings have a life of their own which stems
wholly from the soul of the painter.*

Van Gogh (letter to Théo, no. 439)

B Y now, the painter has learned that with the elements at his command—those he borrows from nature as well as the means of execution which constitute his art—he can, through the image that results from the fusion of these, transmit emotions to others. As we have seen, Poussin organized his paintings with the express purpose of stirring the soul of the viewer.

This organization, which gives the work a unity deeper than any tangible bonds could give it, is found also in other great artists—in Rubens, for example. But there is a fundamental difference between the two. What in Poussin was reasoned out, calculated, seems to surge spontaneously out of Rubens' very being. It is as though his own presence were manifesting itself in the painting, imposing itself upon us with exuberant force. The whole is as precisely co-ordinated as in Poussin, but where the latter brought this about deliberately, in Rubens the effect is as involuntary as is the expression of personality in the lines of a drawing.

289

In his "modes" Poussin sought to express conscious feelings. But Rubens projects his whole being into the painting, even that part of it of which he is not aware. To be sure, both the conscious and the unconscious mind always share in the creation of a work; but the proportionate contribution of each varies with the artist. Poussin surrenders himself to the magic of his art; Rubens is surrendered to us by the magic of his. A comparison between these two artists leads us across the border from the luminous domain of reason into the obscure realm of the subconscious. We must now explore more deeply this latter realm, which so far we have visited only briefly.

1. THE PAINTER AND HIS VISIBLE UNIVERSE

SOME actors are able to impersonate, with consummate skill, the most diverse types; with others the roles they play are assimilated into their own irrepressible and unchanging personalities. This does not mean that the former are more intelligent than the latter, but merely that they use their intelligence as a means of control, while the latter use it as a method of bringing to light and of ordering the spontaneous outpourings of their instincts. It is the latter, therefore, that will afford us a closer view of the workings of the unconscious.

THE UNIVERSE OF RUBENS. Why is a painting by Rubens so obviously and overwhelmingly "Rubensian"? Everything about it seems to contribute to such an effect. There is first of all the dominant red tone, which immediately suggests blood, flesh, the glow of vitality. But the color is only one voice in a chorus that includes also the drawing, undulating, tempestuous, like a swift torrent, and the composition as a whole, which, as we have seen, is based on lines of energy that project their tumultuous rhythm across the pictorial space. And there is, finally, the subject represented—animal, vegetable, and human forms, all pulsating with vital forces, the female bodies in which every feature that can stimulate the sexual instinct is emphasized, the male bodies with swelling muscles. Everything is permeated with life, responsive to its appetites, disdainful of its refinements (plate IX).

This might be the result of a deliberate choice, as in the case of Toulouse-Lautrec, mirroring the artist's own tastes. But a close examination of Rubens' paintings reveals a mysterious unity, as though the universe created by the painter conformed to some secret laws, as rigorous as they are difficult to define. This unity is manifested in a haunting atmosphere, a kind of "ambiance" or "climate"—to use terms that are very fashionable today—an impression of singularity produced by the characteristics that are common to everything this painter shows us as well as by his omission of everything that might divert us from these characteristics.

The things, the living beings and their ages, the time of day, the season—

everything reflects a certain order which,
for lack of a better term, and because this
one has no equivalent, we must call the
Rubensian order. For instance, we are
struck by the abundance of fruit in the
works of Rubens; but we notice at once
how rarely he represents flowers. They
were often introduced into his paintings,
however, by another's brush, for instance
that of Jan Bruegel, who occasionally
collaborated with him on his Madonnas
surrounded by garlands. The fragrance of
flowers is something too intangible for
Rubens; he prefers fruits in heavy clusters,
nourishing fruits, and it is these that he
arranges in garlands.

*Whether Rubens treats a pagan or a Christian subject, he always
rediscovers the same elements borrowed from life.*

258. - *At right:* RUBENS. NATURE DECORATED BY THE
GRACES. Museum, Glasgow

259. - *Below:* RUBENS. HOMAGE TO VENUS. Kunsthistorisches
Museum, Vienna

Photo Braun

260-261. - *BOTTICELLI*. Angels with Flowers. Details from THE CORONATION OF THE VIRGIN. Uffizi Gallery, Florence

In the same way, he dwells on the milk that swells the breast—that of Juno, from which spurts the Milky Way; that of the Virgin, from which there seems to stem a swirl of chubby-cheeked little angels; the hyperbolically multiplied breasts of Isis, the goddess of fertility; and the milk that revives the old man in *Roman Charity*.

His whole art is like an enormous and inexhaustible cornucopia pouring out before us the gifts of nature, as the Magi in his sumptuous *Adorations* pour out their offerings before the Virgin holding the Child. Everything is strewn out and squeezed into the limits of the pictorial space; everything jostles everything else and winds in and out in a farandole, like a chain that makes a thousand turns in order to fill up every corner of the canvas; we see such a chain in the *Homage to Venus* as well as in the wild *Kermesse*. Rubens has no use for the rational categories that separate and set things apart; he likes everything to be connected, from one end to the other, every element to serve as the vehicle of a single force, a force like that which makes the waves of the sea follow one upon the other. Just as the participants in an experiment in animal magnetism were not allowed to let go of each other's hands lest the flow of the force be interrupted, so in a Rubens canvas all the parts are closely linked, the better to transmit the current of life (figures 258 and 259).

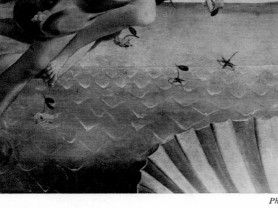

These surging forces that well up, that pour forth without stint, that spend themselves in the rushing impetus of the brush which flies in every direction at once, make their full impact felt when some clash is depicted: Rubens' battles between men or animals, his military battles, his hunts sing a hymn to life, this time in a warlike key. Everything is adapted to, ordered by, this vital force. The light of these paintings is that of high noon, and the season is summer, when the fruits are ripening for the autumn harvest.

Photo Brogi

In both his Christian and his pagan themes Botticelli displays a fondness for flowers, springtime, and youth.

262. - *BOTTICELLI.* THE BIRTH OF VENUS (detail).
Uffizi Gallery, Florence

THE UNIVERSE OF BOTTICELLI. Thus there is a logic, no longer a rational one, but an organic one, which unites all the elements of the painting, both of conception and of execution, combining its attractions in a way that holds the viewer spellbound. But this logic differs from one mind to another, whether the mind is that of a society, of a period, or of an individual. In each case we are transported to a different world.

And how different these worlds can be. That of Botticelli, for example, differs at every point from that of Rubens. Where Rubens' light is full, Botticelli's is fresh and suggests the morning; the powerful forms of the one are contrasted to the graceful forms of the other; red tones, to gentle pinks and blue, violet and greens; tumultuous crowds of plump, rosy children and muscular adults, to slender and graceful young men and women. The juicy roundness of fruit is contrasted to delicate flowers lightly scattered over meadows and over floating robes, or filling the fragrant air with their petals; violent, rushing movements, to the effortless gliding of Venus propelled by zephyrs and scarcely inclining toward the river bank that draws her; heavy drapery, to fabrics so thin that a breath of air flutters them. In Rubens, the season is summer moving toward an autumn in which "the fruits will exceed the promise of the blossoms"; in Botticelli, it is an ethereal spring. Each of these worlds is perfectly homogeneous, each is woven of a thousand different strands no one of which is like a strand of the other; each is alien and impenetrable to the other, each invites us to lead, within it, a different life (figures 260 to 262).

Each of these worlds reveals the innermost essence of a soul. As Louis Gillet says of Titian, in his *Tapis enchantés*, "the painter transforms his life, his feelings, and his loves into the substance of his art." He puts himself "wholly into it, and gives things the air of a dream, the air of being the elements, the words, of a poem."

THE IRREDUCIBLE ELEMENT: RUBENS AND VAN DYCK. There is no question that in thus projecting himself into his work, the painter willy-nilly brings over into it everything he experiences and everything he has absorbed from the society of which he is a part. Taine's theory has overemphasized this dependence, forgetting that great artists, whatever they may owe to their environment, take from it only

Photo Mansell

263. - *Above: RUBENS.* THE TRIUMPH OF TRUTH. From the series "The Life of Marie de Médicis." The Louvre, Paris

Belonging to the same school and the same period, Rubens and his pupil Van Dyck are antithetical throughout, down to their conception of the gesture. The figures of the former grasp things in their hands; those of the latter merely touch them.

264. - *At left: VAN DYCK.* EROS AND PSYCHE. Hampton Court, England

265. - *Opposite page: VAN DYCK.* THE VIRGIN WITH DONORS (detail). The Louvre, Paris

294

the raw materials on which they set their visible seal. They are distinguished from mediocre artists by the worth of their individual contributions. A poet, Théophile Gautier, realized this more clearly than Taine, a philosopher. In his *History of Romanticism*, Gautier does not deny that "while the great masters seem, from a distance, to have been isolated, they did nevertheless participate in the life of their communities, receiving almost as much as they gave, and borrowing from ideas current in their lifetimes." But, he adds, in a sentence that says everything that needs to be said, "they set their indelible seal upon the metal their age provided, and made of it a medal for the ages."

The bumblebee gathers nectar from the flowers; so does the honeybee, but the honeybee alone can transform the nectar into honey. Therein lies the essential difference, which separates the creative artist from the mere craftsman. Thus it may happen in the case of two painters belonging to the same time and the same country, that one may be nevertheless sufficiently different from the other—even if he has been the pupil of the other and been trained in his atelier—that he will create a different world from that of his teacher, provided he too is a great master.

Such was the case with the favorite pupil of Rubens. In Van Dyck, the joyful opulence of Rubens becomes a melancholy distinction. The glowing colors of the teacher yield to the pupil's secret preference for black and white, for the spent tonalities of autumn—coppery golds, subdued dark reds, faded yellows combined with cold blues. The heat of noon on a summer day is replaced with the expiring splendors of a twilight late in the season. The shadows rise, quenching the light.

In this shadowy silence, forms lose their rhythm and assurance; the drawing no longer moves forward, full and compact, like the undulations of an enormous snake; it becomes relaxed, it thins out and flows softly, like the hesitant drifting of smoke. The human figures lose their muscular vehemence; they, too, become thin and elongated, tending toward elegance rather than forcefulness.

Even the movements of these figures reflect a new "spirit." Rubens was fond of showing bodies jostling one another, as in crowds. Whereas gesture, in the Italian painters, is related to the form, just as it speaks to the intellect, in Rubens the gestures are concerned only with matter. In one of the panels of his *Life of Marie de Médicis* (figure 263), Time, grasping roughly at Truth, seizes her bodily with both hands, as one seizes a vase by its handles. In Van Dyck, however, the firmness of the flesh takes on a drooping aristocratic languor. His *Psyche* (figure 264) seems to be floating in water, like seaweed; instead of the density of flesh swelling beneath the skin, the figure has an evanescent weightlessness, scarcely touching the ground on which it is reclining. Psyche seems to have no more substance than Eros, whose foot merely grazes the earth with one toe, though this toe is the only support for his body. And behind them the trunk of the tree rises with the insubstantiality of an underwater plant.

The lightest touch is, for Van Dyck, the natural expression of the limbs. Eros contents himself with letting his fingers hover above the brow of Psyche. In the tranquil harmony of *The Virgin with Donors* (figure 265), where only the pale linen and the skin seem animated, the child Jesus makes a similar gesture toward the face of the man, whose hands, clasped in ecstatic prayer, lightly touch the Madonna's robe. Everything is in half-tints, half-motions, half-realities, in attenuated vibrations suggesting the intangible.

Rembrandt's world of shadows is peopled with old men.   Photo H. G. L.

266. - *REMBRANDT.* PORTRAIT OF A MAN. 1655. The Hermitage, Leningrad

Nothing shows more conclusively than the contrast between these two artists —when everything might have made them resemble each other—that at the heart of each work a constant factor is present; however subtle it may be, it determines the whole effect, gives the whole its significance. This characteristic presence manifests itself now discreetly and now vociferously; we must listen to it, give it our undivided attention, for it is the key to the message addressed to us by the work.

As Rembrandt grows older, his
aged men tend increasingly to
close their eyes to external light, in
order to perceive inward radiance.

267. - *Above: REMBRANDT.*
PHILOSOPHER WITH OPEN
BOOK. c. 1633. The Louvre, Paris

268. - *At left: REMBRANDT.*
PHILOSOPHER MEDITATING.
Bibliothèque Nationale, Paris

269. - *Opposite page: REMBRANDT.*
DOCTOR FAUSTUS. 1650.
Etching. Petit Palais, Paris

THE APPEAL OF THE INVISIBLE: REMBRANDT.   The apparent face of the
painting is there only to enable us to discover its secret face. The painting itself
opens, like a miraculous window cut in the wall of the world in which we live,
into the world beyond—into those obscure regions inaccessible to mere reason.

Poussin dominated these regions from afar; Rubens brought us closer to them
because he was unable to create without bringing organic forces to bear. During
that same seventeenth century, so rich and varied, another genius, Rembrandt,
led man to the very threshold of these mysterious regions which begin where
our knowledge of ourselves leaves off, and which extend into the darkness of
the infinite. No art has ever conveyed so urgent a summons to cross the boundaries
of the visible and enter the invisible; nor has the art of any other painter so forcefully extended the invisible into the unknown.

Where Van Dyck evoked twilight, Rembrandt crossed the portals of night.
The faint shadows become heavy, tenebrous; the actual presence of things is
concealed. In his art there is no trace of the obsession with imitation that had
gripped Dutch painters of the fifteenth century; his youthful works show only a
hint of it, which he soon eliminated, devoting himself thereafter to bearing witness
to that which cannot be copied.

Rembrandt flung the whole world into the crucible of his technique, bringing
it to the point of fusion and subjecting it to his alchemical process, in order to

Whether his old man is Tobit or Homer, he is blind and absorbed in inner meditation.
270. - *REMBRANDT. THE BLIND TOBIT.* 1650. Collection Sir Francis Cook, Richmond

Photo Anderson

271.-*REMBRANDT*. ARISTOTLE BEFORE THE BUST OF HOMER. 1653. Collection Lord Duveen of Millbank, New York

extract from it a new and hitherto unknown substance out of which he was to fashion his visions. There are no flowers here, as in Botticelli, no fruits, as in Rubens, except in rare cases. Rembrandt's chosen materials are somber and nocturnal fabrics, velvet, furs, which offer to the fingers and to the eye an indefinable depth, or else minerals and metals, gold and silver, precious stones, pearls—anything that has slumbered a long time in the bowels of the earth or at the bottom of the sea, and has emerged from these depths only to radiate light. Light, incidentally, ceases to be, for him, a medium that shows what is; it is an emanation, a radiation, having the strange quality given off by radioactive substances.

"Out of this shadow, faces with eyes emerge" (Victor Hugo, *Légende des Siècles: Vision de Dante*, VI). Except for a few studies of young women, whose faces or delicate flesh are also sources of light, Rembrandt, from his early youth, was fond of painting the aged, venerable figures in whom physical life is in the process of being extinguished, and in whose eyes, now that the tumult of existence is calmed, there becomes visible the life of the spirit—another kind of light, which Hugo also was later to see in the eyes of old men (figure 266).

In Rembrandt all the images of the physical world are nothing more than an anticipation of another world, the spiritual one; the sumptuous riches of the real world, whose brilliance he

272. - *REMBRANDT*. HOMER. 1663. Mauritshuis, The Hague

301

is not above capturing, are only a pre-figuring of a higher splendor, whose hovering presence he reveals to us. The eyes of his subjects, always so compelling, tell us of a secret that lies behind them (figure 257).

In his portrayals of St. James, shown praying with closed eyes, and of St. Matthew, shown listening to the invisible angel, Rembrandt transposed his own problem—that of the artist heeding the dictation of his innermost self.

273. - *At left:* REMBRANDT. ST. JAMES. 1661. Collection Stephen C. Clark, New York

274. - *Below, at left:* REMBRANDT. ST. MATTHEW. 1661. The Louvre, Paris

275. - *Below:* REMBRANDT. PORTRAIT OF THE ARTIST BEFORE HIS EASEL. 1660. The Louvre, Paris

Photos Laboratory of The Louvre, Paris

In the dark recesses of his mind, the artist sees the birth of unknown visions, summoned forth by the angel.

276. - *REMBRANDT.* THE VISION OF DANIEL. Museum, Berlin

PASSAGE THROUGH NIGHT. His paintings, if they are studied in their chronological order, disclose a progression, a unity, which is not that of ideas but of a logic of the depths. Around 1633, he painted his *Philosophers*, similar studies of an aged man meditating in seclusion and in shadow, beside a staircase rising into obscurity. Upon the eyes of the figure in each painting—though these eyes are turned inward rather than toward a reality that would only distract them —a window casts a pale light. Ten years later an engraving treating the same subject shows a deepening darkness; the old man has put his hand to his eyes, which are closed, no longer directed at the book and the skull placed before him as allusions to hidden truths. Another ten years, and he executes the etching that has been called *Doctor Faustus*; the figure and the surroundings are the same as before but now the night has opened, and as though from its womb emerges a supernatural glow, which breaks upon the familiar world, shaking it to its foundations (figures 267 to 269).

In about the same period, which was that of his maturity, Rembrandt discovered that the window opening on the world is but a diversion from the true quest, which can only be pursued inwardly. In *The Blind Tobit*, dated 1650, we see once again an old man, but an old man who, his vision extinguished, has turned toward

303

the revelations that come from Being. The blind old man is Tobit, but he is also Homer, and in a work of 1653 we see Aristotle, the embodiment of lucid thought, before a bust of the poet, its eyes blank; the philosopher is exploring with his hands and his eyes the enigmatic skull which conceals the secret of a profound soul (figures 270 and 271).

Ten years after this, Homer appears again; but this time, instead of a bust being scrutinized by a philosopher, he is a living presence. He has no use for the light which illumines the region of evident truths; he contains light within himself, he *is* light. This light emanates from his pallid forehead, from the diffused gold of his robe, and, above all, from the poignant humanity of his face (figure 272).

Compare this Homer with the painter's self-portrait in the Louvre, and you will see the extent to which Rembrandt was picturing himself in the poet. He was also depicting himself, obviously, in his figure of St. James, with his half-closed eyes, and his St. Matthew, who, his eyes lost in meditation, his hand raised to his throat, which has tightened with a sudden revelation, is hearing the "voices of silence"; an imaginary angel is whispering in his ear, disclosing to his spirit the "light ... out of darkness" (figures 273 to 275).

Rembrandt seems to be saying in his paintings what St. John of the Cross wrote: "We are not in this world to see, but rather, not to see." Not to see, that is, what holds our eye unduly when we are not seeking for anything. What we see here is in the highest mystical tradition, reminding us of the words of the Pseudo-Dionysius the Areopagite, whose thought inspired virtually the whole Middle Ages: "The secrets of God appear in darkness more clearly than in the light of silence, the master of secrets. When everything is black ... it floods with its marvelous splendors the souls that have no eyes." This thought, which nourished Christian mysticism, is echoed by the Hindu poet Chandidas, who writes:

The night of the world seems daylight to me, O love,
And the full daylight of the world is my night.

With Rembrandt, painting, the language of spiritual depths, brings us at last face to face with the soul. It opens wide for us the heavy door to an unknown region, which is within us, and which, in its impenetrable darkness, seems at first inaccessible to us. It is only in the last century that Western man has gradually become conscious of the reality of this region, of what it contains, and has set about fashioning new means for exploring it.

2. GLIMPSING THE HIDDEN

ONE of the great accomplishments of contemporary thought is the discovery of the unconscious. Classical psychology had dealt only with sensations, ideas, and logic, but at the beginning of this century, in 1901, Bergson foresaw that "the major task of the twentieth century will be to explore the unconscious, to investigate the subsoil of the mind by specially devised methods."

THE IMAGE, EXPLORER OF THE UNCONSCIOUS. The twentieth century has indeed opened up this vast new territory of the unconscious, which contains the sources, the motivations, the ultimate riches, one might say, of the soul, which was previously known only through the conscious mind, and of which painting is the language. In order to make this discovery possible the Germanic mind had to free itself from its *Aufklärung*, the sign of the ascendancy which the classical spirit had gained over it, and assert its own preoccupations, which were alien to Cartesianism; it had then to embark on the quest to which its own curiosity summoned it. Leibniz had sensed that there was a realm beyond conscious perception, but the new notion actually took shape in Jena with Ritter, Schubert, and Novalis. At one point, Ritter named the "involuntary" as the source of the powers of the imagination. Almost every great German philosopher of the early nineteenth century contributed a stone to the new edifice. But it was a painter, Carl Gustav Carus, who attacked the problem directly, and explicitly affirmed the existence of this region of the soul, the soil in which our emotions and dreams are nourished.

This is not the place to tell the story of this conquest of the human mind—a conquest of itself, this time—and of the new epoch in human knowledge which it

Friedrich's seeming realism barely conceals an anticipation of Surrealism.
277. - *CASPAR DAVID FRIEDRICH.* THE CEMETERY OF THE CLOISTER IN SNOW. Museum, Berlin

Photo Nitzsche

As early as the Renaissance, some artists discovered analogies between the images of art and those of dreams.

278. - *LORENZO LOTTO.* A MAIDEN'S DREAM. National Gallery of Art, Washington (Kress Collection)

ushered in. It now became possible to pass from the psychology of ideas, the instruments of the conscious mind, to the psychology of images, the products of unformulated mental life.

It had been possible to reconstruct that life by means of ideas, but only approximately and mechanically, replacing its vague, continuous flow with fixed data, as clear-cut as cogs in a wheel, and connected through the articulations of the brain conceived in the likeness of a machine. Through this process — logic — everything seemed to have been accounted for, but this was merely a superficial judgment; actually little remained of the profound reality of this nebula, limitless and diffuse, constantly in the act of transforming itself within living time, which is both its habitation and its measure. In the same way, we may account for the bird's flight by analyzing the play of its muscles, which can be dissected, but who can have a true idea of this phenomenon without seeing it with his own eyes?

This direct sight is provided through the psychology of the image. It enables us to gain an understanding that is universally applicable of the obscure impulses that move beneath the surface of our emotional life—an understanding not possible through artificial analyses. Ideas stand outside this life as fixed, unchanging terminal points; images content themselves with reflecting and embodying certain moments from it. Since it is prelogical, the image mirrors psychic life in the process of gestation, sometimes even at its source; it records it, without putting a stop to its development, in the act of being created, before it is enclosed within an intellectual shell.

Indeed, all available evidence confirms that the movements of life first manifest themselves in the conscious mind in the form of images. Before they develop systems of ideas, primitive societies express themselves through myths, which are nothing more than images. The same is true of dreams, which give form, as we sleep, to emanations from the unconscious, without their having to pass through the filter of the conscious mind. Art gives access to these same revelations, inasmuch as it, too, brings together the images that emerge into consciousness without prior intellectual elaboration.

In March, 1898, Gauguin, who was wonderfully prophetic about so many things, wrote to Monfreid about the sources from which a painting springs: "The moment when the most intense emotions are in a state of fusion in the deepest layers of our being, the moment when they ignite, and the thought pours forth like lava from a volcano, is this not the moment—brutal if you will, but great and seemingly superhuman —at which the created work suddenly emerges? The cold calculations of reason have no part in this emergence, but who can tell when the process was begun, in the depths of our being, perhaps beyond our consciousness?" To the extent that inspiration is a surging wave of images, he was right.

But he was merely rediscovering something that Carus, more than sixty years earlier, had established regarding the relationship between dream images and poetic images (the latter can easily be made to include the painter's images). Carus pointed out that in dreams "the soul, in choosing the images that correspond to its emotions, proceeds in exactly the same manner as the poet, who also evokes images reflecting the emotions stirring

Photo Flammarion

The Germanic genius reflects the disturbing revelations of nightmares.

279. - *DÜRER.* THE DESPERATE MAN.
Etching. Bibliothèque Nationale, Paris

in the depths of his soul, and makes them as distinct as possible." It is interesting to note that Carl Gustav Carus was a pupil of the German Romantic painter Caspar David Friedrich, whose seemingly strict realism is strangely reminiscent of the most modern works of some of the Surrealists (figure 277).

It must be understood that the image can reveal our unconscious mind only if it is not transformed into an idea, to which it is, by its nature, anterior. In hyper-rationalistic periods—for instance, in the eighteenth century—both poets and artists have used images only as *a posteriori* means of translating abstract ideas into visual language. But the true poet or artist feels an image rise within him in answer to an expectation, a wish, a need. Then, and only then, is the image authentic. Gauguin knew this when he wrote to Fontainas from Tahiti, in March, 1899: "Now it is night; everything is at rest. My eyes are closing in order to see, without understanding it, the dream in the infinite space that extends before me."

After the image has emerged—and at this point art differs fundamentally from the dream—the artist scrutinizes it, analyzes it, plans how to make use of it and fashion it. With all the resources of his intelligence and experience he begins to explore and exploit its natural riches. Art consists, strictly speaking, in this processing of images; whether they are taken from the outside world or emerge from our inner depths, they are but the raw material with which the artist works. However, he must never lose touch with the primordial impulse that brought the image to the surface.

Even Italian art, perhaps under the influence of Bosch, had a glimpse of the irrational.
280. - *DOSSO DOSSI.* THE DREAM. Museum, Dresden

Goya was the first to reveal the monsters generated by "the dream of reason."
281. - *Opposite page: GOYA.* THE DREAM OF REASON PRODUCES MONSTERS ("Caprichos").
Bibliothèque Nationale, Paris

El sueño de la razon produce monstruos

When the painter is intelligent, particularly when he has a logical mind, he seeks to understand, to account for the images that come to him in moments of inspiration; he forms an "idea" of them. Sometimes he is fortunate enough to be able to confirm and to complete them; sometimes, misled by his aesthetic theories, he distorts and deforms them. It is not impossible, therefore, that the critic should occasionally be more perspicacious than the artist himself about discovering the sources of the latter's inspiration—just as the psychoanalyst can grasp the true significance of a dream which his patient misinterprets, led astray by his wishes or his beliefs.

ANTICIPATIONS OF THE UNCONSCIOUS IN PAINTING. Some of the great painters were pioneers in the exploration of this domain: transcending the limitations of the psychology of their time, they found themselves face to face, thanks to their art, with the extraordinary power displayed by images when they are beyond the reach of rational thought. They were led, thus, to ponder the affinities between painting and the dream. Psychoanalysis raised these questions only at the beginning of the twentieth century, but painters sensed long before that that the visions projected by the imagination, like those seen in dreams, were the products of a region that lies beyond the conscious mind; and in this region they discerned forces which remained intact only if they were not caught in the net of reason.

The earliest glimpses of this hidden world date from the period when art began to be aware of its own nature and its responsibility and to inquire into it—that is, from the Renaissance. Lorenzo Lotto, that curious and restless genius, was scarcely twenty-five years of age when he conceived a strange panel, called *A Maiden's Dream*, which has been acquired by the National Gallery of Art in Washington. This painting is one of a series of Giorgionesque fantasies, the free inventions of reverie unconstrained by logic (figure 278).

The subject of the work is sleep; it shows a young woman slumbering in a half-reclining pose, leaning against the stump of a tree from which rises a laurel bough. Around the woman, nature too is slumbering; the rich glow of the setting sun suffuses the sky, but night is taking possession of the earth and its somber vegetation. Strange beings come to life in the falling dusk: at the left, we see a woman with the legs of a goat peering out from behind a tree; at the right, a satyr lies on the ground, drinking. Overhead in the sky is a cherub, a winged Eros, showering petals upon the young woman.

Whatever may have served as the pretext and the background for this surprising scene, we cannot help seeing in the painting a manifestation of the powers of the unknown that come into play at night, when consciousness loses its grip upon the world. The luminous cherub and the half-animal figures reflect the duality within the unconscious, between airy spirituality and animal instinct.

A few years later, about 1515, Albrecht Dürer produced a more northern, and above all more Germanic, version of the same duality in his etching called *The Desperate Man* (figure 279). Panofsky, who, no doubt correctly, considers this to be Dürer's earliest etching, lists the various interpretations that have been put upon this strange work (in his *Albrecht Dürer*, London, 1948, p. 194). He himself thinks that the picture is a medley of themes arrived at by accident, but he observes at the same time that such seeming incoherence is as revelatory of the artist's ideas and concerns as a composition that is deliberately conceived. Panofsky interprets the engraving as a reflection of Dürer's interest in the theory of the four temperaments, and sees it as picturing the effects of the *humor melancholicus.*

We shall see later, in discussing Hieronymus Bosch (p. 320), that an artist may resort deliberately to a system of allegory while his unconscious makes use of it as a pretext for the projection of private obsessions. Dürer's composition reminds us, in its incoherence, of the mechanisms of a dream. The figure at the left, based on an earlier drawing of the artist's brother, seems to represent the artist himself; at the right, there is a nude woman, rotund and sensuous, sleeping. The other figures seem to be the products of her nightmare: a man, his body contorted with fury or despair, is shown tearing at his hair; above him a strange face, with the eyes of a madman, impassive and almost glassy, stares into the void with an expression of infinite sadness; and finally a man with a satyr's legs, holding a metal tankard, gazes lustfully at the sleeping woman. Whatever Dürer's conscious intention may have been, he has given us an interpretation of sleep as a state in which dark instincts, repressed by reason during our waking hours, are released.

The joining of the Italian with the northern spirit produced a number of surprising engravings, in which, influenced by Raphael, Marcantonio Raimondi and his imitators depicted paradoxical groupings of nude figures, strange beasts, and even monstrous carcasses, such as are usually seen only in nightmares (figure 301). Certainly it is a nightmare we are confronted with in *The Dream,* by Dosso Dossi or one of his school, which was in the Dresden Museum, and which the Duke of Modena had sold to King Augustus III of Poland, calling it "a sleeping woman surrounded by various dreamlike creatures and by phantasms such as a burning city seen in the distance." Under a round moon, we see a gigantic rooster, like those painted by Chagall, an owl, and the spirit of Sleep, and grouped about them fantastic figures like those of Hieronymus Bosch assailing their prostrate prey (figure 280).

Nothing, however, shows as great a foreknowledge of psychoanalysis as that disclosed by Goya in his etching *The Dream of Reason Produces Monsters* (figure 281). Treating a very different theme—one taken from La Fontaine's erotic fable *La Chose impossible*—Fragonard had depicted a similar subject: a harassed angel slumbering in the midst of diabolic creatures such as venture out only in the dark of the night. But Goya, as the title he gave to his etching shows—*El sueño de la razon produce monstruos*—lays his cards on the table, so to speak, making explicit a formulation that until then had remained only a vague anticipation. He conceived this composition in 1797, probably as the frontispiece for the second series of *Los Caprichos.* It shows an artist (doubtless Goya himself), his head down on his sketch, and his piece of charcoal on the table. With the onset of sleep, consciousness has deserted its post, abandoned its control. Bats hover about the sleeper; the blurred space behind him is filled with the muffled beating of their wings: owls, the familiar companions of witches, are beginning to take possession of this shadowy world; and on the ground around him are other disquieting catlike presences....

ART AND THE DREAM. The close relationship between art and the dream was proclaimed by Wagner in his *Meistersinger:*

> *My friends, the poet's only task*
> *Is to record and interpret what he dreams.*

But before that Musset had written (*Lorenzaccio*, Act II, Scene 2): "The painter's life consists in giving reality to his dreams. The greatest painters represented their dreams fully, without changing anything." The spontaneous generation of images in our consciousness, whether the result of dreams, reveries, or artistic inspiration, functions like an outlet through which the fumes from a furnace escape, permitting concerns that are vital to us to manifest themselves, as they can do only at this remove. But, as we have noted, while the images that rise out of dreams are projected on a screen that is not illumined by the waking intellect, those arising out of states of reverie or inspiration are subject to the control and organization of the conscious mind. This organization reaches its height in the emergence of the idea.

Thus there is a continuous process of transition in which the image moves from the unconscious to the subconscious, where it is merely felt, and finally to full consciousness, where it is metamorphosed into the idea. The purpose of this process is to extract the substance of life from the primordial substance, in which it exists in a state of fusion, and to give it consistency and form; then, instead of being passively experienced, it can become the object of conscious observation. Both images and ideas are condensations of matter in fusion, which enable us to get hold of that matter and to manipulate it by solidifying it and cooling it.

Up to this moment man has been merely an actor on the stage of psychic activity; now he becomes a spectator, who judges and reacts. The image merely clothes a state of mind in a garment borrowed from outside reality; as Victor Hugo says in his *William Shakespeare*, "The dream we have within ourselves, we find outside ourselves." Once it becomes an image it can be looked at from the outside. The idea marks a more advanced, more civilized stage, and imposes a rational and unambiguous form on the image, which is still too close to the original undifferentiated emotion.

Between these two stages of "realization" there are exchanges and interactions: the image works upon the idea, modifies it, occasionally challenges its authority; the idea in turn influences the image, diverting it from its natural path, attempting to direct it and to bring it into conformity with itself. Thus it happens that aesthetic theories induce painters to revise the data with which their imaginations have provided them, and to deform their images by making them fit these theories.

THE CHOICE OF IMAGES. There are certain rules governing the choice of the images, from among those found in visible reality, most suitable for expressing the artist's unconscious drives.

Our perceptions of the physical world also take the form of images, by which we faithfully represent to ourselves what is going on around is. But these perceptions and sensations are closely bound up with our affective reactions and emotions (in fact, they are separate from the latter only in theory), which vary according to the outside stimulus as well as the nature of the perceiver. Every image recorded in the memory is suffused with a particular personal flavor that is inseparable from the accompanying emotional state, as has been so well shown by Proust.

Now, the same emotional state can arise in us without an external stimulus. We soon realize that certain emotions that are part of our psychic pattern resemble certain other emotions that are caused by images of external origin. Through this similarity, emotions and images come to be associated, and in a way synonymous. For this reason, in attempting to convey to another person an emotional state that cannot be represented directly, we evoke, instead, certain objects or scenes associated with it. Thus, the image aroused by a certain emotional state may serve to express the state itself.

The artist fashions for himself a repertoire, a selection of images, from among those he likes because they arouse in him his favorite emotions. He ignores, among the images which he is continually receiving from all sides, those which do not move him, and favors those which appeal to his sensibility. As a result, his representation of the world, though it may seem objective to the superficial observer, is inevitably biased, since it is essentially a reflection of his personal obsessions or desires.

This is why it is possible to speak of a dual interpretation of paintings. A work can be "read" superficially, the viewer seeing in it merely a representation of what he sees in nature; it can also be read at a deeper level, and then the viewer does not stop over the representation, but goes on to discover, between the lines as it were, the inner state of the artist of which it is an expression.

Such a reading "in depth" will pay little attention to those elements which come into the painting only through chance or through circumstances, and will concentrate on those which seem to reflect the artist's emotional habits and preoccupations. A familiarity with the history of art will help us to determine those features of a given work which it shares with other works of its time, and those which result from imitation or from temporary influences. Eliminating these will leave us with a number of images or features which, through their recurrence or repetition, point to what we might call the "constants" of this artist's imagination. It is in these features—which may consist in certain characteristic color harmonies, or use of forms, or a particular subject matter—that the secret of a given work is concealed; we are led to it by a kind of statistical survey of the works of a given artist. There is a game in which each player is given a sheet of paper bearing a confused tangle of lines, and asked to darken some of these lines with a pencil, thus bringing to light a form that is hidden in the seemingly meaningless scrawl. Through a similar procedure we may succeed in discerning, out of the infinite variety and richness of the images an artist sets before us, the features of his own face.

We are still confronted, however, with the task of interpreting these features, of charting the inner tendencies of which they are a projection. What was expressive for the artist is more or less expressive for us. While the images he depicts may fail to arouse in us states as intense as the ones he sought to express, they at least

Goya chooses the bloody episodes of his times that correspond to his own secret drives.
282. - *GOYA*. THE DISASTERS OF WAR. "Great Exploit Against the Dead." Etching

steer our emotions into the same path. It is then up to us to follow the artist along that path, for it will lead us to the source of the work, enable us to grasp its true message and know the need it answers. The painter, in this, is kin to the composer, who transposes the music he hears internally into notes, which we need only read in order to hear it in our own minds. It is up to us, then, in the same way to raise within us the silent song the painter has transcribed in his picture. The artist conveys to us something he alone has felt, often only dimly. His work says much more to us than he could possibly have expressed in words.

Will he be able to say even more? It remains with him to disclose to us what he does not know himself and never will know of his own nature, what his conscious mind not only is not aware of but refuses to become aware of.

283. - *GOYA.* BRAVO TORO (or Picador Tossed by the Bull). Lithograph. So-called "Bordeaux Bullfight Series"

3. HIDDEN WORLDS

THE obscure drives of the unconscious, which tend naturally toward the light, like air bubbles that rise inexorably to the surface of a pond, often find the exit barred when they reach the threshold of consciousness. They are rejected, condemned, driven back. Again like the bubble, which, if its way is obstructed, gropes about until if finds another exit, the unconscious drive, diverted from its course, in the end emerges some distance from the goal it had sought. As a result, its exact origin can no longer be determined from its point of emergence, unless we can reconstruct the course it has followed, and infer the cause of the detour. Such is the task undertaken by psychoanalysis.

Its methods are widely known and there is no need to discuss them here in detail; nor do we need to elaborate on the theory it advances to account for the veto imposed by consciousness on anything that might disturb it or contradict its judgments. Psychoanalysis also shows us how a compromise is reached between the prohibited drive that seeks expression and the forces that obstruct its egress. What takes place is technically known as **sublimation**; the prohibited drive resorts to a disguise, or camouflage, in order to enter the conscious zone unnoticed. Prevented from wearing an image that clearly expresses its nature, the drive will choose another that expresses it by the roundabout method of symbolism, which by its very nature is ambivalent.

GOYA AND THE BEAST.   We could study the means by which such repressed drives manifest themselves in a great number of artists. In the simplest cases, the painter chooses from among the objects he observes those which provide a surreptitious outlet for his obsessions.

Goya has already alerted us to his inner drives by giving the title *The Dream of Reason Produces Monsters* to one of his works. What, then, are these monsters that dwell within him? Let us look, in his works, for the shadows—at first blurred, and then fearfully distinct—of the terrible secrets they conceal.

It may be objected that there is no need to do so. Are these works not all explained by history, since Goya drew his subjects from contemporary life, which inspired him with horror? The bullfights—well, that is Spain. The scenes of slaughter—that is the French invasion and the Spaniards' resistance to it, with its resulting atrocities. True enough: but why is Goya the only Spanish painter of his time who made these things the very substance of his art? What accounts for this significant choice? There is blood over everything; men are shown being disemboweled by beasts or by the ruthless sword of a soldier, or impaled upon trees. The obsession with blood is all the more extreme in these black-and-white etchings, where its color cannot be seen (figures 282 and 283).

With these scenes of killing goes a bestial sexuality, eager to add rape to slaughter. It will be objected again that Goya had seen human beings transformed, by war, into beasts. But did he confine himself merely to seeing this? Or did he shudder, feeling a beast awakening in his own depths and stirring with a frightening affinity? For when Goya abandons his frightful realism to treat imaginary subjects, what does he choose? Singular scenes: for instance, he shows, in a small canvas in the Museum of Besançon, the murder of the Archbishop of Quebec, whose disemboweled body is being devoured by naked, hairy cannibals. It will be said that this subject was supplied him by history. Perhaps so, but why did he depict those same savages torturing sobbing women, whom they undress, tie up, rape, and kill in the series of sketches owned by the Marquis de La Romana—sketches apparently painted for his own pleasure, at a moment of relaxation?

A few years later he returned to this strain, in the canvases in the collection of the Count de Villagonzalo. The savages, who seem to have come out of some sixteenth-century German etching, once again brandish heads they have torn from bodies lying on the ground, and ready the knife which will slit the throat of a naked and screaming woman. Then they are shown dancing around an enormous **bonfire**. And these bestial or sadistic scenes always take place in dark, mysterious grottoes (figure 284).

The imagination of Goya, for all the differences of school, epoch, and iconography, discloses surprising affinities with those of certain late-medieval German painters, such as Urs Graf, Altdorfer, and Baldung Grien. They too, at a time

316

The imaginary scenes of which Goya was fond reflect the same savage instincts.

284. - *GOYA.* THE DECAPITATION. Collection Villagonzalo, Madrid

when men's baser instincts were being unleashed, constantly treated scenes of death and of war, figures of savage and hairy men, witches and their Sabbaths. They too were under the maleficent sign of Saturn to whom Baldung gave a face so demoniac in its asymmetry (figure 287), and whose name Malraux used in the title of his book on Goya.

The sixteenth-century Germans were expressing a collective unconscious, that of their tormented race, whose darker instincts were aroused by the disintegration of the medieval order; Goya was revealing dark personal conflicts, which the drama of his time merely served to bring into the open. Whether the unconscious is collective or individual, it seizes upon the earliest opportunity to manifest itself.

When Goya, having secluded himself and his infirmity in his Casa del Sordo, thought of decorating the walls of his rooms, what images did he conceive? Some scene of peace and light, to relieve his isolation? Not at all; gloomier and

deafer than ever, he painted, in the blacks, whites, and greens that were his favorite colors at the time, the sneering, blackened figures of witches, a black dog, a beast howling on a ridge in the wilderness; and finally Saturn devouring his children (figure 285).

Goya was unquestionably taken with this last subject, for he treated it again, in a drawing which shows the same monstrous savage, a giant old man with dilated eyes, whose carnivorous jaws, dripping with blood, tear at a pitifully tiny human body, which he is crushing in his claws. The corpse is seen disintegrating, like a tree cleft by an ax, falling to shreds, its flesh becoming meat.

Goya listened with horror, no doubt mingled with a secret delight, to the voices from the depths which remind man of his animal origins, his terrible bestial stirrings. Cut off from the outside world by his deafness, he was able to hear all the more clearly this interior clamor. His case serves as a particularly striking argument in favor of the Freudian hypothesis, which holds that our

285. - *At left: GOYA.* SATURN DEVOURING HIS CHILDREN. A painting from Goya's house. c. 1818. The Prado, Madrid

In his fantastic visions Goya even more explicitly discloses his obsession with the cruel and the bestial. Saturn, as Goya portrays him, is always present, openly or secretly, in the depths of human anguish; whether he appears in mythical or animal form, he is always the devouring monster.

286. - *GOYA.* THE DISASTERS OF WAR. "Fierce Monster." Etching

318

Photo Lipnitzki

The saturnine face is familiar to artists who are close to the anxieties of the unconscious.

287. - *BALDUNG GRIEN.* SATURN. 1516. Drawing. Albertina, Vienna   **288.** - *COCTEAU.* SELF-PORTRAIT. 1954

mental life has its roots in the unconscious, and that the unconscious is the strong-hold of the baser appetites, which are subdued only gradually, under the pressure of society.

Goya at first submitted to the conventions of the waning eighteenth century. During the early part of his life he, like his brother-in-law Bayeu, painted designs for tapestry, depicting scenes from the life of the upper classes or of the common people. But later, in his maturity, he showed his hand—and showed himself, not merely naked, but flayed. The events of his time, and certain anecdotes from history, provided him with a legitimate pretext for flaunting, in each of his works, the obsessions that haunted him. He could not help revealing this inner abyss; it yawned even behind the countenances in his portraits of the Spanish royal family.

BOSCH AND INTOXICATION WITH SIN. A number of great painters were prey to a similar intoxication, but in order to disguise the fact from others, or even

Photo Giraudon

291. - *At right: HIERONYMUS BOSCH.* HELL. Left panel. Doges' Palace, Venice

The theme of temptation was treated by Hieronymus Bosch in many variations.

289. - *At left: HIERONYMUS BOSCH.* THE TEMPTATION OF ST. ANTHONY. Central panel, detail. Museum, Lisbon

Photo Anderson

from themselves, they resorted to a set of symbols which seemed to resist interpretation. Now, these symbols are precisely the ones psychoanalysis has been able to decipher, in its explorations of the human psyche. One painter who used them was Hieronymus Bosch, whose period—the declining Middle Ages—saw the disintegration of one civilization under the blows of another, which was to succeed it. It was a time (as we have seen in the case of the German painters) in which unconscious forces began to spew forth flames and sulfurous fumes, just as volcanoes, in periods of upheaval, spew forth lava.

Hell and paradise equally express the human anguish in Bosch's imagination.

290. - *At right:* **HIERONYMUS BOSCH.** THE HAY WAGON. Central panel. The Prado, Madrid

Photo Anderson

Photo Braun

292. - *At left:* **HIERONYMUS BOSCH.** PARADISE. Left panel. Doges' Palace, Venice

The mysterious quality of Bosch's paintings was perceived even in the eighteenth century, by Joseph de Siguença, who wrote: "The difference between this man's painting and that of others is this: that others seek most often to paint man as he appears from the outside, while he alone has the courage to paint them as they are on the inside."

Bosch sees man's interior depths as a teeming mass of prohibited desires, just as Freud later saw it. We have learned how much it helps, in seeking out a painter's inner motivations, to study his choice of subjects and the "constants" that are so revealing in them. Bosch's paintings always center around the theme of temptation; for instance, he shows us St. Anthony surrounded by the fiends of hell, harassed by diabolical females, terrorized by inconceivable monsters assailing him by order of Satan (figure 289).

One of his greatest works is *The Hay Wagon*, which he painted about 1485. In it he shows all the classes of society succumbing to the temptations which harassed the hermit saint in his solitude. As an old Flemish proverb has it: "The world is a haystack; each plucks from it as much as he can get." The wagon, heavy with the weight of concupiscence, moves on blindly, crushing some, dragging others in its wake, and surmounted by pairs of lovers whose fate is being argued while a guardian angel and an impatient demon look on. The figure of the wandering Fool in the outer corner is there to remind us of the eternal folly of human beings who stubbornly obey the commands of their sinful appetites (figure 290).

This game is for high stakes, as Bosch's *Last Judgment* serves to remind us. Many painters have treated this subject; but no other painter has displayed the singular bias of seeing the Judgment primarily as a punishment meted out to the damned. The painting which Bosch executed for Philip II has been lost, though its memory is preserved in Hameel's engraving, of which a copy may be seen in Vienna. In the diptychs he did of heaven and hell, Bosch showed the same bias. At the final moment, the choice between the two is no longer in the hands of the individual whose fate is being decided for all eternity. Other painters have dealt with this choice, but again, never as did Bosch, who sees only the second alternative. Forced by the diptych form to represent both according to a solid iconography tradition, he resorts to trickery; in the panels in Madrid and in Vienna he shows heaven as an earthly paradise in which once again temptation occurs.

Heaven and hell are opposed in the two panels in Venice (figures 291 and 292), but if we look closely at these, we find that while Bosch lingers indulgently over the terrors of hell, he is repelled by the idea of having to represent heaven, as the Devil is by holy water. What does he show us? An immensely long tunnel which the elect enter, trembling in their nakedness. At the other end, far away, almost infinitely far, through an opening reduced by distance, shines the light which heralds supreme bliss. But how dark, oppressive, disturbing is the path leading to it![1] Will not the man who has escaped perdition be caught at the last moment, like the character in a famous story by Villiers de l'Isle-Adam, and flung back into the abyss of despair which he thought he had left behind him? This anguishing corridor seems a product of the imagination of Franz Kafka. And the outside panel, which folds in upon this one, instead of showing us the hoped-for goal, once again portrays an arduous ascent toward the empyrean!

Bosch has his paradise; he loves nothing better than to visit it in his hallucinatory dreams, but this too is a trick, the most devilish trick of all. His paradise is depicted in great detail in his *Garden of Delights*. It is actually a garden of earthly pleasures, which are easily detected beneath their camouflage of symbolism. Goya made a pretense of taking his subjects from the outside world, from historical events,

[1] *Semaine médicale* for April 30, 1952, contains a still from a film entitled *Images of Madness*, made by R. Volmat and Dr. P. Roumeguère: it is a drawing by an English patient suffering from depression with paranoid symptoms, which contains the same obsessive image, an interminable corridor with a light at the far end. According to the patient, the execution of the drawing brought her great relief.

where they were actually chosen for him by his instincts: in the same way, Bosch seems to be taking his from the allegories and fables that abounded in the writings of contemporary mystics or from the esoteric works of the alchemists. He too might have been regarded as merely reflecting his time and his surroundings. But taking advantage of a coincidence which deceived his contemporaries, and no doubt even himself, he was actually motivated by the strongest obsessions, which sprang from the secret places of his being.

Charles de Tolnay (*Hieronymus Bosch*, Basel, 1937) and more particularly Jacques Combe (*Jérôme Bosch*, Paris, 1946) have shown, through patient and scholarly analyses, that Bosch's symbols are ambivalent, on the one hand reflecting the prevailing ideas of his time, and on the other susceptible to psychoanalytic interpretation, as revealing his most deeply hidden desires. Jung, in his *Psychology and Alchemy*, contributed a weighty argument in favor of such a dual approach by showing that the alchemists' spectacular rituals and performances, ostensibly to produce magical results, were actually symbols enabling them to explore fundamental psychological truths which it was forbidden to mention or investigate in their epoch.

"Bosch expresses himself so directly through the symbols familiar to him," says Jacques Combe (*op. cit.*, p. 38), "that the symbolism in his works has the function not of a metaphor, but of a complete language, springing directly from the sources at which thought is formed. For this reason it has the expressive intensity of those primitive poems that came into existence in the early stages of a language and were still permeated with the mystery of its formation."

Bosch displays a constant preoccupation with those instincts which jeopardize man's salvation. Is this because he fears the consequences of succumbing to temptations? It seems rather that he is motivated by a secret enjoyment. Crude, even scatological details abound in his works; it has been possible to see him as afflicted with what the modern vocabulary, no longer that of Diafoirus, solemnly calls an "anal complex."

Significantly, he hardly ever treats a sacred subject except for the purpose of gratifying a camouflaged need to profane it. His themes are traditional, but his basis for choosing them is not so normal. He has a penchant for showing Christ as an object of contempt. In the *Ecce Homo*, *The Crown of Thorns*, and *The Carrying of the Cross*, the Son of God, emaciated and pitiful, is shown surrounded by monstrous, leering creatures in whom humanity has given way to a bestiality that rises from man's lowest depths (figure 293). To be sure, there are caricatures in Leonardo, but how much more intellectual they are! To be sure, there is the Flemish carnival tradition, but how much less aggressive it is! Is it going too far to conclude that the artist is on the verge of blasphemy and that he derives an ambiguous gratification from this humbling of Christ which he portrays with such force? Of course, he does not admit this to himself, but his painting admits it to us. No single example taken by itself is conclusive, but taken all together the works show certain constant factors which betray the unconscious drive.

Here, again, it is hard to distinguish the society from the individual. Everything found in Bosch is met with everywhere in his era, the close of the Middle Ages, when the individual, his faith undermined, became aware of his isolation and thought selfishly only of the two dangers threatening him—death and the devil!

Photo Giraudon

Bosch often portrays Christ himself scorned and assailed by the "grimacing tribe," as Ensor was to call it.

293. - *HIERONYMUS BOSCH.* THE CARRYING OF THE CROSS. Museum of Fine Arts, Ghent

Marcel Brion has correctly pointed out, in his study of Bosch, that "the forces of darkness, which the Middle Ages, with its theocentric construction of the world, had relegated to the background, and which the Renaissance attempted to exorcise altogether in the name of Reason, found their outlet in an art that no longer knew either God or the rational will." But this in itself does not explain Bosch: what matters is the new and insistent accent which the scattered features of his period took on as they were sorted out and brought together in his work.

DANGERS OF PSYCHOANALYSIS. Our brief investigation of Goya and Bosch puts too great an emphasis on the unconscious as a negative force, a weight that drags man down to the level of his basic appetites, his animal origins. It seems to confirm the conclusions reached by Freud, whose observation about dreams may be applied to the artistic imagination: "The unconscious takes advantage of the nightly weakening of censorship to seize on the day's leavings, and to express, with the materials they supply, a forbidden wish dream." Indeed, the worlds of Goya and of Bosch may be seen as forbidden dreams.

Freud, while denying that he ascribed a sexual significance to all dreams, nevertheless asserted that dreams serve primarily to gratify sexual wishes; they are projections of the libido, which he defined as the charge of energy with which the self invests the objects of its sexual drives. What these two great painters reveal concerning their unconscious selves seems to accord with this definition.

It must be granted, however, that Freudian psychoanalysis becomes less satisfactory the further it proceeds from its origins. While its founder was an initiator of genius, his stubborn if not obsessive directives to his followers (Freud, it must not be forgotten, was himself never psychoanalyzed, and this omission is disturbing) seem narrow-minded, overdogmatic. Some of his disciples have emphasized the sectarian aspect of his theories by applying them in an almost mechanical fashion. Adler and particularly Jung have admirably overcome this almost grotesquely exaggerated attempt to reduce everything to its sexual basis, and have shown us that the unconscious is far richer and more "human" than the Viennese professor had thought.

There is nothing to be avoided more strictly than the form of scholasticism that tries to fit every work of art into the straitjacket of some theory, or even to deduce its origins from such theory through an ingenious course of reasoning. With the application of a little skillful dialectic anything can be proved. But a great work demands to be studied and contemplated until the submerged echo of the life it communicates to us rises and resounds within us. Logic should not become a substitute for the message of the work; it should merely be used as an aid in translating that message into clearer terms.

We learn from works of art that the unconscious in which they are rooted does not consist in the unvarying recurrence of a few basic impulses, but rather that it is a realm of infinite psychic potentialities. The unconscious consists not only of what reason repudiates and rejects but also of the material ordered by reason, as well as of things that escape and perhaps transcend reason. We shall see certain proof of this later.

Furthermore, it is very rare, if not impossible, that a work created by the whole mind, as a painting is, should be a reflection solely of the unconscious. In the work of art, the contribution of the unconscious is subjected to outside forces, which derive from sources other than the unconscious. It must be said in all fairness that Freud realized this. True, he said that "it happens only in art that a man consumed by desires sets out to make something that will show their gratification, and that, thanks to the illusion of art, this procedure succeeds in producing the affective reactions that would have been produced by genuine gratification." But he added: "The real artist can do more than that. To begin with, he is capable of giving his waking dreams a form that divests them of all those personal features

Leonardo, fascinated by the intricate knots of inter-lacings, introduces them into the most varied themes.

294. - *LEONARDO DA VINCI.* STUDY OF HAIR FOR A LEDA. Drawing. c. 1509. Windsor Castle, England

which might repel others, and that makes of them a source of enjoyment for all." Thus the part played by plastic form is safeguarded. "The artist is also capable of embellishing these dreams, so that their suspect origins are concealed." Whatever reservations we may have regarding the term "suspect," which conveys Freud's bias, this recognition that the unconscious is transcended deserves to be emphasized.

295. - *LEONARDO DA VINCI.* FOLIAGE. Ceiling of the Sala dell'asse, Castello Sforzesco, Milan

Photo Braun

Photo Anderson-Giraudon

296. - *LEONARDO DA VINCI.* Device for the LEONARDIAN ACADEMY. The Ambrosiana, Milan

The moment the artist sets aside his own preoccupations and begins to draft his work, his unconscious is forced to take orders from his conscious mind, and at that moment a new equilibrium is in sight. In the chief essay in which he deals with a great artist, his "Leonardo da Vinci: A Study in Psychosexuality," which he published in 1910, Freud seems scarcely to have made use of his own insights. The essay provides a striking demonstration of the inadequacies and failures of his method. The secrets of the human

The interlacing sometimes becomes a labyrinth. Who would expect to find it at the center of a large Raphael composition!

297. - *RAPHAEL.* The Tabernacle. Detail from the DISPUTA. Vatican

Photo Anderson-Giraudon

Behind his conventional appearance, Raphael holds surprises, for he will paint a suave saint or an asymmetrical, fierce face, wasted by some secret torment.

298. - *Above: RAPHAEL.* An ideal face: Central figure below the Trinity and the Saints. Monastery of San Severo, Perugia

299. - *Opposite page: RAPHAEL.* A realistic face: Figure from the MIRACLE OF BOLSENA. Fresco. Vatican

soul cannot be unlocked with a single key, even the key of dreams. What unprejudiced viewer will see in Leonardo's *St. Anne*, in the Louvre, the vulture that is supposedly outlined by the folds of the Virgin's drapery? This one example is enough to indicate the difficulty experienced by the reader in attempting to verify the assertions made by the great psychologist about the painting. How can we help but think that Freud was merely realizing his own expectations, finding what he hoped to find? In the same way the subject, confronted with the ink blots used in the Rorschach test, sees not what is there, for nothing has been put there deliberately, but the shapes of his own dreams, as in a kind of psychological mirror. Leonardo himself, incidentally, was aware of these mirages which the imagination interprets according to its natural bent (cf. p. 108). The vulture of the *St. Anne* is more reminiscent of the old game of riddles, "Find the Hunter," than it is the result of controlled observation.

Once again: we cannot dictate to the painting the symbols it may conceal; these emerge only as the product of a "statistical" study.

LEONARDO DA VINCI, OR FEAR OF INSTINCT.   What "constants" does such an examination disclose when applied to Leonardo? An obsession with aridity and an obsession with secrecy. The world of Leonardo resembles no other; it seems to originate on some strange, half-dead planet. Ancient mountain ranges are thrust up, their crumbling rocky surfaces and bluish glaciers standing out more and more sharply, in an atmosphere that grows progressively thinner. There are grottoes, which Leonardo mentions in his notebooks among the recollections of his youth, composed of hard rock and impenetrable shadows, suggesting dryness and mystery. Mystery is asserted in his closed faces, like padlocks hung on the inaccessible souls which evade our grasp, our penetration, by their fugitive, glancing, deceptive smiles. It is asserted in the artist's much-indulged chiaroscuro, which blurs every relief, every form, every presence. It permeates all of his cold and enigmatic world.

We encounter this element of mystery in every one of Leonardo's creations—in his handwriting, deliberately reversed to put the curious off the track; in the knots and interlacings of many of his drawings, transforming a head of hair into a complicated pattern with a thousand indecipherable turnings or showing every line of the swirling surface of water; in his fascination with the maze, which is shown in the involved mathematical construct of lines he intended to have as the emblem for the proposed Leonardian Academy, which Vasari refers to as the master's "secret" signature; or in the almost identical labyrinth concealed in the foliage on the ceiling of the Sala dell'asse (figures 294 to 296).

It may be, as someone has pointed out, that these interlacings were suggested to Leonardo by a pun on his own name: Vinci is close to *vincire*, which means "tie, link, connect." But even so it has still to be explained why, among the many images evoked by this verb, Leonardo chose to make use of those which involve the most complicated patterns, ending in the Gordian knot, as it were.

Leonardo's art and his life were dedicated to his secret. First, to the secret of his sensibility lying beneath an icy crust of lucidity, transparent but impenetrable: art for him was *cosa mentale*. And second, to another secret, that of nature, which his intellect was bent upon deducing by catching in reality a net of observation and explanation. His mind was thus suspended between two riddles that fascinated it, one which it perceived within the self—a strong sensibility—and which it kept in check; and the other which it confronted in the external creation, and sought to penetrate. In Leonardo's notebooks we find a sentence of great significance: "The shadow has a power superior to that of light." This statement is true of the visible aspect of his art; it is just as true of its invisible aspect. Why did Leonardo hamper the free play of his sensibility, stubbornly subordinating it to his intelligence? What is the key to his secret? This difficult question can be answered only through a careful psychoanalytic study, which would not be content with mere generalizations. Too often the greatest minds are subjected to presumptuous oversimplifying analyses, by an alleged science which tomorrow will seem as childish as phrenology seems to us today.

We shall confine ourselves to noting a new fact, with which we have just been confronted: the images projected by the unconscious are not simply the products of basic instinctual drives; they also reflect—without the artist's being aware of this or capable of controlling it—a spontaneous tendency to neutralize these drives. Once this tendency begins to operate, the instinctual drives manifest themselves only indirectly, and the mind, free of these influences, comes into full creative play. This no doubt accounts for Paul Valéry's deep and almost fraternal interest in Leonardo.

We cannot say merely that consciousness intervenes after the fact, to control the unconscious, to police it, to retain only the necessary elements from all those it supplies. To all indications this selection and repression take place within the unconscious itself, and consciousness is involved only in bringing the selected elements to the surface and organizing them. The West, with its fondness for simple ideas and direct antitheses, tends to reduce everything to clear-cut, symmetrical alternatives, easily manipulable through dialectic. What a temptation it is to draw a line across the self, with the cloacal unconscious, a dark cavern inhabited by the human beast, below it, and above it the shining edifice of the enlightened mind!

Indian philosophy, less dogmatic, long ago made a closer approximation to reality in all its complexity, for it envisioned an unconscious that would contain the sum of human potentialities, the lowest as well as the highest, the temptation not only of the devil but also that of God. The task of the intellect is perhaps not so much to sublimate the instincts as to bring them to awareness, within the limit imposed by censorship, thus making them the raw material of thought. Only then do the instincts come under the sway of the conscious will, to which they are so to speak made visible.

Jung's great contribution was in showing that the human psyche strives ceaselessly to achieve a balance, to progress by means of unifying its most diverse tendencies. The conflicts among these tendencies are for the most part fought out within the unconscious, and it is there that the highest tendencies must win their victory; this is the goal of human development, to win such a struggle before consciousness intervenes. Images, and particularly the images of art, give us a glimpse of these deep conflicts, even though they come into being at a stage when consciousness has taken over and when every trace of the conflicts themselves seems to have been wiped out.

RAPHAEL, OR INSTINCT MASTERED. What artist suggests greater serenity and purity of heart and mind than Raphael? He does so to such an extent that today we tend to think him insipid, a criticism deserved only by members of his school. The great difference between Raphael and his school is that the latter merely copy his forms in their external aspects, while the master of Urbino gives us images which, though he has brought them to light, are still rooted in and nourished by the soil from which they grew. We have only to observe these images attentively, to feel the intense pulsations of life of which they are the crowning expression. This art, which seems ruled exclusively by Reason, is actually a moving confession, to the extent to which we discern in it the old struggle between Good and Evil that is symbolized in so many human myths. It is these myths that are brought to life in a number of Raphael's works.

Surveying the gallery of figures he created, we are struck at once by two diametrically opposite human types.

The struggle between the knight and the beast, and the creation of monsters play an unexpectedly large part in the imagination of Raphael and his school.

300.- *RAPHAEL.* ST. GEORGE. National Gallery of Art, Washington (Mellon Collection)

There is, on the one hand, the type into whose creation poured all the resources of his lucid mind and refined taste, whose composure seemingly cannot be shaken; on the other hand, there is the type that he creates as though inadvertently, when the shock of reality turns him from his idealism, and his brush creates faces that are not merely naturalistic but tormented, asymmetrical, sometimes even expressing a jarring anxiety against which his art seems otherwise immune. One such is the young nobleman of the *Miracle of Bolsena*, who, literally surprised by the viewer, turns toward him a countenance that seems almost unbalanced, such is the anguish of its look. When Raphael relaxes his control, believing he is merely recording casually observed details, a baffling accent appears in his work, akin to a kind of confession (figures 298 and 299).

Is there then a secret Raphael, who would have us see only the visible proofs of his victory over the problems of existence? What is the "statistical" evidence supplied by his subjects? More than any of his contemporaries he inclined toward the theme of the hero, the knight victorious over monsters—those monsters that, as Goya said, are produced by the dream of reason. The theme of the conquering hero in mythology is one of those archetypes which, according to Jung, has been preserved in the inner depths of our racial memory from time immemorial. It symbolizes the positive forces which free the soul from the negative powers threatening it, as embodied, for example, in the dragon about to devour the princess—whose other name is Psyche. Raphael painted St. George (figure 300) and St. Michael encased in glittering armor and confronting monsters, and St. Margaret after her triumph.

He displays a singular fidelity in rendering the *ugliness* of the beast, considering that he belonged to a school which, chiefly through his inspiration, made an exclusive cult of the beautiful. This man, seemingly the crowning example of the Italian mind's flawless logic, suddenly reveals a fondness for the horrible, enlivened with all the resources of an unrestrained imagination, which is amazingly close to that of the northerners, whose souls could never rid themselves of such tortures. Of course it is possible to trace the source of this invasion of tormented creatures, hitherto more

301. - *MARCANTONIO RAIMONDI.* THE DREAM OF RAPHAEL. Engraving. Bibliothèque Nationale, Paris

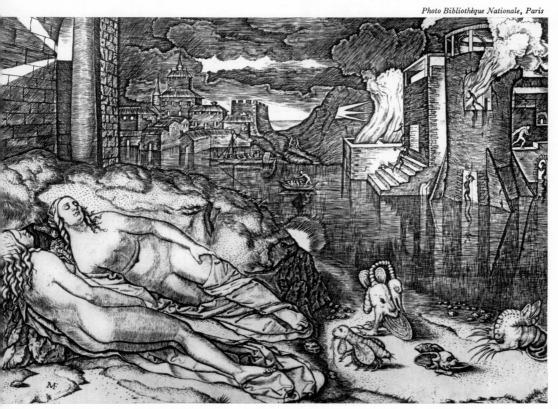

Attila, disorder incarnate, confronting classical civilization, inspired Raphael...

302. - *RAPHAEL*. ATTILA. Vatican

common in northern reveries; it must have come from panels of Hieronymus Bosch in the Doges' Palace in Venice. But while it may be interesting to learn how Raphael was able to gratify an appetite he had, the appetite itself still has to be accounted for. The study of historical sources, so much abused of late in the criticism of both art and literature, explains nothing or almost nothing. It is a good thing to know where things come from; but the important thing is to know why a given artist needed to take them, what the thirst was that he wanted to quench with them; this thirst is what is essential.

The worship of facts which nineteenth-century positivism has instilled into several generations evades the difficult psychological problem, which is the only path into the true core of the human psyche. It was Raphael, almost alone except for a few followers of Giorgione, who sought out and studied the few examples of the Dutch school that had found their way into Italy. And it was he who brought them to life most effectively, with the exception of a few engravers belonging to his school who exploited this vein of the unusual (figure 301). His small *St. Michael* (in the Louvre)—a subject that was echoed in the large canvas he executed in his maturity —is shown giving battle to creatures born of an imagination as unfathomable and diabolical as Bosch's own (plate XI).

Leonardo, who did not overcome these monsters but kept them shut behind a wall of ice, was one of the **few** artists given to such animal lucubrations; he often

...and Delacroix, too. But the romantic artist emphasizes the maleficent power of the barbarian king.

303. - *DELACROIX.* ATTILA FOLLOWED BY BARBARIAN HORDES TRAMPLES ITALY AND THE ARTS. Fresco. 1838-47. Library of the Chamber of Deputies, Paris

sketched such horrible hybrids in his notebooks, and even tried to produce them in the flesh. (There is a story that in his childhood, trying to frighten his father, he grafted the members of various animals onto a lizard, in an attempt to construct a fantastic creature.) The difference between Leonardo and Raphael is this, that the former created his monsters "gratuitously," while in Raphael they are destined to be crushed by the archangel. But, like Bosch, Raphael paints the glow of burning infernal cities on the horizon, cities which Delacroix later places on the shore toward which his *Dante's Bark* is sailing.

Raphael marks the triumph of lucidity—granted; but he achieved this triumph only after struggles whose intensity we can infer from the pale glow cast by his unconscious mind. In his *Attila*, the king of the Huns is shown hesitating before the pure figure of St. Leo, armed only with his spiritual strength. Why did Delacroix choose of his own free will to see Attila, in his study of him, as the terrifying conqueror and destroyer, crushing civilization beneath his horse's hoofs? It is such differences, which often go unnoticed, that lead us to the true inner meaning of a work and to the soul of its creator (figures 302 and 303).

An artist's basic themes and the manner in which they are treated are like iron filings whose position shows the outlines of the invisible field of magnetic force operating within him. In Goya we see the instincts erupting furiously within him, in all their devouring animality; Bosch, more subtle and more surreptitious, could not conceal his secret fondness for certain vices, though he associated them with the idea of sin; Leonardo subdued the instincts and discarded them in a glacial silence that was penetrated only by the voice of the intellect, alien to their clamor; Raphael reveals aspirations that are no longer content to ignore the baser appetites, but must attack them and supplant them. He signifies the triumph of such aspirations. But for the struggle itself, tumultuous, uncertain, we must look to Delacroix.

THE INNER CONFLICT: DELACROIX.   The works of the great Romantic painter express, in the veiled, almost sibylline language of images, that struggle whose vicissitudes are recorded by the conscious mind, which throws all its forces into the fray in order to build, by an effort of will, harmonious life. This goal is achieved through sacrifices, substitutions, and sublimations.

In Delacroix a terrible battle took place. Physically, he was a mixture, his contemporaries tell us, of a somber intensity which reminded them of a tiger or of a savage, and a cold and disciplined dignity, a refined and effortless grace: "The crater of a volcano skillfully concealed under a bouquet of flowers," Baudelaire said. Intellectually, he wavered between unbridled passions, which made him a revolutionary leader, and a Voltairean rationalism, nourished on the humanities and dedicated to a higher order, so that, to those who challenged him, he could say that he was a *pur classique*. He writes revealingly that there is within him "an old ferment, a black depth to be satisfied," a cruelty the equal of Goya's, which intoxicated his imagination; but elsewhere he says: "A great genius is merely a man of superior reason," and he confirmed this by his complete mastery of his means, by the effortlessness with which he made sacrifices, which he regarded as one of the conditions of art, by the importance he gave to "composition, that deliberate and intelligent work on a ground shaken, set in flames by volcanoes." The eternal dualism of light and shadow, good and evil, is reflected in his character to the highest possible degree.

He was aware of it. It is remarkable that at the age of twenty-four he drew up a plan for his life, a plan which became evident to the outsider only after his bodily force had spent itself, with the end of his youth, and he consecrated his maturity to the triumph of the spirit. He wrote in his *Journal:* "If only the soul had nothing to fight but the body! But it also has to cope with its evil inclinations, and its smallest but most divine part has to fight against these without respite." To fight! He uses this word in his motto: "One must fight, or die without honor. *Dimicandum!*" Still, it is his paintings, the images that reflect his innermost depths, that—far more than his thought, for all its lucidity—disclose to us the stages in this battle.

Delacroix gives unlooked-for confirmation to the opinions expressed here. It is rare indeed to find in one man, as we find it in Delacroix, the capacity for intellectual analysis characteristic of a writer, and the ability to project his thought directly as a painter does. But the fact that it is from his paintings, far more than from his literary works, that we are able to gain a clear insight into him—a clearer one, no doubt, than he had himself—proves that the essential conflicts of his life took place in the secret depths which are the source of art.

His first work of consequence, *Dante's Bark*, done in 1822, treats the theme of the wandering bark, familiar symbol of human fate; he casts it into the eternal darkness, and surrenders it to the frenzies of the damned. In the distance we see the burning city of Dis (figure 305).

304. - *DELACROIX.* HOMER WELCOMING DANTE GUIDED BY VERGIL. 1840-47. Library of the Senate, Paris

Dante, a reflection of Delacroix's dreams, having crossed the stormy waters of hell, attains to the serene light of the spirit.

305. - *DELACROIX.* DANTE'S BARK. 1822. The Louvre, Paris

Photo Flammarion

Young Delacroix's imagination was obsessed with massacres in which beautiful women come to a brutal end.

306. - *DELACROIX.* Scenes from THE MASSACRE OF SCIO (detail). 1824. The Louvre, Paris

307. - *DELACROIX.* Study for SARDANAPALUS. Woman Being Slaughtered. Pastel. The Louvre, Paris

A short time later, in 1824, he began the series of what he referred to as his "massacres": *Scio*, then *Sardanapalus* (1827), and finally *The Crusaders* (1840). These are all fire and blood, all women, voluptuous, seeming the more fragile by reason of being fair, made the prey of unrestrained violence, just as in Goya. But with *The Crusaders* the slaughter comes to an end; the river of blood begins to coagulate (plate VI, figures 306 and 307).

By then Delacroix had entered on a new path: in 1833, the *Salon du Roi* in the Chamber of Deputies saw the first of his great decorative works. In these vast compositions, symbolically cyclic, the conflict becomes broader. He was commissioned to decorate the library of the Chamber of Deputies and then that of the Senate. The torrent of passion now rushes into the temples of the spirit. The theme is transformed—it becomes that of civilization struggling against barbarism, of war confronted with thought.

In the Chamber of Deputies he is still hesitant. In one semicircle he shows Orpheus charming the wild beast with his song—the dawn of human effort. Alas, the other semicircle displays the lamentable outcome of history, with Attila assaulting civilization, trampling it; he is shown rising with his ferocious hordes, from a dark ravine, with a dense cloud overhead in which is mingled the smoke from the fires of devastation (figure 303).

In the Senate we see Dante completing his journey; guided by Vergil, he enters the luminous empyrean of the poets, presided over by Homer, to whom Alexander, the conquering warrior, presents his highest trophy (figure 304).

The ceiling of the Apollo Gallery in the Louvre (figure 309) testifies to the consummation of the victory. Here the serpent, timeless symbol of subterranean

The old Delacroix painted Christ calming the waters.

308. - *DELACROIX*. CHRIST ON THE SEA OF GALILEE. Formerly Collection Paul Gallimard, Amsterdam

forces, writhes in violent spasms, struck by the arrow of the sun god, amidst the jubilation of the Olympian deities. The game has been won; the serpent will coil itself at the feet of the crucified Christ, and the raging waves of the Sea of Galilee will strike at the bark of the Son of God; but light dispels the threat of darkness (figure 308).

It must be noted that Delacroix was not a believer. He was nevertheless the great religious painter of the century, for he saw in Christ the embodiment of the light that was the object of his quest. He invokes Christ just as, following Raphael, he invokes the theme of the hero (*Perseus and Andromeda, Roger and Angélique, St. George*) but the *allegory*, which he uses as a vehicle for his thought, is secondary; it only prepares the way for the *symbol*, through which he projects his soul.

"It is a question now," says Sigismond in Calderón's *La Vida Es Sueño*, "of achieving the highest victory: the victory over the self." Delacroix's whole *œuvre*, his very life, may be called such a victory. Its highest point is reached in his *Jacob Battling with the Angel* (Saint-Sulpice, Chapelle des Saints-Anges), completed in 1861, two years before his death. This work is a spiritual testament, as Barrès pointed out in his *Mystère en pleine lumière*, whose title ("The Mystery in Broad Daylight") serves to express the task of the work of art as we have been dealing with it here. On the ceiling we see St. Michael finally crushing the dragon.

Skeptics will say: "Why look for this hidden meaning in the painter's subjects? Aren't they often prescribed for the artist anyway?" It so happens that we know how persistently Delacroix tried to dodge the task he had been assigned: portraying the procession to Calvary, and the descent to the tomb. His heart was not in it, and he did not rest till he had arranged to treat the themes that expressed what he felt most deeply. On one side, we see Heliodorus driven from the temple by the Angel (another subject treated by Raphael): he is shown collapsing, defeated, amidst all the material treasures he had lusted for—gold, jewels, rich fabrics. Opposite him, Jacob is attacking the Angel. With all the strength of his massive body he struggles, lifted out of the stream of humanity which flows past him. He wrestles with the Angel all night long, "until the breaking of the day." He will bear the marks of the struggle but, victorious, he will be able to say: "I have seen God face to face, and my life is preserved."

Perhaps in no other work has the unconscious revealed with such marvelous effortlessness the fate of which it is the instrument, the fate of man, and shown how man can find his consummation in the wound he receives, when wrestling with forces stronger than he. In this hand-to-hand fight, intelligence is not a primary factor. Everything needed is already there, in the depths of our being, and it is these depths that art expresses, with the help of intelligence. It is not surprising that this most perspicacious and clear-minded of painters should have communicated this truth to us in one of his works. And the keenest of his admirers, Odilon Redon, also a great mind and a great talent, goes so far as to assert: "Nothing in art is done by the will alone. Everything is done by docile submission to the demands of the unconscious."

THE MYSTIC FLIGHTS OF EL GRECO. The unconscious is the as yet un-developed life of the spirit, but it is a complete life, rooted in man's biological nature

Symbolizing Delacroix's inner conflict and its conclusion, Apollo, god of light, annihilates the monsters of darkness.

309. - *DELACROIX.* APOLLO CONQUERING PYTHON. Sketch for the ceiling of the Apollo Gallery in the Louvre, Paris. 1850. Museum of Fine Arts, Brussels

and yet having access to the divine. Through this life, as Indian thought teaches us, man can go beyond the I and attain the Self, where individual problems are transcended in a unity that is reconstituted outside the phenomena and processes of nature that is pure essence (*puruṣa*), Being, what man calls God. This vast conception illuminates the role of images—that is to say, of art—in so far as they are the visible manifestations of the unconscious, from which comes and toward which goes "everything that strives to manifest itself, i.e., to have a form, to display its power, to define its individuality." Thus run Mircea Eliade's comments on Indian philosophy in his *Technique du Yoga*, and by a significant coincidence, these words also define what we have just seen to be the task accomplished by art.

In contrast with works like those of Bosch and Goya, in which the artist plunges into the unconscious to a depth that approaches the organic, there are others which seek to evade human limitations altogether by reaching the heights. Rembrandt exemplifies this in his turbulent art. But his total humanity cannot be kept to a single direction. In this sense, El Greco is a purer example of the effort to ascend. For him painting is a form of *super*-naturalism, if we take this Baudelairean term to imply the exact opposite of the plunge into the lower depths which is Surrealism. Under El Greco's brush everything expresses, in visual terms, a prodigious effort to escape from the world in which we are prisoners of our senses: his elongated forms (whether these derive from Mannerism, or, as has been somewhat naïvely maintained, from the artist's astigmatism, hardly matters; what counts is the use he made of them), which soar upward, before our eyes, in a swift movement like that of a flame; his compositions, which are the reverse of the solid pyramid firmly planted on the ground, tapering off, instead, at the bottom, and opening out like a fan, at the top, toward the sky; his themes—Pentecost, the Assumption, the Resurrection—or his figures that seem to be stretching themselves, throwing off their flesh-and-blood wrapping and denying the law of gravity (figure 310 and plate X).

His canvases strongly suggest a blazing mass: as fire consumes matter, its energies—heat and light—are released and mount upward as flames, scarcely deterred by the debris of combustion, by the ashes they leave behind. Irresistibly, each canvas is drawn toward the heavenly lights, as in the one where the soul of Count Orgaz, transparent as a genie in a bottle, a bubble seeking the surface, hastens upward (figure 311).

The light in El Greco is, like that in Rembrandt, beyond the night. It is a light revealed only to mystics who no longer call the solar radiance by that name. El Greco saw it as a beacon out of the darkness, as he saw those lights that he noted in the inscription on his *View of Toledo*, which "from a distance, and however small they may be, seem to us large." This light explodes within total darkness, creating phosphorescent effects that endow the familiar world with a new appearance and intensity, suddenly transfiguring it, as though a veil were torn away. Like the mystics of his time, El Greco sought to break through the boundaries of the physical world, the normal world of the senses.

WHERE THE SPIRIT RULES: VERMEER. There are men for whom this physical world is so transparent that they do not feel the need to break out of it, to burst it open. The unearthly light is within them, in their hearts; they illumine things

El Greco's forms and compositions suggest a will to ascend.

310. - *EL GRECO.* VIEW OF TOLEDO (detail). **C**asa del Greco, Toledo

343

simply by looking at them. These men enjoy peace of mind, for their unconscious knows only those lofty spheres where everything is radiant; the dregs remain at rest on the bottom. For such men the very idea of conflict is meaningless: they have nothing to struggle against. For this reason they do not try to escape from reality. They find in it only what they have put there themselves—light. Such an artist is Fra Angelico, Vermeer, or Corot. The gullible take them for realists. Fra Angelico so easily makes the transition from the gentle Fiesole landscapes to the sweetness of the eternal meadows, where the flowers are not bent by the passing of angels' wings. But we cannot analyze them all here.

Vermeer will serve as an illustration. (I have attempted to give an account of his spiritual experience in my *Poétique de Vermeer*.) His early painting, *The Procuress*, is dated 1656—it is one of the few works of his that are dated; he was only twenty-four years old when he painted it. Everything in it has a density that is physical: the subject, suggesting sensuality, the barter of flesh for cash; the composition crowded within its frame, though that frame is larger than those of the later paintings will be; the rich scale of colors with its harsh reds and greens (figure 312).

The only other dated Vermeers are *The Astronomer* of 1668 and *The Geographer* of 1669. Twelve years had gone by, and the painter, at thirty-six, was close to the end of his career; he was to die in 1675. He had become aware of peace and order; the crowded space has yielded to emptiness, but an emptiness that is at the same time strictly delimited: the regular box formed by the walls of the room is viewed from the front, and everything in it is ranged horizontally or vertically. Silence prevails: the solitary figure is shown absorbed in meditation. Within the white walls of his room, resembling the cell of a monk, he has discovered that his thought has no limits, that it can soar, with the map or chart as a pretext, toward distant regions, even toward the infinite it conceives of. The physical world is reduced to its simplest expression; it complies with the rules of the mind in order not to distract it, to enable it to rise upon its invisible wing (figure 318).

The path that leads from *The Procuress* to *The Geographer* can be reconstructed: after the first works in which the window upon the external world is still wide open, after the scenes of love, of drinking bouts, and sensual pleasure, such as he portrayed in *The Soldier and the Laughing Girl* and in *A Couple with a Wine Glass* (figure 313), Vermeer's universe comes more and more to be permeated with the music which in *The Music Lesson* (figure 314) serves as the new and subtler bond between the young man and woman. As its sound dies away, time seems to have stopped, so as not to disturb the reverie of women writing or reading messages that seem to come from unknown places far away, beyond the street, beyond the city, perhaps from one of those countries that occasionally appear on a map hanging on the wall.

Everything is concentrated in the soundless palpitation of the spirit; and the spirit itself seems to be concentrated, made palpable or at least symbolized in the precious globule of the pearl, from which a gentle glow emanates. The color, for its part, no longer features the reds and greens that were displayed in the earlier, livelier scenes; the ineffably pure harmony that now epitomizes Vermeer for us is a combination of limpid blue and luminous yellow (plate XII). Young women with smooth, rounded foreheads, pearls with an underwater translucence, milky-white walls, the dying sound of music—all these comprise an atmosphere of serenity (figure 315).

The irresistible soaring of Count Orgaz's soul is emphasized by the horizontals separating the lower from the upper part of the painting, and by the narrow opening between the clouds through which the soul passes as though shot from the mouth of a cannon.

311. - *EL GRECO.* THE BURIAL OF COUNT ORGAZ (detail). Church of Santo Tome, Toledo

Vermeer's evolution can be followed year by year. All references to physical life and its pleasures are gradually transmuted.

312. - *VERMEER.* THE PROCURESS (detail). 1656. Museum, Dresden

It is interesting to compare Vermeer's *Woman Weighing Pearls* with Pieter de Hooch's *Woman Weighing Gold*. De Hooch was no doubt attempting to imitate Vermeer; he brought over everything he could perceive or understand of Vermeer's painting onto his own canvas: the shape and arrangement of the room, the gesture of the woman holding the delicate scales, even her fur-lined cloak. But the imitator failed to perceive the underlying spiritual message of Vermeer: his own spirit was deaf to it. He did not understand the tranquillity lent to Vermeer's painting by the

As Vermeer matures he gradually simplifies and purifies his subjects and compositions; this development culminates in female figures shown against plain backgrounds.

313. - *At right:* VERMEER. A COUPLE WITH A WINE GLASS. c. 1658. Gemäldegalerie, Braunschweig

314. - *Below:* VERMEER. THE MUSIC LESSON. Buckingham Palace, London

315. - *Below, right:* VERMEER. THE PEARL NECKLACE. c. 1662. Museum, Berlin

Photo Bruckmann-Giraudon

Photo H. G. L.-Giraudon

Photo Rijksmuseum, Amsterdam

316. - *VERMEER.* WOMAN WEIGHING PEARLS.
c. 1662. National Gallery of Art, Washington (Widener Collection)

unbroken wall; he cut into his with a door opening onto other rooms that arouse the viewer's curiosity, and replaced the smooth whitewash with an overrich embossed texture. He did not understand that the window must remain closed to outside distractions; that the color, avoiding the harshness of overintense tones, must subtly carry out the dialogue between the subdued blues and yellows; and that the painting of the Last Judgment, which hangs on the wall in the background of the Vermeer, adds a solemn overtone to the anecdotal balancing of the little scale. Finally— and this is the most important thing of all—De Hooch failed to grasp that the essential element in the scene was the pearl. Out of common greed, he substituted for its marvelous silent presence the clinking gold pieces, thus banishing at one stroke the magic of the unconscious, and leaving behind only the crushing weight of material facts. The fragile, crystalline poetry of the scene is shattered (figures 316 and 317).

Anyone still in doubt as to the hidden meanings, the implicit language which the painter uses instinctively in bringing together the elements that comprise his work, anyone who still maintains that our interpretations are "literary," will perhaps be convinced by Claudel's lines on the pearl. In these lines, the poet was unwittingly describing Vermeer's art and its inner meanings, though he thought he was merely describing the pearl: "...pure and round, it frees itself, immortal, from that ephemeral being that has given it birth. It is the image of that lesion which the desire for perfection causes in us, and that slowly results in this priceless globule... It does not sparkle or burn; it touches; a fresh life-giving caress to the eye, the skin, and the soul....A sort of soul attains utterance. A kind of dawn, a kind of hunger for the light. It is no longer the brilliance of the mineral; it is an intimate tenderness that flows out" (Paul Claudel, *The Eye Listens*, pp. 275 and 278).

Not a single word need be altered. The passage, though it does not deal with Vermeer, could not conceivably be more apt, keener, more perceptive, as an analysis of his art.

PAINTING, OR SPIRIT MADE MANIFEST.   "A sort of soul attains utterance" —does not this phrase sum up the powers that I have been attributing to the

The same subject treated by Pieter de Hooch changes in meaning, for all the outward similarities. The details are lacking in simplicity, and gold pieces take the place of pearls.

317. - PIETER DE HOOCH. WOMAN WEIGHING GOLD.
Museum, Berlin

painter's art? A kind of soul that attains visibility, if you prefer, at the same time as it attains beauty.

The curve we have plotted is complete; in the works of the great masters we have seen the scope of the unconscious, of its resources as they are embodied in images—from its roots, plunging into the soil, to its crown, soaring into the light. Is not the unconscious merely a new word for that quality, once called the soul, which is opposed to the intellect?

The requirements of logical exposition may, however, have created the illusion of an orderly ascent, with each of the painters we have discussed marking a different level of altitude. In reality the path followed by the individual artist is more complicated, involving unexpected wanderings and regressions. If we had followed Vermeer to the end of his career, we would have found that in his last years, during an illness that probably hastened his premature death, he lost some of his unerring precision. While his technical skill increased with experience, gradually the strength needed to impose his inner law upon the universe waned; his world was invaded, as a garden is by weeds, by too much detail, too many complications imposed by reality, which once again asserted itself; and once the dam was broken, everything was submerged by realism. As his compositions became more complex, his colors degenerated, and the pure chords of blue and yellow were marred, tending toward maroons and browns, which, according to child psychologists, reflect physical deficiencies, sickness. Regardless of what may have been said on this subject, I am convinced of this degeneration. *The Studio*, which dazzles us by its perfect technique, and the *Allegory of the Old Testament*, where a heavily explicit language has replaced the communication of the ineffable, as though the magic had evaporated, despite their technical proficiency, mark the stages of a regression.

The same is true of Watteau. I shall not repeat here the arguments I developed elsewhere (*L'Univers de Watteau*, published with Hélène Adhémar's *Watteau*, Paris, 1950), but will merely state that Watteau in his youth succeeded in expressing in his paintings the indefinable spiritual state in which carnal desire is transmuted into gentle, timid hope, shading into nostalgia, thus sublimating the ardent instincts of adolescence, and extracting from them only a delicate and slightly morbid fragrance.

The rising curve of Vermeer's art culminates in his savants mentally confronting the infinite in their narrow cells.

318. - *VERMEER.* THE GEOGRAPHER. Städelsches Kunstinstitut, Frankfurt

But as he moved closer to his death, which was also terribly premature, he came under the pressure of reality. His avidity for it grew more intense, more detailed; his work is redeemed by his nervous delicacy, but nevertheless the preoccupation with reality caused him to lose his magic. A comparison between the two versions of the *Embarkation for Cythera* will serve to illustrate this (figures 319 and 320). We may wonder whether, had Watteau lived longer, he might have escaped the perils of this realism, which lay in wait for him, threatening to raise its too noisy voice and drown out the song of the spirit. It is this song, infinitely various, and mysteriously contained in the signs used in painting, that it is important to decipher.

4. PSYCHOLOGICAL EXPLORATION

IN creating his works, the artist has opened a window on his soul. We cannot expect to find in it the clarity which is the exclusive appanage of reason. Instead, what we discover are tendencies, obscure impulses, and currents, among which our eyes, even after they become accustomed to the dimness prevailing in these recesses of the mind, find their way with difficulty. Our exploration must proceed with caution.

LIGHT AND SHADOW. Why, then, do we not confine ourselves to that area in which clarity does prevail? Because it gives an incomplete, and hence misleading, impression. It would be easier and more reassuring to pretend that nothing exists outside this area; man did that very thing for a long time. Indeed, it is certain that to venture beyond it involves many risks. Nevertheless we must undertake this exploration; the human mind has never ceased to confront uncertainty in its effort to extend the boundaries of truth.

The psychology of art, which seeks to chart this primordial chaos of the soul, must never lose sight of the difficulty of its task and must take all the necessary precautions. More than twenty-five years ago Dr. Allendy wrote: "So long as the need for artistic creation was accounted for entirely by conscious, logical, volitional factors, only a limited aspect of the question was being dealt with. The recent great advance in our understanding of life lies in the introduction of emotional factors which have their roots deep in the unconscious, among the most basic impulses of living matter.... The new psychology faces new problems, which have no bearing on the value of a work, but relate to the unconscious scope of art, the purely emotional sources of inspiration, its essential significance, the nature of mental images, their unconscious symbolism, the need to create—all of which raises new specific questions which new specialists will have to study, applying contemporary thought to the domain of art" (*Formes*, No. 1, December, 1929, p. 30).

Between the two versions of one work Watteau's sensibility underwent a change.

319. - *WATTEAU.* EMBARKATION FOR CYTHERA (detail). The Louvre, Paris

The individual pair of lovers has become a worldly "kermesse," or outing.

320. - *WATTEAU.* EMBARKATION FOR CYTHERA (detail). Museum, Berlin

It is important to be aware at the outset of the difficulties of the enterprise. Access to the obscure depths of the soul to be penetrated can be gained, as we know, only through the ambiguous mediation of the image, a spontaneous symbol, illogical but demanding. Now this symbol, as specialists have discovered, is complex and elusive by nature; it is polyvalent, lending itself to many interpretations, whose diversity and apparent contradictions are sometimes repugnant to the mind, which naturally seeks unity. An idea, in order to be clear, can have one, and only one, meaning; it may even be said that it was with this end in view that the mind fashioned ideas as its instrument. But the symbol is only partially detached from the various associations and sense impressions out of which it arises.

On the other hand, the symbol, despite its complexity, is far more stable and constant than it might at first be thought. Once a connection has been established between a given reality and its outward sign, this connection will always prevail; it will be seen universally, as we have already shown. Otto Rank and Hans Sachs describe this property of symbols: "The formation of symbols is not a matter of chance ... it is governed by laws, and results in typical and general patterns which transcend the borders of space and time, of sex and race, and even cut across the major linguistic divisions."

But let there be no mistake about this: it is not the same *meaning*, but the same *meanings*, that link a given symbol with a given object. Psychoanalysis has attempted to explain, through the mechanisms of condensation and transference, this changing character of the symbol: a given symbol may have a certain meaning, which will be encountered in all periods and in all places, but it can also have other meanings, and, more important, it can have them simultaneously! We must not forget that the symbol is registered on our consciousness in the form of an image, which remains alien to the rules of logic. Thus, errors of interpretation lie in wait for the psychologist at every step. He can avoid them only if he never isolates any one symbol present in the soul of an artist from all the others; only through such a joint confrontation can he put his finger on the general tendency common to all, on the affinities among them that help in placing them. And even then another complication may arise: it is not impossible that a given symbol may serve as the channel of expression for several separate impulses operating on different levels.

THE COLLECTIVE AND THE INDIVIDUAL. Nor is this all: the soul of which we catch a glimpse in the images that rise to its surface; this soul which speaks to us indistinctly through these images, whose intonations, the pressures it exerts, we begin to discern; this soul which gradually takes shape before our eyes—whose soul is it? The artist's, of course. But what does this mean? For the last century and a half we have been accustomed to regard the artist as an entity contained within his own ego, a person apart. We tend to forget that the life of each one of us is bound up with that of his epoch; certain individual characteristics distinguish the former from the latter, but often the distinctions between the two are slight—far more often than our pride is willing to admit or our consciousness to perceive. Every artist is an integral part of his time, and often of a school of art.

The work of art, being an exact reflection of the artist's inner life, records with equal fidelity those elements deriving from the uniqueness of that inner life, and those deriving from the influences at work upon it. The former elements predominate when the personality of the artist is strong and independent, but also when the historical circumstances allow them to be dominant.

In the course of the centuries, civilization has moved away from the collective stage in which primitive societies existed and toward the individualism of the modern era. During the Middle Ages, the artist projected his own identity only against his will, so to speak, for he was dedicated to a common faith which he strove only to interpret submissively. Not so in recent centuries, when originality has been cultivated to the point of exaggeration, when it has become the criterion of value; today it is individuality that seeks priority. Gide's injunction: "Make of yourself, patiently or impatiently, the most irreplaceable of creatures," has become the maxim of an epoch whose art seems to testify only to the irreducible autonomy of each individual.

Each race and each century extracts those elements from reality which correspond to its feelings and which express them, without the artists' being aware of this. These elements are further sifted by each individual artist and adapted to his own needs. He may transform them radically, even to the point of making them into their opposites, but he will in each case take some position in relation to them.

The individual and the collective are found together in great artists. Whatever personal elements contribute to the inspiration of Hieronymus Bosch, it reflects that of the declining Middle Ages, which is also reflected in Van der Weyden's work.

321. - *VAN DER WEYDEN.* THE LAST JUDGMENT (detail).
Hospital, Beaune

355

Hieronymus Bosch reveals his secret preoccupations to us; but at the same time he reveals those of the fifteenth century, of the waning Middle Ages. How are we to tell at what point he achieves independence, separates himself from his time? For his soul is the soul of his race, whose characteristics are common to all the northern schools, so different from the Italian, for example. And more than that: beyond himself, beyond the Middle Ages, beyond the northern schools, Bosch's canvases embody and communicate an anguish common to the entire human species (figure 321).

The individual unconscious is thus inseparable from the collective unconscious, a new concept developed only in the course of recent decades. Jung has shown that many of our archetypes are survivals of the most primitive mentality, that of the earliest races of men.

As in the Assyrian ziggurats, each level serves as a foundation for the next. A comparative study of the images begotten by the mind reveals, to begin with, certain constants that are universal, found in every time and place, and consequently to be considered as inherent in the species; others, whose application is more circumscribed, then appear, which are characteristic of certain groups, certain civilizations, nations, social classes. Still others belong only to a given epoch and define its particularity. Finally, the individual projects himself, crowning the whole and giving his own particular emphasis to the themes of the collectivity, or rather the various collectivities with which he is connected. And within the individual's private projection, it is possible to distinguish among his successive chronological periods, each with its different problems and different methods of coping with them.

It is clear, in the light of the foregoing, that all narrow and systematic methods must be rejected. It is not sufficient to see each work, as Taine does, as the product of a given race, milieu, and epoch. Nor is it possible to regard as adequate a method that exalts above everything the individual, seeing the artist of genius as a sudden, spontaneous phenomenon which cannot be accounted for and whose strength renders him immune to all influence.

So far we have dealt only with the unconscious. But the conscious elements too can be investigated—the ideas the artist forms, as well as the ideas others have formed for him, which he has been

322. - *PISANELLO.* ST. CHRISTOPHER, AND DRAPED WOMAN. Collection Koenigs, Haarlem

Photo Giraudon

taught, which he has acquired from his family, his social and intellectual milieu. The same complex structure will be found at both levels, the conscious and the unconscious. Every individual is the product of influences to which he has been subjected internally, by the unconscious, and externally, by ideas; but he is also an ego that strives to master itself, to assert itself, that aspires with all its being to belong only to itself.

Thus the work of art must be read at several different levels, superimposed one on the other but encompassed simultaneously in our vision. Each level is a curious admixture of conscious and unconscious elements, but it is not impossible for us to distinguish between them, as the eye sometimes does in scanning the successive levels of a visual object, preserving at the same time the total impression. Provided this total impression is kept intact, analysis may discover the presence of the various components. Such a process of analysis will be outlined in the following sections.

The drawing styles of various schools reveal national characteristics.

323. - French School. A SAINT. Late fourteenth century. The Louvre, Paris

324. - Flemish School. Study for a DESCENT FROM THE CROSS. Fifteenth century

Photo Giraudon

Photo Giraudon

RACIAL ELEMENTS.   The canvases of Bosch and of Delacroix that we have discussed demonstrated that the most universal human characteristics are expressed by artists and in works of art. If we narrow our field of investigation, certain racial characteristics manifest themselves. The term "race" has fallen into disrepute because it has been made the tool of politics. It would be absurd to fall into the opposite error by denying the existence of a concept so self-evident, even though its nature is difficult to define.

The fact is that, for reasons which science has not yet succeeded in elucidating, certain human groups are distinguished from others by specific characteristics. Are these distinctions the result of heredity, of centuries-long adaptation to certain climatic conditions, which also determine the nature of plants, or of the slow action of a culture that remains constant? Whatever the reasons may be, the fact remains that human groups are distinguished one from another; and each group has its own psychology, largely determined by unconscious processes. Any arguments that may be advanced against this statement are refuted by the evidence supplied by art. Its images provide a silent testimony that is perceived at a glance.

Even drawing, which is more complex and more flexible than any handwriting, has certain expressive constants that are characteristic of particular racial groups. These are so evident that they supply the expert with an empirical basis for his diagnoses: what specialist would ever confuse a fifteenth-century Flemish or German drawing with a French or Italian drawing of the same period (figures 322 to 324)?

The Flemish artist's strokes are angular, abrupt; he does not control his line rationally. His gaze merely follows the successive forms and directions it perceives. He is little concerned with bringing these into any kind of harmony. The German artist's drawing is characterized by its complexity, by a harsh and tormented quality manifested in sharp turns, curlicues, and a proliferation of vehement, cramped details. By contrast, the Italian effortlessly brings his forms into harmony with the models provided by solid geometry. As for the Frenchman, he too reveals himself as concerned with intellectual qualities, with organization and consistency, but his harmonies are less pronounced than the Italian's; they are more flexible, gentler, more unexpected and more uncertain, and at the same time more graceful.

Are not the traits we thus discern profoundly characteristic not only of schools of art but of human groups? Yet they can be read here as clearly as in handwriting, which also varies distinctly from one nation to another, and is a revelation of national character. Various influences and geographical circumstances might result in transitional styles, which may at first appear to defy racial classification; but a patient and expert analysis will detect the fundamental characteristics beneath the seeming heterogeneity.

Needless to say, racial or national traits are revealed ever more clearly when the analysis is not confined to line drawings, but is based on all the elements of a painting. Such revelations are in the nature of a work of art; we find them in sculpture and even in architecture. Germain Bazin has published a study ("Dieu est-il Français?" in L'Amour de l'Art, January, 1931) in which he demonstrates the traditional antithesis between the French and the German mind as manifested in the faces in medieval art. Particularly instructive is a comparison between the representations of the prophet Jonah, at Bamberg, and of St. Theodore, at Chartres: the mystery of the two racial temperaments—attracted to each other because they are complementary, and at odds because they are so dissimilar—seems to be fully revealed in these two figures (figures 325 and 326). The French figure, product of a gentle and fertile land, where living is easy, presents a relaxed and serene face, with an open and calm expression, promising a ready response, instilling confidence. The German, who from time immemorial has had to wrest his living from a land covered with impenetrable forests, having poor soil and an unfriendly climate, has developed strength and a massiveness; he is defensive out of distrust, and aggressive; he finds it difficult to organize a body of conflicting qualities, in which violence and anguish go hand in hand. If much larger classifications—as, say, the art of China and of Europe—could be compared in this way, each would appear undoubtedly as a distinct mental universe, almost totally incompatible with the other.

Photo Archives Photographiques

The characteristics of various people are reflected in the types invented by their artists.

325. - PROPHET JONAH. Bamberg Cathedral   **326. - ST. THEODORE.** Cathedral of Chartres, south portal

CULTURAL ELEMENTS.   The character of culture, which is determined both by geographical factors and by chronological development, can be similarly inferred from works of art. Take, for example, three works, each representative of a different Mediterranean culture—the first, a product of the Mesopotamian genius, the second of the Greek, and the third of the Christian. Each, we will find, has a characteristic image of divinity, which tells us at a glance the nature of man's relationship with his world in that particular culture; a study of the relevant texts would inevitably lead to the same conclusions, only more slowly and laboriously. In the Assyrian example, a figure representing the Southeast Wind, or the demon Pazuzu, whose animal traits anticipate those later used to portray the devil, the artist expresses the fear of the supernatural, of maleficent powers that threaten man with enslavement and suffering. The Greek artist, in the pure, smooth contours of his head of

Photo Flammarion   *Photo Giraudon*

The soul of a culture is disclosed in its images of gods. Assyrian magic contrasts with Greek reason.

327. - Assyrian art. THE SOUTHEAST WIND. The Louvre, Paris   **328.** - Greek art. ATHENA PARTHENOS. Reduced from Phidias' gold and ivory statue. Museum, Athens

Zeus, expresses the perfect harmony man has achieved, through reason, between the laws governing his thought and those governing nature. To this harmony the Christian artist adds the glow of love, of sympathy, in the fullest sense of that term, that God willed between Himself and man by His assuming human form and sharing in human suffering. These three images, embodying three major human traits, speak with great eloquence when placed side by side (figures 327 to 330).

The analysis can be pushed further if we examine successive stages within a single civilization. How did the Christians represent, and hence conceive of, Christ on the cross, over the centuries? We know what a profound upheaval in the Western soul was caused by St. Francis of Assisi; nothing illustrates it more vividly than three works of art executed within the narrow confines of only two generations. Lucca was the birthplace, in the thirteenth century, of one of the earliest schools of Italian painting; a number of large crucifixes, at that time placed above the rood beam in churches, were produced there chiefly in the workshop of the Berlinghieri.

The crucifix executed by Berlinghieri the Elder, master of the school, today in the Pinacoteca at Lucca, shows a Christ whose image no longer bears the hieratic Byzantine features. Instead of being garbed, as always formerly, in a long robe, He is almost nude, with only a cloth draped about His loins, His martyred flesh displayed; but His face on the cross still has the fixed, impassive expression that was the mark of divinity. In that period the Church was primarily concerned with stamping out the Monophysite heresy, and with proving that Christ was not confined to a single, divine nature, but that He actually suffered the physical agonies of the crucifixion (figure 331).

The crucifix now in the Pinacoteca at Perugia, which is attributed to the Master of the St. Francis Crucifix, was executed a generation later. What a transformation! The divine body is shown contorted with agony; the torture the flesh is undergoing is emphasized by the drooping of the head; the face displays the ravages

There is just as great a difference between the ancient Zeus, serene and impassive, and the medieval Christ who became flesh and subject to human suffering.

329. - ZEUS, after the statue by Phidias at Olympia. Ny-Carlsberg Glyptotek, Copenhagen

330. - Burgundian CHRIST. Late fifteenth century. The Louvre, Paris

Photo Giraudon

From one generation to another, sensibilities can be discerned in works produced in the same workshop. From impassivity the Christ passes to the extreme of agony.

331. - *BERLINGHIERO BERLINGHIERI.* CHRIST ON THE CROSS. Thirteenth century. Museum, Lucca

332. - *MASTER OF THE ST. FRANCIS CRUCIFIX* CHRIST ON THE CROSS. Museum, Perugia

of pain. Suffering is expressed even more forcefully in an admirable crucifix now in Florence, that originated in the Berlinghieri workshop. Here the face is lined, the mouth twisted, and the eyebrows are drawn together in a spasm (figures 332 and 333).

In the Perugia crucifix, the figure of St. Francis, shown in miniature, engrossed in contemplation of the pierced and bleeding foot of Christ, indicates the source of the compassion and love that illumines the work. The faithful no longer feel obliged to conceal God's assumption of the human condition beneath an appearance of grandeur and remoteness. Just as St. Francis experienced the wounds of Christ in his own flesh, sharing in the tortures willed by Him, so the painter strives to make the believer share in this community of suffering. The same feeling is expressed in the fresco of Notre Dame de Chauvigny (Vienna), dating from the end of the eleventh century; it shows all the Christians helping Christ to bear His cross, which has become a collective burden.

333. - *Opposite page:* Workshop of Berlinghieri. CHRIST ON THE CROSS (detail). Thirteenth century. Florence *(Photo Brogi)*

SOCIAL ELEMENTS.   We may narrow our investigation further, by confining ourselves to the evolution of a more restricted group, for instance, a class in society.

At the end of the eighteenth century the French middle classes were on the verge of attaining the goal they had long pursued: under repeated blows, the monarchy, too closely associated with the hated and envied aristocracy, had been shaken to its foundations, and was about to be eliminated. The Revolution was being prepared. To enlist the support of the masses against the common authority, the bourgeoisie vigorously denounced the luxury in which the upper classes lived, contrasting it with the wretchedness of the common man. The great publicity given at the time to the episode of the Queen's necklace and the extraordinary effect of this on public opinion was characteristic of this campaign, which today we would call one of political propaganda. It was expressed far more spontaneously in the art of that time, far more unconsciously, and yet just as strikingly (figures 334 and 335).

As the power of the bourgeoisie had increased, it had imposed upon the public its

334. - *DAVID*. BATTLE BETWEEN MINERVA AND MARS. Second prize of the Academy, 1771. The Louvre, Paris

Photo Viollet

tastes in decoration and architecture, which in the eighteenth century became sober, even austere. The superficial historian would ascribe this trend to the excavations at Pompeii and the rebirth of the classical style. Actually, this rebirth was itself put to the service of an ill-defined but powerful aspiration. The bourgeoisie exalted the Roman virtues, those of the Republic, because they echoed virtues of its own which it intended to put to use.

The Neo-Classicism of the second half of the eighteenth century had as a corollary the deliberate elevation of figures such as Brutus and the Horatii: the intention of all this is quite clear. Soon the façades of bourgeois houses were to set a new trend toward severity, resembling the disapproving faces of the rising class, proud of its thriftiness. It was a class fond of recalling the gesture of the Roman matrons who donated their jewels for the good of the Republic. The massive stone buildings, with their severe proportions, the elimination of ornament, the smooth, bare surfaces, embodied the new spirit in society.

But no sooner had the bourgeoisie achieved its goal, overthrowing the regime

David reflects first the tastes of the eighteenth-century aristocracy, then the more austere ones of the rising middle classes

335. - *DAVID*. LICTORS BRINGING THE BODY OF HIS SON TO BRUTUS. 1789. The Louvre, Paris

Photo Alinari

336. - *A. J. DERKINDEREN.* PORTRAIT OF MALLARMÉ.
Rijksmuseum Kröller-Müller, Otterlo

337. - *RENOIR.* PORTRAIT OF MALLARMÉ.
The Louvre, Paris

The portraitist reveals himself at the same time as he represents his model. There are as many Mallarmés as painters who portrayed him.

338. - *MANET.* PORTRAIT OF MALLARMÉ. The Louvre, Paris

which had denied it the place it strove for, no sooner was it at last in the saddle, after repressing the rage of the proletariat it had unleashed, no sooner had it supplanted the aristocracy as the ruling class, than all this austerity, all this ostentatious thriftiness evaporated. The bourgeoisie, now bent on wearing the very garments of the class it had driven out, did not bother to create a new style of its own; it sought only to preserve and to revive the obsolete style of the *ancien régime*, which

Photo Viollet

339. - *At right:* Photograph of Mallarmé

340. - *Below: GAUGUIN.* PORTRAIT OF MALLARMÉ. Engraving. Bibliothèque Nationale, Paris

Photo Flammarion

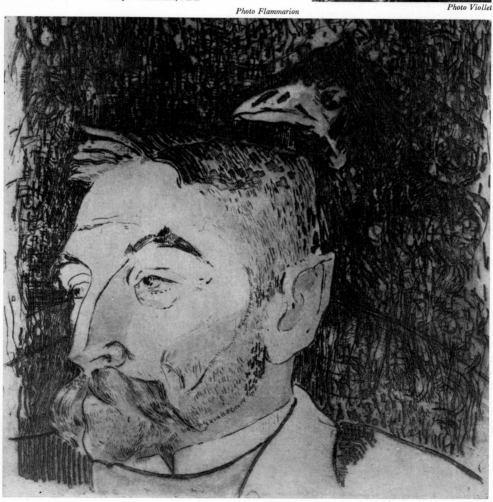

it continued to abuse in words. The unconscious, as it was manifested in art, displayed no such hypocrisy: it led the bourgeoisie to move into houses not furnished by its efforts, but filled with copies of works of past periods, from Henri II to Louis XV; as for the period of Louis XVI, in which the bourgeoisie had played such a large part, its style was not nearly so much appreciated, for it was lacking in opulence; it was criticized for not being rich enough.

The Second Empire, which marked the apogee of the bourgeoisie, saw the emergence of a style that is the negation of the ideal this bourgeoisie had flaunted before its triumph. Its excessive ornamentation, its lavish use of precious materials and minute decorative detail, served only to testify to the prosperity of the middle classes, who now had at their disposal the requisite marble and gold, as well as the human capital represented by man-hours. Thus, the evolutionary curve of a social class and its interior motivations are clearly manifested by works of art dating from two different phases of its history (figure 33).

INDIVIDUAL ELEMENTS.   A final narrowing down of our field of investigation will bring the light of analysis to bear on the individual and his irreducible particularity, which the nineteenth century tended to make the very substance of art.

In the genre that would seem to require the maximal renunciation of self, that of portraiture, in which the artist is compelled to concentrate everything on capturing the essence of another human being, his personality nevertheless asserts itself equally with that of his model. Th. Silvestre, commenting on Delacroix's *Portrait of Bruyas*, says shrewdly: "M. Bruyas, having been subjected to Delacroix's preconceptions and prejudices, seems to us both more like the artist and less like him than we ourselves are; for the nature of the painter here ferments in that of the model like leaven in dough."

The poet Mallarmé had his portrait painted by three great artists—Manet, Renoir, and Gauguin. To be sure, we find in each work certain physical features of Mallarmé which the three artists were unanimous in recognizing. And yet, what a diversity! The different men, bearing only the slightest resemblance to one another, appear before our eyes, and we are compelled to admit that the artist is as completely present in each painting as is the poet he is supposedly portraying. The latter, for all his fame, becomes largely a pretext for the artist's revealing of his own personality (figures 336 to 340).

The upper-middle-class Manet, worldly and interested in social relations, sees Mallarmé primarily as the eloquent host at his Tuesdays in the Rue de Rome. The dreamer nonchalantly stretched out on a sofa, following with his eyes the wisps of smoke rising from his cigar, has merely interrupted for a moment the brilliant talk with which he dazzled his visitors. He seems to be murmuring his own lines addressed to "an immoral poet":

> *Je vais avec ce blond cigare*
> *Allumer ma verve un instant.*

(With this blond cigar I shall/Kindle my verve for a moment.) His face sparkles with wit, displaying the liveliness and keenness of his mind.

This Mallarmé, almost a man of the world, in whom Manet perceives the keen vibration of his own nerves, becomes, when portrayed by Renoir, placid, almost dull by contrast. His tight coat, his florid face, his well-trimmed goatee, suggest the unobtrusive civil servant, the teacher of English occasionally booed by his pupils, whom he is unable to control. A petit-bourgeois like Renoir, who came from a family of craftsmen, in this portrait Mallarmé suggests physical health and vigor, and seems a man somewhat harassed by the petty burdens of social life, but accepting them as a sound discipline against which it would be futile to rebel.

Mallarmé is seen in still another, entirely different light by Gauguin. The reassuring plumpness is gone; the cheeks are hollow, sunken, unshaven; a secret torment is expressed in this bony face, with the curved nose and the sharp features. Just as in the painting *Nirvana* a strange haggard figure rises behind Meyer de Haan (in the same position as the angel in Rembrandt's *St. Matthew*!), so here Edgar Allan Poe's raven becomes the emblem of the poet, denying him peace of mind, a dark presence whispering in his ear its "Nevermore." (Gauguin borrowed it from Manet's engraving *The Raven*.) This artist, who sought escape from a devouring frustration in the exotic, the mysterious, perceives that quality in the raven's cawing. He always looks for the primitive origins beneath the veneer of civilization. Here he finds an echo of them, in the poet's strangely pointed ear, like that of a devil or a faun, the same faun that we find in Mallarmé's poems. Did Gauguin invent this ear? Not at all; in an interview a few years ago, the poet's own niece confirmed the detail to a newspaperman, observing that she too had a similarly shaped ear, and that it was a family trait whose atavistic origins her uncle had admitted.

We have emphasized previously the importance of the artist's power of selection. These portraits of Mallarmé are an illustration of it. Each of the three painters saw qualities in Mallarmé that were actually present, at least potentially, in the model. Just as each species of animal chooses, from among the infinite variety of food offered by nature, only that suitable to its particular needs, so the artist can assimilate only that nourishment suitable to his intentions; and these intentions, which he defines through his selection of images, by the same token characterize him.

ELEMENTS DERIVED FROM THE AGES OF MAN.   Each man has his "constants," to which he owes his continuity; but each man also has his variables. In each of us many potential selves stir, sometimes moving toward fulfillment, often dying stillborn. We are many different persons, successively, as we grow older. Painting, a faithful recording instrument, bears witness to these successive stages, which are all variations on a single theme, that of the self.

Théodore Rousseau is regarded as an overliteral realist, and in our day is in disrepute for this reason. But this verdict ought to be reconsidered. Twice in the course of his career he set up his easel at the same spot, before the same view: near the Col de la Faucille, facing the Mont Blanc range, which towers on the horizon, gleaming with snow and ice. One rarely sees two paintings so dissimilar, although the subject is exactly the same. The reason for this dissimilarity is that one expresses Rousseau's youth, and the other his old age.

The first time he painted the scene, in the fall of 1833, Rousseau, then at the height of his Romantic fervor, perceived only the terrifying presence of powerful, unleashed forces, threatening to spend themselves in upheaval, in destruction; overcome by his Romantic conception of nature, he seems to be echoing the cry of Chateaubriand's

341. - *Above: THÉODORE ROUSSEAU*. THE ALPS SEEN FROM THE COL DE LA FAUCILLE. 1833. Formerly Collection A. Roux

342. - *At right:* Panorama of the Alps. Gex-la-Faucille

René: "Rise, ye longed-for storms!" The jagged old silver firs, the sharp rocks, ravaged by erosion, in the foreground, part to reveal a wind-swept plain above which black clouds are piling up. A storm is in the making, its lightning illuminating the Alpine range, whose serrated outlines, emerging from a chaos of brilliant lights and heavy shadows, bear witness to their ancient battle with the elements. His nerves attuned to this explosion of terrestrial energy, Rousseau throbs with impatience; nature, like a wild horse, is driven along in frenzied leaps by his panting, intoxicated imagination. The exclamation he uttered before this scene has come down to us: "Long live God, long live the great artist!" (figure 341).

Years went by; the man changed. One summer day in 1863 he found himself in almost the exact spot where he had experienced such feverish emotion. But now he was filled with the serenity of age, of approaching decline. He had less than four years to live, and he dimly sensed the imminence of death, of the moment when his dwindling strength would be gone and his dust would return to dust. Now he does not hurl himself bodily into nature, ravaging it as he goes; he knows he is almost nothing, but a conscious nothing, deeply moved by the cosmos (figure 343).

370

This time he prefers to stop, listen, look! He has discovered contemplation. Now it is his turn to be overwhelmed. This time he does not think only of space, of the smallness of these rocks, these trees, tiny for all their closeness, in relation to the vast expanse. Their dramatic forms are lost in a dazzling, limitless radiance. Nature now becomes only the infinitely small flung into the infinitely vast. How much vaster the sky seems now through being empty, indifferent, outside the scale of human passions! And the peaks themselves are now but mocking variations on the line of the horizon.

Thus the same man, lending his voice to the universe, utters first a strident cry and then a calm whisper. These two paintings tell us more about Rousseau, and about his interior struggle, than any explanations that could be advanced. "O silent power that speaks only to the soul...."

PAINTING, MIRROR OF THE SPIRIT. It is because painting is the language of the soul, of the unconscious, of this vast sea on which thought, at the center, is but a tiny island, that it can achieve such extraordinary scope in revealing to us all there is to know of men or a man.

Consciousness is indeed an island at the center, rather than a peak rising above the unconscious: the sea converges upon it from all sides, exerting a continuous pressure; but the conscious mind yields to this pressure, opens itself to the unconscious, only at certain points. For the most part the unconscious, though it surges against the mind, assailing it as waves batter a coast and sometimes modify its contours, never breaks through into consciousness.

Painting, closer to the sensory sources, is less capable than words of rendering ideas, and never undertakes to do so without running a risk, but it is the chosen intermediary of everything outside conscious thought. It plunges into the depths.

Whereas the conscious mind can translate certain emotions more or less easily into ideas, painting renders them in their original purity, before the intellect has transcribed them into its clear but often unrepresentative language.

Above all, painting readily reveals everything that escapes the grasp of the intelligence, which is further removed from the organic sources of life. The intelligence picks flowers off the surface of life,

Art reflects the ages of man. In thirty years Rousseau shifted from the passionate visions of his youth to the serenity of old age.

343. - *THÉODORE ROUSSEAU.* Drawing for a VIEW OF THE ALPS FROM THE COL DE LA FAUCILLE. 1863

and makes bouquets of them; painting not only picks the blossoms but takes their roots and even some of the soil that has nourished them. The painter is aware only of the enchanting effect of the corollas he is grouping together; unwittingly he brings with them the tentacles covered with the earth from which they drank up life and which gave them their colors. The flowers gathered by painting are fresh, alive, heavy with perfume, very unlike those picked by the intelligence, which cuts them off neatly at the base of the stems, thus dooming them to wilt in the vase.

Every work of art, provided it is sincere and authentic, provided it is not the product of imitation or an exercise in theory, conveys a message from the unconscious. Only in our time, which has cast light on hitherto obscure areas of the soul, has this been fully realized.

Not long ago a school of painting arose which sought to exploit the opportunity the painter has to make direct contact with the unconscious. André Breton in his *Second Surrealist Manifesto* proclaimed that this school was no longer primarily concerned with "producing works of art, but with illuminating the still unrevealed and yet revealable part of being, where all beauty, all love, all virtue, which we know only imperfectly, glows with intensity." Unfortunately, Surrealism has fallen prey to the mechanization that human beings, in their laziness, always end up by substituting for living experience; it has often degenerated into artificiality and convention. Nevertheless it has produced some amazing works—those of Max Ernst and of Tanguy. The latter in particular has truly "visualized" the bottom of the abyss where nascent form, the protozoa of the plastic universe, takes shape in the dim light where an indistinct glow hovers in space, and Medusa-like creatures or algae, inchoate beings, drift undulating by. No other paintings ever have given us a more vivid illusion of witnessing the very birth of the image, its setting out on its future course (figures 52 and 375).

But if there are depths below, there are also "depths" towering above us. We have seen that when man wishes to transcend the too rigid boundaries of his reason, when he strives to make contact with realities that he apprehends but that are beyond his conscious grasp, to confront that which can for him be only a presence—that is, something ineffable—he resorts once again to images. In this unfamiliar realm words are of no avail; the image alone can enter there, and it is by means of images that religion has always communicated what lay beyond the reach of words. Plotinus, as we may recall, saw in the image a means of attaining that condition he called ecstasy —a state transcending the positive data of the senses or of logic. The great mystic painters, from El Greco to Rembrandt, have demonstrated the power art has of confronting that darkness which results not from a deficiency of light but rather from the deficiency in our vision, incapable of bearing such radiance.

Art gives us a glimpse into the mystery of the universe—and into our own.
344. - CHINESE LANDSCAPE

CHAPTER SEVEN

ART IN OUR LIFE

Art teaches us not merely to see, but also to be; it makes us what we are!

Bernard Berenson

Art is the mediator between nature and man. The primitive model is too great, too sublime to be grasped directly.

Caspar David Friedrich

THE final question to be raised regarding the work of art is perhaps the most important of all: the role it plays in our lives. Barrès once said that nothing is truly important to us unless it is somehow bound up with our fate, and we have seen already how closely art is linked with it. Time and again, in the course of this investigation, we have come up against man and his essential pursuits, as though art were a series of mirrors continually reflecting the human countenance in its many aspects and from many different angles—as many as humanity, in its infinite diversity, displays.

Do we not run the risk of losing our way, of remaining uncertain in the face of so many possibilities? Before we conclude our study we must get to the heart

373

of this problem, and attempt to define the deep human purpose that lies behind art's variety of aspects.

Aesthetics provides various answers to this question; and before going further we shall review these answers in the light of what we have learned in the preceding chapters.

A painting—since it is from the field of painting that we have chosen our examples of the work of art—appears at first as an image; therefore, what we have said about the role played by the image in psychic life also applies to the painting. But a painting differs from images that merely record our sense impressions, like photographic plates; it also differs from dream images, which are beyond our conscious control. A painting is a creation devised by a human being, it is a work. The product of a collaboration among the artist's sensory, intellectual, and practical faculties, it retains the essential characteristics of all three. At the same time, though it is created by the mind, it becomes separated from it, and takes on an autonomous appearance, immutable, and perceivable by others.

Is this all? The painting bears the indelible mark of the purpose man assigns to it—that purpose he conceived when he went beyond the stage of *homo faber* and attained the stage of *homo aestheticus*, as it has recently been called. The painting no longer conforms to a practical function, but to a need for beauty, or at least to the idea of beauty arrived at by the artist; therefore it presupposes a scale of values.

Thus the painting contains in itself the justification for the various points of view from which it is considered: the psychological point of view, in that it is an image; the formal and plastic point of view, in that it is a work; the aesthetic point of view, in that it expresses a quest for beauty. Only by combining all these points of view shall we be able to encompass it in all its complexity.

1. THE FUNCTION OF THE IMAGE

THE images we harbor within us are only echoes of the outside world, as it is perceived directly or preserved in the memory. In this sense they reflect the milieu out of which they spring and which nourishes them—the external world. Painting reflects this world more fully than other images, for it requires the total participation, both spontaneous and conscious, of a creator. The artist can produce the work only with the help of the visual recollections stored up in his memory; but he uses them as he chooses, either reproducing them faithfully (or imagining that he is doing so), or transforming and rearranging them in accordance with other intentions.

Thus there comes into being this extraordinary plant, which has its roots in the visible world, but at the same time springs from a human being. It is, in varying degrees, a reproduction of the former and an emanation of the latter. For the

In the simplest case the artist records what is a source of pleasure in nature.

345. - *WATTEAU*. THE SHOP SIGN OF GERSAINT (detail). Museum, Berlin

viewer, therefore, it is partly a reminder of something already known, and partly an expression of something previously unknown, which is given form and a visible aspect in the painting. It is indeed a strange plant, drawing its nourishment from two different soils, which seem to be separated by the most impassable barrier, and yet sending the vital substances extracted from these two soils into a single homogeneous product, something entirely new—a flower that is pure fragrance and color.

The painted image is both representation and symbol. We can find in it a resemblance to its model, but also an analogy with its creator, from whom it cannot be separated; the product of his action, it will, once it is completed, in turn act upon him.

It is this duality that we shall now try to define more closely.

IMAGERY AS EVIDENCE OF SELECTION AND REJECTION. The image that is a painting depends, until it is completed, on the man who paints it. Then one day it gains its independence, and by the same token, its power. From that moment on, its creator and its viewer alike are dependent upon it. Already belonging to the external world, it will belong doubly to the inner world of the artist, because, having been created by it, it also creates it.

It owes its existence to this inner world. The image is born, as we have seen, out of an obscure and complex need of the painter. In the simplest cases, the image is a direct response to his wish, conscious or unconscious. He puts into it what he thinks will gratify him most, in order to enjoy this quality, but also to record it, to prevent it from eluding him, to preserve this source of pleasure or emotion for all time—a landscape, a spray of flowers, a face. This is what we mean when we speak of realism (figure 345).

Dreams, too, which have not been fully explained by psychoanalysis, are peopled with residues, or rather with the overflow from our waking life, with impressions so vivid that their traces linger in our minds. However, it is still to be explained why one visual impression rather than another produces such a strong effect: the reason is that it answered an expectation.

Thus the painter projects into his work both his desires and the nourishment he draws from nature to satisfy these desires; through the work he realizes what he seeks. Occasionally, he expresses an aspiration he shares with society—an ideal or a faith. In such cases the image serves merely to illustrate the precepts of a dogma, of a text. The Christian art of Byzantium best exemplifies the powerful coherence with which a religion can be made manifest to the faithful. But sometimes it is a deep urge, inherent in the painter's own personality, that seeks visible form. Then the image is no longer in competition with the word; its sovereignty is uncontested when it sets for itself the task of bringing to light the dimmer reaches of the soul (figure 346).

It achieves this latter goal by linking up the inner world and the outer, for in such cases it makes use of analogies between an emotional state and physical reality, by which means the latter can represent the former. The painting may seem merely to depict a familiar, or at least a possible, sight; but we have seen the extent to which it can, beneath this camouflage, render psychic realities that cannot otherwise be visualized. They disclose themselves by indicating their preferences, like Achilles looking for weapons among the gifts brought to the daughters of Lycomedes.

Up to this point, the image has aided the soul to affirm what it likes. But the image can also serve as an instrument of elimination: as an outlet for those elements of which the psyche seeks to rid itself. This function is that which Aristotle in his *Poetics* so lucidly described as catharsis, the purging of passions. Like the dream, art—anticipating the technique perfected by Freud and Breuer—externalizes those elements that encumber the soul; in the same way, according to ancient medicine, harmful humors were driven out by being concentrated in an abscess, which eliminated them from the body. The idea is conveyed by the very term "expression."

The most lucid creative artists have perceived this eliminative function of art, which is the inverse of the selective action discussed above. In his *Dominique*, Fromentin has his hero say, significantly: "I felt a craving not to be somebody, which in my opinion is absurd, but to produce something, which seems the only justification for our poor lives.... I shall try; my purpose will be not to add to my own human dignity or my enjoyment, not to benefit ... others or myself, but *to expel from my brain something that disturbs me*."

Photo Flammarion

Sometimes art discloses the painter's most secret aspirations, such as those of the crippled Maria Blanchard who was obsessed with the idea of motherhood.

346. - *MARIA BLANCHARD.* MOTHERHOOD. Musée d'Art Moderne, Paris

It is as though the psyche felt clogged by certain obsessions, painful or forbidden, or crippling merely by reason of the excessive importance they assume, and as though it could find relief only by "realizing" them, embodying them, through "transference" into an object which at once represents them and fixes them. Such an object thus serves as a liberating outlet (figure 347).

Art in its beginnings was closely allied with magic; in this latter-day function it again seems to serve as a means of exorcism. The artist acts instinctively in the manner of the sorcerer, who causes a sickness or an evil to "pass" into a stone or a tree and keeps it locked up there. In the case of a prohibited desire, the artist deceives his conscious mind by replacing the real object of this wish with a fictitious one which will afford him the longed-for gratification.

The exchange that goes on continually between the artist's psyche and the externalized reality which is his work is a source of strength, allowing him to gratify certain of his inner desires or, conversely, to neutralize or even to eliminate certain others. We must keep in mind that in doing so, he may be acting in the name of whatever group he represents, as well as exclusively on his own account. Indeed, this kind of emotional breathing, the inhalation of life-giving elements and the exhalation of waste, often serves the interests of the body of society.

IMAGERY AS A MEANS OF SELF-DISCOVERY. Life constantly aims at a balance; but this balance, like life itself, is perpetually changing: it is dynamic. A permanent state of balance has continually to be restored, because it is continually endangered. Nevertheless a man's life is characterized by a specific orientation; though it makes a thousand detours dictated by circumstances, it tends always toward a definite goal. It is like drops of water on a pane of glass, whose meandering course conceals only imperfectly the inexorable force to which they are subject. Each life, since it is in a continuous state of development, is inevitably faced with uncertainties; often it is driven backward, and sometimes loses its way, with the result that it is not fulfilled. Jung has coined the term "individuation" for this dramatic process.

In this process of individuation, the work of art plays an important part, whether the artist speaks for the group to which he belongs or only for himself. In the first place, the work enables the artist to realize himself, in the sense of actualizing what otherwise would remain merely a potentiality, and thus to liberate the mind by fulfilling its aspirations. But the work of art does more than that: thanks to it, our

Photo Royal Museum of Fine Arts, Antwerp

The painting, usually an expression of the artist's wishes, sometimes serves to exercise the demons haunting him.

347. - JAMES ENSOR. INTRIGUE.
Royal Museum of Fine Arts, Antwerp

348. - *ANDRÉ MASSON.* CRANIAL VILLA. Drawing. 1938

inner states, or rather, our impulses, take on objectivity and form, thus emerging from their more or less obscure condition. In this, art serves an essential function. The animal, governed by instinct, merely submits to the laws of those instincts; its life is indistinguishable from its experiences and the acts into which it transforms its impressions and feelings. It is not free because it cannot divorce itself from its impulses; it is, in fact, nothing more than one continuous impulse. By contrast, the man who aspires to freedom can stand off and look at his life; he can not only set his own powers to work, he can also modify these powers. He can externalize the substance of his inner life and treat it as an external object. To be able to do so, he must make a representation of it, to place it before himself as an object for his eyes or his thought. In this way he is able to take a position in relation to himself, thanks to his marvelous ability to split himself in two, simultaneously to be, to live in a certain state, and to contemplate it, make it subject to manipulation and transformation.

Once a vague feeling has been transmuted into an idea or an image, it can be scrutinized or contemplated. As Valéry put it, a part of our own substance becomes "the possible object of another's attention." We are simultaneously the observer and the thing observed. In becoming visible to our fellow men we become visible to ourselves. For language—whether that of ideas or images—introduces us not only to others, enabling them to know us, but also to ourselves, enabling us to act upon ourselves or react as we would to a stranger.

The idea defines the object clearly, but schematically. The image compensates for its lack of explicitness by remaining closer to life; it is more active, more capable of playing upon our emotions. It is like a mirror, enabling us to see ourselves, to contemplate ourselves in living, visible form.

Though unable to elevate a reality to full consciousness—something only an intellectual concept can do—the work of art nevertheless effects an actual contact with, and often takes possession of, reality. Its scope might be compared with that of the phenomenon of clairvoyance. However repugnant this phenomenon may be to the logical mind, which cannot account for it, it must be granted that besides the multitude of experiments proved fraudulent, some remain uncontested. Can we frame some sort of explanation for them? It is probable that in such cases the unconscious apprehends a reality that escapes the conscious mind; and in certain individuals endowed with an abnormally nervous constitution such apprehensions are extremely vivid. Incapable of understanding rationally a message which is by its nature unintelligible, the medium interprets it as an image from the external world, on which he concentrates his attention and which he deciphers intuitively.

We have seen that the image can convey hidden meanings which are banned by conscious thought and morality; in clairvoyance it discloses meanings that the mind cannot apprehend. It produces a kind of trance, in which we are brought into contact with matters of deep significance that are otherwise inaccessible (figure 348).

This may account for the powers ascribed to the Tarot Pack, coffee grounds, or the dowser's rod, which obviously have no visionary capacities in themselves, but which serve as vehicles for the phenomenon of internal perception. The modern psychologist proceeds in a similar way in using the Rorschach test. The ink blots, through the associations they arouse in the patient, touch off interpretations into which the unconscious projects itself, and which the physician translates into precise language, whereas in the case of Tarot cards or coffee grounds the patient himself, i.e., the medium, "reads" his own mind. This aspect of the psychic powers of the image is still unexplored; it will doubtless prove fruitful some day. Even now, the painting can to some extent avail itself of these powers.

IMAGERY REACTS ON ITS CREATORS.   The urgent and powerful force that stirred within the artist's unconscious depths has entered the visible world through the medium of the painting; born within him, it nevertheless now acts upon him from the outside. For it has become an image, and every image affects the sensibility, arousing a thousand echoes in it. Even though the image has been created in the artist's own likeness, he now responds to it as to a new and alien fact; possibly he reacts to it even more intensely than he would to the experience which it expresses.

Thus in the work of art, man is split in two, as it were, and enters into a dialogue with his own reflection. The inner drive, once it has been embodied in the work, is seen from the outside, and touches off the same mechanisms of association as do external appearances which are produced without human intervention.

There is no doubt that its image of the deity expresses, as we have mentioned earlier (cf. pp. 359 ff.), the aspirations that lie dormant in the soul of a people. But once such aspirations have been expressed, this people will react to the image as to a permanent and all-powerful visible presence. After determining the aspect of its deity, it will in turn be overdetermined by it. Louis Hourticq has noted this ricocheting action in his *Vie des Images*. Sometimes the action is unconscious: the image arouses, produces, in those who contemplate it, a disposition toward the particular emotional life expressed by the image. Sometimes the action leads to logical interpretation: many religious beliefs came about as a result of attempts to understand paintings whose original and true meaning had been forgotten.

Hourticq cites the examples of St. Catherine's mystical marriage and the invention of St. Wilgeforte; equally striking is the case of St. Erasmus, referred to by Emile Mâle. Originally he was the patron saint of sailors, and was pictured with a cable wound around a pulley. But the original meaning of this attribute was gradually forgotten; only the image remained and it demanded an interpretation. The pulley came to be seen as the instrument of the saint's martyrdom, and a legend was invented according to which it was used to disembowel him. By a further process of association, St. Erasmus gained the reputation of curing colic. The new myth was suggested simply by the image itself (figures 349 and 350).

Our inveterate rationalism always seeks for a lucid motive behind each of our actions and creations; just as we tend to believe that to execute a work of art is to give material form to a concept fully elaborated in advance in the mind, so we tend to suppose that every image is the conscious representation of an idea. The opposite is true: ideas, like states of mind, are often suggested to us, even imposed upon us, by works of art.

In such cases the images are no longer mere reflections, signs inscribed upon the visible by the inner life; they themselves give rise to and account for that inner life. Through them, unformulated contents are suddenly projected onto a screen; while the intellect cannot always decipher these contents, they never fail to have an effect upon the emotions. By means of images, individuals and groups seek to fashion counterparts of themselves, in order to perceive what they are; but these transcriptions, which make them at long last visible to themselves, become the point of departure of a new process. For now that they have before them this version of themselves, of their own inner reality, which hitherto they had experienced but not understood, they begin a dialogue with it, which will serve as a basis for subsequent modifications.

One stage of the existence of this individual or group has been embodied in this particular image, but by the very fact of being projected it has, as it were, achieved fulfillment; and so its originators begin to anticipate a new stage, determining the direction the future evolution will take upon this earliest image, from which they have taken their bearings, so to speak. Man acts upon and through his work; but the moment it comes into being, it begins to react upon him as though it were a new, independent, and unpredictable force. A truly dialectical process is touched off: the painter, whether interpreting his own thoughts or those of his group, imagines that he has projected his own "thesis" in the painting; but the moment his work becomes separate from him and its appearance fixed, permanent, he looks upon it as an "antithesis." Then he must work out a compromise, a "synthesis," between what he is, what he believes himself to be, and the unexpected revelation contained in the work, in what he has put into it—an unwitting revelation of part of his psyche he had not known before, which suddenly confronts him. Our brief survey of the evolution of the main themes of Delacroix's art (cf. pp. 335 ff.) has shown how an artist, uncertain of his own destiny, can take as a guide the direction that emerges from his own works: they make him aware of a course which had been only a vague possibility before it came to be expressed in those works.

AN OUTLET FOR THE SPIRIT. What we have been saying is true not only of individuals but also of entire peoples. In either case, art assumes, from this, a primordial importance. Far from being a mere embellishment of life, a luxury or an ornament, an idle pursuit, art answers a profound psychological need. No society can do without it. In our civilization, where art tends to be only a refined pastime practiced by an elite, the motion picture has become a crude substitute for it, in this respect. It is upon that screen that the modern unconscious projects its myths, clothing them in living shapes. The movies evoke its desires, its lusts, and its aspirations, and it exorcises its anguishes through them. The public

The image not only embodies, it also creates, myths. An ancient Byzantine Christ with a long robe was later interpreted as the figure of a bearded female and gave rise to the legend of a holy princess, martyr, and virgin, who is sometimes called St. Wilgeforte.

349. - ST. KUMMERNIS. Romanesque statue from the Engelberg Cloister, Switzerland

believes itself to be a mere spectator at motion pictures, but in reality it is the chief protagonist of the drama, which is that of itself. In the picture that unreels before its eyes, it finds not so much a spectacle as a partner who carries on a silent dialogue with all the avid and fascinated eyes that stare at the screen from the shadows of the theater. More recently, it is the television screen which, by introducing its living presence into every home, has tended to make up, in our modern interiors, for the absence of altars, chapels, or icons which confronted men of the past— of antiquity as well as of yesterday—with painted or sculptured images embodying the interior concerns.

The modern form of this confrontation is disappointing, unfortunately, for spiritual forces scarcely play a part in it, and its materialism appeals to the lowest instincts. This is why the frustrated public is once again turning to art, as evidenced by the tremendous popularity of a painter such as Van

St. Erasmus, patron of sailors, was represented with a cable wound around a pulley. This detail was misunderstood, giving rise to the invention of his martyrdom.

350. - *POUSSIN.* MARTYRDOM OF ST. ERASMUS. Vatican

351. - *LURÇAT.* THE STORM. 1928. Private collection

Gogh, whose appeal seems universal, judging from the hold he has on so many uneducated persons not motivated by aesthetic curiosity. This phenomenon would cast light on many things, if we were to study its causes and its relation to certain moral needs, which are left ungratified today, and which seek for gratification.

Man cannot dispense with that form of psychic breathing which art provides. Liszt said: "My music is the breathing of my soul." Indeed, the contemporary world suffers from a kind of suffocation. Not so long ago one saw at country fairs a figure called "the bronze man," who was entirely coated with a liquid that gave him the appearance of a statue; though aping the pose of a statue, he aroused the admiration by his living appearance. This attraction became a thing of the past when it was discovered, following several accidents, that the metallic coating obstructed the respiratory process that must be carried on through the skin if life is to continue.

Our twentieth century might be likened to a "steel man," enclosed in a shell of materialism, shiny and hard. This man of steel will perish, too, through having failed to realize that his deceptively solid armor has deprived of air a soul that needs more than words and ideas as nourishment.

There are many signs that modern man is seeking, with the means available to him, to rediscover the lungs that images provide and that are the only way in which our inmost being can gain access to the air it requires. Psychoanalysis, that psychic cultivation of unconscious images, has achieved excessive importance in modern life, particularly in the civilization that claims to be more modern than any other, the American. In America psychoanalysis has become a panacea, a super-stition, almost a form of idolatry!

As long as man has existed, from the time of the magic of caves, it is art that has had the task of assuring a free traffic in images and in their meanings. To the extent that it has become self-conscious about its spontaneous processes and subjected them to dogmatic and one-sided definitions, it has failed in its task; self-conscious-ness is a disease with which we are afflicted as art is. Surrealism was aware of its task, but it too drifted into the use of arbitrary formulas, rejecting the spontaneity which alone could have justified it. Only a few Expressionists, such as Rouault,

Occasionally art translates the hidden feelings of a whole epoch; the period between the two world wars saw the emergence of the theme of barren and anguished solitude.

352. - *BERMANN*. AT THE CITY GATES, AT NIGHTFALL. 1937

and those whom Louis Chéronnet called "the oneiromancers" (dream interpreters) —for example, Chagall—have succeeded in performing to some extent this essential function (figure 353).

Never have human eyes been as avid as they are today; never have they searched so desperately; for art has been removed from them. The lamentable misunderstanding that was realism, fostered by the sordid misconceptions of the nineteenth-century middle classes, has led art into a kind of suicide. Reacting against realism, and attempting to restore art to health, the modern school has lost contact with the public and shut itself off within the closed circle of its own eccentricities.

As a result painting has become a technique applied to particular means; it has lost the sense of its function and become an infinitely rarefied form of play for specialists, for mandarins who scorn human society and take refuge, as though on a desert island, in a solitary concern with themselves and their own intellectual virtuosity. The same charge often applies to literature. But a society whose highest and most indispensable activities have become atrophied or distorted is bound to decline.

The appeal sent forth by Van Gogh cuts across the whole history of painting, and has broken down the walls erected by aesthetic theory; this is why, no doubt, it is heard by so many today, even though they do not clearly comprehend its significance. In the face of those who remain deaf to his cry, even though they profess admiration for his work, Van Gogh proclaims the enduring human role of art, a role to which it is entitled, and which we are entitled to have it fill. Assailed by images, but deprived of their natural aid, modern man is moving toward a crisis the nature of which can easily be foreseen (figures 351 and 352).

2. THE FUNCTION OF THE WORK

A LTHOUGH the work of art is essentially an image, it is not simply that. In order to be more than an inconsistent, ephemeral daydream—in order to become a visible and permanent reality, offered for our attention and contemplation—the image must assume some substantial form, be embodied in some suitably fashioned material. At this point begins a new chapter in its existence and demands.

THE WORK STARTS FROM AND IS ORGANIZED AROUND THE IMAGE. The work of art is not merely an image in the mind; for the artist and through him it becomes a thing, an object. Since the etymology of words so often reveals their true meanings, let us not neglect that of the term "object," which lends its full force to the new existence bestowed upon the work: object = *ob-jectum*, that which is thrown before. The work of art is, indeed, something the artist extracts from himself, in order to make of it a material reality, which can then be placed before its creator and its viewers.

Some painter-poets record the rhythms of their dreams in their art.

353. - CHAGALL. OBSESSION. 1942

Men have always known that the work of art is not simply a mirror reflecting what is put before it; that it is the product of a form of transubstantiation which makes it independent and its consequences unpredictable. Once again, language is revealing. In Greek, the word for "image" is εἰδωλον, in medieval Latin *idolum*, i.e., idol. The inflection in meaning—from the primitive sense of "image" to something looked on as a fetish—is meaningful in itself. The idol is fashioned in the likeness of deity, the work of art in that of a model, physical or moral. But both become *objects* of a special cult; they are worshiped for what they are, not for what they are deemed to represent.

Pascal was struck by this surprising phenomenon whereby the work is substituted for that of which it is supposed to be merely a copy: "How vain is painting," he wrote, "which arouses our admiration for its resemblance to things that we do not admire!" (figures 354 and 355).

Photo Giraudon

Pascal was surprised that paintings should be admired for their resemblance to things which ordinarily we do not admire in themselves...

354. - *CHARDIN.* COPPER WATER HOLDER. The Louvre, Paris

The work of art, however, also transcends the person who fashions it. Once the artist has created it, it possesses an existence all its own, which will continue irresistibly even after it has lost all contact with him, after he has fallen into oblivion.

Prehistoric man knew this when he endowed his rock paintings with magical powers which neither the models for them nor the artists who made them possessed. The iconoclastic movement shows that at a certain point the Church was terrified by that distinctive and independent power the image acquires once it attains visibility. For from then on the image has a form which defines it and makes it autonomous; and, as we know, every form is inseparable from a state of mind which is latent within it, and thus creates the illusion that it is animated by that state of mind. The Church needed images to give material reality to religious beliefs and thus to influence the illiterate members of its flock; but it reacted, at times with great violence, against the tendency of believers to worship these images themselves rather than that which they were intended to communicate. Lactantious said: "Images and religion are incompatible." This is not simply because the statue diverts to itself the adoration it is meant to arouse toward God, of whom it is the symbol; the Church also sensed that the statue was capable of arousing an aesthetic emotion which, instead of increasing religious fervor, might turn souls away from it toward specifically aesthetic pleasures. Toward the end of the fourth century St. Nilus, writing to a high dignitary of the Empire, condemned the ornaments intended "only to give pleasure to the eye." This remark is highly significant. It expresses a shift in the preoccupations of the Church, which no longer fears merely that the worship of God might be transferred to His human apparition, but which realizes that the work of art arouses specifically aesthetic pleasure, and is apprehensive lest this pleasure assert itself independently of religion. St. Augustine, too, describes his fear that beauty and the enjoyment it gives him may induce him "to sin"; he dreads the moments, he says, "when the song moves me more than the content of the song" (figure 356).

The mental image can, and often does, remain imprecise, vague; it stops halfway between representation and allusion; it evokes more than it shows; it suggests the remembered quality of a visual apparition rather than the apparition itself. It is the work of art that "informs" the image, i.e., endows it with a well-defined and immutable form, lifting it into a different plane: "*Forma dat esse rei*" (the form gives being to the thing"), say the scholastics. Art sets the image out in space, reserves for it a certain spatial area which it occupies visibly and permanently, gives it the consistency of a particular material and a certain combination of colors, gives it a "configuration."

By this means, as Gestalt psychology has recently established, the image becomes an integrated whole, which by the very fact of its being created resists anything that threatens its nature or existence. Edouard Claparède's definition of form applies fully to the work of art: "An autonomous unified whole, which displays an internal consistency and is governed by its own laws." This integral quality is evidenced in the fact that each part of the work is determined by the whole to a far greater extent than the whole is determined by the sum of its parts.

Thus the "plastic" existence of the work of art is essential. Its outward appearance is more than a mere translation of the spiritual reality it embodies. The moment the artist, bent upon

...Pascal did not understand that a painting contains much more than what it seems to represent.

355. - *DELACROIX*. STUDIO CORNER: THE STOVE. The Louvre, Paris

Photo Giraudon

translating this reality, conceives the idea of the outward appearance his creation is to have, that appearance acquires its own life and value. From that moment on it can be judged on its merits alone; it answers certain requirements and arouses certain emotions, which are inherent in it and which need no other justification.

Its entry into the world of space and matter confers upon the image the right

Photo Alinari-Giraudon

Fear of the powers of the image was so great that Byzantine art reduced it to simple decoration tinged with symbolism.

356. - Mosaic on the ceiling of the king's chamber. Detail. Palazzo Reale, Palermo

to become a work of art, i.e., the fruit of human labor, born of the collaboration between the brain that conceives it and the hand that fashions it. According to Lamennais, "Art is for man what in God is the power to create." In other words, it lies in the capacity for giving reality and consistency to the possible. This is, incidentally, the original meaning of the term "art."

THE WORK TENDS TOWARD BEAUTY. But this original meaning of the term has gradually given way to one more familiar to us, which carries a different connotation. Art is, indeed, essentially man's creative activity, but it must at once be added that this activity is disinterested, subject to no external, utilitarian purpose. It is directed solely at realizing a specific type of value, which has been called beauty. Kant, in his *Critique of Judgment*, defines it in his somewhat ponderous fashion: "Beauty is the teleological form of an object in so far as it is perceived in that object apart from any practical purpose." Today the concept of beauty has become inseparable from the concept of art.

For us, art results from a creative act, but an act which has no other goal save that of its own consummation, i.e.—since its goal cannot exist outside it—that of its own perfection. However, a hierarchy of sensory values is required to enable us to distinguish between perfection and an approximation to it. We may again cite Kant, who says: "Taste is the faculty of judging an object or a mode of representation according to the satisfaction it provides apart from any interest." Poussin, before him, had said: "The purpose of art is delight." This satisfaction, as Kant calls it, or delight, as Poussin does, presupposes a range of qualities capable of arousing this feeling with varying degrees of completeness.

Photo Durand-Ruel

No formula, no theory contains the secret of beauty. After Poussin, Delacroix and Ingres were agreed that beauty is Vergil's "Golden Bough," a gift of the gods.

357. - *DELACROIX.* SIBYL WITH THE GOLDEN BOUGH. 1845

Thus the nature of the work of art gradually emerges: it is an image representing or expressing that which man perceives within him or outside him, or rather, that which he perceives within him in relation to that which he perceives outside; but this image, in order to become art, must be organized into a coherent and independent whole, which has no goal beyond its own consummation. Whether this consummation has been achieved or not, man can decide only

391

through an assessment of value—a specific value which is called the Beautiful.

The judgment involved is qualitative, since in the realm of the spirit values cannot be measured without being experienced. Hence they cannot be made to fit some fixed and mechanical standard. That is why all formulas for achieving beauty that have been devised by theoreticians have proved false. No such prescription, no measure or proportion, not even the famous golden section, will automatically produce beauty. For each of these solutions works only if the artist is capable of endowing it, investing it, with the required value. It is not the formula itself that produces beauty, but the excellence with which the formula is carried out. Formulas may facilitate the undertaking, they may serve to eliminate hesitation or floundering in the face of obstacles, but in the last analysis it is the undertaking itself and its quality that alone determine the result. Beauty, as Poussin said, is "the Golden Bough of Vergil, which no one can discover unless he is guided by destiny" (figure 357).

Thus a value judgment is as much a part of the work of art as is the process by which it is realized. The good and the beautiful can never be pinned down in an equation; they can be achieved only by a surge of creative power, indefinitely sustained; without this they do not begin to exist. And a new and genuine act of appreciation is required, on the part both of the creator and of the "consumer," to endow the work with lasting value.

For those who thirst after absolutes nothing is more disappointing and irritating than the impossibility of exactly defining this value, which is nevertheless self-evident to anyone who perceives it. But we must resign ourselves to this state of affairs. Fingers are not made to grasp liquids, and even less to taste its flavor. Ideas, too, have their limitations. And disappointing as these limitations may be, they are the sole guarantee of our freedom.

THE WORK, INSTRUMENT OF OUR FREEDOM.   The specialist or the historian can account for various characteristics of a work of art, he can show the influences of which it is the result, the necessities to which it has responded, and how it has been "determined." There it is, that crushing determinism, the realization of which is sometimes so depressing. There is only one way to escape from it: this is provided by quality, by our perception of quality, our judgment of quality.

The problem has never been more urgent than in our day, when cybernetics, the fabrication of mechanical brains, confronts us with the disquieting prospect of a robot capable of surpassing the mental efficiency of a man. It is purely a question of mechanical efficiency, however; the robot can equal or even outdo the human brain in the number of mechanical associations it can make; but it will always be confined to what can be measured, to quantity.

Now, quality is something else again: it cannot be achieved by an increase in numerical strength, but only by mutation. Hence it will always remain inaccessible to machines; their dominance will always stop short of quality. "Art is freedom itself," Proudhon said. Man may be subject to all kinds of pressure from his environment; but through art he gives form to the very pressures to which he is subjected and in turn subjects them to a scale of values which is free, by definition, and which evaporates the moment we try to give it the character of necessity, to make it the inevitable consequence of a particular principle.

This is why quality evades all the automatic devices designed to ensure it. For quality cannot be conquered, it has to be deserved. It has never been obtained by known and tested, that is to say, infallible, methods; it must be re-created afresh each time, by an effort of which the result cannot be predicted in advance. Imitation, even of the most excellent models, is always and has always been a sure guarantee of failure, precisely because its results are predictable.

Art, together with morality, is the last stronghold of exclusively human values, which will never be vanquished by the influx of determinism. Pascal long since noted that man "is nobler than what kills him, because he knows that he dies; while the universe is completely ignorant of the advantage it has over him." Are we not forced to conclude, then, that man is greater than that which determines him because he is capable of judging it, while the forces to which he submits are inevitably blind?

Art is for this reason one of our most precious possessions, one which safeguards our will to live and perhaps even life itself, because it utilizes that capacity which makes it worth while to be human.

At the end of our survey, as at its beginning, whether art is regarded as a source of beauty or merely an image that is projected, it is more than a superficial pastime, diversion, or pleasure. It goes always to the deepest roots of our existence. Its disappearance would destroy, no doubt irremediably, man's innermost psychological and moral balance.

BEAUTY VERSUS EMOTION. The requirement of quality is so essential to art that it justifies the two directions by which quality is achieved. These two directions are incommensurable, and this duality is the greatest obstacle encountered by those theories that attempt to reduce art to a single principle. For the work of art can be evaluated, on the one hand, in terms of the functions performed by the image, i.e., in terms of its capacity for expressing emotions and states of mind, and communicating them to others, even when it is imitating nature. Then we measure artistic value according to intensity—the quality of the intensity, to be sure, but the chief consideration is the power to express, to suggest. On the other hand, it is possible to evaluate a work of art in terms of its "plastic" characteristics; then the "conquest" of form is the essential consideration—the quality of the form, that is, its harmony.

Thus we see again, this time in its true light, the problem of form and content, which we encountered earlier, observing then how unsatisfactorily it was formulated. It is now expressed more correctly, in the light of the opposition between an art that emphasizes emotional force and an art that emphasizes plastic form. There is indeed an opposition between the two, for emotional force is often achieved by a violence that disturbs the hedonistic quietude which is the condition of formal perfection, and the converse of this is also true.

This is why Rembrandt was incomprehensible and shocking to the disciples of Winckelmann; and this is why the Expressionist vehemence of Rouault gives so many of our contemporaries pause. Now, a century later, we hear the same

Photo Marc Vaux   Photo Giraudon-Bruckmann

Beauty may come from two opposite sources, from consummate harmony as well as from expressive intensity, which some call ugliness. For beauty actually resides exclusively in quality.

358. - *ANDRÉ MARCHAND.* CRUCIFIXION. 1942   **359.** - *GRÜNEWALD.* CRUCIFIXION. Gemäldegalerie, Karlsruhe

charge of "ugliness" as was hurled against Delacroix by Victor Hugo, in referring to the painter's female figures. Hugo was judging according to a standard of beauty based on form. The text of the charge is worth quoting, for in it Hugo, for all his reservations, glimpses the duality inherent in the ideal of the beautiful: "He has expressiveness, but he has no sense of the ideal. Now, I reject expressiveness without beauty, as well as beauty without expressiveness." As for Delacroix's female figures, he says: "They are perhaps the ideal of Eugène Delacroix; but not one of them is the ideal of the human mind" (Maurice Tourneux, *Delacroix devant ses contemporains*, p. 32).

We may ask the cause of this strange duality of beauty, although each of the two conceptions is based on an acceptance of qualitative values. How is it possible for beauty to be pursued by two such different, in fact irreconcilable and even contradictory, methods, one aiming at emotion, and the other at plastic effect? Once again, only psychology provides an answer to this aesthetic problem. What is important is not to decide theoretically as to which of the two methods is more valuable, but to recognize that human nature itself implies such a duality, which

360. - *Opposite page:* *MASACCIO.* HOLY TRINITY. Santa Maria Novella, Florence

seems to reflect two kinds of minds, two essentially different temperaments. One might say that there are, on the one hand, vitalists eager to express themselves passionately, and on the other, formalists bent upon working out constructions.[1] The art historians, to whom this dichotomy is familiar, see it as epitomized in the contrast between the Baroque and the Classical artists. As late as the nineteenth century this contrast was strikingly embodied in Delacroix and Ingres. For what we have here are not two aesthetic theories, freely chosen and developed, but an inner determinism, as a result of which some artists are fated to express themselves only in terms of intensity and others in terms of harmony (figures 358 to 360).

This particular instance shows that even where a physiological imperative seems to determine man's course, art maintains its freedom, for its value is equal in either conception, and beauty is attained in equal measure by both, the only consideration that counts being the creative quality.

361. - A CONCEPTUAL CHILD'S DRAWING. Collection Dr. Minkowska

RATIONAL AND SENSORY TYPES. Child psychology confirms that the duality in question reflects the existence of two distinct human types, which can be discerned from childhood on, though there are of course many intermediate types as well. The existence of these two basic types—the rational and the sensory—is confirmed, in the case of adults, by the Rorschach test. Dr. F. Minkowska speaks of the types (as manifested in the drawings of children) as two different worlds (figures 361 and 362).

The distinction between the Classical and the Baroque artist is suggested in the words of Dr. Minkowska: "Each of the two worlds has its own particularities. One is dominated by the mechanism of separation, of what Bleuler called 'Spaltung';[2] the other, by that of joining, connection. The first world tends to immobility,

---

[1] Maine de Biran, in his *Division des faits psychologiques et physiologiques* (1823), referred to this duality. According to him, "the major and the only real difference between systems of thought" lies in the difference in their fundamental principles; and there are only two such principles, "substance and force.... All the doctrines of philosophy, ancient and modern... can be reduced to one or the other...."

[2] Wölfflin uses the term "discontinuous."

and compensates through precision for what it loses in dynamism. The other, oriented toward movement, often errs through impreciseness of form" (*De Van Gogh et de Seurat aux dessins d'enfants*, Paris, 1949, p. 63). Now, this difference can be found even among "*very young* normal children," just as it has been demonstrated among the greatest artists.

We might be justified in speaking of an intellectual type and a sensory type, each oriented toward a different one of the two great possibilities open to man. We discover elements of both in man's basic attitudes toward the universe and toward himself. The world appears to him as an object of knowledge, and even as a reason for acquiring knowledge, for knowledge is indispensable to man if he is to find his way about in the world. Now, two modes of apprehension are possible, depending on whether the sensory or the intellectual faculties are put to use. The first, the sensory mode, seeks being; the second, the intellectual mode, seeks knowledge.

To explain: Sensory knowledge, which is predominantly intuitive, tends toward

There are families of minds in art, which are disclosed even in children's drawings. The main distinction is that between conceptual and sensory types.

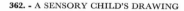

362. - A SENSORY CHILD'S DRAWING

an association with the object so close that we could call it fusion; a surge of participation and love makes it possible to experience this object, as though we ourselves had become it, as though we had been integrated into its existence. The highest degree of such knowledge is found in the mystical states of ecstasy in which the subject tends to lose himself in God in order to discover Him.

For the artist, sensory apprehension of the world means cleaving to life; following its rhythms in order to assimilate them; surrendering to and even letting himself be invaded by the forces he discerns around him, and opening his whole sensibility to them. Sensory apprehension tends to use art for the purpose of achieving communion with the world or that part of the world which interests it, and to let itself be carried by the current of reality. We have seen that the East is familiar with such a submission to reality, which has strongly marked its conception of art, and which is found wherever its influence has been exercised.

By contrast, intellectual apprehension tends to separate itself from its object (*ob-jectum*), even to move as far away from it as possible in order to keep it under its lucid scrutiny, and thus to be able to determine its limits and its form. For what this type of apprehension seeks is to define and to characterize the object, i.e., to grasp it in its permanence and universality—apart from life, one might say, and shorn of those variations which go against the typical and the immutable. This tendency was carried to its extreme in the Platonic theory, which asserts the presence of an absolute truth, the Idea, beyond the appearances that always accompany, in varying degrees, the ephemeral event. In this view life is only a source of disturbance and accident, a factor causing variability and uncertainty which must be eliminated as completely as possible, in order to attain to the stable structure which constitutes the essence and the truth of reality.

It is clear that an art of the first type will be based primarily on music, which renders the variable modulations of living time; and an art of the second type on architecture, which works with materials as nearly permanent as possible, and reduces everything to a question of forms and their relationships. Such is man's dual position in the face of the universe. Will we find the same conflict in his attitude toward fate?

LIFE: EXALTED OR REJECTED. The first type of art is intoxicated with life, with its rhythm and intensity; it lets itself be carried away by it as by a runaway horse, losing itself in the sensation of speed, of passionate participation (plate XV). It is always closely allied to an obsession with death, for such a rapid consumption of existence brings us closer to death. And the contrast with the somber fact of mortality serves to heighten the brilliance and the devouring fire of life. This succession of beings, things, moments, this breath-taking πάντα ῥεῖ (everything is in flux) is at once a cry of despair and a spasm of enjoyment, the latter all the keener through being precarious, having to be savored, consumed as fully as possible. This may lead to an almost morbid fondness for portraying destruction, those ruins which stimulate the eternal romantic in man because they suggest dramatically the pathos of his transitory existence. Life and death become inseparable aspects of a single reality: from the end of the Middle Ages to Baudelaire and Félicien Rops the figure of Death, or its shadow, has constantly

Painters exalted by a sense of life are led to cherish ruins, which remind us of the value of each passing hour. Occasionally a Hubert Robert enjoys imagining ruins that do not as yet exist

363. - *HUBERT ROBERT.* VIEW OF THE GRANDE GALERIE OF THE LOUVRE IN RUINS. Private collection

accompanied the portrayal of the nude splendors of the female body (plate XIII).

The other type of art rejects degradation, and in ignoring it, is led inevitably to ignore the changing aspects of life. It dreams of escaping from time—that tide which sweeps all things before it, exalting them and exhausting them simultaneously. It would grant existence only to pure space, a space uninvaded by time, and organized in accordance with the eternal forms. It conceives of these forms as immutable, forever fixed, and attempts to achieve with them the most unshakable balance. It often makes use of the solid triangle, set firmly on its base, or the square. It takes shelter in a factitiously frozen image of the universe, which conceals its precariousness.

Everything in this art is well defined, that is, definitive. It strives always for perfection, for perfection is an ideal state no longer subject to change. The Romantic cherishes ruins, as the evocation of mortality, but the Classic banishes all suggestion of them. The tombs of the Ceramicus in Athens, with their serene

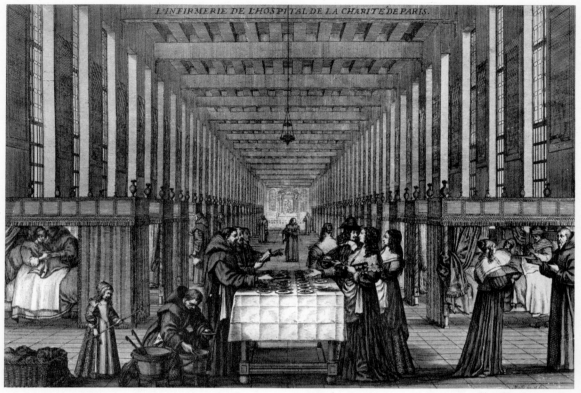

Italian art and the classics it inspired render space by the geometry of lines: an intellectual problem...

364. - *ABRAHAM BOSSE.* INFIRMARY OF THE HÔPITAL DE LA CHARITÉ. Seventeenth century.
Bibliothèque Nationale, Paris

figures representing an eternal farewell, remain the perfect example of an attempt to negate death in the very face of it (plate XIV).

Nothing flows in this art: neither time, nor space. To Ruisdael's landscapes, rushing toward the horizon like a stream toward the rapids that will engulf it, Poussin opposes a nature in which everything is ordered and interwoven, space being apportioned and made use of according to a definitive plan that must not thereafter be revised or disturbed.

The conception of an infinite space, open to all the winds that blow, suggests death, whereas the grouping of clearly defined units about a center or an axis suggests the security of a structure hermetically sealed off from outside disturbances. Every image, in this art, becomes a closed world, complete, perfect, self-sufficient, which no longer hopes for nor fears anything.

The Classical use of perspective, which by one cast of its tightly woven net imprisons all the visual elements scattered about in space and compels them to converge toward a single logical point, a necessary terminus for the gaze as well as for the mind, is the master stroke of this effort at systematization. Nature reveals that its disorder is only of the surface, and that actually it is constructed according to a geometric theorem. To this concentration upon a definitive point, aerial perspective opposes the openness of the distant horizon, toward which everything is imperceptibly drawn, shading off continuously into the distance, and, once there, is dissolved. In the conception of space, each element is in transition, gradually tapering off and finally being lost in infinity. The two contrasting techniques strikingly illustrate the two fundamental attitudes of the human mind (figures 364 and 365).

The Classical artist recognizes only one material element, the most solid, the most durable—stone. He seems bent upon reducing all others to it; at least he neglects them, and this is why his painting seems always to be tending toward sculpture or architecture. The Baroque artist, on the other hand, surrenders himself to the air, to the winds, to water and its rapid or violent flow, to fire and its leaping, devouring flames. His favorite material is cloth, whose softness is stirred by the least breath of air.

3. THE FUNCTION OF ART

VIEWED through the centuries, art is infinitely diverse, disclosing so many different and even contradictory directions that is provides us no hope of discovering a definition that might serve as a common denominator, a unifying principle. Art has as many faces as has human nature itself; each type of temperament contributes its resources and particular predispositions. We may, however, ask

...Northern art resorts to sensory means: keen vision, atmospheric perspective.
365. - *LUCAS VAN VALKENBORGH* (Flemish, sixteenth century). VIEW WITH THE CHÂTEAU DE BRUXELLES

whether all of them, though by different means, do not pursue the same end. If it were possible to uncover this common end behind the variety of expression that is dictated by the diversity of human temperaments, if it were possible to define it in its unity, we would have fathomed the ultimate purpose of this human activity, art.

DISPARITY BETWEEN THE I AND THE UNIVERSE.   This question is fundamental, for it bears upon the problem of our existence and its equilibrium: art is an attempt to preserve this equilibrium. The question leads us to the heart of the basic duality in our fate, that between the inner life and the outer, between direct internal experience and indirect sensory experience of the external world. On the one hand, each of us is "himself"—the permanent stratum that underlies what we experience, and that accounts for the unity, autonomy, and permanence of the I. On the other hand, each of us is also an echo of something else that acts upon him, something that is not himself—what German philosophy since Fichte has designated as the non-I, the universe into which man has been flung, within which and with

Photo H. G. L.-Giraudon

which he must live, which is nevertheless alien and external to him (figures 366 and 367).

This non-I is for us the great riddle and the great menace; we can survive only if we adjust ourselves to it, for it is the source of all the dangers that threaten us and all the defenses available to us. Consequently we must both know it—i.e., have an effective concept of it based upon our perceptions—and act upon it. Even when we achieve a mode of coexistence with it, by which our survival is secured, there remains a disturbing disparity between the subjective, that which we

Sometimes painters abandon themselves to the dizzy contemplation of a universe infinite and unmeasurable; the Germanic genius especially, uninfluenced by the lucid mastery of the Latins, grows intoxicated with vegetation and limitless space.

366. - *At left: ALTDORFER.* ST. GEORGE AND THE DRAGON. 1510. Pinakothek, Munich

367. - *Opposite page: ALTDORFER.* BATTLE OF ARBELA (detail). 1529. Pinakothek, Munich

402

experience directly, and the objective, that which we conceive, of which we form an approximate, empirical idea that must be continually revised.

Gradually, through force of habit, we come to regard the relationship between the two worlds as normal and natural. But the moment we halt, in our dizzying flight through life, we become aware of the fact—and this is a deep source of man's unhappiness—that while the inner and the outer worlds coincide empirically, the two are in reality incommensurable: our inner experience unfolds in time, the outer world unfolds in space. The two worlds—incommunicable to and impenetrable by one another—come together only at points of conflict and inter-action. One is spirit, the other is matter. Mankind has always been preoccupied with this antinomy, which in Christianity became that between the body and the soul. Possibly man's essential aspiration is to cease being a foreign object, projected like the hunter's bullet into the flesh of the world, and compelled to penetrate it without ever truly becoming one with it. Man dreams of a more secure link than this "accident" by virtue of which he is able to exist only within an environment absolutely alien to himself (figure 368).

Human thought has tried over thousands of years to pierce the impervious wall between the two worlds through knowledge, in order to understand the universal, and discover a principle of brotherhood with it. Philosophy was stubborn in its pursuit of this aim; but all it succeeded in formulating was a view of the world more pretentious than the ordinary one, which is formed empirically on the basis of our sensory experience; the philosophical view lays claim to absolute knowledge, but has never succeeded in making a breach in the wall.

Even if it were possible to conceive an exact notion of this universe, this "reality," would such knowledge do away with the fundamental antinomy between man's nature and the nature of the universe? Would it bridge the gulf that man himself cannot cross? Only religion has attempted to form a common bond between the two—a bond for which we long as soon as we cease to be content with the mere fact of our animal existence. This is why the gods—those of the Greeks, for example —were created in man's likeness, and why in our Christian civilization God was thought to have created man in His own image. The basis for the profound union between man and his universe was thus discovered outside the physical world, in its very principle, its Creator, and man's separation from the "other" was done away with. Yet Christianity regards this principle of unity as being even more "other," so incommensurably "other" that, quite unlike the inhabitants of the Greek Olympus, it remains unknowable and inaccessible. We can attain to God only through the mysterious bond of love, which reaches out across an infinite chasm. Thus a wave of faith in the divine Presence makes up for the impenetrability which persists. According to Indian thought, we can unite with the Godhead only at the price of abandoning, annihilating our own selves.

ART LINKS THE INNER AND THE OUTER WORLD.   In addition to religion, philosophy, and science, man has always used art as a means of breaking through this impassable wall. Now, art and art alone is truly equipped to mediate between the inner and the outer worlds, to carve out a path leading from one to the other; and this is why it is indispensable and irreplaceable. Art alone provides a path toward unity, not at the price of renunciation but, on the contrary, by an assertion of what we are.

This duality between inner and outer that man perceives and that he experiences as a split is present in the work of art, emphasizing the twofold, heterogeneous character that makes of it a link between those two realities. This link, moreover, is polyvalent: for it connects not only the I and the universe, by giving rise to the image in which the two are jointly and inseparably embodied, a fact expressed in the ancient maxim, *homo additus naturae;* it also connects the artist and his fellow men, for it enables him to communicate himself to them, and enables them to perceive and to experience him as a part of themselves.

Therein lies the miracle of the work of art—a miracle that is not sufficiently noted, but which accounts, nevertheless, for its powers, in a far more fundamental sense than all the aesthetic doctrines invoking the principles of pleasure, play, or ideal beauty, at the same time as it accounts for the aesthetic doctrines themselves, as too rigid systematizations of partial truths.

The work of art is, first of all, a symbolic image expressive of a psychic reality, and the word "symbol" is used here in its original connotation, which derives from $\sigma v\mu\beta\acute{a}\lambda\lambda\epsilon\iota v$, "to throw together, to unite." Originally, the word $\sigma\acute{v}\mu\beta o\lambda ov$ denoted a coin which two contracting parties broke between them, the two jagged parts serving thereafter to identify each to the other. The work of art is in the same way a link connecting two elements hitherto regarded as incompatible, which recognize themselves in it, as broken pieces of a single whole.

It is often supposed that the work of art merely reproduces natural appearance; but no matter how realistic the painter believes himself to be, we know that it is himself, his character, his very essence that he reveals; that he gives himself away in the manner in which he approaches reality in order to transcribe it, and in the choice he makes among its elements. If he attempts not realism but the reverse, and seeks to express himself, to translate himself to others, though he essentially is unknowable to any but himself, he will have to find the elements of the language he needs in appearances borrowed or derived from the visible universe.

Thus the artist cannot reproduce the outer world without by the same token revealing his inner world, and vice versa. In the work of art, each world lives only through the other, each can be conceived only with the help of the other, thus creating between them a third reality, which is consubstantial with each (figure 369).

Here we have the connection, the bridge thrown across the great void, the opposing banks of which are occupied by man and by the universe. A means of joining the two has at last been discovered, and this joining is not a fugitive contact, a momentary spark. It is more durable even than the two things it brings together; the man who reveals himself in the work and the natural appearances reflected in it may change or fall into oblivion, but the work will remain in existence, thanks to the durable material which has been given a permanent form.

A third order of being has thus come into existence: an order which is determined both by what is within us and by what is outside, which has reality for both, and the unique substance of which contains elements of both, inseparably joined, as the characteristics of the parents are joined in the child. The work is a fruit: it exists only when it has detached itself from the creative act and become independent, entering upon a life that is solely its own. In it the I and the non-I are no longer separated.

This is no doubt the reason so many writers have been tempted to compare artistic creation to love, to man's effort to unite with the other, with that which is different from him, in order to make it his own and at the same time to give himself to it. But love, whether human or divine, is only a striving, not a result.

There can be no doubt that love endows artistic creation with an almost super-natural force; and it is evident that this love reappears in the viewer's enthusiasm for the work of art and its riches. But though art is fed by this striving, which is both irresistible and desperate, it goes beyond it. The work of art takes up a permanent habitation in that darkness which is illumined for only a moment by the spark of love; it does not merely break through the night, as love can; it dispels it forever with its durable light.

Sometimes art expresses man's anguish before a universe alien to him.

368. - *Opposite page:* DÜRER. MELANCHOLIA. Engraving. Bibliothèque Nationale, Paris

Sometimes it achieves a perfect fusion of the inner and the outer worlds, so that the latter seems to be but an image of the former's dream.

369. - *Below:* WATTEAU. ENCHANTED ISLAND. Private collection

For the work of art is a thing, an object, implanted in the physical world, and possessing the characteristics of an object—mass, matter, form, an appearance perceivable through the senses; yet at the same time it exists only because it is subject to a scale of human values. In it, material reality cannot be distinguished from spiritual reality, any more than content can be from form. It is not possible to apprehend one without by the same token apprehending the other. In the same way, when two substances are united chemically and suddenly give rise to a third, analysis will no doubt discover in it traces of the component bodies; nevertheless the new substance now exists, has properties of its own, its own incontestable reality. The work of art, too, enables the viewer to reconstruct the two sources, which may become objects of his curiosity; but the work of art is something outside them, self-sufficient and self-contained: it exists by itself and by itself alone.

KEY TO CLASSIC AND BAROQUE.   In the light of this the two tendencies of art, the Classic and the Baroque, are seen in their true aspects: the work of art, this bridge arching between the banks of the I and the non-I, does not necessarily reach its highest point exactly halfway between the two; the summit can be closer to one bank or to the other, depending on the nature of the artist.

Some races, some epochs, some individuals display an authoritarian drive, seeking to reduce everything to the scale of the human—for races like the Mediterranean ones, particularly the Greeks, nature is so sober, so naturally ordered and intelligible, and so unobtrusive that man, facing it, feels himself the king of creation; in some epochs civilization, at its apogee, proclaims itself master of its own conception of life and the world, of its own truth, and enjoys a miraculous balance between its conceptions and its possibilities. These are examples of culture in its Classic phase.

At such times nature is assumed to be in harmony with the laws of reason, and man even imagines that he is not imposing these laws upon it but merely freeing it from its own seeming disorder. He moves effortlessly within the known and reduces everything to it. Having climbed to this luminous peak, he brings up to his level the two unknown regions he surveys from this height—the mystery of the universe and the mystery of his own interior life. What he cannot contain in his grasp, he denies or ignores. He makes the whole world conform to himself, i.e., he disciplines it and makes it fit at all costs the natural forms within his mind— the intellectual forms of ideas, the plastic forms of images; he has a secret aversion to the free play of forces, for they inevitably introduce change and disorder into the authoritarian balance of his architecture (figure 372).

Baroque art, taken in the broadest sense, is the opposite. In Europe it was characteristic of the races living in Germany and the northern areas: there, nature, with its

The Baroque German genius dreams of a return to primitive nature and its instincts. The Latin genius of Italy aspires to rise to the pure zone of the mind. These two pictures of dances, in which we recognize an element of sly coincidence, symbolize the opposition between the two: earthly paradise and love on the one hand, disembodied paradise and love on the other.

370. - Opposite, above: CRANACH THE ELDER. THE EARTHLY PARADISE. National Museum, Oslo

371. - Opposite, below: FRA ANGELICO. Dance of Angels from THE LAST JUDGMENT (detail). Convent of San Marco, Florence

The Classic artist, like the architect, combines static elements; the Baroque artist projects movements in vast space by means of gestures, beams of light, clouds.

372. - *Opposite page: GIROLAMO DEL PACCHIA.* ANNUNCIATION AND VISITATION. Early sixteenth century. Academy of Fine Arts, Siena

373. - *Above: PIETRO DA CORTONA.* ANNUNCIATION. Seventeenth century. Church of St. Francis, Cortona

Analogous to the works of the Italian Arcimboldo, this Flemish "metamorphosis" naïvely embodies man's eternal desire to recognize himself in the universe and to recognize the universe in himself.

374. - *JODOCUS DE MOMPER THE YOUNGER.* WINTER

inexhaustible fertility, fostered by the humidity, is more powerful; there, swarming shadows extinguish the light. Baroque art characterizes also periods of decline or uncertainty, when traditional forms are threatened by the rise of new forces. Under such conditions, man is brought into contact with the irresistible movement of life; he feels its currents within himself, and is intoxicated with the notion that for all his insignificance he is participating in this raging storm, and is able to vibrate in unison with it, thanks to his sensibility. He abhors the petty prison of form, which prevents life from sweeping everything before it as the universal rhythm of its force requires. He wants art to express interior and exterior realities that are greater than man himself—realities which in their irrepressible development break out of the containing structures of reason as well as the contours drawn by the hand (figure 373).

Over the centuries, the same geographical or historical factors have appeared in hundreds of different combinations, but analysis always discovers at work in them the subjective elements mentioned above, or the pressure of circumstances. Thus, as has been pointed out, every civilization, and every art, has gone through a period of Baroque art following a period of balance and maturity. At the same time, some schools of art favor the Baroque, or resist it, more strongly than others; some permit it to flower, and others confine it to a brief and inconsequential manifestation. The nature of a people is sometimes contradicted by its historical circumstances, and sometimes reinforced by them. As a result, a whole range of possibilities opens before us in history (figures 370 and 371).

Our definition of the function of art does not imply that either one or the other attitude shall be dominant; although the scales utilized by art for weighing man's inner world against his outer world are never at precisely the same level, they are always connected by an essential bond. The two worlds may show different relative weight; but what matters is that art is always able to compound from them a third, homogeneous reality—the work (plates XIV and XV).

THE ONE AND THE INFINITE.   Man is always confronted with two infinites —the universe whose nature remains alien to him, and the unconscious mind with its unfathomable depths. Equipped with a lucid mind, he cannot help being aware of the action of these two forces upon him and his action upon them. To survive and develop, he was compelled to form systematic answers to these two riddles, answers which he has revised in the light of experience, and which remain partly factitious and partly effective. But for all his awareness man remains alone, assailed from both sides by unknown powers which he cannot fully understand no matter how he improves and refines his means for exploring them.

But is it enough merely to be active during his brief span of life? Does it satisfy him merely to enjoy life, and try to understand it? Lucidity is not a consolation; on the contrary, it makes him more clearly aware of the fact that he is an alien element in the universe, and that he is unable to penetrate even that unconscious which he knows is a part of himself. His conscious mind confirms that he is a single being and he tends, physiologically and intellectually, to reduce everything to that unity which is his own person, his I. Now, this man who is defined by oneness, unless he succumbs to physical or mental degradation, everywhere runs up against the infinite, that is, against the most violent negation of his own nature. There is an infinite outside him, that of space and of time, of reality. There is another infinite within him, that of life and of the soul, which extends into the unconscious. How can these two unknowables, the one and the infinite, possibly be joined?

Yet a junction between them does exist, in the work of art whose unity is formed in man's likeness and which nevertheless, like a magic mirror, reflects the infinity of the universe which contains him and the infinity of that dark life which he himself contains. In the work of art these two infinities are reconciled and related to man's own inherent oneness.

Man's work of art is himself, legibly; it is what is not himself, visibly. Like the conscious mind which creates it, it has a well-defined presence, and yet it opens up unlimited vistas. Through it, without renouncing his human condition—indeed, by asserting it, imposing it upon this creation born out of himself—man nevertheless establishes a closer contact wich the outside world, so much so that its secrets, as well as the secrets of his inner world, are revealed to him beneath the appearances represented.

Is this an illusion, a mirage, as are, according to some, the ecstasies in which the mystic believes he transcends himself? No, for the work of art is more durable than the moment it records, than the man who creates it, than the appearances it evokes. It has grasped the ungraspable, it has arrested transience in its course; it gives us all this, yields it into our keeping.

Man, who is forced to witness the crumbling and dissolution of all that he knows and experiences, and who suffers from this universal relativity, aspires to escape from transience and to discover some firm ground, which will at last give meaning to his life, justify it. He finds this meaning in the work of art, for thanks to it he has access to an absolute, which is infinitely varied in its embodiments, but which is self-evident by virtue of its substance and its value, which he calls Beauty.

To be able to create the work of art, to be able to experience it—is this not one of the reasons why we find life worth living?

APPENDIX

THE PSYCHOLOGY OF ART

Not the obvious, material, aspect of the work of art, but its inmost spirit....

Baudelaire

Art can open a vista into the depths of the unconscious.

375. - *TANGUY.* LANDSCAPE

416

376. - *LORENZO LOTTO*. FRAGMENT OF PREDELLA. Church of Asolo

THE PSYCHOLOGY OF ART

> *To discern the inner vision of the artist ... in the*
> *work—such is the purpose of psychological analysis.*
> *And this vision soon leads us to the state of mind*
> *out of which it arises.*
>
> *Karl Jaspers*

1. ART AND THE HISTORY OF ART

BECAUSE the work of art, beyond what it represents, and even beyond what it is as a result of the development of its formal resources, happens to be the vehicle of man's inner life, with all its rich connotations; because the work reflects the entire range of this inner life, from its conscious core to the outer limits of its immense unconscious nebula, historical analysis can serve only as a preliminary approach, and formal analysis can only partly explore it. These must be supplemented by psychological analysis.

BEGINNINGS OF ART HISTORY.   Many generations passed and many efforts were made before this was realized. For a very long time, the study of art was merely a province of history. At first, it was motivated by unsystematic curiosity: it was merely a narrative, an accumulation of raw materials and unverified facts chosen at random, and was confined to anecdotal "lives of the painters," based on oral traditions rather than documentary evidence. Aesthetic theory had not risen even to the level of historical criticism; following the lead of philosophy, it evolved, on the margins of that field, its logical system of beauty, conceived as an absolute. Such was the background of men like Vasari and Alberti.

Not until the nineteenth century did the history of art emerge as a separate discipline. However, as is the case with all new sciences, it was conceived in the image of the older, parent science, history proper, which gave it a considerable advantage, particularly as it made use of history's well-tested methods. But the too-ready application of these historical methods to the study of art was bound to lead to fundamental errors. Art history, striving to be scientific, aimed at the objective observation of certain facts. The early art historians conceived of the facts in their own field as being a specific variety of historical data, having a bearing on art and its evolution; as a result they proceeded to apply the general principles of historical research to their own specialized sphere.

In doing so they overlooked an essential difference: the facts that are the objects of historical research always belong to the past; they are no longer in existence, hence can only be inferred, and must be reconstructed with the help of documents. But art history deals with facts of another kind—facts that came into being in the past, but that have survived it, and hence can be and must be experienced directly.

Consequently, the written document, which is of essential importance in history, can serve only as subsidiary or preliminary, though extremely useful, material in the history of art. Unfortunately, generations of art historians, blindly imitating the methods of the parent science, were led paradoxically to give more importance to documents, contracts, signatures, and dates than to the work itself. The latter was treated as a kind of abstract, almost unimportant means of conveying the data concerning it, which took precedence over it! Though the work was not completely forgotten, the chief purpose of this type of art historian was to situate it in time and space, assign it to a specific period and school, with as much accuracy as possible. When this historian had indicated a relationship between certain works, a bond arising out of common sources and influences, he felt he had said everything there was to say about them.

There are still art historians who look upon this as the only valid method. To go beyond it is, in their eyes, to enter the domain of aesthetics or, worse still, "to indulge in mere literary judgments...."

ART HISTORY DISCOVERS THE VISUAL.   All this is not to suggest that written documents are unimportant; but it is necessary to relegate them to their proper place. Whereas, in history, they constitute almost the entire source material, in the history of art they can serve only as a vital preliminary stage. The history of art in the true sense of the term begins with the visual sources.

André Michel, author of the famous *Histoire de l'Art*, formulated his task as follows: "To analyze, to study the work of art *directly*, to place it in its environment, to elucidate it by means of all the contemporary documents that can help us understand it." This marked a great step forward; but it was still to be established that such an analysis required methods of its own, that merely to describe the work, without considering its significance, was not enough. To make clear that the facts to be studied are of a visual nature (or auditory, in the case of music) is to arrive at the proper point of departure for art history, but not yet to define its purpose. The student of art has now liberated himself from the basic misunderstanding. He is no longer exclusively concerned with the written source material. He attends to the importance of the works themselves; but he has not yet arrived at a clear distinction between the archaeologist and the art historian.

The École des Chartes, founded in 1847 (though its beginnings go back to 1821), led the way, in France, in the historical analysis of art. It took a great step forward by admitting that in addition to the exploration of archives, the looking up of contracts, and the deciphering of old texts, it was necessary to study the work itself. Its researches, however, were confined to architecture. One of the founders of the *Monuments Historiques*, Pérignon, observed that historical monuments do not lie, and that the history exhibited through the development of architecture may be more trustworthy than any other.

Despite all this, purely historical facts were still given precedence over all other phenomena. In the study of the various styles and their visible characteristics, the purpose was always to gather data that would fill in the gaps in the written record, that would provide the same kind of information as the documents did— namely, information about places, periods, and influences. The field of historical research was enlarged by the application of archaeological methods, but no attempt was made to go beyond it.

To be sure, the art historians of that time were sensitive to the beauty of the works they studied: it is enough to recall the emotional fervor André Michel communicated to his audiences. But this was a purely personal reaction, which had nothing to do with the scientific task at hand—a kind of compensation, so to speak, which he granted himself at the conclusion of his labors. One wonders, finally, whether such an approach puts history at the service of art, or whether it does not merely use art as a means toward contributing to our knowledge of the past. For the work of art, viewed in this way, is simply a new instrument for historical exploration; though art is regarded as a manifestation of an independent human activity, which warrants being studied separately, that study is actually only a branch of general history.

The dangers of such an approach are obvious. Historical research can never explain the work of art, since it is confined to performing the important but preliminary task of placing it, of determining the circumstances attendant on its birth. We must never forget that the work of art is first and foremost an artistic phenomenon, and only secondarily a historical one. But the attempt to subject art to scientific analysis led to art history's subordinating itself to the already existing science of history.

A similar development took place in the realm of aesthetic theory, which succumbed to the same temptation. Instead of making use of existing theories and

their methods, it made itself subordinate to them. In 1853, Flaubert declared: "Aesthetics is still waiting for its Geoffroy Saint-Hilaire" (*Correspondance*, 1, p. 338). Aesthetic theory pinned its hopes on psychophysics—Fechner published his *Elements* in 1860—and sought to base its generalizations exclusively on empirical data; this tendency gave rise to what Vernon Lee called, at the beginning of this century, "empirical aesthetics." Where aesthetics took a different direction it surrendered to the obsession with history. Attempts were made to treat aesthetics as a branch of sociology: Burckhardt published his *Esthetik und Sozialwissenschaft* as early as 1895.

HISTORICAL STUDY OF VISUAL CHARACTERISTICS. Thus, both in the realm of aesthetics and in the realm of history, art abdicated its own basic reality, led away by the siren voice of science. A reaction might have been expected. The way was paved for it by those who were called "connoisseurs"; carrying on the work of such forerunners as Waagen, Morelli, Crowe and Cavalcasselle, this group in turn gave way, in the mid-nineteenth century, to the "experts," who demanded that the work of art be perceived in what in philosophical language would be termed, barbarously but expressively, its "specificity."

The connoisseur, or the expert, continued to work closely with the historian, whom he assisted. He too ended up by classifying the work, placing it in time and space. But his methods emphasized the work itself, its visible aspect, its physiognomy, as it were, rather than the historical source materials. The expert strove to recognize the work of art, to "identify" it, and the latter term is revealing.

This pursuit of the "identity" of the work of art, the recognition rather than the cognition of it, was to lead to a still closer scrutiny of the work itself, and to a more precise realization of the sole objective of the study of art. The great generation of Friedländer, Hulin de Loo, and Berenson did not confine itself to unearthing invaluable documentary material. By insisting upon direct observation of the works, by demanding that art history be first and foremost a visual experience, these men emphasized the fact that art is the product of a unique human activity, and that the realization of this uniqueness must take precedence over all other considerations in the study of it.

In the second half of the nineteenth century a new trend further enlarged the field of art history. Political theory and philosophy, with Auguste Comte's positivism, placed an increasing emphasis on the social aspects of life. Taine introduced the new point of view into the study of art. In his *Philosophie de l'Art* (1865) he declared: "The work of art is determined by a complex of factors, defined by the general spirit and patterns of living in a given period." Thus he stressed the importance of space and time, but he also added certain new factors—those of race, of environment, and of the historical moment—which clearly bore the mark of the natural sciences.

MODES OF EXPRESSION

For some artists, painting is primarily a means of recording natural appearance.

377. - *Opposite page: SAMUEL VAN HOOGSTRAETEN.* MAN AT THE WINDOW. 1653. Gemäldegalerie, Vienna

This new trend had far-reaching effects. Taine did not content himself with cataloguing and placing works in time and space; he also strove to account for those distinctive traits which constitute the *visible* character of a work, and which enable experts to identify it. Thus he moved from a mere description of a work's appearance to an attempt to penetrate its meanings. Unfortunately, he conceived his insights and explanations in historical, not in artistic, terms; his method was applied with the sole purpose of showing that the work of art is inseparable from the environment in which it comes into being. Taine continued to see art only as a fruit from the tree of history; though the fruit had characteristics of its own, it was still a product of the tree. The study of art remained heavily weighted on the side of knowledge of the past rather than on the nature of art itself.

Many years were to elapse before Benedetto Croce put history in its proper place. According to Croce, the work of art can be understood only in the light of its causes, which are historical; but its value is determined only by its effects, and these effects are of a purely aesthetic nature. A complete judgment of the work cannot omit either of these points of view; indeed, "true historical interpretation and true aesthetic criticism coincide." Croce's lucid theory was not set forth until after 1900; it marked the conclusion of a half-century of gropings in various directions.

It was first of all necessary, in resisting the encroachments of history, to arrive at a clear statement of the nature of art.

THE SO-CALLED SCIENCE OF ART AND THE PROBLEM OF FORM. A new term made its appearance at this time, "the science of art," in German *Kunstwissenschaft*, to which the works of Dessoir and Utitz lent so much brilliance.

The purpose of the new "science," in the minds of its founders, was to liberate the study of art from the grip of aesthetic theories of beauty, and to base it on an objective investigation of the work. Here, finally, the history of art, which had been smothered by history proper and by aesthetics, came into its own. The new designation of "science" contributed to the general acceptance of a field of research specifically concerned with art; it was no longer thought of as a branch of those other disciplines, but in the end served as a link between them.

The essential step was about to be taken. The way had been cleared by the archaeologists, who had pointed out the importance of style, as well as by disciples of Taine, who had steered the study of the work of art toward an explanation of the characteristics that determined it. The invention of photography contributed greatly to the increasing tendency to look upon the work of art as a visual phenomenon. Because photographic reproductions were still possible only in black-and-white, attention was centered on form, to the detriment of color; the study of the latter lagged behind, even in the case of paintings.

MODES OF EXPRESSION

Sometimes, concerned chiefly with lines and volumes, the painter reduces nature to the play of forms.

378. - *Opposite page: SCHOOL OF FONTAINEBLEAU.* Sixteenth century. VENUS AND CUPID. Private collection

The twentieth century thus focused art history upon a new field of exploration. Having gravitated toward the study of the artistic phenomenon, it now tried its hand at defining it. What is the work of art, it asked, but an organization—accomplished through the collaboration of the sensibility and the intellect—of sensory data, visual data in all the plastic arts (space) and auditory in music (time)? And what is this organization if not the giving of form to the raw materials of perception? With this definition, the science of art won complete autonomy. The study of forms was no longer a more or less indirect means of increasing our knowledge of the past; it was the new goal, in which the science of art which originated at the end of the last century at last found its own clearly defined justification.

The problem of form is assuming an ever-increasing importance in contemporary thought, not only in relation to art but also in relation to our intellectual life. Psychology, having long since abandoned the eighteenth-century view of the mind as a mere repository for sensations in their various combinations and arrangements, has gradually come around to the theory that certain patterns pre-exist in the mind, where they are nourished by and in turn impose their structure upon the perceptions.

Aesthetics could not have remained unaffected by this revolution. In Germany Friedrich Vischer, with his *Aesthetic Formalism*, and Max Dessoir, with his *Morphology of the Beautiful*, paved the way for the Gestalt theory that was developed around 1912. In France Etienne Souriau defined aesthetics as a "science of form," while Paul Guillaume developed his *Psychology of Form*. A strong intellectual movement in this direction resulted, from the various theories of form (among them those concerning the Baroque, which created such a great stir thanks to Wölfflin and Eugenio d'Ors) to the sudden emergence of certain "plastic" tendencies that were to bring painting all the way from Cubism to abstract art. The same movement extended into literature where it led to the debate over "pure poetry." As Valéry put it, there was "a remarkable drive to isolate poetry from everything that was not itself." One has only to replace the word "poetry" by "art" in this luminous formulation to define the radical change that had taken place in the study of art.

From W. Deonna's *Les Lois et les Rythmes de l'Art* to Louis Hourticq's *Vie des Images* and Elie Faure's *History of Art*, whose fourth volume is called *The Spirit of the Forms*, the same preoccupation sprang up everywhere. In Germany it inspired Riegl and Wölfflin, in England Roger Fry, and in France Henri Focillon, whose *Life of Forms in Art* achieved great popularity.

Thus the history of art carved out a domain for itself; it was the domain of form, whose evolution shows certain rhythms, perpetually recurring, that are independent of historical processes. Form was seen as deriving from an internal principle, no longer from circumstances extraneous to its own nature; it was freed from the bondage to space and time, in which Taine's view had kept it.

Deonna and others outlined the stages which inevitably marked every artistic movement. Focillon recognized an age of experiment, a Classical age, an age of refinement, and a Baroque age; but, avoiding the pitfalls of aesthetic theory, he deliberately refused to distinguish among these successive stages in terms of value-judgment. He simply showed the existence of each, without judging any one of them as superior to any other. Thus form, recognized now as the substance of the work of art, imposed its own laws concurrently with the laws imposed by history.

FORM AND CONTENT. Tremendous progress had been made; the science of art could now be regarded as an independent discipline. But the exclusive preoccupation with form which the new science displayed threatened to confine the work of art within too narrow limits, to reduce it simply to its structure and appearance. Elie Faure had shown that there was such a thing as a spirit of forms. Focillon went further; attacking "the conventional distinction between form and content," he asserted that "the fundamental content of form is a *formal* content." This was bound to lead to a conception of art as only an apportioning of space, and of art history as a study of the laws governing the various types of apportionment. It is true, however, that Focillon himself avoided such a conception in his keen and perceptive analysis of the masterpieces of art.

At the same time attempts were made to apprehend the essence of the work of art through a study of its contents. (This line of exploration was characteristic of France, whereas the exploration of form was carried out primarily by German writers.) Here again historical considerations played an important part. A new science of iconography came into being, which did not confine itself simply to listing the characteristics of a given subject matter, as was done by A. N. Didron and the Reverend Cahier in the nineteenth century. Emile Mâle concentrated on the sources of subject matter, its evolution, its interactions; and, more important, he set himself to discover the moral causes behind the choice of a particular theme as well as behind the method of representing it. Thus, at the dawn of the twentieth century, he opened a new vista in the psychology of art. He opened his *Art religieux après le Concile de Trente* with the firm declaration: "In this book I shall not deal with the grammar, nor with the style of the arts, but with their thought."

Henri Focillon, seeking to prevent possible excesses on the part of the iconographers, who might have become intoxicated by the magnificent results achieved by Emile Mâle, asserted that the intention of a work—the artist's conception, that is, as evidenced by his choice of subject—could be separated from its realization —its forms—only by artificial means. According to Focillon, the creation of a work does not consist, as is often believed by the layman, in giving a visible appearance to an idea that has been completely elaborated in the artist's mind. Form is not a kind of translation, nor a "plastic" garment for an idea; it is not added after the fact. Focillon very wisely pointed out that the artist feels and thinks directly in terms of form, as others think in words.

Content and container are inseparable; one exists by virtue of the other. Focillon defined the part played by the medium: "What an error to see in it a passive repository of our dreams, a mere receptacle! Our dreams begin to come alive only when they find a place in it. It multiplies them as it brings them into the world."

All this had to be said, asserted, in order to vanquish an error born of a long-established habit of thought. However, it would be just as dangerous to go to the other extreme, and to conclude that the only riches the work of art contains are those that are not formal. In the Middle Ages, Emile Mâle says in answer to this, "all that was required of the work of art was that it disclose the soul!" Is this not more or less true of any other period?

PSYCHOLOGICAL STUDY OF VISUAL CHARACTERISTICS. The over-emphasis on "plastic" values was bound to produce a reaction. It will be a salutary

MODES OF EXPRESSION

Painting may be primarily an expression of life; for some, life is expressed by expansive movements, by a soaring into space; for others, life is expressed by secret forces, which open on the invisible and its mystery.

379. - *Above: FRAGONARD.* THE RENDEZVOUS. Frick Collection, New York

380. - *Opposite page: ALTDORFER.* NATIVITY. Museum, Berlin

one if it manages to avoid the opposite extreme. It must be granted, however, that this reaction has had help from a movement, stemming from the biological sciences, in favor of the psychological approach, which has only recently been disavowed by physiology. This confirms once again the truth that in a particular period currents of ideas in the most diverse fields are linked together by secret bonds.

The need for a psychology of art had already asserted itself when, in 1927, Henri Delacroix, following Müller-Freienfels, gave this title to his masterwork. It is also the collective title of a series of works by André Malraux which has attracted considerable attention. The psychologist of art has a difficult task; he has to cope with a great number of problems. He proposes to find evidence within the work of art of the will of the artist to create an image of himself that preserves the complexity of the original. As we have seen, the work of art reflects, first of all, the artist's conscious mind, i.e., the theories, ideas, and intentions that make it possible for him to define himself. In it we also perceive the influences the artist's time, his society, his teachers have had upon him. But the work of art also contains his personal preoccupations and attitudes, as reflected in his temperament. We see in the work a complex interplay of external pressures and internal impulses, which the artist seeks to balance one against the other. In addition to these conscious and semi-conscious elements, the psychologist of art must distinguish the presence of the more or less unconscious impulses which determine the artist's so-called "inspiration" as well as the movements—unlike those of any other artist—of his hand.

Careful, like the archaeologist, not to confuse the various strata, the psychologist of art, equipped with historical knowledge, has to determine which of the elements in a given work are the result of imitation—which reflect the influence of the artist's milieu, which the art of previous centuries, and which that of his own time.

When all these elements have been sorted out, there remain those characteristics which, according to their number and importance, are a measure of the individual worth of the artist. These irreducible traits, which recur constantly, define his personality; they reveal his deepest inclinations, his obsessions. "To catch a glimpse of a poet's soul," says Baudelaire, "or at least of his principal preoccupation, look for the word that occurs most frequently in his works. That word conveys his obsession." There are similarly "obsessive" images in painting

We shall have to analyze these distinguishing features, which the expert learns to recognize for the practical purpose of authenticating the work, in order to perceive those elements in the work which most clearly reflect its creator's character, as he wished to communicate it to us. And once we have perceived them, we shall have to observe them as they evolve in the course of his life and the transformation he undergoes. On the basis of the various forms they assume, we shall be able to go further, to see the artist's personality gradually take on a definitive aspect in response to the ceaseless challenges of life.

2. ART AND PSYCHOLOGY

WHAT are the resources available to the psychology of art in carrying out this complicated task? This question is less difficult to answer than it might at first seem to be: its resources are all those that psychology has developed. The psychology of art must borrow from the older science, to the same extent that art history borrowed from history. The resources thus made available to it must be ordered and disposed to fit its special purposes.

VISUAL SENSATIONS AND PSYCHOPHYSIOLOGY. A systematic investigation of the psychology of art will go back to the sources, and begin with a study of visual sensations and their effects. This study was begun long ago by psychophysiology. The nineteenth century inherited from the preceding century the theory that all our scientific knowledge originates in sensation. Beginning with experimental investigations of the sense of touch carried out by Weber in 1851, the Germans made outstanding contributions in this field, culminating in the founding of Wundt's Psychophysiological Laboratory in Leipzig. Fechner, whose *Elements of Psychophysics* came out in 1860, studied the pleasurable sensations aroused by certain forms and proportions; similar studies were made with respect to colors.

While these laboratory findings are instructive, it took all of the nineteenth century's notorious credulity to suppose that such analyses could cast light on the problems of art. The seeming scientific objectivity of the conclusions drawn from these experiments was based on two premises. The first—a premise dear to contemporary materialism—was that a strict parallelism exists between subjective and objective phenomena; it was thought possible by measuring the physical causes of sensations to draw inferences as to the sensations themselves, and the emotions they aroused.

Now, this assertion does not correspond to reality, as has been shown by several authorities, among them Dr. Sollier, at the beginning of the present century, and later, Souriau. These writers emphasized particularly the disparity between objective and subjective sensibility: while the former can be studied by outside observers, the latter depends entirely on the subject's own evaluations, so that there can be no common ground between them.

The second premise in question is also characteristic of an age steeped in materialism: it was the illusory notion that it was possible to determine through analysis the sensations that make up the universal impression produced by a particular painting, and that this impression is merely the sum total of these sensations. As though psychic realities could be taken apart and rearranged at will, like a piece of rock smashed into bits which are then reassembled!

The illusion that underlay this idea was so patent and led to so many errors, that it was as a reaction to it that the Gestalt theory was developed, around 1912. The cult of analysis had led to such an impasse; a synthesis cannot be broken down like an arithmetical sum. The impression the work makes upon the viewer is an indissoluble "Gestalt"; the sensations figure in it as its original components, but their coming together creates an affective complex which has new characteristics of its own, by which it is defined, and which can be perceived only in it. Wertheimer has shown that a perception is not the sum of its parts, that it is from the outset a new Gestalt. Rubin, Koffka, and, in France, Paul Guillaume have gradually developed a "theory of form," which has replaced the old analytical study of sensations with a synthetical study of universal structures.

This is not to say that the psychology of sensations and the valuable data with which it can supply us are to be ignored; we have only to recall the results that have been achieved in our own day by Henri Piéron. However, the psychology of sensations must be supplemented by a concept of the organized impression that is produced by the work of art, in the study of which the psychology of form plays an indispensable part.

But the psychology of form, too, accounts for only one aspect of these phenomena.

SENSORY COMMUNICATION AND EMPATHY.   In art, the creator does not confine himself to organizing a complex of pleasing or moving sensations, nor does the viewer confine himself to perceiving such a complex. Something more takes place: the intuitive communication of a certain inner state. Here, sensation is merely the mode of contact by which an almost magical transference is effected between one mind and another. This phenomenon is even more difficult to analyze.

Hume, however, sensed the existence of such a phenomenon, when he remarked on the tendency of the imagination to spill over onto external objects and to associate with these objects the internal impressions they provoke. Jouffroy also had glimpsed the phenomenon in question when he spoke of "sympathy." Taine, for his part, in his *La Fontaine et ses Fables*, said that in looking upon a landscape we cannot help "making ourselves conform to the unspoken idea that seems to permeate all things and unify them." And Féré, drawing an analogy with electricity, spoke of "psychomotor induction."

Artistic communication is accounted for most fully by the theory of *Einfühlung*, or empathy, which we owe to Vischer, Lipps, and Volkelt. According to these writers, such communication is due to an impulse of the viewer to re-experience the forms in which the artist has represented his own interior impulse. It is also considered, in broader terms, as the projection of a state of the artist's soul into his work, by which it is in turn projected upon the viewer.

The credit for this discovery is most often given exclusively to the Germans; it must, however, be noted that Baudelaire, with the intuition of a genius, had perceived the same phenomenon in various of its aspects. He mentions a communion between the artist and nature: the purpose of art, he wrote in 1865, is "to create a magical suggestion which will contain both the object and the subject,

MODES OF EXPRESSION

The rendering of life leads to the expression of the soul and its deepest yearnings, such as mystic ecstasy.

381. - *EL GRECO.* RESURRECTION. The Prado, Madrid

the world outside the artist and the artist himself" *(L'Art Philosophique)*.[1] He also referred to the communication between the artist and the viewer: "Truly artistic works are an inexhaustible fountain of suggestions" *(Richard Wagner et Tannhäuser à Paris)*. In his comments on the Salon of 1846 Baudelaire explained this power of the work of art: poetry, he says, "is produced by the painting itself; it lies buried in the viewer's soul and the genius is he who has the power to arouse it." Baudelaire thus perceived in essence the theory which the Germans developed and systematized.

THE MECHANISM OF EMOTIONAL ASSOCIATIONS. Psychology not only enables us to gain a better understanding of the work of art and of its effects, from the sensory shock produced by a color or a line to the universal involvement of the viewer's inner being; it also casts light on the way in which it produces these effects.

It was pointed out in a previous chapter that except in theory there is no such thing as a simple and objective sensory datum. Actually every sensory impression that reaches the mind immediately arouses a thousand responses, resonances, endless overtones. What we perceive provokes instantaneous echoes in our sensibility as well as in our intellect. The artist instinctively controls the range of these echoes, which are responsible for the effect the work of art has upon us. Certain colors and lines, either separately or in combination, set the soul of the viewer vibrating, just as the sight of a printed note in a score suggests the sound of which it is the sign.

The key to these associations is supplied by the infinitely complex play of associations stirring in the memory. Baudelaire noted this; for instance, in his article on Delacroix, in 1863, he wrote that "he is the most *suggestive* of all the painters, the one whose works ... provoke the most thought and bring to memory the greatest number of feelings and poetic ideas that we have known before, but have believed to be buried for ever in the night of the past."

The whole of Proust's psychology is based on these resonances that each perception sets up in the memory, which immediately links the present impression with the past, giving it an unlooked-for coloration, differing with each individual according to his temperament and his experiences. The instant a sensation rises to consciousness it is enriched with a mass of unpredictable new elements. Claudel, who next to Malraux had the deepest insight into art, admirably expresses this process of enrichment in his *Introduction to Dutch Painting:* "The sensation has awakened the recollection, and the recollection in turn activates successive layers of the memory, assembling other images around the initial one."

Some of these associations are fundamental, common to almost all men, and relevant to man's very nature. Child psychology, through the work of Piaget,

---

[1] Byron, whom Baudelaire greatly admired, refers to the same phenomenon in *Childe Harold's Pilgrimage* (III, 72 and 75):

> *I live not in myself, but I become*
> *Portion of that around me....*
>
> *Are not the mountains, waves, and skies a part*
> *Of me and of my soul, as I of them?*

Wallon, Claparède, and others, has cast considerable light on the interior processes that transmute the sensory raw material. But the psychology of the child often varies from one period, or from one local or social group, to another; consequently, a part of this interior language will be inaudible to the ears of outsiders. The fund of associations mankind has in common is gradually transformed through education, habit, experience. Each civilization has its own particular emotional hopes, to which the instinct, as well as atavism, no doubt contributes. This suggests the important role that may be played by sociology. Charles Lalo has observed justly that "since Dubos, Herder, and Taine, we have been obliged to realize that there can be no psychology of art without a sociology of art, which is its necessary complement."

It would be dangerous, however, to account for everything in terms of mechanisms, however subtle. The human being and his states of mind are not compounded simply; to see them as based on a set framework of associations of ideas or emotions is to view them superficially. We cannot ignore the soil in which these phenomena are rooted. Delacroix reminds us that "man has within himself certain innate feelings that can never be gratified by the objects of nature, and it is to these feelings that the imagination of the painter and the poet gives form and life."

What does this phrase "innate feelings" mean? Man's soul, like a bronze bell, can respond to that which sets it in motion only with the resonance that is characteristic of it alone, and that defines its very individuality. Whether the shock transmitted by the senses is due to an outside cause or, rising from the interior emotional depths, is perceived directly, whether it is violent or gentle, the resonance it produces is always an individual one.

INDIVIDUALITY. The artist sometimes deliberately develops this unique resonance, seeking to "express himself in his work" (this is almost the general rule in our time); sometimes, as was the case in the past, he merely performs a task assigned to him, and all he can do is to leave his imprint on it (for this the law of his own nature requires). But in both cases we are witnessing a projection of the artist's inner nature onto a form which gives it material substance, makes it visible.

What, then, defines the particularity of this inner nature? How is it revealed? The work of art displays, first of all, that species of lucid organization in which the artist's intellectual convictions, his values, come into play. He has formed a certain idea of the world and of himself, of reality and of art, to which, inevitably, he tends to make his work conform. This is the conscious, reasoned, even systematic part of his creative effort. This is also the part which most clearly reflects his environment. For the ideas he adopts are most often echoes of those prevalent in his time, even if he gives them a personal inflection.

Once again the history of art must go outside its own field, must trace the history of ideas, their evolution and the deeper meaning of this evolution. When it does so, it soon realizes that the artist, in his language of images, is producing a version of these ideas equivalent to that produced by thinkers and writers and scientists in their verbal language. He is contributing a *vision* of the world which

must inevitably be compared with the *conceptions* of it formed by the thought of his time. Thus the abstract aesthetic of Romanesque art reflects the a priori idealism that prevailed in the early Middle Ages, as typified by the ideas of St. Augustine, whereas the positive aesthetic of the Gothic period reflects the Aristotelianism and the beginnings of experimental science that prevailed in the thirteenth century, the former typified by the thought of Albert the Great and St. Thomas Aquinas, the latter by that of Roger Bacon.[1]

The artist takes the ideas of his time for granted; sharing them automatically with his contemporaries, he cannot realize the extent to which they determine his own views; we realize it only in the perspective of history. Nevertheless, his "I" is not entirely the product of external forces; he also answers to certain inner impulses, which are a part of his most basic individuality. Claudel emphasized this point: "It is not in anecdotes of external behavior that we must look for our explanations. Every great work of art, like the creations of nature, is a response to an inner necessity of which the artist is more or less aware."

This necessity is composed, in part, of his innate inclination, of everything latent in him that strives to manifest itself, to become actualized in his life as well as in his works. Here, the psychology of temperament and character, or character-ology, can supply a fund of data. From Sheldon to Le Senne, from Klages to Dr. Carton and Gaston Berger, increasingly numerous studies have dealt with the various human types, and their affinities to certain forms, which they either prefer or create instinctively. Graphology provides us with eloquent examples.

But a human being is not made up only of his inclinations; such a definition would be too theoretical. Every man who lives accumulates experience. From the moment of birth, his will to live is measured against reality; he is the result of conflicts, joys, and sorrows, harassing problems which he has to solve in order to move forward and which affect his very nature, shaping it continually on the anvil of experience. This makes for a complex constitution, open to perpetual mutations, and reflecting conflicting internal forces seeking a balance—the individual's various drives and impulses, his appetites and his efforts to repress them.

PSYCHOANALYSIS AND THE EXPLORATION OF THE DEPTHS.   We have seen previously how at this point psychoanalysis entered the picture, for it is this branch of psychology that has undertaken, with varying success, the exploration of mankind's depths. Psychoanalysis has demonstrated how the conscious mind tends to obstruct this task of exploration, by replacing the truth of the unconscious with interpretations that suit its own purposes. To get at the unconscious, psychology must use a roundabout method, that of associations.

For this reason, psychoanalysis has sought to determine, particularly through the evidence of dreams, the laws that govern the recurrence of certain images which

[1] I have developed this idea in greater detail in my essay "La Pensée médiévale et le Monde moderne," in *Cahiers du Sud*, 1952, No. 312.

MODES OF EXPRESSION

In modern times, the emphasis on inner life leads to a searching inquiry into the individual soul.

382. - *GOYA.* THE DUCHESS OF CHINCHON (detail)

arise in the mind when it is not under the control of consciousness. Gradually a whole symbolism of the imagination has been formulated, one which still contains many uncertainties and some errors, but which has achieved increasing insight.

Baudouin, in his remarkable *Psychanalyse de l'Art*, issued in 1929, has shown the amazing results psychoanalysis can achieve when it is applied to the work of art. Because of his clinical background he was primarily concerned with the effect of certain works of art on his patients; what we should be interested in, rather, is the imagination of the artist himself. Dr. N. N. Dracoulidès, in his *Psychanalyse de l'artiste et de son œuvre*, published in 1952, deals with this problem, but his approach is narrower than Baudouin's very broad and human treatment.

The uncertainty from which psychoanalysis, working in several, sometimes conflicting, directions, still suffers compels the psychologist of art to proceed with extreme caution; the new science is still too unsure of itself, and too much inclined to take refuge in automatic formulations. However, we have seen how, by selecting judiciously from among the conclusions reached by Freud, Jung, and Adler, it is possible to cast a vivid light on the artist's unconscious, on this deepest part of him which is the source of his profound desire to translate himself, to express himself, to *be* in the objective form of the work of art.

A kind of statistical study of those images most often appearing in an artist's work will indicate the magnetic field of his sensibility. But at this point a new danger arises: that of ignoring the incessant change that is characteristic of all living things. Consequently, psychology must trace this evolution which never ceases; then only will we gain insight into the development of a particular life, the causes of its restlessness, the quest that defines it, the pursuit of a particular goal or balance or gratification—in short, its meaning.

LIMITATIONS OF THE PSYCHOLOGY OF ART.   Such then is the program that may be outlined for the psychology of art. But does not this expose it to some major criticisms? "To pursue such an investigation," it will be said, "is that not to divert attention from the work of art in order to concentrate it on its creator? Is it not to lose sight of its true significance, which is Beauty? Is it not to ignore effort by virtue of which the work tends to become an independent reality, an aesthetic object that exists only for itself?" Such an objection would be valid if the psychology of art were to become an end in itself, instead of a mere means toward deepening our insight into the work of art and enabling us to discover everything it has in it. One of the motives for an artist's creating a work is certainly his will to express himself and to translate his complex nature into a form that will have validity in itself. Only our insight into the man can give us a sure means of access to the message contained in the work. By avoiding those errors into which our spontaneous, subjective reaction might lead us, we are actually showing greater respect for the artist; to know his true nature is to open ourselves to it, to become receptive to him.

The psychologist must not commit an error similar to those committed by the historians who treated paintings as mere historical data, confirming conclusions reached by other methods. He has the same duty to be humble: to subordinate himself to the work of art and its effects, to provide us with a clear insight into

MODES OF EXPRESSION

Whatever his main goal, the painter always seeks to exploit the qualities of his technical resources, but the conception of what is a picture varies infinitely with the times.

383. - *Above: TITIAN.* VENUS WITH MUSICIAN. The Prado, Madrid

384. - *Below: RAOUL DUFY.* Watercolor after the above. 1949

the elements that the artist strives, consciously or unconsciously, to communicate to us.

"Then, your primary goal is comprehension," it will be objected, "whereas the work ultimately aims at providing enjoyment, delight, as Poussin said? Must we not *feel* it, rather than gain insight into it? Does not your study of causes lead to a determinism which submerges that freedom that finds its highest refuge in artistic creation?"

The study of art has by rights only one province, that of the causes of the work, of those elements which may have affected its development. But the student of art must realize that all he learns is at the service of another kind of study, one alien to his, and which belongs only to criticism—the province of the "how" and no longer that of the "why," which properly makes use of those elements which the study of art has isolated. Here begins the realm of quality and here the study of art ends, as the solid ground in an outline of the contour of the sea. By defining those historical and psychological elements that are viewed as components in the work of art, and that are in reality only its causes, the study of art removes beyond all possible ambiguity the result of the work—its *value*.

DETECTING THE IRREDUCIBLE.   To explain is gradually to eliminate all that is not that ultimate reality which is the true object of contemplation. History, by isolating those elements in the work of art that are the product of contingencies, made it possible for psychology to attack the more essential elements. Psychology, in its turn, while rejecting determinism, stops before that which eludes it. The task of psychology is to isolate pure quality, wherein resides the freedom of the work and its beauty.

For although man is not the master of the elements imposed on him by life, which presses on him from all sides and molds his own nature, he is the master of the value he ascribes to these elements in his capacity as spectator, or of the value with which he endows them in his capacity as creator. Whatever the pressures to which he may be subjected, he always preserves his capacity to judge them, to determine their value, aesthetic or moral; and by this token he remains indomitably free.

The more insight the history of art gives us into the necessities that form the artist, the more nearly it liberates us from the temptation of formulas, theories, and fashions, because it shows us that these things, being subject to perpetual change, are relative and vain. The only permanent thing is quality, which cannot be reduced to a formula or a definition.

Only the sorcerer's apprentices will try to reduce harmony to particular measurements, or to confine it to a "golden section," when actually it is inseparable from the results that are sometimes achieved with its help. What a deception, to judge the success of a work by the principles it applies or the ideas it expresses! Tables of formal values, the rhetoric of expression, aesthetic dogma—all are meaningless unless they serve as a basis for quality; the quality with which a man may one day endow them can justify them, but by themselves they can never create quality or even account for it.

Comprehension of a work of art, insight into it, does not penetrate its secret but, rather, delimits it with precision. It defines it, in the original sense of the term, by fixing the boundaries beyond which it begins. It dissolves the shell that might have been taken to be transparent, but is actually the opaque envelope of the work. Then only do we perceive the true brilliance of the gem it encloses, and experience its fascination. Then it is time to be silent, in order to attend to its voiceless speech.

INDEX

INDEX

An asterisk indicates a page with an illustration

———

447

8:00 p.m.
7

Not to be
taken from
the Library—
no tracing

8:00
14

4:30
14

9:05
14

8:45
15

2:45
16

5:15
16

8:20
16

8:00 a.m.
17